TRIPLEX

TRIPLEX

Secrets from the
Cambridge Spies

Edited by
Nigel West and Oleg Tsarev

Yale University Press   New Haven & London

Designed by James J. Johnson and set in Ehrhardt Roman types by Keystone Typesetting, Inc., Orwigsburg, Pennsylvania.
Printed in the United States of America by Sheridan Books, Inc.

Library of Congress Cataloging-in-Publication Data

TRIPLEX : secrets from the Cambridge spies / edited by Nigel West and Oleg Tsarev.
p. cm.
Includes index.
ISBN 978-0-300-12347-0 (alk. paper)

1. Espionage, Soviet—Great Britain—History—20th century—Sources. 2. World War, 1939–1945—Secret service—Sources. 3. Great Britain. M16—History—20th century—Sources. 4. Great Britain. M15—History—20th century—Sources. 5. Blunt, Anthony, 1907–1983—Archives. 6. Philby, Kim, 1912–1988—Archives. 7. Cairncross, John—Archives. 8. Spies—Great Britain—Archives. 9. Spies—Soviet Union—Archives. 10. Soviet Union. Narodnyi komissariat vnutrennikh del—Archives.
I. West, Nigel. II. Tsarev, Oleg.
UB271.R9T75 2009
327.1247041092′2—dc22
2009009949

A catalogue record for this book is available from the British Library.

This paper meets the requirements of ANSI/NISO Z39.48–1992 (Permanence of Paper).

10 9 8 7 6 5 4 3 2 1

Contents

PART III. John Cairncross's Documents   189

PART IV. NKVD Reports   250

Acknowledgments

We owe a debt of gratitude to our translators, Didna Goebbel and Geoffrey Elliott; to the D Notice Committee in London; and to the SVR Declassification Committee in Moscow.

Note on the Translation

The documents reproduced in these pages were translated into Russian in Moscow by the NKVD and now have been translated back into English.

Abbreviations

ACSS	Assistant Chief of SIS
AFHQ	Allied Forces Headquarters
AO	Auslandorganisation [Nazi]
ARO	Aliens Restriction Order
ASP	Advisor on Security Policy
BAOR	British Army of the Rhine
BJ	BLACK JUMBO, British code name for intercepted diplomatic communications
BUF	British Union of Fascists
CIA	Central Intelligence Agency [USA]
CID	Committee of Imperial Defence
CID	Criminal Investigation Department
CMA	Competent Military Authority
CP	Communist Party
CSS or C	Chief of the Secret Intelligence Service
DB	Director of MI5's B Division
DCSS	Deputy Chief of the Secret Intelligence Service
DDMI	Deputy Director of Military Intelligence
DD/SP	SIS Director of Security
DMI	Director of Military Intelligence
DMO	Director/Directorate of Military Operations
DORA	Defence of the Realm Act
DPP	Director of Public Prosecutions
DRR	Defence of the Realm Regulations
DSO	Defence Security Officer
ECGD	Export Credit Guarantee Department
FAE	Italian Fascist Party
FO	Foreign Office
FORD	Foreign Office Research Department
GAF	German Air Force
GC & CS	Government Code and Cypher School
GCHQ	Government Communications Headquarters
GRU	Military intelligence service [Soviet]
HO	Head Office of the Secret Intelligence Service
ISK	Intercepted machine ciphers
ISLD	Inter-Services Liaison Department
ISOS	Intercepted hand ciphers

JIC	Joint Intelligence Committee
KID	SIS code name for colonial intelligence
LCS	London Controlling Section
MI5	Security Service
MO	Military Operations
MOI	Ministry of Information
MOPR	International Labor Defense of the Communist International
NID	Naval Intelligence Division
NKVD	Soviet intelligence service
NSDAP	Nazi Party
OSA	Official Secrets Act
OSS	Office of Strategic Services [USA]
OTP	One-Time Pad cipher system
PIC	Palestine Intelligence Centre
PCO	Passport Control Office
PUS	Permanent Under-Secretary
PWE	Political Warfare Executive
RCMP	Royal Canadian Mounted Police
ROVS	Russian All-Military Union (White Russian intelligence organisation)
RSS	Radio Security Service
RWM	Reichswehrministerium (Ministry of the German National Defence Force)
SA	Sturmabteilung; Nazi Party stormtroopers
SCI	Special Counter-Intelligence
SD	Security Service [Nazi Party]
SM	Special Measures: MI5's term for covert recording devices
SHAEF	Supreme Headquarters Allied Expeditionary Force
SIB	Special Intelligence Bureau
SIME	Security Intelligence Middle East
SIPO	Security Police [German]
SIS	Secret Intelligence Service
SLC	SIS Controller, Special Liaison
SLO	Security Liaison Officer
SLU	Special Liaison Unit
SOE	Special Operations Executive
TWIST	Deception committee
VCSS	Vice Chief of the Secret Intelligence Service
WRNS	Women's Royal Naval Service
WW	Censorship intelligence
WWS	Military Economy Staff [of the German High Command]
XK	SIS code name for Communist activity
XX	Name of the committee, also called the Twenty Committee, that supervised MI5's double-agent operations
XXX	TRIPLEX, code name for material extracted from diplomatic bags

TRIPLEX

Introduction

TRIPLEX was, and remains, one of the most closely guarded secrets of the Second World War. No reference to it has ever been published, and the official multi-volume history *British Intelligence in the Second World War* contains absolutely no mention of this source, which is still highly classified in Britain. Ironically, the only documents to describe the source are to be found in Moscow, where they were sent by Anthony Blunt, one of the very few Security Service (MI5) officers entrusted with the task of supervising the XXX (TRIPLEX) operation and distributing the intelligence product: material extracted illegally from the diplomatic bags of neutral missions in London.

The Soviet spies recruited from Cambridge University were known in Moscow as the Ring of Five and consisted of Kim Philby, Donald Maclean, Guy Burgess, Anthony Blunt and John Cairncross. What made the network so remarkable was that they all knew one another. The only outsider was John Cairncross, a formidable intellect but a cantankerous, socially insecure Scot who, despite his undoubted talents, made himself unpopular in successive Whitehall posts, including the Foreign Office, the Treasury, the Secret Intelligence Service (SIS) and the Government Communications Headquarters (GCHQ). Although Cairncross had been taught French by Blunt, had been approached to spy by Burgess, had shared a room in the Foreign Office with Maclean and had worked alongside Philby in SIS's Section V, he had never realised that he was not operating alone.

Much has been written about all five, whose collective espionage has become a byword for treachery and betrayal, and both Philby and Cairncross have published their own self-serving autobiographies, *My Silent War* and *The Enigma Spy*. All escaped prosecution in Britain, with Burgess and Maclean fleeing to Moscow in May 1951, followed by Philby from Beirut in January 1963. Cairncross, implicated inadvertently by documents left behind by Burgess, resigned from his post in the Treasury in 1951 and finally confessed to a joint MI5-FBI interrogation team in the United States in 1963. The following year Blunt accepted an offer of a formal immunity authorized by the attorney general and gave first Arthur Martin and then Peter Wright of the Security Service a version of how the group had operated and what it had achieved.

In retrospect MI5 concluded that Blunt's apparent co-operation was considerably less than comprehensive and that he had engaged in an elaborate charade to protect suspects who had not been compromised and to steer the molehunters towards individuals who had already come under investigation.

MI5's belated conclusion that it had been duped by Blunt led to an intensive reappraisal of everything he and Cairncross had admitted to, but the unsatisfactory result was clearly less than the whole story. How much damage had each of the spies inflicted on the various branches of Britain's secret establishment that had employed them? Guy Burgess had worked for Section D of SIS, then the Security Service, where his brother Nigel was a wartime officer, and finally the Foreign Office. Donald Maclean had pursued a glittering career as a diplomat, first in Paris and then in Washington, DC, and Cairo, ending as head of the American Department in the Foreign Office. The longest-serving war correspondent in the Spanish Civil War, Kim Philby had joined Special Operations Executive (SOE) from the *Times* in December 1940 and then, in September 1941, had seized the opportunity to transfer to SIS, where his journalistic skills ensured swift promotion. By the time he was dismissed in November 1951, he had headed the Iberian sub-section of the counter-intelligence branch, taken control of the anti-Soviet division designated Section IX, run the SIS station in Istanbul and been appointed SIS's liaison officer in Washington. John Cairncross had moved uneasily from the Foreign Office to the Cabinet Office to Bletchley Park, where he removed thousands of ULTRA decrypts, and to SIS before ending up in the Treasury. As for Anthony Blunt, he admitted having haemorrhaged to his Soviet contacts every secret that had passed over his desk in MI5's headquarters while he was based there between June 1940 and October 1945.

Between them, the notorious Cambridge Ring of Five represented the most thorough hostile penetration of Britain's various intelligence agencies, with SOE, SIS, MI5 and GCHQ falling victim to a highly sophisticated scheme orchestrated with some scepticism by uncomprehending controllers in Moscow, who found it hard to accept their astonishing good fortune. Bewildered by this extraordinary group of apparently ideologically motivated volunteers, NKVD analysts scrutinized the thousands of handwritten letters, typed reports, original classified documents and photographs for clues to an elaborate deception, but eventually concluded that the material was authentic and that these unlikely adherents to Communism were exactly what they claimed to be, zealots who had made a total, lifelong commitment to Stalin. While Soviet intelligence became convinced of their credentials, MI5, SIS and GCHQ undertook lengthy damage assessments to establish as precisely as possible what secrets had been contaminated. Unfortunately, in relying on inadequate interviews with Blunt and Cairncross and the public comments of Philby and Burgess, these appraisals proved far from complete. As for Maclean, he made no comment after his arrival in Moscow, leaving the molehunters in London and Washington, DC, to speculate about what he had compromised. The only accurate answers to the conundrum were buried deep in the cellars at Dzerzhinsky Square.

While some of the material sent by the Cambridge spies to Russia has survived in its original form in the NKVD's (later the KGB's) archives, far more was translated into Russian and filed for future study by Soviet personnel who could not speak English. As paper became a precious wartime commodity in Moscow, the blank sides of many of the original documents were recycled as typing paper and thereby lost forever. In 1995 some of the first original communications from the Cambridge Five were released by the KGB and formed the basis of *Deadly Illusions*, written by the British historian John Costello and his co-author, Oleg Tsarev, who pulled off another coup in 1998 with *The Crown Jewels*, a collection of declassified files containing original English-language material supplied by the Five at the height of their activities during the Second World War. This initial publication led to the release of a further batch of secret papers that had been translated into Russian, and includes some highly significant reports from Philby, Blunt and Cairncross that have been chosen for this volume, together with a selection of intelligence appreciations written by NKVD analysts and based in large measure on material supplied by the Cambridge Five.

These documents, translated from the Russian, are doubly valuable, first, because they illustrate precisely what was compromised by the British traitors and, second, because they shed astonishing light on what Philby, Blunt and Cairncross thought would be of special interest to Moscow. Because of their highly privileged access to the state's most secret files, the Cambridge spies were in the extraordinary position of deciding for themselves what they should remove for Stalin. Unlike other agents, the Five were self-directed, in the sense that they provided their NKVD contacts with a wealth of classified papers, reports, memoranda, minutes, intercepts and photographs and neither sought guidance nor accepted direction in respect of what they selected. The documents are additionally significant because most have either failed to survive the intervening years or have been considered too secret to be declassified. The one exception is Jack Curry's official history of MI5, but, as we shall see, the early draft removed from the Security Service Registry by Anthony Blunt is the unexpurgated version, whereas the edition released by the Public Record Office at Kew has been sanitised. Indeed, it would be difficult to imagine the circumstances, however enlightened, in which the Security Service would be willing to release pages listing the identity, code names and locations of the agents that it had recruited inside foreign embassies in London. Understandably, the MI5 officer who compiled this particular report begged Anthony Blunt to ensure its destruction as soon as he had read it for fear of compromising the organisation's star assets. His wasted plea was, of course, ignored, and the result is the appearance in Moscow of a document that probably was considered too dangerous to entrust to MI5's own archives.

This material is published here for the first time, finally allowing researchers to see practical examples of the Five's duplicity at a working level, historians an opportunity to reassess the Five's impact on the Cold War, and the general reader to see how almost all the various branches of the much-feared British secret establishment succumbed to hostile penetration.

PART I

Anthony Blunt's MI5 Documents

A
nthony Blunt's time in the British Security Service, between June 1940 and October 1945, was marked by betrayal on a truly breathtaking scale, although the MI5 molehunters who pursued him between May 1951, when Burgess and Maclean defected, and April 1964, when he finally confessed, were never able to determine precisely what he had given away. This collection of documents represents the first confirmation of exactly what he supplied to his Soviet contacts, and when.

The first four documents are relatively routine Security Service reports based on surveillance of neutral diplomatic personnel in London; they give a flavour of the period and illustrate MI5's preoccupation with the leakage of information to the Nazis. The files include a detailed dossier on a dubious Swedish naval attaché, an account of prominent Britons suspected of having fallen under Japanese influence and a hugely sensitive list of agents reporting from inside foreign embassies in London. The officer who compiled this last item begged Blunt to destroy it immediately, for he had always tried to avoid identifying, and potentially compromising, so many valued sources. Needless to say, Blunt sent the entire list straight to Moscow. The final document is the secret MI5 history that was prepared for internal consumption only, but was copied by Blunt, as can be seen by the accompanying letter addressed to Guy Liddell, then head of MI5's counter-espionage branch, designated B Division, for whom Blunt acted as personal assistant.

1   *The Swedish Naval Attaché*

[Blunt's first document is an MI5 report on the Swedish naval attaché Count Johan G. Oxenstierna, who was quietly removed from his post at the request of the British government at the end of 1943 and replaced by the king's grandson, Prince Bertil. Oxenstierna was suitably indignant about his treatment and the

British ambassador in Stockholm, Victor Mallet, pressed his case, as did the British naval attaché, Henry Denham, but the Foreign Office was adamant about his removal and equally insistent that the precise nature of his offence should not be disclosed. Oxenstierna had been responsible for the leakage of secret information, but the Foreign Office was not prepared to be specific beyond a reference to his inquisitiveness about a naval stabiliser recently installed on destroyers. Certainly there was no mention of TRIPLEX, or the illicit copying of the contents of the naval attaché's dispatches in the Swedish diplomatic bag, and the issue has remained a mystery to this day. The count was from an exceptionally well-connected Swedish family, being a cousin to the Wallenbergs, and his removal, under the threat of being declared persona non grata, continues to be highly controversial.]

To the Head of B Division, Captain Liddell

I feel obliged to report to you on what we currently know about the Swedish naval attaché Graf Oxenstierna. Over the past week a large amount of information has been received which shows that he is up to no good.

A considerable amount of TRIPLEX material consisting of reports by Oxenstierna to his Admiralty has become available to us. The content of these reports is based almost entirely on the *Weekly Naval Notes,* issued by the Admiralty. This bulletin is classified 'Secret', and I know that it is provided to the military attachés of neutral countries on condition that it will not be sent abroad. This condition seems to me very naive, and if the material in the bulletin really is of value to the enemy, I think that we should put pressure on the Admiralty to deprive neutrals of this privilege.

The material covers a large number of topics, principally:

1. Detailed accounts of the naval areas of landing grounds in Salerno
2. Operations on Corsica and Sardinia
3. Operations in the Adriatic and the Aegean
4. Tactics of convoy ships
5. Information about the Italian navy
6. Ship damage reports
7. The activity of the aircraft carrier *Victorious*
8. Defence installations on merchant vessels

Besides the material that Oxenstierna got from the *Weekly Naval Notes,* there are one or two items he apparently obtained privately: (1) The use of torpedo nets on merchant vessels. Apparently Oxenstierna got this material from a crew member of a merchant ship, although the material does not identify the source. (2) Material about American and English aircraft carriers. According to Oxenstierna, this material was partly obtained from the press reports. An additional paragraph states that 'information about the number of English aircraft carriers is impossible to get' (from public sources), and that therefore he will try to obtain it elsewhere. (3) A comment on the difficulties experienced by the Royal Navy in finding crews for their ships. (4) A comment on the use of monitors in the landing on Sicily. This information was obtained by Oxenstierna 'privately'. (5) A brief note about the rebuilding of Russian ships.

In addition to the TRIPLEX material mentioned, we have received a long report from the navy about Oxenstierna's conduct. The report is dedicated in part to an incident that took place in December 1942 on which we have some other information partly collected by TRIPLEX. At that time Oxenstierna received permission to make a trip on HMS *Brecon,* and some of the information he obtained then fell into our hands through TRIPLEX. It is now known that Oxenstierna used very dishonest methods during his trip in order to obtain access to a secret device known as stabiliser and in order to find out what it did. Although it was taken for granted that he must not see it, Oxenstierna first tried to draw the captain into a conversation about it. Then he was found attempting to get access to it in order to ferret out what it was. He also tried to persuade the officer of the watch to allow him to see it. Finally he told one of the midshipmen that the captain had given him permission to see the stabiliser. The captain states that he does not remember giving such permission, and Oxenstierna did not tell him that he had seen the stabiliser. In February 1943 he wrote a letter to Brown Brothers asking for a detailed description of their stabiliser, but they declined to provide it.

This incident throws some light on the methods Oxenstierna uses to obtain information.

The Admiralty's report contains other information about Oxenstierna using similar methods. A good example is an attempt by Oxenstierna to get the secret of a device called HEDGEHOG out of Captain A. Noble, a device on which Oxenstierna, as it turned out, was well informed, although he had never been told about it officially. It is also known that he was in contact with various naval officers and with Wrens [women in the WRNS, or Women's Royal Naval Service] in the Admiralty. Among other things, his assistant Prince Bertil has close ties to a Miss Pamela Hunter, who is employed in top-secret work with Captain Lodchins.

The Admiralty has just sent us another report showing that Oxenstierna tried to obtain cards for the Sperry Gyro-Compass by writing to the manufacturers, who told him he could have them only if he obtained an export licence. On 30 June, Oxenstierna wrote to them again, stating, 'I am taking the necessary steps to obtain an export licence.' In view of this, the compass cards were duly dispatched, but as far as the Admiralty was able to find out, no licence has been applied for, let alone granted. According to the Admiralty, the cards are not of great importance, but it is another instance of Oxenstierna's underhand methods.

Another one or two minor points might be mentioned. Some secret TRIPLEX items, dated 5 October 1943, show that Oxenstierna received material from the director of the [Swedish] Joint Intelligence Service in Stockholm, Landkvist, to be secretly passed to one 'R.L.' 'R.L.' was required to pass on this information in English in order to conceal its Swedish origin, while Oxenstierna was ordered to do his best to cover his tracks. The Admiralty is sure that 'R.L.' is the Norwegian colonel Roscher Lund, who is known to have close ties to Oxenstierna and to exchange information with him (I was given some further details on this point that do not concern the issue at hand). It is possible that the information was meant solely for the Admiralty itself and that in this case Oxenstierna was an 'honest broker'. On the other hand, the way this was handled does look somewhat secretive.

According to information dated 19 October 1943 received from TRIPLEX, Oxenstierna sent the Admiralty in Stockholm a short message about the air raid on London that took place the night before. This message was obviously based on his own observations. In the message he remarks that the air attaché will send a more detailed report on the raid.

Finally, TRIPLEX material of 21 October 1943 contains a letter from the head of the naval staff in Stockholm to Oxenstierna, in which he asks the latter whether he has any information about the advantages of destroyers with 'a direct and protected walkway allowing the crew to move between bow and stern should the ship be seriously damaged'. The writer had heard that such a facility had been fitted on French destroyers. There is also a reference in the letter to a German secret weapon that would be deployed from November and that would allow the Germans to 'destroy' southeast England.

Based on this information it is obvious that:

a. Oxenstierna is obtaining more information than we would wish, and
b. he is duplicitous.

Most of this information was received through TRIPLEX and therefore cannot be utilised, but some of it—namely, his breach of the export licence law and the episode on the *Brecon*—can be used as a reason for demanding Oxenstierna's recall. The Admiralty proposes to instruct the naval attaché in Stockholm to see Landkvist privately and tell him that it would be very opportune to transfer Oxenstierna to another post, since otherwise we might declare him persona non grata and take steps officially. This seems to be a perfectly satisfactory solution unless you consider it better to protest officially with the aim of warning the other attachés here. The downside to the proposal is that it may worsen the already delicate position of the British naval attaché in Stockholm.

2 Japanese Suspects, October 1941

[MI5's Japanese Section contained a file note on Japanese intelligence in the United Kingdom and persons investigated on suspicion of working for Japanese intelligence, among them the 19th Baron Sempill, a veteran of the Royal Naval Air Service who had been employed after the First World War to organise the Japanese Naval Air Service. Further details of the Sempill affair may be found in Richard Aldrich's *Intelligence and the War Against Japan* (Cambridge: Cambridge University Press, 1996).]

Agent's Report from TONY
20 October 1941

The Japanese have an extensive intelligence network throughout the British Empire. It is run mainly through their embassies and consulates, which act as collecting points. The consulates are mainly concerned with ship movements and, in the UK, with bomb-damage reports. The Japanese network is an important component of the Axis intelligence system. Apart from direct intelligence, the Japanese Embassy in London has certain connections with British subjects from whom it obtains valuable information; this is transmitted to Tokyo. It is difficult to determine to what degree these sources are acting wittingly, but the fact that they are perhaps acting without hostile intent does not diminish the danger that the information they provide will reach enemy hands.

The most important individuals linked to the embassy are Lord Sempill and Professor Grotwohl. Lord Sempill makes no secret of his pro-Japanese sympathies and has often done favours for members of the embassy staff. He has been connected with Mitsubishi for ten years, which has usually paid him £300 per annum. Following the outbreak of war, Mitsubishi proposed stopping these payments, but at the special request of the Japanese naval attaché they continued for some time, albeit at a lower level. In a letter on this subject a director of Mitsubishi described Lord Sempill as someone who was of 'direct and indirect benefit' to the military and naval attachés in London.

In 1924–25 Lord Sempill was in very close touch with the Japanese naval attaché, for whom he collected information on bombs and aviation. Sempill does, of course, have access to secret files of the Air Ministry, and it is likely that he passed some of this information to the naval attaché, although it is not clear whether Lord Sempill was aware that this information was in fact secret. On 30 September 1940, Lord Sempill undertook to the Admiralty not to discuss any official matters with the Japanese. Since then, however, he has maintained contact with them, and there are grounds [telephone taps] for supposing he has not broken off his contacts. It should also be noted that Lord Sempill was one of two directors of the Anglo-German Club when it was organised in 1930; that he was a member of the Council of FCK and was connected with [illegible]. He is also known to have been extremely indiscreet in conversations with his friends on official matters. We cannot conclude from the foregoing that Lord Sempill is consciously acting as an agent for the Japanese, but the risk is a serious one, given that he holds the position he now does in the Admiralty.

Professor Grotwohl is a German by birth, but—although the technical aspects of his nationality remain obscure—he was granted a British passport, his father having been naturalised in 1869. From 1903 to 1912 he worked as professor of French at the Universities of Bristol and Dublin. Since then he has earned his living mainly as a freelance journalist and as an unofficial advisor for various embassies and private individuals. He has worked for the *Daily Telegraph* as well as for various provincial papers; at various times has been on the payroll of the Greek, Romanian and Saudi Arabian Embassies; he was later connected with the Poles and with the Turkish and Argentine Embassies. For quite a long time he has had a more or less permanent position drafting letters for Mr Lloyd in the Foreign Office, a job for which he is paid. He had a very close relationship with Dr Siebert, doyen of the Nazi press corps in the UK. For the last several years, however, his main connection has been the Japanese Embassy, and there is a large amount of extremely detailed evidence to demonstrate that information that he passes on to them is then relayed on to Tokyo as being of great significance. There is no reason to suppose that Grotwohl is especially concerned to pass information to the Japanese in order to damage the interests of UK, but everything suggests that he is an intelligence 'hireling' and will get information from any source, and pass it on to any other source, if there is something in it for him.

It was for this reason we were alarmed at his close friendship with Sir Edward Grigg, MP, on the one hand, and, on the other, at his regular use of the Japanese Embassy as the centre of his activities in London. We therefore took steps to warn Sir Edward Grigg, and he is now, to some extent, being used as a conduit for passing disinformation to the Japanese.

Other interesting connections of the Japanese fall into a different category. Arthur Frances Henry Edwards, who worked in Chinese Customs from 1903 to 1928, is now openly employed by the Japanese Embassy as an advisor at a salary of some £4,300 per annum. It appears that the cost of this was borne equally by the Manchurian government, the Japanese government and the South Manchurian Railway. It appears that his job includes receiving the latest Japanese news from Baron Kano and passing it on to British circles in order to assess their reaction, which in turn is reported back to Baron Kano. He would often talk to Mr R.A. Butler after he had received a letter from Kano and in many cases acted as an emissary between the ambassador and Butler and the prime minister. When Butler left the Foreign Office, Edwards stated he had established a new connection, but we do not as yet know how it operates. Edwards is in close touch with Sempill and, like the latter, advocates a policy of appeasement with the Japanese. Together with Kano and the previous Japanese ambassador, he has tried to enlist the aid of Mr Ernest Bevin and Sir Francis in the conclusion of a pact between China, Japan, the USA and Great Britain. Lord Sempill's speech on his subject in the House of Lords was based on a memorandum compiled by Edwards. We assume that Edwards's attitudes are pro-British and that he is seeking to bring about better mutual relations between Great Britain and Japan, but as a paid employee of the Japanese Embassy, he is probably obliged to pass on to his masters information that he picks up in British government circles.

General F.S.G. Piggott is a close friend of Edwards. Until 1930 he was military attaché in Tokyo. He makes no secret of his firm pro-Japanese views, and since he enjoys unrestricted access to a certain department of the War Office, it is suggested that his friendship with Edwards should be viewed as a cause for some concern. General Piggott would never, of course, act disloyally vis-à-vis Great Britain, but he is so blinded by his absolute belief in the Japanese and his conviction that they can do no wrong that there is a certain danger in his relations with them.

Another friend of Edwards is Commander McGrath, a director of Cannon Boveri. McGrath was a near neighbour of the former Japanese ambassador in Bucharest, and we know that he had many talks on Japanese policies and the British attitude towards relations with Japan with Edwards and the ambassador.

The last member of the group is Mr George Sale of the firm of Sale Tilney, who undertakes export-import business with Japan. He is known to all those mentioned above, and there is evidence that his commercial interest in the maintenance of good relations between Great Britain and Japan compels him to adopt something of a pro-Japanese attitude. There can be no doubt that from the circle of connections listed above the Japanese are in a position to obtain an extremely significant amount of valuable information on military work in England.

3 *Neutral Attachés in London, September 1943*

TOP SECRET
No. 3 Source T. Bag
No. 19 of 12 September 1943
Film no. 1

In August 1941 the Security Service presented a memorandum to the JIC [Joint Intelligence Committee] recommending that the activities of the attachés of neutral countries in the UK be circumscribed (see JIC/4&1, 24th Session of 8 August 1941). The matter was re-examined at the prime minister's request in July 1943 (see JIC 1045/43 of 16 July 1943).

It was recognized that the security measures taken on the basis of the JIC paper of 1941 had been effective in that the risk represented by the neutral attachés was not great. Since then, however, the Security Service has received new information indicating that the situation may not be as satisfactory as had been assumed and that it might be necessary to take more severe measures. The issue will in any event become more serious in connection with the need to ensure maximum security for the preparations that will be undertaken in the UK in the coming months. A document recently captured from the Germans showed that the enemy was unusually well informed about production figures and aircraft construction in Great Britain. The German report was evidently based on information from a large number of sources, some of it possibly emanating from the reports of neutral air attachés in the UK. No particular points can be directly tied to information that, as far as we know, is available to these attachés, but there is now evidence that some of them are in receipt of detailed information that could prove useful for the Germans in compiling reports of this kind. For example, most secret and sensitive sources recently provided information that the Swedish air attaché, Major Servell, had sent back long, well-compiled reports on air matters that included detailed information on certain types of aircraft, general facts on tactics, etc. We know him to have reported that he had 'precise details on the production of fighters and bombers in the UK'. It is interesting to note that when he returned to Stockholm recently, he was thanked for his reports. We are also aware that when he visits aerodromes and other air establishments, he gets information on matters about which he is not supposed to know. In short, he has many friends who are well informed on technical questions and who probably give him, perhaps unintentionally, more information than is desirable.

The Spanish air attaché, Colonel Sartorius, also has certain connections with aviation experts, from whom he certainly gets information. His report could not have been used directly in the German documents, since it is dated in early June, while Colonel Sartorius did not arrive until July. But his activities clearly represent a threat for the future.

It may also be worth mentioning the Swedish naval attaché, Count Oxenstierna, who has on several occasions used illegal means to obtain secret information. In some cases he was successful, while in others all his efforts proved fruitless. It is understood that the Admiralty is considering whether to make an official or an unofficial demand for his recall. We have no evidence that any of these attachés are consciously working for the Germans or even that they have pro-German sympathies, but even a neutral attaché such as Major Servell, who is pro-British and generally sympathetically inclined towards the Allies, represents in a certain sense a major threat for the security of the country, perhaps even more so than an attaché who is overtly hostile towards us. It is easy for him to get close to officials or civil servants who have important information, and the latter will be much more inclined to speak freely to him than to someone who is hostile to the Allied camp. The danger this represents is not that the attaché will pass the information on to the enemy directly, but that in being forwarded to his government, the information can leak to the enemy via German agents or through intercepts of neutral communications. There is, unfortunately, very clear evidence that information reaching Stockholm or Madrid reaches both the Germans and the Japanese. The same information can also leak via the Argentine, since we know the Germans have access to reports sent by Argentine diplomats in Europe.

The foreign ambassadors and envoys in London represent one further risk. For instance, the Spanish and Turkish ambassadors both mix with a very large number of senior British officials from the various services and government departments. The Spanish ambassador's dispatches are known to be regularly passed on to the Japanese, and there is evidence that information reaching Ankara is also being leaked to the enemy.

In view of the foregoing it is suggested that more stringent precautions be taken to prevent the attachés of neutral countries and heads of missions from obtaining information that could be of interest to the enemy.

The Security Service proposes to undertake more vigorous investigation of the individuals who seem to represent the greatest risk, but there are also some general security measures that might prove effective:

1. The three ministries principally concerned (i.e. War Office, Admiralty and Air) should be required to limit as far as possible the trips they lay on for neutral attachés. In this connection, the issue of reciprocal action being taken obviously arises, but we suggest that under current circumstances the risk of information leaking out is far more serious than any benefits that may be gained from trips made by British attachés overseas.
2. When such trips are made, the official acting as escort must take pains to see that the attaché gets access only to those parts that he is scheduled to see of the establishments he visits.
3. The Security Service can compile a list of the British official connections of the various attachés and heads of missions. These people should be strongly warned against passing information to neutral attachés.
4. If the Admiralty decided to make an official demand for the recall of the Swedish naval attaché, this may serve as a warning for other attachés in London.

Steps are already being taken to supply certain attachés and heads of missions with misleading information. This will help to some extent to distort the intelligence they supply. However, such steps are not 100 percent effective and can never be a substitute for appropriate security measures.

4   *Diplomatic Missions in London*

Minutes of a Meeting of the Committee for the Deception of the Enemy, 1943

Themes Proposed for Dissemination Through Private Conversations

Content:

The rearmament of England is now complete; that of the USA is proceeding at top speed.

During the next few months strong land and air forces will be directed towards the final defeat of the Axis countries. Our only problem is providing enough ships to do the job. Control of the Mediterranean enables us to use the much larger vessels that were previously forced to take the long route around Africa.

Italy can be forced to leave the war by an intensive bombing campaign. In any case, the Alpine barrier makes Italy a cul-de-sac that we cannot use for our invasion of the Continent. For the same reason, attacks on Sicily and Sardinia will be futile. They are not bases for a further offensive. After the liberation of Tunis, new major operations will begin in the western and eastern Mediterranean, possibly simultaneously. We will certainly attack the Dodecanese and Crete, and an invasion of Greece may follow. On the other hand, [General] Giraud is very insistent that we attack from southern France. All that said, the main blow has to come from the west. England is the only location with the resources to assemble and supply the strong expeditionary forces necessary for the final operation—the invasion of Germany.

The strength of the German air forces is decreasing rapidly, and the fighter squadrons are no longer able to operate along the continental coastline. This enables us to defend landing sites simultaneously in at least two locations as far apart as Trondheim and Bordeaux.

Our absolute air supremacy in areas close to England allows us to make airborne landings in the enemy's rear and to take several Channel ports. A hundred million people hungry for retribution are ready to welcome us to occupied territory. The invasion will be a massacre, not a military campaign.

Objective:

To divert attention away from the central Mediterranean.

Italy is inaccessible.

1. Those who think that after the conclusion of operations in Italy our next step will be the invasion of Africa are wrong. The Alps make it impossible to penetrate into Germany from Italy.

Germany is our target. The Bolshevik danger.	2. Germany is the country against which we must direct our forces. It is the only way to achieve a comparatively quick victory. Moreover, if Britain is to have its rightful seat at the table in the post-war world, we cannot risk Russia occupying the entire German territory while our army is busy on other fronts.
The Italian cities must disappear from the map of Europe.	3. In any case, to knock Italy out of the war does not require invasion. By the time the Allied Forces in North Africa and Egypt meet in Tunis, the combined Allied air forces will match the capacity of the entire German air forces in the Mediterranean, in Russia and in western Europe. Moreover, VK's Bomber Command is getting stronger every day. Italy will be the main target for two powerful air fleets, attacking simultaneously from the south and the north. The bombings of Warsaw and Coventry were child's play compared to what the Italian cities are about to suffer. Germany will be in no position to defend Mussolini against this, and his regime is bound to fall.
Sicily and Sardinia can only be a burden.	4. It follows that an invasion of Sicily and Sardinia would be useless. These islands cannot be used as jumping off points; their occupation would only tie down considerable land forces and we would be forced to feed their population.
Control over the Mediterranean and neutralisation of the airfields of Sicily and Sardinia.	5. The main objective of our operations in North Africa is the opening of the Mediterranean for navigation. As soon as we have liberated Tunis, the Allied air force will be strong enough to neutralise the enemy's airfields on Sicily and Sardinia, just as the enemy's air force was able to neutralise our airfields on Malta for a while. We have already made preparations to send our convoys through the Gulf of Sicily again.
Ships—the key to an invasion.	6. As soon as our convoys can get to the Far East through the Mediterranean instead of going around the African coast, we will get access to several million tons of extra shipping capacity. This would enable us to begin and conclude an invasion of the Continent at any point from northern Norway to eastern Greece.
New objectives for Allied forces in Africa.	7. Although Tunis will remain the main base for our air strike capability in the Mediterranean until Italy is forced out of the war, we will not need to keep a large army there. The end of the campaign in Tunis will free a pool of experienced soldiers for use elsewhere; this will provide us considerable extra flexibility.

The 10th Army and the Dodecanese.	8. With the liberation of the Caucasus by the Russians, the 10th Army will no longer need to protect the oil fields of Iraq and Iran. There can be no doubt that the Axis powers are concerned about what happens to the Dodecanese.
The 6th Army and Crete.	9. If a firm decision is taken to launch an offensive against Europe, the operations will combine an invasion of the Dodecanese under Wilson's command with a simultaneous attack by Montgomery on Crete; the latter is only two hundred miles away from Tobruk, and there are a large number of ports along the coast that can be used by the 8th Army as starting points for an invasion.
Advantages of an invasion of Greece.	10. The next step will be the full occupation of Greece. There are many arguments in favour of launching the attack on Europe through the Balkans. Greek and Yugoslav partisans are in position to do serious damage to the enemy's communications immediately after an Allied landing. We will be able to deprive the enemy of the chrome he so badly needs, and control of Greek air bases will enable us to bomb the Romanian oil fields, with the result that the German military machine, already creaking, will be brought to a complete halt.
Southern France is also an interesting target.	11. On the other hand, the use of our experienced North African armies for an invasion of southern France is equally tempting. All Algerian ports have now been brought back into operation, and as soon as we have thrown a bridge across the Lionsiumu Gulf, we will be able to get one of Europe's first-class railway systems under our control and to use it for further advances to the north.
The growing power of the French army in North Africa.	12. Giraud and other French generals who have joined us are trying their best to convince us to begin an offensive on French territory from the south. They are sure that the majority of the population will join us in the common struggle, and their views now carry much weight, since they have at their disposal the better part of twelve divisions that are being rapidly re-armed with modern American technology.

Objective:
To suggest a cross-Channel invasion of the Continent for this summer.

BOLERO.

13. The rebuilding of the French North African army means that there is no need for us or the Americans to send new divisions to the Mediterranean theatre of war. England will thus be turned into a huge armed camp ready for the decisive invasion of the continent. We expect to have an American army of at least a million in England and the world's strongest air force by the summer.

The great offensive.

14. Controlling the entire North African coast, we will be able to deal a heavy blow to the Axis powers in the southern part of Europe, but the fatal thrust has to be delivered from the west. Morocco, Algeria, Lebanon and even Egypt are not in a position to be used to launch the vast army that will be needed for the great offensive. The UK, more specifically England, is the only location on table to assemble and train such a large force.

Several regions have to be attacked simultaneously.

15. It should, however, not be thought that the entire army will be focussed just on one target. The fact that we have to use the ships we have at our disposal and cannot pick and choose specific vessels means that we need to invade the continent at several points simultaneously and spread the flotilla in a way that will maximise the impact and the effectiveness of each landing.

Mass production of special transport ships for carrying tanks.

16. Special craft will be needed to carry out each initial landing operation. Special tank transporters are being successfully built at the moment. The new shipyards of the American 'king of shipbuilding', Kruger, are now working at full capacity and producing a huge number of ships.

Our objectives in western Europe.

17. Having landed on the coast, we will be able to support operations in north-west France by attaching major river and motorboat flotillas to the navy. We will carry out operations that are the exact opposite of those at Dunkirk. If we land on the Dutch islands at the mouth of the Schelde River, a large amount of our reinforcements and ammunition can be taken across on coastal vessels and sea barges, since the voyage will be little more than one hundred miles. This enables us to free up a large number of ships for supplying other strong points, in Norway, in the Bordeaux region and possibly in Denmark.

The use of troop transports by plane.

18. The German air force is no longer what it once was and cannot be everywhere at the same time. Once we are able to deploy the Allied air force effectively to move large numbers

of troops, we will be strong enough to penetrate to the enemy's rear and to seize the ports. The German air force is bound to put up stiff resistance, but since its effectiveness has been seriously impaired, our convoys of landing troops and matériel will not encounter serious opposition.

Iceland as a base for the invasion of Norway.

19. I regard Norway as an exceptionally good base. The Germans have been badly affected by their losses in Russia, and they are trying to make up for them by any means possible. They are already lowering the quality of their garrisons in Norway. Now that they are no longer threatening Iceland, we can turn the latter into a base for the preparation for an invasion, and at the right moment we can use the garrison there as an expeditionary force for the invasion of Norway.

Removing Finland from the war and joining up with Russia.

20. If we manage to send supplies to the Finns via Norway, they will be only too glad to leave the war. Then we can join up with Russia and close the noose around Germany more tightly, attacking its ships in the Baltic and causing it damage from the north. It seems to me that many of our young people are already tired of being taught the principles of mountain warfare, but they will realise later how useful it will prove.

The 'Pincer Movement': invasion of France from the north and the south.

21. All this sounds very optimistic, and I admit that the enemy's submarines still present a very serious danger to our plans. But even if heavy losses in the future prevent us from carrying out our plans to the full, we will still be able to conduct at least one major operation from England and another from the Mediterranean. If we really had to limit ourselves to these two operations, I would be in favour of an invasion of western France from England, simultaneously with a landing in southern France from North Africa.

Secret weapons.

22. However circumstances develop, when the time comes we must shun no means and use everything at our disposal, including scientific inventions that have never before been used in war. Moreover, every red-blooded citizen in occupied territory will consider it his duty to kill at least one German so as to be able to say he 'did his bit' in the final defeat of Hitler and his regime.

Notes About Agents Under the Direction of B1(g)

To Major Blunt, B1(b), from Mrs A.W. Pitt, 25 May 1945

SPAIN

EMBASSY:	JP is in the minister's office.
	DUCK, who will probably remain there until the end of FRANCO's regime.
	HOW [Home Office warrant]
CONSULATE IN CARDIFF:	JPs—dismissed.
PEPPERMINT:	He will probably try to stay there as long as he can.
ARMESTO PASTOR:	He has to be considered an intermediary rather than an agent. He will stay here indefinitely, since he is professor of Spanish language at London University. He is currently the 'cultural-educational attaché'.

ARGENTINA

PLOVER:	Secretary-typist. She is unlikely to stay here indefinitely, since she wants to return to Gibraltar with her mother.
LEZICA ALVEAR and FLORES PIRAN:	The connections with them are more or less official. It has to be assumed that any information they provide is with the knowledge of the minister.

CHILE

ALVARO MUÑOS:	He has lived here for a very long time and is unlikely to return to Chile. He does not like the other members of the embassy and is inclined to supply information even though it is about his own country

COLOMBIA

HALE:	Secretary-typist. Probably is staying indefinitely.

PORTUGAL

ALPACA:	Clerk. Probably is staying there indefinitely.

PERU

GRANDE:	Is going to leave; is preparing to take the post of consul general in New York any time now.
RUMBA:	As an employee in the public relations office of the Latin American Section of MOI [Ministry of Information], she has met and become acquainted with all Latin American diplomats here, and she can be contacted at any time, although she is now working only part-time for the ministry and will soon leave there completely.

The sources presently available for information on the activities of foreign diplomats here are the following:

1. BJs [BLACK JUMBO is the British code name for intercepted diplomatic communications]
2. TRIPLEX
3. Special Material
4. Special Facilities
5. Domestic Agents
6. Other Agents

The end of the war in Europe will influence the quantity and quality of almost all these sources, with differing results:

1. BJs

Will continue to be important sources but probably will not be as fruitful in the future. With the current difficulties of courier links between [foreign diplomatic] missions, it is possible that they are currently sending more material in cipher than they will do once movement becomes relatively easy again. The result of this change will be twofold. First, the cipher telegrams will contain less important material; second, fewer telegrams will make breaking the cipher more difficult.

It should also be mentioned that the lifting of exit restrictions from the UK will make it easier for missions to use OTP [One-Time Pad cipher system]; it will be easier and more secure for their couriers to move around with diplomatic bags.

2. XXX [TRIPLEX]

It is very likely that this source will largely disappear. At present we depend on various conditions for obtaining XXX, and these are likely to change in the near future. Once exit restrictions are lifted, couriers will travel more frequently, and the missions will thus have less reason to give their bags to the Foreign Office for shipment to their respective capitals.

The limitation of airline traffic has already restricted our access to diplomatic bags in transit; this avenue is likely to be closed completely. However, the censorship checks on passengers, which sometimes can be used to separate a courier from his bag, will probably be relaxed as well.

3. Special Material

During the war, as we found out to our detriment, this was almost useless and sometimes even positively dangerous. The sad story of our negotiations with SIS on this issue showed that we cannot do anything to improve the situation unless we take on the whole job ourselves and make more extensive use of mechanical recordings. If some sort of merger between us and SIS occurs, this change may be made more easily. If this does not happen, in my view we will have to put pressure on SIS to allow us to take charge of special materials, and simultaneously review the practical possibilities of doing this on the necessary scale. Preliminarily, Saffery should be asked what technology he has in reserve in case we make some proposal of this kind.

4. Special Facilities

Recent research into the security of specific targets has shown that where switchboards are concerned, the danger of discovery is greater than we had previously supposed. This danger will be more serious under normal circumstances once any neutral or Allied government can simply send over a technical specialist to test its telephone systems, and it is clear that where there is a switchboard, it will be easy for such a specialist to discover what we are up to.

Unfortunately, most embassies do have switchboards, although in some cases there is a direct line to the head of mission himself. It thus seems that for the present we will limit ourselves to the use of special means in a few cases only—for example, the Spanish Embassy—where there is a direct line. It might, however, be worth obtaining from Saffery a list of all foreign missions where they could be used.

5. Domestic Agents

Generally speaking, the servants in the embassies are not in a position to obtain high-quality intelligence. They can provide details on the social life of the mission and some visitors' names. In some cases they have been of really valuable service in the sense of obtaining the contents of wastepaper baskets, which have given us either valuable documents or material useful for breaking ciphers. Most embassies, however, are careful to burn such material, and we cannot hope that many of them will be as productively insouciant as the Spanish during the war.

Mr Dickson, moreover, has pointed out that the difficulties of finding suitable agents and putting them in work will grow immensely. During the war, many agents were willing to carry out this kind of work out of patriotic conviction, but they are now hesitating to continue after the war either on moral grounds or because they are trying, quite naturally, to secure better-paid and more-permanent work for the future. It must also be assumed that it will soon become easier to find servants and that therefore the competition for a particular post will be greater. The current position in regard to domestic agents is as follows:

a. Brazilian Embassy: A solid agent, who probably will stay there and who in the past has obtained good documents and the plain texts of important cipher messages.
b. Persian Embassy: Our agent there may stay at his post. He reports on various activities and official work but does not supply any documents.
c. Swedish Mission: The agent is over sixty years of age, has worked for the Swedes for more than thirty years and is very loyal towards them. During the war, he worked well for us for purely patriotic motives, but it will be difficult to convince him to continue betraying his masters during peacetime unless some specific case arises and we will be able to assure him that, from the national point of view, there are truly serious reasons for him to do so.
d. French Embassy: An especially good agent, who, however, will find it difficult to stay there for various reasons.

e. Turkish Embassy: A good agent, who will continue to work for us; but here, too, as in the majority of the Middle Eastern missions, conditions are so bad that it is unlikely that any English servants will stay there for long.

f. Spanish Embassy: A good agent, who has only just started this job. He has a great advantage in speaking Spanish and other languages and may be extremely valuable. His work, however, is badly paid there, and I assume that we will have to give him a generous addition to his salary if he is to work for us in the future.

g. Lebanese Mission: An agent whose work has been efficient, but only in the form of reports about official activities and various individuals. His conditions of work there are very bad, but the agent could be convinced to stay there. If this does not succeed, maybe he could be used for other work.

h. Dutch Embassy: The agent is a trustworthy man, but he has limited intelligence opportunities and can give reports only on bureaucratic issues.

i. Independent French Agency: Apparently a very good agent, who has the useful post of secretary-typist. She will probably stay in this job, although she might want to go back to Spain, where she originally came from, if there is a change of government there.

It is absolutely clear that if we intend to develop work with this type of agent, we have to be prepared to spend much more money. If we need to ask agents to stay at their posts and not look for more solid and better-paid work, which is easy to find, it seems to me that we need to offer them not only appropriate compensation for now but also some form of security for the future—i.e. we have to be in a position to tell an agent that if he starts a job, or remains at his previous post for us, and as a result of this gets into a difficult situation, we are ready to provide for him for, say, six months to a year, until he finds something else.

There is another problem in this connection—that of Dickson's position. At the moment he is, so to speak, 'on loan' to us by the Ministry of Labour, and he will naturally return there after the end of the war. His experience in this kind of work is so great that it is extremely unlikely that we could find someone else to provide such competent leadership. On the other hand, if he is to stay, he will have to give up his post in the Ministry of Labour and become a permanent employee of the Security Service. In my personal opinion, that should certainly happen.

6. Other Agents

They are so varied that it is impossible to give any generalised information about them. At the present the following are working for us:

Spain

DUCK, who may stay at her post as long as the Franco regime lasts. Her achievements cannot be listed and her value may remain significant even though she recently lost her job in connection with diplomatic reports and cipher telegrams through no fault of her own.

PEPPERMINT, may stay here, but his value is not too high. At present, he usually reports about dubious Spaniards who come here and from time to time about

South American diplomats. However, his potential probably could be developed further.

1038 is a good agent, but his links with the embassy are not as good as they used to be.

PEACOCK may be more of an intermediary than an agent. He has just been appointed cultural-educational attaché, but his own political views at the present moment are apparently so pro-Franco that he will hardly be very useful for us. He is about to retire from his post at London University and thus may not settle here, as we had assumed until now.

Latin America

RUMBA used to work in the Department for Public Relations in the Latin American Section of the Ministry of Information, and she knows all Latin American diplomats here. She will probably leave the ministry soon but will retain some of her old connections.

Argentina

PLOVER, a secretary-typist at the embassy. She is unlikely to stay indefinitely, since she wants to go back to Gibraltar.

With Lezica ALVEAR and Flores PIRAN connections are of a more official nature, and they will not give us information without the knowledge of the minister.

Chile

SEAGULL, almost entirely anglicised and definitely staying here. He will give good information about the other South Americans and even about his own country.

Colombia

Hale, secretary-typist; she may stay here and will give us all information at her disposal, although her information has not been of too much use.

Portugal

ALPACA, clerk. May stay here indefinitely.

Peru

GRANDE, may leave at any moment to take a post abroad.

Sweden

LEMON has been an invaluable agent in giving information on various attachés. Her situation may become less useful now that Karlson [has] left, and Servell may be sent home in order to avoid a scandal.

Switzerland

ORANGE has agreed to stay in the diplomatic service as we proposed and will, of course, be mostly in England, although he may have to go back to Switzerland for a couple of years during the next five years. His connections to other diplomats in London and his political intelligence should supply us with extremely valuable information in regard to international intrigues in England after the war. If, for example, a peace conference were to be held in London, he would be a most important agent.

Poland

BRIT has wide-ranging connections with Polish diplomats, politicians, journalists, etc., and apparently can obtain good information on their intrigues.

Belgium

BUSS, a Belgian diplomat, who in time will go back to Belgium but who is prepared to continue working for us there if he is able to overcome the practical difficulties involved.

Holland

LYONS, no comments available.

B1(b) / AFB, 28 May 1945
A.F. Blunt

To Major Blunt, B1(g)
From: J.G. Dickson, 19 April 1945

Here is the note you said you would like to have concerning our conversation this morning. We have always tried to avoid keeping any lists of such an incriminating character, and I would be very grateful if you could destroy it as soon as possible.

Brazilian Embassy: The agent is a butler, thirty-nine years of age. He was installed in his job by us in 1941 and is still working there. There is no prospect of his leaving, and he would like to work with us after the war. He is someone without any imagination, reliable and staid, and sends us exact lists of connections and random 'portions' of used papers.

Persian Embassy: The agent is a doorman-messenger, over sixty years of age. We installed him in this job at the beginning of 1941, and since then he has been working for us. He will probably stay at his post until retirement and wants to continue helping us after the war. He has sent us quite voluminous reports during the time of the preceding ambassador, but since the present ambassador arrived, his post has been of relatively little interest, and the fact that we are not seeing so many reports is not the agent's fault.

Swedish Mission: The agent is a doorman and a telephone operator, sixty years of age, known to you. He has been at his post for over thirty years and has helped us on a rather vague basis for two years. He is a man of high principles, passionately desirous of helping his country during the time of war, but reluctant to betray the mission officials, who have behaved well towards him. I assume that he will continue to do all he can for us after the war if we convince him that it is important.

French Embassy: The agent is a footman about twenty-eight years of age who has worked for us for more than three years and, at his present post, for three years. He is a useful agent but does not do too much for the execution of long-term assignments. You know of his reputation owing to his personal links with LIND in the Swedish operation. His conditions at work are rather bad, and it will be difficult to convince anyone to stay there for long during peacetime without some incentive.

Turkish Embassy: The agent is a footman, thirty-three years of age, who is known to you. He has been working for us since 1941 but has been at his present post for only a few days. He is a satisfactory agent and will continue working with us after the war if he wants to, but his present conditions of work are apparently such that an English servant will hardly stay there for long.

Spanish Embassy: The agent is a footman, thirty-eight years of age, who was recruited by us in 1944 and has been at his present post for only a few weeks. His reputation is known to you; he speaks Italian, Spanish and very fluent French. We have received little from him at the two posts where he has worked for us, and so far it is difficult to evaluate him properly as an agent. There is no reason to assume that his current masters will want to part with him. He will not want to continue working for us after the war on the present conditions, but I think he will do so if he is given some incentive.

Lebanese Mission: The agent is a butler fifty-seven years of age, recruited by us in 1942, who has been at his current work for three months. He is an excellent type of butler and a satisfactory agent, although a little hot-tempered and reluctant to be directed. He may be able to help us after the war, but conditions in his present job are so bad that perhaps no good English servant would stay in it for long, although his masters and he himself seem to be quite content with each other.

Dutch Embassy: The agent is a factor, fifty-five years of age; he has worked for us for a year and has been in his present job for five months. He is a former regular soldier and a Metropolitan Police officer. He is extremely loyal and wants very much to help us, but he is incapable of playing any kind of role and is more of a policeman than an agent.

French Independent Agency: The agent is a senior secretary-typist, forty-three years of age. She is Spanish, and because she worked for the Republican government in Madrid, she was not allowed to return to Spain. However, she does not belong to the left wing, and while she does not like Franco, she does not like the other Spanish political leaders either. She has been working for us for two years and has been at her present post for more than a year. There is no reason to assume that she will be dismissed, and although she is not that fond of the woman in charge of the AFI at the London Department, her job is very good, and she is not thinking of leaving there. She will probably go on helping us after the war, until a change of government allows her to return to Spain. She is a rather frivolous woman but a satisfactory agent and has given us information about the leaking of information on the D-Day preparations, which I think evoked some alarm in Whitehall.

The list given above does not include agents in reserve, those carrying out purely political duties or those who help us from inside various employment agencies.

5 *MI5's History*

[A history of the Security Service was supplied to Guy Liddell, then director of B Division, MI5's counter-espionage branch, who was known administratively simply by the initials 'DB'. Accordingly, his personal assistant, Anthony Blunt, was 'PADB'. The document was written by Jack Curry, and he refers in passing to two members of F Division, (Sir) Roger Hollis and Graham Mitchell. Both remained in the Security Service after the war and were appointed director-general and deputy director-general, respectively. This document was the first draft of a longer document that was declassified and released to the Public Record Office at Kew and then, in 1999, published as a book with an introduction by Professor Christopher Andrew. The relative disadvantage of this version, rather than the one stolen by Anthony Blunt, is that portions deemed to be still sensitive have been redacted. Curiously, this quite normal procedure is not acknowledged in the text, and the book contains a misleading 'Publisher's Note' to explain that a blank space had been left in 'a small number of instances where the original text cannot be deciphered'. In reality, these passages were deliberately deleted, and a comparison between the censored version and this draft serves to highlight matters of interest, such as the statement that SIS kept the Dutch chief of police on its payroll.]

DB

I understand you wanted one or two members of B Division to read this. I would be very pleased to have their comments, if any, and I also propose to send the paper to Hollis, who should ask Mitchell to read the sections dealing with the BUF [British Union of Fascists] in Chapter III. I should be grateful if this could be done fairly quickly and the papers returned to me by 15 July.

35/6

J.G. Curry
Room 707
To be delivered by hand or in sealed envelope
Sent to: Mr Hollis, Mr Mitchell. I shall be grateful for their comments. To be sent with the file to DB by 15/9.

      Hart 3/8
      Hunt
      Hall

Note: This history of the Security Service has been written for the exclusive use of the senior staff of the Service and is not to go outside this organisation in its present form. It contains references to Cabinet papers, which are not to be quoted or referred to in communications to any other organisations. The same applies to certain references and opinions expressed by various senior public figures at different times. Such matters have to be included in a review of this nature since they have a material bearing upon the development of the organisation and its constitutional position, which cannot be properly evaluated without taking them into account.

We need to decide whether an abridged version of this review should be prepared, omitting the references of a more secret nature, and be used for familiarisation within a wider circle inside the organisation and for the information of individuals outside it.

This is a draft of the chapter headings:

The Security Service
Chapter I: Functions and Structure
Part 1. Introduction
Part 2. Functions, or Duties and Powers
Part 3. General Principles and Their Application to the Duties of the Security Service

The general nature of the organisational structure. Powers. Activity of a consultative nature. Links with other institutions and authorities in the UK, the Dominions and the Colonies and with Allies. Functional links with SIS. Functional links with SIS stations in London and in operational areas. The scale of the Security Service.

Chapter II: Changes Related to External Events in Peacetime and During the War Years, 1908–31
Part 1. The German Threat in 1908–14
Part 2. The German Espionage System in the 1914–18 War
Part 3. Events in Germany, 1918–31
Part 4. Communism and the USSR, 1918–31
Part 5. Personnel

Chapter III: Changes Related to the Development of Right-Wing and Left-Wing Politics in International Affairs, 1931–39
Part 1. Communism and the USSR, 1931–39
Part 2. The Nazi Menace, 1933–39
Part 3. Italian and Japanese Aggression
Part 4. Personnel

Chapter IV: Changes Related to the Second World War, the First Phase
Part 1. The Phoney War Up to the Fall of France
Part 2. The Crisis Following the Fall of France and Up to the Attack on the USSR

Chapter I
Functions and Structure

Part 1. Introduction

The history of an organisation cannot be correctly understood without a clear
picture of its functions and structures: what it does, or is supposed to do, and
how it is structured and adapted to carry out the tasks with which it is charged.
In the case of the Security Service, which was earlier known as MI5, experience
from its establishment in 1909 to the present day demonstrates that although its
principal functions were recognized from the outset and have remained unchanged, the internal structure of the organisation has changed frequently. Virtually all these changes have been a result of the need to adapt to changing circumstances. For our purposes it is expedient to begin by looking at certain
general principles that define the work of the Security Service and then to examine their application to conditions as they now exist and as they existed in the
period under review.

Our aim is to define for future use the experience that has been acquired, the
problems that arose, the structure adopted for resolving them, and the degree of
success or failure in our day-to-day operations.

Part 2. Functions, or Duties and Powers

ii. General Principles and Their Application to the Security Service
Every arm of government has its defined functions, i.e. powers and duties. If these
are not clearly delineated, confusion will inevitably arise, whether internal (i.e.
inside the organisation) or external (in its relationships with other institutions).

Under the British constitutional and administrative system, with its logical improvisation, a precise definition of function is often impossible. The confusion that this engenders sometimes has consequences which are seriously harmful to the public interest, but it can also at times make for flexibility and make it easier to get rid of deadwood and help new shoots to grow.

If an arm of government has powers but does not have corresponding duties, abuse of power may result. If it has duties but without the powers needed to carry them out, the inevitable result is poor-quality work and confusion. Thus, good organisation implies the correct combination of rights and duties.

Functions may be administrative, executive or consultative. Where functions are purely consultative, there are no rights of an executive nature, and the duties are limited to tendering advice to the authorities who have the executive power and duties.

Responsibility for the King's Peace, for the maintenance of law and order, including the detection and prevention of crimes, lies with the Home Office and the police, who work under the general supervision of the home secretary. Responsibility for the detection and prevention of a particular type of crime— espionage and sabotage by agents of a foreign power—rests with the Security Service, operating in close cooperation with the police. All these responsibilities flow from that component of the royal prerogative that relates to the maintenance of the King's Peace.

This formulation does not provide us with a precise definition of the related duties, but it is quite clear that the key words in relation to the connections between the Service and the police are 'co-operation' and a 'gesture of goodwill' (*sic*) and that the responsibility of the Service in matters of espionage and sabotage is broader than that of the police as a whole or of any individual department of the police, which is confined to its own sphere of jurisdiction.

For the most part, the police in Great Britain are part of the system of local government, which is a legacy of British liberty, although the home secretary exercises a coordinating authority over the entire country. He himself, or through others acting upon his advice, exercises the royal prerogative. The king is bound by decisions of the courts. This stems from the Magna Carta of Norman times, which decreed that the 'good laws of Edward the Confessor' would be maintained, and, going back even further, from the coronation oaths of the Saxons, which bound the sovereign to observe certain stipulated laws, thereby limiting *pro tanto* his executive authority.

These precedents form the basis of the law that is the essence of our constitutional and administrative system, in which one can see both the origins and the result of the Englishman's empirical and pragmatic thought processes.

This, then, is the context in which the Security Service operates and in which it has continued to adapt itself to changing conditions in response first to German aggression, then to the emergence of Nazism and Fascism and, latterly, international Communism. In the face of this sharply contrasting spectrum of challengers, it is hardly surprising that it has often proved very difficult to define the organisation's functions. This doesn't mean that we should not try.

On the contrary, it is vital they be reformulated periodically as the organisation adapts itself to changing circumstances, if only to avoid confused thinking, as far as possible, and to indicate the path along which development might best proceed.

Duties

The main function of the Security Service is to detect and prevent espionage and sabotage by an enemy in peace and in war. In the phraseology currently employed within the Service, the term detection
[page missing]
officers of hostile armed forces, and they are actions that could attract a death sentence.

It is accepted that a spy or saboteur should be brought to trial, but not the enemy officer on whose orders he was acting, even if in wartime this officer could be taken as a prisoner of war. If he is captured on British-occupied territory, he can be treated as a spy, and not as a prisoner of war, if he operates under cover. Nevertheless, the very fact that an enemy officer participates in a criminal conspiracy in itself justifies the work of the counter-intelligence service, which will pursue the fullest possible investigation of the officer and the organisation to which he belongs. Knowledge of this organisation is also highly desirable as a means to more important ends.

This knowledge consists of the intelligence information that the counter-intelligence organisation makes it its aim to obtain so as to facilitate further measures to counter the activity of the hostile service. This activity is an integral component of the enemy's military operations and can have an important influence on the course and even the outcome of the war; in the fight against this activity the Security Service carries out functions that extend beyond the limits of the law and belong more to the field of military operations. When a counter-intelligence service uses information obtained in this way in order to deceive the enemy, it moves entirely into the field of military operations.

Thus the functions of a counter-intelligence organisation are of two kinds: legal, which puts them in the area of responsibility of the home secretary and the law officers of the Crown, and operational, which places them under the direction of the authorities responsible for the conduct of the war.

There can be differing assessments of the role played by intelligence and counter-intelligence in determining the outcome of a war (hence, in some wars, determining the fate of a nation), and the value of what they actually accomplish varies from war to war. But the military authorities have no reservations at all about the exceptional value of a good information service, one component of which is intelligence, or an organisation for collecting information via spies. (Conceivably this component might come to play a lesser role given the development and huge advantages of aerial reconnaissance.) The great commanders of history, including Napoléon, placed a very high value on secret agents and to some extent owed them their success.

The Germans' success in the Franco-Prussian War of 1870 can be attributed to the fact that they had at their disposal a well-developed spy network, an area in which the French lagged behind; by the time the French attempted to build a counter-intelligence service from scratch, it was too late. The circumstances of this campaign—the precursor of the contemporary wars of nations—generated the widely held view in military circles that a development such as the German intelligence system (which was partly based on the police, which represented an important component of the modern state and which was a characteristic product of the industrial age) required that counter-measures needed to be taken in time of peace as well. A country supported by such a system and under threat of military attack cannot simply create an effective counter-intelligence service from nothing after hostilities have commenced.

When it was formed in 1909, the organisation of the British counter-intelligence service was therefore designed with two goals in mind, the one, legal; the other, operational. This was a comparatively simple concept, appropriate for the circumstances of the time, and was seen to maximum effect in August 1914. There was a straightforward, essentially military problem, which gave the opportunity to find a clear solution. In proposing to the Cabinet the formation of MO5, later MI5, as an integral part of the Operative Division, the Committee of Imperial Defence [CID] was aiming to enlist the support of the civil power, principally the Home Office, the police, the Post Office and Customs, to cope with the situation of evident German interest in the east coast of Britain, a situation reminiscent of a similar sort of curiosity in the run-up to the Franco-Prussian War.

The counter-intelligence service was thus founded as an integral part of the military machine with the job of co-ordinating the work of these civilian organisations and steering them in the direction of measures for detecting and preventing espionage and subversion.

Purely military objectives are subordinated to the state's supreme leadership, which determines its strategic plans in accordance with its political (or politico-economic) objectives. Thus, in theory, and sometimes in practice, the counter-intelligence service may be subject to the directives of authorities responsible for the political direction of affairs—namely, and especially in peacetime, the foreign secretary. In the final analysis, it is of course answerable to the directives of the Cabinet, and possibly for this reason, and also because no single ministry can take on responsibility for it, the head of the Security Service is appointed by the prime minister.

As the 1914–18 war unfolded, some new and hitherto-unforeseen factors acquired significance in the political and economic spheres. This was to some extent at least the consequence of the conditions created by the industrial revolution and its concomitant social changes and technical development. The most noteworthy were the Allied propaganda services and the naval blockade of Germany and the German-occupied countries in Europe, systematically enforced as part of contemporary approval of the conduct of economic warfare.

These factors and the role they played, combined with Germany's defeat in 1918, taken together with the inability of the German General Staff and its intelligence arm, headed by Colonel Nikolai, to counteract, try as they might, the forces that had led to the undermining of German morale, were undoubtedly among the reasons that forced Ludendorff and other German military thinkers to develop a new view of warfare. There is a considerable body of literature on this subject, but for our immediate purposes we can summarize it by saying that, turning Clausewitz's theory on its head, they claimed that to consider war the continuation of policy by other means was no longer valid. They taught that policy, i.e. foreign policy, had to serve the strategic interests and goals of the German Reich; from this they proceeded to the doctrine of total war, from which in turn there developed the theory of 'Permanent War' (*'Krieg in Permanenz'*). All this squares with the concept of German hegemony as a national goal, with Nazi racial ideas of the 'continuous commonality' and the concept of a German state encompassing all Germans past, present and future, both those living in Germany and those living beyond its frontiers.

Moreover, Ludendorff's 'sealed train', which delivered Lenin to Russia, engendered a new idea about how to undermine the enemy from the rear, an idea that was further refined and used by the Nazis, [although it] was not new to the practice of warfare and although it acquired a new name, that of 'fifth column', and to a certain extent took on a new shape. Far from being a new technique, it was employed, for example, in the wars between the Greek oligarchies and democracies. It was familiar to MI5, which had responsibility for counter-intelligence work in the 1914–18 war, and it took on a new form in the war between the modern democracies and today's highly organised totalitarian state.

The term 'Fifth Column' is used broadly in the press and in public discussion, but we have no precise definition of how it was understood by German intelligence operators, the Abwehr [military intelligence], or [Heinrich] Himmler's SIPO and SD [security] organisations, both of which resorted to Fifth Column methods, or the shape it took in various pre-war organisations that used different types of propaganda in a bid to influence British attitudes to Germany's aggressive policies. We need only look at the results in our own country, in Norway, where Quisling typified certain forms of this sort of strategy, in France before the war and in Ireland in the autumn of 1939. Information on German theory and practice in relation to the Fifth Column will be examined in more detail in later chapters to provide a fuller commentary on their significance. We will examine more exhaustively the related issue of the extent to which Communist Parties may play a similar role. For the present, we need to focus our attention on the problem posed by the Fifth Column on the way the counter-intelligence service should shape its organisations.

Fifth Column activity may be illegal, as in many instances in the 1939 Polish campaign, as described by the Polish General Staff. It may, on the other hand, be entirely legal, as in the case of the pre-war Anglo-German Fellowship, which was formed at the instigation of the Germans but financed for the most part by leading British businesses. Another example, again from before the war, is the British Union of Fascists, which received subsidies from German and Italian funds. Where it is illegal, the Security Service needs to uncover information on individual agents and their organisations. It also has to take preventive measures through internment or otherwise to render them harmless. We have not seen on British soil any cases of Fifth Column activity co-ordinated with enemy military operations, and we have no knowledge of any active plot to this end. If such a situation were to occur on a scale sufficiently large to have an influence on military operations, it would require the taking of military measures augmented by actions by the Security Service, and the question then arises of whether the Security Service has the capability to acquire the relevant information and take preventive measures ahead of time. This involves a serious responsibility, perhaps the most serious responsibility imposed upon the Service.

In the case of Fifth Column activity that is not prima facie illegal and that in a free democratic system cannot simply be declared illegal, the duties of the Security Service are of necessity confined to the acquisition of intelligence.

The functions of the Security Service thus comprise:

1. in peace and in war, uncovering espionage and sabotage by an enemy or potential enemy, as well as any active plots and organisations of a Fifth Column nature
2. in peace and in war, prevention of espionage and sabotage by an enemy or potential enemy and illegal activity by a Fifth Column
3. acquisition of information on enemy intelligence, the enemy's methods of spying, its organisation of sabotage and Fifth Column activity and the means used
4. organisation and development of methods to deceive or mislead the enemy
5. passing on to the relevant British authorities such information as may come its way on the political, economic, strategic and tactical secrets of an enemy or potential enemy

From points 1, 2 and 3 there flow executive functions, in the same way that the detection and the prevention of crimes are the executive functions of the police. Point 3 covers functions that are supplemental to those enumerated in points 1 and 2, in exactly the same way that the police acquire information on other forms of organised crime. The functions under point 4 cannot be differentiated from military operations and match the duties of Military Intelligence and the [General] Staff. The role played in this by officers of the Security Service is sometimes of a pure intelligence nature and at other times of an operational nature.

These, then, are the duties of the Security Service. However, it is not the principal executive authority in these matters. In certain respects its rights are limited, and in other respects it has no authority and can act only as a consultant.

Part 3. The General Nature of the Organisational Structure

It is appropriate at this junction to take a very brief look at the general nature of the structure of the Security Service, i.e. the machinery put in place to deal with the issues enumerated above.

This machinery has two aspects: the internal organisation of the Security Service and the Service's place in the structure of government. In both, the Service has undergone important changes. In the early stages, beginning in 1909 and through the whole of the First World War, it was an integral part of the War Ministry, although the nature of its functions, as described above, inevitably broadened the scope of its activity—even though this was carried out mainly or wholly in a consultative capacity—into the areas of responsibility of other government institutions and departments, in particular those of the Home Office and the law officers of the Crown. After 1918 the position gradually changed, for two principal reasons. One was that the transition from a state of war to a state of peace had the natural and obvious result that while the War Ministry ceased to play an active part in the conduct of the affairs of state, and MI5, as it was still called, ceased to carry out those of its executive functions that had been aimed at disorienting the enemy in furtherance of military operations, MI5's functions of a legal nature, i.e. uncovering and preventing criminal acts of espionage, remained in force.

From 1909 through 1917 or 1918, MI5 devoted almost all its attention to counter-measures against German intelligence. No other intelligence service presented a threat to us in the near or even in the remote future, and given the need for it to husband resources and to concentrate attention on the one really significant danger, no serious effort was made to detect espionage activity by any other power, if indeed it existed.

Following the Russian Revolution, MI5 created Section 6, whose task was to deal with the issue of Russian espionage; it did not deal with problems connected with the Comintern and its secret agents, which, other than the issue of Communist subversion in the armed forces, remained the province of the Metropolitan Police Special Branch.

After 1931, however, the Scotland Yard team dealing with Comintern secret agents was transferred to MI5, whose responsibilities were extended to include the interrelated targets of Communism in Great Britain, the Comintern's secret agents and the agents of Russian military intelligence. This was the second reason for the gradual shift in the organisation, since the consequence of more extensive functions was that the everyday work of MI5 began more definitely and more regularly to obtrude upon the area of responsibility of the Home Office, an obtrusion that also brought about closer ties not only with the Metropolitan Police but also with the county forces and other police departments in the UK, as well as those of the Dominions, the Colonies and India, all of which were dealing with intelligence questions related to these three objectives. In turn, this had an influence on MI5's relationships with other departments, including the ministries responsible for the Dominions and the Colonies, the Foreign Office and the Service departments; the latter were directly concerned with the existence of Communism among their personnel and Communist propaganda in the armed forces.

After 1934 a further step was taken in this gradual process of change, when MI5 was asked to investigate the British Union of Fascists and other Fascist organisations in the UK.

The reason for this change was that there were grounds for assuming that the BUF was not a purely British political party and that it had ties to similar foreign political organisations and was mainly financed by Mussolini. The links between the BUF and the German Nazis led to further investigations relating to the NSDAP [Nazi Party], which in turn provided information about the first stages in the work of a German 'Fifth Column' (although the term was not used at the time). This took the form of propaganda conducted by numerous German organisations aimed at influencing British public opinion on issues related to the aggressive policy being followed by Hitler in Europe; intelligence product on these matters obtained by MI5 was of interest to the Foreign Office.

The Foreign Office had nominal responsibility for financing the Security Service, and its subvention was taken through the House of Commons on the Foreign Office vote, but for all practical purposes the Service had a direct relationship with the Treasury. The complexity of the interrelationships with the Foreign Office, the Treasury, the Home Office and the Service departments suggested to Major General Vernon Kell and other members of his staff the desirability of having some sort of more centralised control. Their sense was that none of these departments felt directly responsible for the Security Service in the inter-war period, highlighting an anomaly that at another time might have been less vivid. One of their submissions declared that the Security Service should be under the supervision of a minister who had a central position but who did not have responsibility for any particular department. In support of this it was pointed out that if the Security Service made a recommendation on security to one or another [Service] department and it was rejected, there was no one else to whom the Service could turn, and that if some security issue were to come before the Cabinet, there was no one there who could represent the security point of view. It was suggested that it would not be appropriate to place the Service under the Home Office or any other specific department. In his report on the Security Service in 1940, Lord Hankey noted that he had been aware for twenty-five years of General Kell's desire to attach the Security Service to the Committee of Imperial Defence so that it would come under the jurisdiction of the prime minister. Lord Hankey added that as secretary of the Committee of Imperial Defence, he felt it would not be right to burden the small secretariat of the Consultative Committee with such a large sub-department.

The year 1940 saw the formation of the Security Executive, headed by Lord Swinton as minister without portfolio, and the Security Service reported to him through the new executive, details of which will be found in Chapter IX. These, then, were the changes in the nature of the Security Service insofar as it concerns its relationship to the most important parts of the government system.

Further changes will be examined in the chapter covering the 1939–45 war.

As far as the internal organisation of the Service is concerned, a 'Review of the Crime Prevention Department,' compiled at the end of the First World War, noted that

> . . . the work and consequently the organisation divides naturally into two main branches:
>
> 1. the investigation of cases where there is a definite suspicion of espionage, and
> 2. the creation of a legal and administrative system designed to hinder and, if possible, neutralise such efforts.

The first branch deals with cases of hostile espionage, and the second with its prevention.

The report goes on to describe the formation of a third branch, incorporating a secretariat and 'an extremely important element in the form of a Central Registry for recording all counter-intelligence information in the possession of HMG [His Majesty's Government]'.

This third branch eventually became the unit that dealt with all aspects of internal organisation and finance. During the First World War the preventive branch acquired two additional units. One dealt with port control issues, the other with liaison on counter-intelligence matters with the Dominions and the Colonies. During the war and in the subsequent period, many small changes were made, especially in designations. For instance, the administrative branch was designated successively as C, K, O and A. This makes it difficult to describe the development of the three main branches and their subsidiaries without getting bogged down in a mass of detail. This is made even more difficult by the fact that after the war, when the organisation was substantially downsized, the demarcation lines between the counter-espionage and the internal administrative branches became so blurred that the counter-espionage section virtually disappeared, with the exception of work being done under the supervision of the deputy director on wartime legislation and the vetting of candidates for jobs in Service departments, Civil Service candidates, people applying for naturalisation and applicants for jobs in British missions overseas. It should be noted that in this context, and elsewhere in this report, 'vetting' means checking the Security Service records for traces of unfavourable information, not 'positive vetting'.

With one exception, the preventive branch vanished for all intents and purposes when peace came. For example, its principal functions, such as the internment of enemy citizens and the port control carried out by MI5 staff, naturally ceased. The exception was D Branch, which developed during the 1930s, its staff seconded from the War Office, the Admiralty and the Air Ministry. They were responsible for the security of munitions plants and aircraft public buildings, as well as the gas and water mains and the electricity grid, all of them possible targets for spies and saboteurs. The responsibility for counter-espionage and the detection of spies in matters relating to Communism, when the target was transferred from the Special Branch in 1931, rested with the investigations branch, which had hitherto been rather more narrowly focussed as a purely military counter-intelligence unit.

As this branch began to be more involved in matters relating to the Communist Party, the BUF, the NSDAP and the Italian Fascists, the dividing line between the preventive, the investigative and the intelligence aspects of the work ceased to exist, and both the preventive and the investigative tasks became in their entirety the job of the one branch, which at the same time developed an overwhelming interest in the acquisition and application of intelligence data.

So it was that when war broke out in 1939, B Division, as the investigative unit was then called, took on most of the work related to the prevention of espionage, except for vetting issues and matters related to port control, including passenger entry and exit.

The investigations branch had two important sub-sections. One of them handled the recruiting of secret agents for counter-intelligence purposes, to obtain information on organisations such as the Communist Party, the BUF and the like. Certain of the intelligence sub-sections also directly recruited agents of a different kind. These sub-sections incorporated the surveillance teams. In fact, these sub-sections had been created in the War Ministry at the instigation of then Captain Kell, and a CID [Criminal Investigation Department] officer named William Melville, MVO, KCB, was employed to run it, and he took up his duties on 1 December 1903. Prior to and during the First World War this sub-section ran active surveillance on German agents and reported on their activities, but its main job later became external surveillance of Russian agents and Communists and also, from time to time, Japanese, Germans and other suspicious persons. The conditions of this current war have provided fewer opportunities for this type of operation, since enemy agents have generally been captured soon after arrival, or their work has been carried out under British control.

The changes that have taken place since the start of the war will be examined in more detail in the final chapter.

Chapter II
Changes Related to External Events in Peacetime and Wartime

Note: Chapters II to V describe the issues facing the Service during the entire 1909–45 period and outline the structure created to deal with these issues at different points in time. The report's aim is not simply to describe how the organisation was built but also to explain how it responded to external circumstances, within the UK in relation to other parts of the government machine and abroad in relation to developments in hostile states and the actions of their intelligence or their agents, e.g. the Comintern.

Part 1. The German Threat, 1903–14

1. The Creation of MI5 Under the War Office and Admiralty, 1908

In the long years of peace that followed Waterloo, Britain had no intelligence service (other than a small organisation specially created in the Boer War). Nor did it have a counter-intelligence organisation or a security service. The General Staff did, however, have a small section that handled intelligence work; it came under the DMO [director of military operations]. In 1908 this section was being run by Colonel J.E. Edmonds (later the official historian of the Great War). He had made a study of the German army ever since his time in France during the German occupation after the war of 1870. In 1891 he was able to acquire an insight into the methods adopted by the German General Staff as a result of the situation at that time, when there was an exchange of information in regard to Russia between them and the British General Staff. On returning from a visit to Russia, made for the Intelligence Division of the British General Staff, Colonel Edmonds was ordered to report at the Ministry of War in Berlin and thus got in touch with a number of officers, including Major Dame, head of the German Secret Service in the Herwathstrasse. The Nachrichtendienst then had two branches, one of which conducted operations in France, the other in Germany. Colonel Edmonds and Major Dame maintained a personal friendship and contact until 1900, when the latter was removed from his post for being too pro-British. He was replaced by a Major Bose, who was known to be anti-British. Shortly after this, Colonel Edmonds learned from several sources that a third branch of the German Secret Service had been formed to deal with England. Among the sources from which confirmation of this information was received were reports from a British officer serving with the international contingents in Beijing and reports from French officers connected with their own secret service.

Detailed information was received about the German methods of collecting intelligence in peacetime, including, inter alia, a study of maps and points of military importance (such as docks, bridges, magazines, railways and other objects that were intended to be damaged on or before the outbreak of war). Intelligence of this kind was obtained from German official sources, including those of attachés, diplomatic and consular officials, and officers and officials making official visits, as well as from officers and scientists sent on secret missions. All this was supplemented by the purchase of secret information and espionage.

These peacetime methods gave place in time of war to a system under which secret agents were employed in the midst of the enemy forces in the rear. Thus, in 1870 there was a German collecting agent at Lyon who forwarded all dispatches to Geneva, whence they were telegraphed to Germany. Other agents were employed to effect demolitions, and a third class [of agents] were instructed to travel to the enemy frontier, where they were distributed to act as guides for the invading German army. These three classes of agents were apparently employed by the Germans with success in the campaign of 1870 and played an important part in the initial successes of the Germany army.

In 1908 it was reported that information had been received from a number of private individuals who indicated that a German espionage system on the lines that had been successful in France was being developed in England. It was emphasised that the War Office had received no reports from the police but that some Chief Constables had made inquiries when asked to do so; they had, however, made the General Staff understand that it was not their business. Late in 1908 the War Office had learned that the section of the Nachrichtendienst that had been set up to act against England had established a branch in Brussels for this purpose and that the head of the Brussels branch was coming to England via Ostend. They therefore asked the head of the Criminal Investigation Department to allow his men at Dover to watch for the man among the arrivals by boat, but that officer felt compelled to refuse on the ground that the man was not a criminal and that if the matter leaked out there might be awkward questions in Parliament. The director of military operations, who was informed of this, considered that since the information which they had received indicated that the man was coming to interview certain new agents who were British subjects, it would have been useful to learn the names of the persons with whom he got in touch.

The subject was discussed between the director of military operations, the chief of the General Staff and the secretary of state for war. The Admiralty was also interested. On the one hand, it was difficult for those at the Admiralty to obtain the intelligence they wanted from Germany, given the organisations that had been set up by the German police and security units, and, on the other, they were being approached by individuals seeking to sell them intelligence on Germany, and they felt it undesirable for the Admiralty to be in direct contact with such individuals.

At the same time, they were not as well placed as the War Office to investigate cases where espionage was suspected, and they had thus sought Colonel Edmonds's help in certain cases of this nature. After a discussion of these issues Colonel Edmonds prepared a paper on the German and French systems of espionage in peacetime.

2. The Creation of MI5—The Minutes of the Committee of Imperial Defence

Against this background the prime minister decided in March 1909 that a sub-committee of the Committee of Imperial Defence should examine the question of foreign espionage; the information presented to it included the facts mentioned above. The sub-committee's members were Mr Haldane, Mr McKenna, Sir Charles Hardinge, three Service representatives and Sir Edward Henry, the commissioner of police. Its remit was to make a brief review of the nature and scale of foreign espionage being conducted within the country and to report on whether it would be desirable to establish an official link between the Admiralty and the War Office, on the one hand, and the police and Postal and Customs authorities, on the other, with the aim of ensuring appropriate surveillance of the activities of foreigners suspected of espionage or of being secret agents. It was also asked to propose measures that might be desirable to take to expand the powers required to investigate persons suspected of espionage. The sub-committee was further asked to report on the desirability of making changes to the system for procurement of intelligence from overseas as it then existed in the Admiralty and the War Office.

The committee was presented with information on a large number of cases in 1908 and the first quarter of 1909 in which Germans had been suspected of involvement in various forms of espionage in our country. It was stated that certain German officers had let slip inadvertently that they had been assigned an area of Britain for intelligence purposes, and that individual Germans had been observed making sketches and topographical notes. It was reported that in one instance a number of Germans of a military bearing had been living for eighteen months in a house in Hythe; two or three men had stayed there for about two months at a time before being replaced by others, so over the eighteen-month period about twenty different men had been seen. They had used the house as a base for tours by motorcar, and their interest in Lydd and the surrounding area had been especially noticeable. The general impression conveyed by the facts noted in a number of such cases and by the overall climate of the times was such that the situation was felt to resemble that in France before the German invasion in 1870. The view was expressed that France's defeat in 1870 was attributable in large measure to its lack of an appropriate intelligence organisation, and it was taken as given that the great generals of the past, such as Frederick the Great, Napoléon and Wellington, owed their success to a great extent to a carefully developed espionage system. Immediately after hostilities commenced in the 1870 war, the French had attempted to set up a counter-intelligence organisation from scratch, but it had been too late, since the creation of such an organisation required preparation and steady development under peacetime conditions.

Among the material submitted to the Sub-Committee on Foreign Espionage was a statement by Captain Temple of the Admiralty. He noted that the Admiralty was not organised to investigate cases of espionage but that it had looked into certain cases from which it was clear that Brussels was the headquarters of a mail-forwarding organisation that throughout 1908 had placed advertisements in the *Daily Mail* suggesting that retired officers, engineers and clerks seeking to augment their income by contributing to the *American Naval Review* should apply to a box number in Brussels. A letter to that address produced an offer to pay £50 for a report on artillery matters that, according to the newspapers, had been lost in Portsmouth. There was no information to indicate a link between the box number in Brussels and the German government, but contact had been established with an individual who used that number. He presented a list of questions on what information was required, from which it was evident that whoever had compiled the list was very well informed on artillery questions and extremely familiar with Admiralty reports. The same man gave his supposed agent, who had replied to the *Daily Mail* advertisement cover addresses in Basle and Ostend. It was against the background of such facts that the Special Intelligence Bureau (henceforward SIB)—the precursor of MI5—came into operation.

The sub-committee had before it a number of papers reviewing precedents going as far back as the Armada and the threat of invasion by Napoléon, including a description of the position under common law and the Crown Prerogative. These included a memorandum from the home secretary proposing amendments to the Official Secrets Act of 1889 (henceforward OSA). He pointed out that the main provisions relating to espionage and similar crimes were contained in section 1 of the act. However, this section was extremely complicated, and in his 'Review of the Criminal Law', Stephens had been highly critical of the drafting, pointing out that it had created eighty kinds of act, all of which would become crimes only if specific circumstances were proven, but that while such circumstances almost always existed de facto, they could only rarely be proved de jure. The act did not grant the right of search, a right that the home secretary was convinced was highly desirable.

It was pointed out that in the conditions obtaining in 1908 and 1909 it was impossible to take measures to prevent the Germans from carrying out intelligence operations and that these had been conducted in Britain almost openly. The sub-committee discussed the question and suggested an amendment to the 1889 act. It was further proposed that a Secret Service Bureau be set up to counter espionage and to act as a screen between foreign spies and government representatives; a press control law be applied with the aim of preventing the publication of specified documents and information; communications on intelligence matters between the Admiralty, the War Office and the Secret Service Bureau, on the one hand, and the Post Office and Customs, on the other, should be handled outside the customary official channels via special officers of the latter two departments, to whom correspondence would be sent directly; in view of what reports received indicated about the importance given by the German General Staff to sabotage operations at the outset of hostilities, the Home Ports Defence Committee should investigate how vulnerable points (including wharves, radio stations, private shipyards and railway bridges) were guarded, with a view to assigning responsibility.

It was also proposed that one officer, who was to be relieved of all other duties, would be appointed to concentrate solely on intelligence issues; that the registration of aliens introduced by acts of Parliament in 1798 and 1804 should be revived; and that there should be a meeting of an unofficial nature between representatives of the Home Office, the Post Office, the War Office and the Admiralty.

At a meeting in August 1909 in the office of Sir Edward Henry at Scotland Yard, further proposals were made for the formation of the Secret Service Bureau. It should be noted that such were the vision and mindset of those times that the proposals went no further than the appointment of a retired CID chief inspector in the guise of a private detective, whose name would be used as cover for the bureau's operations. At the same time, the War Office nominated Captain Vernon Kell of the South Staffordshire Regiment (he was to retire from active service for the purpose), and the Admiralty put forward Commander Cumming. These two officers shared premises leased by the retired chief inspector, but after several months it was decided that it was impractical to run intelligence and counter-intelligence operations under the same roof.

3. Creation of the Special Intelligence Bureau (SIB) in 1909

The Security Service, as it is now known, thus began life under the name of the SIB, which began operations in 1909; its staff consisted of one officer, Captain, later Major General Sir, Vernon Kell. The report of the preventive branch written after the 1914–18 war begins: "The work and hence the organisation of such a bureau fall naturally into two parts.

1. the investigation of cases in which there is a definite suspicion of espionage
2. the creation of an administrative and legal machine designed to counter and, where possible, prevent such attempts"

4. Developments from 1910 through 1914

In March 1910, Captain Kell was assigned a clerk to assist him. In January 1911 another staff member and a secretary were added; it was not until December 1912 that Captain Holt-Wilson joined. He later became head of the Espionage Prevention Section and also dealt with matters relating to port control and liaison with the Dominions and the Colonies.

One of the most important achievements of the SIB in this early period was the preparation of a report compiled at the request of Lord Haldane, then secretary of war, in order to assist him in presenting the new OSA to Parliament. The report cited twenty-one cases in which espionage had been suspected but which had not been investigated satisfactorily because of shortcomings in the 1890 act.

The passing of the 1911 act allowed the work of the SIB to be placed on a satisfactory legal footing and enabled SIB to develop as an effective counter-intelligence organisation for safeguarding the security of the state.

In layman's terms, the new law provided that it was a crime (if done with the intent to damage the security of the state) to enter or to approach a Prohibited Area as defined in the act or to make sketches, plans, models or notes intended to benefit an enemy. In order to prove intent to damage the security of the state and thus secure a conviction, it would be sufficient if it was clear 'from the circumstances, his behaviour or its consequences, as given in evidence' that this was the accused's intent. A person committing a prohibited act or found in a Prohibited Area, as Lord Haldane explained when he tabled the bill, would need to satisfy the court that his actions were innocent in intention. It thus became possible to take active measures against German spies that would not have been feasible under the old OSA or common law.

Another most important element in the development of the SIB was the creation of conditions under which the correspondence of suspected German spies could be opened and examined with the authority of the secretary of state. There had always been a firm conviction that the right to intercept correspondence in this way should be used as sparingly as possible, and the Post Office always claimed that it would be highly undesirable if the public's faith in the integrity of the mails was shaken. The postmaster general went so far as to state in a memorandum to the sub-committee that it was extremely doubtful whether in cases of espionage examination of the mail would yield anything useful, since it was unlikely that a spy would send or receive letters of any significance without using ways to disguise the fact. Despite this attitude, the home secretary was given such rights, and they played an important role in enabling the SIB to uncover a network of German spies active in the UK. In his book *The Crisis,* Winston Churchill recalls his involvement in the case when he became home secretary in 1910. It should be noted, by the way, that the original purpose behind setting up an official organisation to handle the transmittal of correspondence had been to create the opportunity for its head to monitor and examine undesirable communications! Churchill also writes about measures taken by him to protect naval magazines against sabotage upon the outbreak of war.

The SIB's policy was not to do anything that might alarm the network of German agents operating in our country in peacetime but rather to obtain all available information on their organisation so that it could be struck at once and destroyed when war broke out. This policy did not mean that overt actions were not taken in cases where individuals were caught red-handed. In February 1914, for example, a German officer was arrested while attempting to take the plans of a British cruiser and other papers out of the country.

The methods that followed from the general policy required the development of close co-operation with the police (in order to rectify the situation that had been disclosed to the sub-committee) and use of powers from the home secretary for the interception of correspondence of German spies, who, as it turned out, contrary to the opinion of the postmaster general cited above, used the mail for correspondence, which made it possible to expose their network in the UK.

At the same time, some success was achieved in the field of aliens' registration, but this had to be done unofficially since the authorities, evidently concerned about mustering the requisite Parliamentary support on a matter affecting civil liberties, were still not ready to come out publicly with proposals to take official steps to this end. This unofficial registration was carried out by the police at the instigation of the SIB in 1910. This covered only the Metropolitan area and the east coasts of England and Scotland. The census in 1911 showed that there were some forty-two thousand adult males of Austro-Hungarian (*sic*) origin in England and Wales, and extrapolations from this suggested that, as a result of the unofficial registration, eleven thousand of them were in the coastal areas and that the data were 'quite complete'. Even these approximations were made under rather difficult conditions, since the home secretary had insisted that all the information was to be gathered confidentially and that no foreigner was to be asked questions 'of an intrusive nature'. Moreover, the registrar general considered that information included in census returns had been obtained in confidence and that the police must not allow it to become known that it was being used for registration purposes. This considerate attitude towards the liberty of individual foreigners in our country was even reinforced by the argument that obtaining such data confidentially had an advantage, since it was important that a potential enemy should not know that information on him was being noted down. On the basis of information obtained via this partial registration, foreigners were divided into different groups, the most important of which were known spies, persons suspected of spying and Germans and Austrians who needed to be watched because they were known to be army officers or for other reasons.

Part 2. The German System of Espionage in the 1914–18 War

1. The SIB Becomes MO5 Under the Director of Military Operations

The main point to remember about SIB is that it was established as a military measure to protect military departments and the country from the attempts that would very obviously be made by German intelligence to obtain information, and that over a number of years prior to its establishment, active attempts were indeed made against both the army and the navy. The SIB operated under Captain Kell as a secret organisation but reported to a section of the DMO [Directorate of Military Operations] in the War Office, and at this point it is therefore convenient to examine the structure in the War Office, of which it formed part.

Until August 1914 there had been no military intelligence department. Intelligence functions lay with the DMO. The directorate had six sections, with MO5 responsible for policy on various issues, including censorship, foreigners and the civilian population in time of war, as well as legislation relating to the General Staff.

With the outbreak of war in August 1914, the DMO began to expand rapidly, with MO5 showing the fastest growth because of its wide range of functions, including responsibility for intelligence work. On 17 August 1914, MO5 was split into eight sub-sections, with MO5(g) now placed under the command of Major Kell, who was responsible for counter-intelligence work, issues concerning aliens and monitoring of British citizens' foreign travel. In April 1915 there was a further reorganisation with the partial implementation of a plan to create separate Ia (intelligence) and Ib (counter-intelligence) staffs through the establishment of a special intelligence department under Brigadier General Cockerill, who ran MO5, MO6 and MO7, with Lieutenant Colonel Kell in charge of MO5. In November 1915, MO5 was again reorganised by the addition of port control officers.

2. Creation of the Military Intelligence Department—MO5 Becomes MI5

In December 1915 an Intelligence Directorate reporting to the CIGS [chief of the Imperial General Staff] was set up alongside the DMO. As a result, MO5 became MI5 and absorbed the MO [military operations] sections from MO2 through 9.

'A Historical Note on the Activities of the Military Intelligence Department During the Great War of 1914–18' describes MI5 as follows: 'The history of the organisation known as MI5 begins in October 1909, when it was resolved by the Committee of Imperial Defence that Captain V.G.B. Kell should be designated as head of MO5 to conduct an investigation of German espionage in the UK. He was later given three officers to assist him, who were transferred to the reserve for this purpose, and a small team of office staff.'

This organisation operated in secret but reported to the colonel in charge of MO5, who acted as its paymaster, military superior and head.

On 4 August 1914 its staff comprised nine officers, five civilians, four female office staff and three police officers. In August 1914 it was put under the colonel i/c [in charge of] MO5 as sub-section MO5(g). Its duties were defined as military policy in relation to the civil population, including aliens, and ensuring compliance with DORA [Defence of the Realm Act] regulations insofar as they concerned the MO Directorate.

Before the war all aliens living in the UK had been registered, with the exception of those in the East End of London, and lists of those who were suspect or who were known to be German spies were drawn up and passed to the chief constables. With the declaration of war, these individuals were arrested, and it may therefore be assumed that German intelligence in the UK was totally disorganised.

With the outbreak of war, the rules worked out principally by the CID sub-committee (one of whose members had been the colonel i/c MO5) came into force, wherever possible in the form of orders in council. This necessitated a major increase in staff. The section was not housed in the War Office, where it retained only a single room as a postal department.

On 1 October 1914, MO5(g) was divided into three sub-sections:

MO5(g)A—Investigation of espionage and of persons suspected of espionage

MO5(g)B—Co-ordination of overall policy of government departments in relation to aliens and issues relating to DORA on the Aliens Restrictions Order (ARO)

MO5(g)C—Registry, personnel, administration and port control

On 11 August 1915, following the creation of a new sub-section dealing with port control, it was decided to reorganise MO5(g) into the following four sub-sections. One new sub-section was designated MO5(e) and dealt with issues of military policy in connection with the control of civilian passenger movement from the UK and, within that, with matters of port intelligence and the issue of military permits. MO5(g)A became MO5(g), MO5(g)B became MO5(f) and MO5(g)C became MO5(h).

With the formation of MO5(e), the system of military control over civilian movements through mainland ports, the significance of which was growing steadily, was placed on a new footing. The whole of this work, which later came to include the creation of Military Permit Offices [MPOs] in London, Paris, Rome, New York and Brussels, was directly supervised by MO5(e), with MO5(h) handling the administration.

In January 1916, when the General Staff was reorganised, MO sub-sections (a) through (d) became MI6, and (e) through (h) became sub-sections of MI5.

On 21 September 1916, MI5 was created from MI5(g) with the aim of co-ordinating counter-intelligence measures throughout the British Empire.

On 15 January 1917, MI5 was created from MI5(g) to deal with counter-espionage throughout the British Empire.

On 23 April 1917, PMS2 (Parliamentary Military Secretary Department, Section 2), a section of the Ministry of Munitions originally formed from MI5(f) on 19 February 1916 to deal with matters relating to aliens and others working in munitions plants and auxiliary military establishments, rejoined MI5 as MI5(a).

On 1 September 1917, MI5(b) was merged with MI5(d).

On 1 August 1919 military control of home ports ceased and overseas stations were put under MI1(c).

On 1 September 1919, MI5(a) merged with MI5(f).

On 31 March 1920, MI5 was reorganised as follows:

MI5(f) became MI5(a);
MI5(g) became MI5(b); and
MI5(h) became MI5(d) and was renumbered MI5(o).

Colonel Sir Vernon Kell, KBE, KCB, who had headed MI5(g) since August 1914, became head of MO5 in March 1915 and remains head of MI5 today.

Since its formation MI5 has acted for the Admiralty and (after its creation) the Air Ministry on all matters concerning counter-intelligence and all related preventive measures.

3. The History of MI5's Development After the 1914–18 War

Following the end of the war, the internal history of MI5 is recorded in the form of the reports of A, D, E, F, G and H Branches. These may be requisitioned by those wishing to familiarise themselves with matters in more detail.

The intention of compiling an overall report was not followed through on. What follows are very brief notes of events during the 1914–18 war.

The three main branches were F (Prevention), G (Investigations) and H (Secretariat, Administration and Registry).

The head of F Branch was Lieutenant Colonel Holt-Wilson, who also ran A (Aliens in Military Establishments), D (Imperial Special Intelligence for Overseas Territories, including matters relating to Ireland and the Far and Near East) and E (Port and Border Control). Various changes related to these sections are described in the above-mentioned historical account of the Military Intelligence Directorate.

The main guiding principle behind the organisation of the prevention side of the work was to establish a level of control and monitoring that would make espionage easier to detect and thus, in one way or another, create the opportunity of throwing the operations of hostile intelligence into confusion. This control was established in accordance with DORA and the regulations arising under it, by complete registration of all aliens at the start of the war, and by monitoring their movements in accordance with the Aliens Restriction Order by checking passports and visas and port inspections, by checking papers, by cross-checking with card indexes and by monitoring communications through postal and telegraph censorship.

As had been decided by the Committee of Imperial Defence, the Home Office became responsible for implementing the AROs, while the administration of the Defence of the Realm Regulations [DRR] was the job of officers known as competent military authorities (CMAs), who were appointed by the Army Council for this purpose. These officers exercised jurisdiction within a defined area in accordance with orders issued by the Army Council and transmitted through the Horse Guards at the General Headquarters, Great Britain.

The powers of the CMAs, who were usually commanding officers in the various districts into which Great Britain had been divided, were in practice significantly restricted, and the Army Council's control was in fact dependent upon the preventive branch of the Special Investigation Bureau, or MI5(f), as it eventually became known.

The CMAs obtained information to a greater or lesser extent from regional intelligence officers on the General Staff. MI5(f) was responsible overall for the preparation of special intelligence measures, and it thus had an interest from a policy point of view in a number of directives whose administrative aspect was of no concern to it. Of more direct concern to it were three categories of the regulations—namely, those relating to espionage, to local restrictions for special espionage purpose and to personal restrictions for special espionage purposes. These included such matters as the right to prevent persons suspected of contact with the enemy from boarding ships and the right under DRR 18B to impose restrictions of a personal nature on dissidents or dangerous persons who, not being subjects of a hostile country, could not be interrogated by virtue of the Crown Prerogative.

The CMAs were empowered under an order in council to prevent certain persons from entering or residing in defined areas 'in certain eventualities'. Only the CMAs were empowered to issue orders under DRR 14, while orders under 14B were issued by the home secretary 'acting on a recommendation'—to quote F Branch's report—'from the CMAs, guided by MI5(f)'. It had become clear that local CMAs were unable to resolve these issues satisfactorily, and the home secretary refused to act on their recommendations.

Inasmuch as MO5 was subordinate to the DMO (it later became MI5 under the supervision of Military Intelligence), papers on the last war stress throughout the military nature of all the forms of control cited above.

Effective work on the prevention of espionage included the establishment under DORA of a system to monitor the several hundred individuals who were considered dangerous, the tabling from time to time of draft laws, liaison with the Censorship and other government departments, the vetting of personnel engaged on secret work, the vetting of persons entering or leaving the UK or visiting British war zones abroad, compiling lists of individuals known to be suspect, general oversight of merchant sailors and the internment of enemy aliens.

From the start of the war a small number of enemy aliens who figured in MI5's lists had been interned; at its peak in October 1915 the total of those interned exceeded thirty-two thousand.

The report of G Branch runs to nine volumes and is written in a prolix style. There is no concise exposition of the cases investigated before and during the war, nor is there any indication given of the extent to which MI5 succeeded in obtaining a complete overall picture of the German intelligence organisation with which it had to deal. An investigation in the immediate pre-war years had demonstrated that the German organisation was active in our country and was especially interested in acquiring intelligence about the navy. After numerous investigations a certain number of cases were exposed, but in line with the policy described above, the main part of the German organisation was kept under observation, and with the outbreak of the war twenty-one of the twenty-two people known to our authorities as spies were arrested. During the war it was stated, and it was confirmed after the Armistice, that the arrest of these spies completely incapacitated the German intelligence organisation, which was unable to begin to operate effectively until 1915. One result was that the Germans got no intelligence whatever from our country and did not have accurate information about the dispatch of the British Expeditionary Forces.

In November 1914 a case that received more attention than most was that of Karl Hans Lody, a German officer who, to obtain military intelligence, had managed to travel around England, Scotland and Ireland without arousing suspicion. It ended with a court-martial, and he was shot in the Tower of London.

In 1915, cases involving three groups of spies, several individual cases, were brought to trial. In all, ten men were shot, one hanged, five sentenced to hard labour and four interned under DORA.

Six of the men involved were Germans, including British and American citizens of German origin; the rest were of various nationalities, including five Dutchmen, one Russian, one Brazilian, one Uruguayan and one Peruvian.

The year 1915 saw the investigation of four groups of spies. The first involved four people, one of whom was interned, and the rest, deported.

In the second group, a Swedish woman was sentenced to death but reprieved, and a Danish man and a Dutchman were deported.

In the third, a Spaniard and a Dutchman were sentenced to death but reprieved, and a German was jailed for ten years.

In the fourth case, an American woman received the death sentence but was later released and extradited to the USA for further questioning at the request of the American authorities. A Dutchman was deported, and a Frenchman was interned. In this fourth group, spies connected with it had ties to the USA, and as a result of investigation, steps were taken against certain of their collaborators there.

Five spies were arrested in 1915. Of these, a Spaniard was released for lack of evidence, a Norwegian journalist received the death penalty but was reprieved, a Brazilian journalist was interned and a woman—a British subject of German origin—was sentenced to penal servitude.

It is an interesting feature of their operations that at the start of the war the Germans relied to a significant extent on persons of German origin but that after 1915 they steered away from this and for the most part recruited individuals of various other nationalities.

No clear explanation is given of how contact with the German intelligence service and its agents was first established, but evidently one of the first sources of information was a British subject whom the Germans had attempted to recruit and who duly reported the attempt to the authorities. Another lead came via an officer who had overheard a conversation in a railway compartment. Important information was obtained when the suspect was searched.

These first steps were complemented by exploiting the authority given for secret opening of mail, which had led to the exposure of the entire German network at the start of the war.

The reports indicate that during the war the most important sources of information about German espionage came from MI1(c) (or SIS) and also via the Censorship. One of SIS's most important sources was the Dutch police, whose chief was on their payroll. As a result, a significant amount of information on German agents travelling through Holland (which was evidently a major centre of the German Nachrichtendienst [intelligence service]) came into British hands.

In certain instances, information was received from agents abroad, which led to addresses in neutral countries being targeted by the Censorship and in turn to the exposure of agents writing or sending cables to these addresses.

In one case, a man described as the best agent sent in by the Germans during the war arrived in the UK from Hamburg via America and France in 1919. His cover was as representative of two well-known American firms, and en route here he had dealt with real commercial matters in France and received a letter of recommendation to British firms from the American head of a French company of standing. In another case, a German agent in Holland representing a Dutch firm of tea merchants dispatched young Dutchmen to the UK as commercial travellers selling tea but armed with instructions to collect detailed information on ship movements. He was also connected with the dispatch of sailors from Holland for the same purpose and had a further link with a firm of Dutch cigar merchants, some of whose representatives were his agents.

Information that came to hand in 1917 gave a detailed description of the directions given to German intelligence in Scandinavia. They cited the importance of obtaining information from businessmen arriving from hostile (i.e. Allied) countries, as well as from merchant navy captains and crew. The directive also proposed identifying neutral firms who might hire German commercial representatives who could pursue genuine commercial business in Allied countries; it was also stated that experience had shown that women were less likely to fall under suspicion than men. It was recognized that the principal risk for all agents lay in their communications, but it was claimed that German chemistry had minimised that risk. MI5's experience showed that German intelligence used secret writing and artificial codes in overt letters, as well as cable code. There was no evidence of radios being used.

When German intelligence realised that its agents' covers had been blown, it changed its methods; as it did so, MI5 too took steps to change its rules to make it easier to counter hostile agents. As a result of this duel, by the end of the war the Germans had come to rely to a significant extent on information obtained orally from people travelling between the UK and neutral countries.

The scope of MI5's work gradually increased, shifting from the simple exposure of espionage to the practice of impersonating enemy agents in order to pass disinformation to the enemy. In one case, their plant went under the name of a German agent after, unknown to the Germans, the agent had been jailed. Significant sums of money were received from the Germans for false information.

Double agents were also used to deceive the enemy in regard to sabotage. This involved insignificant and non-threatening acts of sabotage that were none-theless sufficient to satisfy the enemy that its agents were in full swing.

The challenge was to prevent the enemy from finding out what had happened and sending in new agents, who would be difficult to discover and who could pose a threat.

As a consequence of these preventive measures and MI5's work on exposing espionage, together with its deception efforts (insignificant as these now seem in scale compared to the experience in the Second World War), as 1918 drew to a close, MI5's reputation stood very high.

The reports emphasised that MI5's functions were of a consultative nature, a fact that defined its relations with all government and military departments. This meant, for instance, that it was the police who, acting upon information obtained from MI5, were responsible for pursuing all cases involving enemy es-pionage agents. Many such agents were actually interrogated by Sir Basil Thomson in his office at Scotland Yard. MI5 representatives were present, but responsibility for legal proceedings was obviously that of the police. Nonethe-less, there were a number of cases in which MI5 officers interrogated espionage suspects in Cannon Row police station.

This division of responsibility led to a certain amount of rivalry, possibly envy, between Sir Basil and MI5, and it can be said that in this respect at least, the system had significant drawbacks.

MI5A dealt with all matters concerning the employment of aliens in defence plants and all other kinds of auxiliary military establishments. It also dealt with the importation of labour from abroad for employment in defence plants.

MI5D was responsible for co-ordinating special intelligence organisation op-erations with the Dominion, Indian and Colonial authorities and for co-ordinating the work of special intelligence missions in Allied countries. It also handled correspondence with the Middle East and Asian countries on matters of espionage, incitement to mutiny and treason.

MI5E was responsible for 'military policy related to control of civilian pas-senger movements into and out of the UK; control of Military Permit Offices in London and Paris; and control by Military Permit Officers abroad'. In relation to neutral countries, liaison with the MPOs was handled via MI1(c).

MI5H acted as MI5's secretariat and administrative department, and in-cluded its Registry. The Registry maintained all counter-intelligence informa-tion at the disposal of the British government. The names and addresses of indi-viduals around the world were entered in a card index, and as the war progressed, the volume of information obtained from all sources and on case-related matters grew to the point where the Registry became a powerful weapon in the intelligence armoury.

As the Prevention and Investigations Sections gradually subdivided, the need for specialisation grew, and a whole range of women—secretaries and filing clerks working in A, D, E, F and G Branches or involved with them—grew into a group of specialists with a good command of their areas whose specialised knowledge contributed to the success of the organisation.

The head of H Branch was responsible for hiring personnel, including operational staff, secretaries and Registry technicians, and the reports contain commendations from other section heads for their work in these important jobs. In an appendix to the H Branch report dealing with the work of women in MI5, the importance of the role they played at home and abroad is emphasised, and it is also underlined that work in the Registry based on special knowledge was an important part of the intelligence process.

It appears that MI5 did not have such a strong position in relation to the questioning of suspicious individuals arriving in British ports from neutral countries. In some cases, travellers who came under suspicion were interrogated by a number of officers representing the Home Office, the War Office, the Admiralty and Customs, as well as MI5, and in one case in Harwich, an MI5 officer found himself side by side with the other officers around a semi-circular table with the suspect in the middle. The aim of this set-up was to speed up the questioning of arriving passengers, but the results were not always satisfactory, especially when time was short and some middle ground had to be found between the conflicting interests of the various departments. (These control techniques may be compared to the completely different way interrogations were handled in the LRC, or Camp 020, in the Second World War.)

4. The Growing Recognition of the Concept of 'Total War' in Modern Conditions

Two books on German intelligence, both particularly germane to our theme, were written after the 1914–18 war. The first, *The Nachrichtendienst, the Press and Popular Attitudes in the First World War,* was published in 1922. It appeared in English in 1924 under the title *German Intelligence;* its author, Colonel Nikolai, had been the chief of that service. The second book, compiled in 1921 by the General Staff in the War Office, i.e. by officers of MI5, was not published, but was confidential and intended for official use only. Its title was *The German Police System in Relation to the Organisation of Military Security During the War.*

MI5's book, based on information from all available sources, including documents, interrogation of German agents and POWs and evidently inquiries conducted in Germany after the war, pulled together vast amounts of information on Nikolai's work, which it characterised as a defence of the activity of the German General Staff and its intelligence bureau in relation to state security. The aim of MI5's book was to underscore the all-embracing nature of a state intelligence and security organisation in modern warfare and to draw from this the moral that every security organisation needs to be maintained at a sufficiently high level in peacetime as well. The book claims that in fighting for its existence, the modern state has to be ready to attack its enemy by any means at its disposal, whether moral, intellectual, or material and commercial, as well as by propaganda, espionage and sabotage.

The book suggests four functions for a security organisation: political, defence, public safety and economics. The first three cover the field of foreign affairs, the security of naval military and air forces and munitions, as well as security against political warfare on the enemy's part; this includes responsibility for measures to combat revolutionary and pacifist propaganda, and leaks.

In taking the line it did, MI5 adopted in its book Nikolai's point of view that the war had proved that combat between states had outgrown the narrow bounds in which the issue was resolved by force of arms and had become a trial of all of a state's strengths in the political, economic and military fields, 'and by no means last, a trial of the very spirit of a nation'. The purely military intelligence service had been superseded by an all-embracing state intelligence service, which dealt with all matters that might give the state an advantage over an enemy in one or other of these fields.

The authors of the MI5 book stated that the need to study the German intelligence system followed from the fact that it was too closely tied to the German system for organising security in wartime; a close link had also been demonstrated between the German military intelligence service, or Abwehr, and the Nachrichtendienst intelligence organisation. The close ties between the intelligence service and the German secret police had its origins as far back as the Franco–Prussian War of 1870, and it was demonstrated that there was nothing unusual in the fact that in 1914 the Geheime Feldpolizei [Secret Military Police] continued using the same methods as in 1870. In 1914, German counter-intelligence work was handled by special sections in the German Admiralty (Admiralstab der Marine), by Abteilung [Department] G, i.e. the *geheim* or secret section, and by Abteilung S.V. of the German General Staff. Abteilung S.V. worked in close co-operation with the seven central police departments in the provinces and regions of the German Empire, while the Admiralty section was almost exclusively connected with the police department in Hamburg. During the war the secret police organisation was extended and developed not only in Germany but in the occupied territories, where the term 'Sicherheitspolizei' [Security Police; SIPO] was used. In the absence of detailed information, the compilers of the MI5 book had to make assumptions in describing certain aspects of the German organisation, but it is noteworthy that there was a certain degree of co-operation between the Nachrichten or intelligence organisations, on the one hand, and the Abwehr or security sections on the other, as well as between the Abwehr sections and the Geheimfeldpolizei and other units of the German police. As the war progressed, these organisations grew and developed, as did the steps taken to improve the co-operation between them. This is especially interesting given the changes, similar in principle but dissimilar in their details, that occurred under the conditions of a totally different internal situation, in the Nazi state during the Second World War.

As the basis for its analysis of the role played by the German police and security service organs, MI5's book highlighted the fact that the German General Staff and the German military and other authors were almost unanimous in their view that Germany's defeat had not been the result of any shortcomings of the German army. On the contrary, they claimed that the explanation was to be found in Allied propaganda, in a [misplaced] trust in plausible promises and in the increase in influence of the Allies, and that the blame thus lay with the nation, not the army; with the civilian population, not the soldier.

German military specialists therefore set out to study measures that could be applied to control the civilian population in wartime. In the future, political, economic and financial security were to be given the same attention as had previously been devoted to the purely military problem.

This question is of primary importance in the context of the impetus given to such issues by the formation of the Nazi Party and its system for control over the home front in Germany via the Party organisation, the Gestapo and the entire Reichsicherheitsamt [Reich Security Bureau] during the Second World War.

It may also be noted that, as was pointed out at the time, i.e. in 1921, during the 1914–18 war the German General Staff had been of the view that the Social Democratic Party had undermined the soul of the nation with the support of Jewish liberal elements, that there had been many traitors in the population as a whole and in the Reichstag [parliament], and that the Allied powers had concentrated immense resources against Germany's political and social weaknesses, which had been played up by Allied propaganda. It was claimed that the propaganda campaign was conducted with an unlimited budget and stopped at nothing in its aim of perverting the German people's national feelings. The opinion was therefore expressed that the German General Staff needed to take certain steps, as security measures, in order to combat this tendency, and Ludendorff assumed personal responsibility for doing this; he used the services of Nikolai and the Abwehr; the Abteilung took responsibility for censorship and other internal security measures.

In their general conclusions, the MI5 authors quoted Nikolai extensively in his own defence. Apart from everything else, he said: 'The General Staff never came to terms with the fact that Abteilung S.V. turned out to be unprepared for its tasks and undertook them without sufficient knowledge. The General Staff studied the war from a purely military point of view. No attention was paid to higher aspects, especially military economics and the shaping of public opinion, and as a result, no steps were taken to create the necessary structure. Both public opinion and the powers that be looked to only one authority—namely, the chief of the General Staff of the Field Army—to take whatever action was needed.' In this connection he quotes Ludendorff as saying that a profound feeling of responsibility forced the General Staff to begin to make creative efforts.

Both the German General Staff and the MI5 analysts seeking to describe the situation evidently came to the conclusion that there was a connection between the General Staff's use of its security apparatus and police system and the weakening of German morale. While the General Staff explained away the defeat as the result of inadequate organisation and poor co-ordination of state resources as a whole, the MI5 analysts obviously concluded that in part it had come about as a consequence of over-centralised and over-militarised control and draconian measures that engendered resistance and dissatisfaction among the German people. They recalled that Ludendorff had ratified all of Abteilung S.V.'s actions.

The report of MI5 now under discussion (*The German Police System in Relation to the Organisation of Military Security During the War*) also contains a detailed description of the work of Abteilung S.V., whose duties included procuring secret intelligence, preventive measures (or security), and liaison with the foreign armies (*Fremdenheer*) and political sections of the General Staff. There was great interest in this whole question as a result of its influence on the subsequent developments in Nazi Germany and the reaction to these developments in our country. This latter point is reflected in the attitude towards the problems for British security created by Nazi Germany before and after the outbreak of the Second World War. This question will be a principal theme of our later chapters on the work of MI5, or the Security Service, but at this point we need only draw attention to the fact that a distinctive feature of the Nazi regime was measures to reinforce German resistance and German morale inside the country by the use of secret police methods and abroad by its use of propaganda in peacetime as well as in war to develop pro-German sentiment, along with its support for political parties modelled on the Nazi's, such as [Oswald] Mosley's Fascists. In the final analysis these parties represented an important component of the Nazi Fifth Column in countries that were invaded, and their leaders became known as the Quislings of occupied Europe.

Both these books indicated the growing awareness by both countries of the concept of 'total war' in contemporary conditions and the completely different approaches to it in Britain and Germany. In both countries the intelligence services understood that they would be affected by it, but in Britain these lessons were swiftly forgotten.

Part 3. Developments in Germany, 1918–31

The MI5 report reviewed above did not have the desired effect, and for a number of years after the war the Security Service in our country was reduced to a minimum. Sir Vernon Kell remained in charge, but he was left with only a handful of staff.

In the year immediately following the war, contact was maintained with the BAOR [British Army of the Rhine] intelligence staff, and information was obtained on the steps taken by the German General Staff to retain an intelligence service under the cover of commercial intelligence, an initiative in which they had been helped by some of the major German industrialists, including Krupp, Thyssen and Vögler, who had underwritten part of the costs. The fact that German heavy industry was under less control by the Allies than by German official departments made games like this easier to play. But a more important factor was that as the foundation stone of Germany's military potential, German heavy industry also represented the most suitable channel through which to acquire commercial information with a bearing on the military potential of Germany's past and future enemies. It was reported that officers of Abteilung S.V., the High Command's intelligence section referred to above, were employed in an industrial intelligence organisation of this kind known as the Deutsche Ubersee-dienst, an officially recognized organisation whose stated aim was the acquisition of commercial information to facilitate Germany's export trade. The Uberseedienst operated legally for some time, but towards the end of 1921, according to reports received, legal operation was supplanted by illegal activity organised by officers of the German General Staff. It was reported that in many cases people working for the Uberseedienst did not know that they were doing anything more than getting genuine commercial intelligence, since the information they were being asked to provide was of an industrial nature. However, it included those aspects of industry, knowledge of which would be of great help in evaluating the strength and war-preparedness of other countries. The Uberseedienst was especially interested in factories connected with the aircraft industry, as well as plants capable of manufacturing tanks. Other similar organisations went under the name of Ostdienst and Wirtschaftsdienst. The latter was connected with the Wirtschaftspolitische Gesellschaft, an information bureau financed by Krupps and run by a woman called Margarete Gaertner.

She was in correspondence with various individuals in the UK and collected information for propaganda purposes, i.e. for campaigning against the Versailles Treaty. Those connected with the Uberseedienst included [Hermann] Goering, as its representative on aviation matters, and Freiherr Freitag von Dernighofen, who later came to notice as head of the Abwehr's sabotage [unit], Abteilung G, in the Second World War. Linked to the Uberseedienst was an organisation called the Nuntia Bureau; it was suggested that this subsequently formed the core of the Abwehr's intelligence directorate, Abteilung 1.

Other lines of inquiry pursued by MI5 in this connection related to the use of German consuls in Britain for intelligence purposes and to issues concerned with how German journalists were able to get hold of secret reports, often on political or strategy subjects.

In the context of the time, the problems were not easy, since the field of commercial intelligence was extensive and it was not always easy to distinguish between overt legal work, on the one hand, and secret intelligence activity, on the other, especially when the same individuals were engaged in both. This was particularly relevant in regard to official representatives such as consuls; diplomatic immunity presented a serious hindrance to the collection of information for counter-intelligence purposes.

Part 4. Communism and the USSR, 1918–31

Following the Russian Revolution of 1917, a unit of G Branch ran an investigation into Russian, Finnish, Polish and Czechoslovak officers and also investigated activity relating to Bolshevism, strikes and pacifism in the UK. It also screened individuals of the above nationalities arriving in or departing from the UK, as well as all passengers arriving from or departing for Russia. In 1919 it was proposed that the section dealing with Bolshevism issues be transferred to Scotland Yard.

While MI5 thus retained responsibility for matters related to Communism in the armed forces, the Communist movement outside the armed forces was, until 1931, the responsibility of Scotland Yard.

Part 5. Personnel

On 4 August 1914 the staff consisted of:

9 operational officers
3 civilians
4 female clerks
3 policemen

At the Armistice the numbers were:

In the Central Department:

84 operational officers (military and civilian)
15 male clerks
291 female clerks
23 policemen
77 support staff

In the Home Ports Control staff, the [Military] Permit Offices and missions to Allied countries:

49 principals (military and civilians)
7 male clerks
34 female clerks
255 policemen
9 support staff   A total of 844

By 1929, MI5 had been renamed the Defence Security Service [DSS], Sir Vernon Kell was its head and Lieutenant Colonel Holt-Wilson was his deputy. At this period there were two branches, A and B.

A, headed by Major Phillips, had three principals and dealt with administration and espionage prevention measures. B Branch, headed by Mr Harker, was responsible for investigative work; it had five male and one female principals. There was also a three-man observation team for watching suspects and for obtaining information by confidential means.

This very small staff was responsible for all aspects of counter-intelligence work against Russian, German and other organisations. Given its small scale, it obviously could not handle a great deal of investigative work, and the SIS structure on whose services MI5 relied to obtain information from overseas was also too small to be able to cope with a large volume of work. The methods available to the DSS—namely, mail opening and the use of agents in the UK—had very obvious limitations. Very definite constraints arose in connection with the general climate both internationally and in Whitehall. This was not conducive to the recruitment of capable and ambitious officers, and Sir Vernon Kell must be given credit for the fact that the organisation did not die but was in fact in a position to grow when the tide turned.

Chapter III
Changes Connected with the Emergence of Right- and Left-Wing Politics in International Affairs, 1931–39

Part 1. Communism and the USSR, 1931–39

In 1931, MI5's position changed completely following an inquiry conducted by Sir Warren Fisher in conjunction with Sir Robert Vansittart, Sir John Anderson (at the time permanent under-secretary of state at the Home Office) and Sir Maurice Hankey.

Its functions were expanded to add to its existing remit—security measures against Communism in the British armed forces, measures to counter espionage and sabotage at docks, munitions plants, aerodromes and other state or private-sector plants of significance to national defence and measures to uncover Russian espionage—the study of Communism in all its manifestations in the UK.

Until then, the study of Communism in the UK, with the exception of those aspects related to the Security Service, had been the province of the Special Branch at Scotland Yard, which was not part of the Special Section and which, in addition to all other investigative procedures at its disposal, had the right to open mail under Home Office warrants.

There were thus three organisations in the UK concerned with obtaining intelligence on international Communism and the Comintern and its agents—namely, Section V of SIS, MI5, and the Scotland Yard unit referred to above.

This situation let to some lack of co-ordination and duplication of effort, while no one organisation was fully informed about the subject as a whole. For this reason, the staff involved in this area at Scotland Yard were transferred en bloc to MI5.

The decision that MI5 should take on this task by virtue of 'its position as the joint Security Service' was transmitted to Sir Vernon Kell by Sir John Anderson, who insisted that the changes should come into effect on 1 October 1931. Sir Vernon agreed, subject to its being approved by the Imperial General Staff and the heads of the defence departments. It was decided to retain the title 'MI5' for administrative convenience, since it allowed the service, 'without conflicting with its existing organisation, to carry out assignments at the request of the [Joint] Intelligence Committee and the heads of the defence departments'.

The fact that this change had been made was later communicated to 'all units of the British police and the other authorities concerned'. No detailed reasons for the change, or any statement as to what it actually meant, were recorded within the Security Service or, as far as can be determined, in other departments.

Part 2. The Nazi Threat, 1933–39

1. Problems Created by Germany

The problems created for the Security Service by Germany in this period fall into the following categories.

a. the NSDAP and its organisations abroad (Auslandorganisation [Foreign Organisation] / AO);
b. the Nazi Party and its ties with the Fascist movement in Britain;
c. general intelligence in relation to Hitler's policy and preparations for war; and
d. German espionage, 1933–39.

[A.] The Nazi Party and the AO

In practice the Nazi threat attracted almost no attention from the Service between 1931 and 1933, and very little when Hitler and the Nazi Party came to power in Germany.

A year later, however, Section B of the Central Directorate informed the head of the Service that the activity of the organisation set up in Britain by the Nazi Party merited particular attention.

At the same time, although nothing was known of any direct connection between the two organisations in relation to subversive activity, the growth of the BUF under Mosley justified the Home Office's taking a close interest in his movement. At the beginning of 1934 it was decided to task the Service to carry out observations and report on the Fascist movements. There seem to have been two reasons for this. First, the various departments of the police were not in a position to investigate these movements from such a broad perspective as the

Service was, and second (which may have been the main reason), there were firm grounds for supposing that the BUF was to a significant degree financed by the Italian dictator; at the same time, it was noted that the BUF had certain contacts (evidently stemming from 'ideological sympathy') with the Nazis.

Several months passed before it was decided to begin an active investigation into the BUF; the investigation began only in April 1934. It soon showed the existence of close sympathies with and personal contacts between members of the AO in London and certain of the main people on Mosley's staff. It also revealed that while the BUF was financed by Mussolini, there were elements within it whose leaders, W.E.D. Allen, William Joyce, Raven Thomson and an Australian-German named Pfister, had closer ties and sympathies with the Nazis. It is, however, noteworthy that when these contacts showed signs of getting out of control, Mosley issued an order forbidding any contacts with foreign organisations other than those under the direct control of his headquarters.

These events and the general political situation on the Continent, especially the *Gleichschaltung* in Germany and Hitler's assumption of the supreme military and civil authority following the death of Hindenburg, when he combined all the functions of the state in himself and thereby assumed dictatorial powers, together with developments like the Night of the Long Knives, served jointly to compel us to pay close attention to the potential significance from Britain's point of view of all aspects of the growth of the Nazi Party.

The almost simultaneous coincidence of the Night of the Long Knives with the severe beatings meted out to their opponents by Mosley's Fascists at Olympia had a double effect: it discredited Mosley's movement in the eyes of many who had tended to sympathise with it, and drew attention to its great similarity to the Nazis.

Although the attention of our department was concentrated appropriately on both the German and the British organisations, there were significant difficulties in getting permission to investigate the activities of either organisation in Britain by the only means by which our department could at that time obtain information (other than by sending in penetration agents), i.e. mail intercepts, authorisation for which was refused for some time on the instructions of the home secretary.

We then happened to receive a report on the arrest of a German in Switzerland in January 1934; among his papers was the London address of the AO in a context in which all indications were that it was an address also linked to the Gestapo.

Sir Vernon Kell then had an informal talk with Sir Russell Scott, PUS [permanent under-secretary] at the Home Office, and asked him whether he considered that the Service should take any special steps in relation to the Nazis in Britain. Sir Russell replied that unless in the ordinary course of our business we were to discover any instances of subversive propaganda or other actions inimical to the interests of our country, we should leave them in peace. For that reason the home secretary could not authorise mail intercepts, at least at the present time.

Captain Liddell subsequently conducted further investigations and in June 1934, calculating that it would be easier to get authorisation to open mail sent to addresses in Germany than mail coming into London, requested and obtained permission to intercept mail being sent to two addresses in Hamburg, to which, as he knew, the AO branch in London sent correspondence.

The basis for his request was that the centre of the Nazi Party in Britain appeared to be an office representing the German secret police.

Thus, in the final analysis, a random arrest in Switzerland turned out to be the decisive factor in overcoming the home secretary's reluctance to make it possible for us to obtain intelligence about the Nazi organisations on British soil and led to the accumulation of extremely extensive and graphic material on the nature of the Nazi state and its aggressive tendencies.

(As explained below, Home Office mail intercept warrants were used against less significant BUF members, but the Home Office steadfastly refused to give authorisation in the case of Mosley himself.)

With the benefit of hindsight it is quite obvious that official and broader circles both failed to understand the nature of the Nazi Party and the role it had played in events in Germany after it came to power. In the light of subsequent events it is easy to understand that Hitler's overtures to Britain were simply part of his overall plan for German hegemony.

The picture that was gradually built up from information reaching our department as the result of our observation of the AO showed that the Hitler machine was using all the resources at its disposal to create a good attitude towards Germany in Britain and even to encourage, when possible, a spirit of pacifism, while Germany itself was rearming, and its people were readying themselves for the war that Germany was later to start.

It was only in 1935 that a detailed investigation was commenced of the further ramifications of overall Nazi policy represented by the AO branches established around the world (with the exception of the one in Russia, as far as the records show).

A report on this matter was compiled by Section B in 1935.

It showed that the AO's aim was 'to rally all Germans abroad and all Party members travelling around the world into one large bloc', and it stressed the potential represented by an all-encompassing Party organisation that had absorbed the entire state apparatus. One result was that outside Germany the Nazi Party could use its unprecedented power over the individual to channel the efforts of any Party member in whatever direction it desired.

It was pointed out that as long as the Führer sought friendship with Great Britain, each individual German was obliged to speak and act with this objective in mind, but it could not be forgotten that under certain conditions the full might of this machine could be exerted in the opposite direction. This machine was an instrument that could be used for espionage, intelligence and even sabotage.

The idea of demanding loyalty from all Germans who had settled abroad pre-dated Hitler, but it was unlikely to be easily discarded.

This was even truer of the concept proclaimed by Baldur von Schirach of the Hitler Youth: 'raising in the hearts of our young people an altar on which stands Germany'. The question posed by Hitler and his friends to all the Germanic peoples was whether this broader patriotism would exert more material and emotional influence than would their older allegiances.

The report was used as the basis for discussion with the Foreign Office, the Home Office and other government departments. Numerous supplementary re-ports were presented describing the Nazi Party organisation. In the event, the matter was remitted to the Cabinet for review, but no proposals were made for any steps to curtail the AO's activities on British soil. However, when the German government proposed appointing Otto Bene, *Landesgauleiter*, or head, of the AO in the UK, as German consul general in London, the Foreign Office objected and the German government recalled him.

At the beginning of 1935 the German government reintroduced compulsory military service, bringing in a new law under which 'every German man and woman is obliged to serve the Fatherland in time of war'. The law applied to Germans who also held British or other citizenship. It provided that Germans with dual nationality residing in foreign countries who failed to register for military service in Germany would be punished. (There was some evidence that the Nazi Party was used in monitoring compliance with this law.) The introduction of this law had a significant psychological effect on Germans living in Britain. It was reckoned to underscore the nature of total war in the future.

At the same time, SIS provided intelligence on the massive scale of Germany's rearmament. In March 1936, against the advice of his generals, Hitler ordered the reoccupation of the Rhineland. Information received by MI5—in particular, intercepted correspondence of the Nazi Party in the UK—showed that he had been influenced by communications from the AO in London, including messages from leaders of the German Chamber of Commerce, who forecast that if Germany were to take such a step, the British government would not resort to military action.

Influenced by this climate, the officers of our Section B felt that the latest changes in the international situation compelled the Service to examine more closely than at any time since 1918 the issues that were of most immediate relevance to it.

They drafted a paper in the middle of 1935 on the opportunities for sabotage available to organisations established on British territories by the totalitarian governments of Germany and Italy. It was sent to the DSS of the Joint Intelligence Sub-Committee of the Committee of Imperial Defence.

The paper stated that the opportunities for the AO and the Fascisti all'Estero

[Italian Fascist Party; FAE] to organise sabotage were sufficient to merit their being drawn to the attention of the minister of defence co-ordination and that in view of the growing amount of information on these organisations, it would be desirable to review certain questions relating to the acceptance of persons of German or Italian origin for service in the armed forces or in government establishments or firms connected with the manufacture of ships, aircraft or military supplies.

It was also pointed out that the steps MI5 would need to take to keep a satisfactory watch on these organisations would entail significant costs and increases in staff.

The memorandum cited the official view of the Nazi constitution, in which the state, the Party and the armed forces are under the personal control and command of the Führer, and also referred to views expressed under the aegis of von Blomberg, the Reich's war minister and the *Oberbefehlshaber* of the Wehrmacht [German army], on the relationship between National Socialism, the Wehrmacht and the so-called *Wehrpolitik*. It was held that 'from the standpoint of National Socialism', *Wehrpolitik* meant 'co-ordinating the nation's armed forces, directing and reinforcing in them the will to self-determination and developing all their inherent political possibilities. As Head of State, leader of the Party and Supreme Commander, Adolf Hitler is the Master of Germany, possessed of virtually unprecedented authority. There will no longer be any division between the higher leadership or foreign policy and the direction of military strategy, and the organisation of the entire people for military purposes will be centralised.'

The new army was the creation of Adolf Hitler, and together with other organs of the Party and the state, must act in accordance with his will in the cause of 'educating' the 'new' German people.

The memorandum went on to point out that Hitler's intentions had been spelled out in *Mein Kampf* and that his actions spoke louder than his words. All his actions showed that his goal, which had never changed, was the acquisition of power in order to increase Germany's strength until no one would be able to resist it; that the concept of law as it was understood in Anglo-Saxon countries was totally foreign to him; and that he would not hesitate to commit any crime or use any force to achieve his ends.

These were the circumstances that dictated that the significance of the AO for Great Britain, its Dominions and its Colonies required investigation.

The memorandum also pointed out that judging by his conduct of the Abyssinian War, it hardly needed to be said that in international affairs Mussolini's principle was the use of force without limit or restraint.

Further, according to reliable information, in 1935, when it had been anticipated that Britain and Italy might go to war, the leaders of the National Fascist Party planned to use their organisation to sabotage British airfields and aircraft in the Mediterranean.

The nature of British official thinking and the total failure to understand the real position is epitomised by the fact that at the time, a significant number of Italian workers were employed in the civilian organisation that serviced the British airfield in the Middle East. It was assumed that some of them were members of the Italian sabotage organisation.

The memorandum was reviewed by the Joint Intelligence Sub-Committee, which once again recommended a heightened focus on the potential danger of the Nazi and Fascist organisations in Britain and the empire as a whole.

It pointed to the need for the Service to continue to look into these problems and suggested that detailed plans should be worked out for dealing with members of these organisations in case the military departments took certain precautionary measures in relation to the armed forces and in relation to plants and firms engaged in secret and general defence work.

It also recommended that the Dominions and the Colonies be warned about this particular danger and that the Service give them guidance on special measures to safeguard their own security.

However, the Service was not authorised to increase its staff either to carry out these specific tasks or to organise counter-intelligence work in response to the case that had been presented.

In 1937, Section B prepared some further comments on the AO (see Bibliography), which they sent to the home secretary, the foreign secretary and the heads of the War Office, the Admiralty and the Air Ministry. Copies were also sent to the Dominions, India and the principal Colonies and later to the [US] State Department and the Deuxième Bureau.

These comments dealt with the issue of the AO more broadly than before, and they highlighted the questions of principle relating to sovereignty which followed from the fact that it was an offshoot of the Party-government machine on British territory; it was pointed out that the AO branches operated as subordinate units of the German police system.

E.W. Bohle, *Gauleiter* of the AO, had been appointed its leader, and the AO was now part of the German Foreign Ministry.

The paper also analysed earlier statements about the role it was assumed the AO was supposed to play in wartime, as well the role it was quite obviously supposed to play in achieving the Nazi leader's ends.

It also disclosed that Germans were to be allowed to take another nationality while retaining German citizenship if this was considered in the interest of Germany. In this context, German citizenship was regarded as compulsory, while the supposed adherence to another state was viewed as a mere technicality.

Early in 1938 a report was received from the RCMP [Royal Canadian Mounted Police] on the activities of the AO in Canada. It had been complied in the same spirit as ours and provided further important details on the Canadian Society for German Culture, or German Bund (whose members were almost all Canadian-British subjects of German origin); the society, as the report explained, was also a branch of the Nazi Party.

It was explained that the AO exercised active control over the society, and extracts were quoted from a secret circular sent to the heads of the society's divisions in Canada stating that 'the Bund has been recognized by the AO, but for certain reasons this cannot be openly confirmed in documents or even reported to the members'.

Information had also been received that a questionnaire had been circulated inquiring which of the local leaders were German citizens, and the approach taken to dual nationality was the same as in Great Britain.

This issue was important in Canada because between April 1925 and March 1936 almost one hundred thousand Germans had immigrated there. We received indications of the role that the Nazi Party expected its members to play in America as intermediaries between Nazi Germany and the American people. Information also came to hand suggesting that despite American objections to the formation of a Nazi Party in America, such an organisation was in fact functioning separately from the German-American Bund.

Section B exchanged information on local Nazi Party organisations with the authorities in Australia, New Zealand, South Africa and certain colonies and provided them with copies of British memoranda and other general information on this subject. It was natural that the issue would acquire especial significance in two former German colonies in South Africa—namely, Tanganyika and South-West Africa—both of which are discussed in the 'Additional Material on the AO Issue, 1935'.

The police authorities in Pretoria and East Africa later reported to us on the situation in their respective areas.

The close connection between the Nazi organisation in the USA and the development of the AO convinced Section B staff that these ramifications must in the final analysis put the 'Germanism' of the Nazis on a collision course with the established order both in the USA and in the British Empire. It was therefore considered desirable to set up an exchange of information with the US authorities, and at the beginning of 1938, steps were taken towards this end. Underlying this was the thought that such an exchange (even within these narrow limits and on comparatively unimportant issues) would set the stage for closer cooperation, possibly on more important matters, between UK and US government representatives.

B. The Nazi Party and Its Ties with the Fascist Movement in Britain

B Branch's investigation of Fascist movements in Britain, including the BUF, began in April 1934, and over the next two years, frequent reports on the matter were sent to the Home and Foreign Offices. The information they contained was summarized and updated on the basis of more recent information in a booklet prepared by our department in July 1941.

In the early years of our investigation, we did not have at our disposal all the information contained in the booklet—in particular, on the use of this kind of organisation as an instrument of German military strategy for sabotage from within.

Given the conditions of the time, we were unable to foresee this clearly, and although we had a vague feel for the general nature of the threat, it was more as a political than as a military factor. The experience of other European countries gives a better picture of the issues, but even today (1945) we do not have a full picture of the German plans for using such organisations as a Fifth Column. There can be no doubt whatsoever that when the German army invaded Holland, certain of the National Socialist Parties there played a role previously mapped out for them by the Germans; similar things happened in Norway and elsewhere. It should, however, be noted that where a Fifth Column was deployed, its role in a war situation in which German military superiority was decisive was a secondary one. On the other hand, when the Germans retreated from the countries of western Europe, they sought to use members of local National Socialist Parties as stay-behind agents, but with little success for the obvious reason that the people concerned were almost without exception well known as collaborators.

This will be discussed later, and for the present we draw attention to it in order to emphasise that from a purely military viewpoint, the investigation into the activities of the BUF was wholly justified by subsequent events.

There were, however, major difficulties in the way of the investigation, since, especially in the first phase, the Home Office was unwilling to grant intercept warrants for the mail of the BUF leadership; it gave its consent only in the case of certain of Mosley's less prominent followers. Once it became known that Mosley was in close contact with Mussolini and Hitler, and also that he was receiving a subsidy from the former of around £100,000, and when it could be assumed, although it had not yet been established, that he was being subsidised by the Nazi Party, Section B started to insist on a carefully concealed examination of his correspondence, but the Home Office resolutely refused.

After his arrest, it was discovered that certain of his bank accounts had been managed in such a way as to camouflage the nature of certain financial transactions via which the BUF received funds. As stated in the booklet, Sir Oswald clearly wished to make it impossible for the finances of the BUF to be investigated, and the persons conducting the examination had to be satisfied with the comment that most of the funds had come from 'unknown sources'; only a small portion came from members' dues. It is thus very clear that if it were feasible, the issue of the financing of the BUF and the possibility that it received funds from Nazi sources merits further examination.

C. General Intelligence on Hitler's Policies and Preparations for War: Political Intelligence

Inquiries into the BUF and the investigation of German espionage, which were normal functions of our department, thus led to an investigation of the activities of the AO.

Taken together, these various lines of inquiry served as the basis for a more general intelligence effort that concentrated on the organisation of the totalitarian state in Germany as a threat to British security.

We summarise below some of the principal issues arising from this intelligence, which was obtained from sources in the German Embassy in London or in touch with it. We do so to give a general outline of the problems facing the Service in its formative period in the inter-war years and to demonstrate the efforts that were made to tackle these problems, albeit with a totally inadequate staff.

Towards the end of 1935, the director put B Branch in touch with a representative who had a number of contacts in German official and diplomatic circles, with the aim of obtaining information on the German intelligence system and Nazi Party activity in London.

At the beginning of 1936, this representative told us that he was cultivating friendly relations with Wolfgang von Putlitz of the German Embassy in London. Von Putlitz was a German diplomat of the pre-Nazi school and had studied at Oxford. He totally disagreed with Nazi methods and in 1936 concluded that the Nazis' aspirations would lead to a war, with disastrous consequences for Germany. He convinced himself that if he could persuade the British government to take a hard line with Hitler, he could prevent the catastrophic consequences he envisaged. He was not an 'agent' in the ordinary sense; he reckoned that if he passed on certain information relating to the Nazis' aspirations to our representative (who he thought was in direct contact with Sir Robert Vansittart; the latter did indeed see his most important message), he could exert a certain amount of influence to steer British policy in the right direction. His thinking was reinforced by the fact that when he passed on information about the Germans' intention to appoint Otto Bene, the *Landesgruppenleiter* in London, as German consul general in Great Britain, certain steps were taken. His appointment was regarded by our department as highly undesirable from the security viewpoint. It would mean official recognition of the Party and therefore probably lead to a situation where it would not be possible to take any measures whatever against the AO without complications, especially at a time of crisis. The Foreign Office concurred in this view and let it be known to the German authorities that they would not welcome his appointment.

Von Putlitz therefore had grounds for believing that his information had produced a result which appeared highly desirable, since the Nazi Party had received a rebuff on a matter it took far more seriously than the British perceived it to take.

At the end of 1936, von Putlitz was adamant that the British government should make every effort to insist that German troops should leave Spain. He said that such a demand would come at the right psychological moment, since the Reichswehr [German army] was also insisting that the forces be withdrawn.

Around this time he also communicated a number of interesting facts on

[Joachim von] Ribbentrop's attitude towards the abdication [of Edward VIII]. He said that Ribbentrop had ordered the German press in London not to mention it. The motive was, not as had been wrongly thought, to display tact vis-à-vis the British people but to remain in Edward's good books; he reckoned the king to be 'a certain winner'. Ribbentrop even attempted to send the king a message to the effect that 'the German people supported him in his struggle'. When the king gave up the crown, Ribbentrop's dispatch to Berlin stated: 'The king's abdication is the result of the machinations of dark Bolshevist forces against the young king and of a leader's will. I shall report further details orally to my Führer.'

He gave strict instructions that no one in the embassy was to report on the matter to the German Foreign Ministry, upon which von Putlitz remarked, 'We are helpless in the face of such nonsense.'

In September 1936, von Putlitz told us that war with Russia was 'as inevitable as an amen in church' and that people were assuming that events had developed beyond the stage where the Wilhelmstrasse or the more sensible Reichswehr circles could have any influence on their course. Opinion in Nazi circles was that the moment would soon come when Germany's comparative superiority in armaments would began to decline and that the optimal date to launch an attack on Russia must not be missed. These circles were convinced that Britain would not lift a finger if Germany were to attack Russia. It may be noted here that judging from general information, [we can guess that] when Ribbentrop arrived in London as ambassador, he was counting on being able to align British sympathies with Germany on an anti-Comintern platform. When this mission failed to achieve the desired effect, his attitude towards Britain changed noticeably. Around the same time as abdication was in the air, von Putlitz found out that Berlin was providing large-scale financial support to the opponents of [Léon] Blum in France. He spoke of 8,500,00 francs being paid in one week for one operation, and this had found its way into French pockets.

When Ribbentrop arrived in London, he was accompanied by a large staff, including members of his *Dienstelle*, adjutants, secretaries and 'detectives of the Schutz Staffel' [SS]. According to von Putlitz, members of the embassy staff had discovered that their desks were being searched at night, and he felt that he was working, as he put it, in a 'real madhouse'.

Returning to the embassy after a talk with the prime minister, Ribbentrop declared, 'The old fool doesn't know what he's talking about.' He told his staff that his mission in London was to keep Britain neutral in the imminent confrontation with the 'Red Army'. Von Putlitz said the Reichswehr had obtained useful experience in Spain and discovered that some of its weapons (incendiary bombs were mentioned) that had been tested there had turned out to be unsatisfactory. Hitler determined the dates and gave orders to a reluctant Reichswehr and Foreign Ministry.

An attempt was made to get von Putlitz to give our representative information on the activity of the Nazi Party to the extent that he could see it from the embassy, and also on any case of links between the attachés or other embassy staff and illegal underground activity; over the course of 1936 and 1937 all indications were that these were on the increase. During this time many communications received from von Putlitz on matters concerning German foreign policy were passed to the Foreign Office.

In November 1937 he told us that Ribbentrop was more anti-British than ever and wanted to give up his London posting. Hitler, however, had said, 'He always wanted to go to England, so he can stay there!' At the same time, Hitler commented that Ribbentrop was a 'foreign policy wizard'.

At the beginning of 1938 we learned from von Putlitz that following a decision by Hitler, allegedly encouraged by Ribbentrop, the policy of seeking friendlier ties with Britain had been abandoned, and Ribbentrop had given orders to that effect to his subordinates, explaining that this meant that their aim must be to weaken and, in the final analysis, bring about the downfall of the British Empire.

At the same time, the Italian government decided that the Committee on Non-Intervention in Spain had imposed impossible conditions and that it should be disbanded. This point of view was expressed to the German government, and the Party leaders agreed with it. The Italian government accordingly agreed to send fresh Italian forces to Spain and took a position of open participation in the war there, rejecting the 'farce' of the Non-Intervention Committee. It was suggested that this decision had not been palatable in military circles in Germany and that this had been one of the decisive factors in the recent crisis in that country. This information was passed to the Foreign Office, and we were informed that it matched information received from other sources and that it had made a considerable impression on the foreign secretary.

At the same time, i.e. in early 1938, von Putlitz informed us that orders had been given to step up work on the organisation of espionage against Britain. The Abwehr's Abteilung had issued orders to that effect to the military attaché in London, and the German consuls in our country had been asked to pass messages and to give the names of agents suitable for the procurement of military secrets.

In mid-February 1938 we passed to the Foreign Office a brief summary of the views expressed by von Putlitz. He reckoned that the army would henceforward be an obedient tool of Nazi foreign policy and that after the last purge the Nazis now had full control over the army. Ribbentrop's foreign policy would be aggressive and audacious. The first target—Austria—had been partly attained. Austria would 'fall into Hitler's hands like ripe fruit'. After he had reinforced his position in Austria, Czechoslovakia would be the next step. In the opinion of German official circles, a block of 130 million well-organised people with armies ready to march when ordered to do so (Germany, Austria, Italy and Hungary) would come face to face with the two great powers of Western democracy, whose peoples did not want to go to war. It was perfectly clear that Hitler and Mussolini had done a deal involving help from Germany in the Mediterranean and Germany's having a free hand in central Europe.

Von Putlitz felt that Britain was losing its trump cards. If it had previously taken, or even now were to take, a firm stand and threaten war, Hitler could not call its bluff—i.e. he would be unable to give the impression of taking a stronger line than would be justified by Germany's real strength at that time.

The German army was not yet ready for serious war. Von Putlitz emphasised time and time again that the British did not understand the aggressiveness of people like Ribbentrop and mistakenly applied their own standards of thinking and diplomacy in dealing with them.

He said that in his opinion, given the weakness of Britain's position, war had now become inevitable—i.e. it would begin as soon as Hitler felt himself to be strong enough. The view in Nazi circles was that we were now at the beginning of the Napoleonic period; major events would occur, and occur with great rapidity. Ribbentrop had stated in the German Embassy in London that 'the minute the war comes, we will be at the Bosphorus'. He also spoke of his hope that Yugoslavia would fall under German and Italian influence. Throughout 1938 we continued to send the Foreign Office messages from von Putlitz and other sources on Hitler's aggressive policies and preparations for war. In mid-August, von Putlitz, who had been transferred to the German Embassy in The Hague, sent us a secret message that decisive action was being planned. With the agreement of SIS, we sent a representative to make contact with him, and he told us that a document dated 3 August and signed by Ribbentrop had been circulated to German embassies and missions abroad. It was called an 'order', consisted of four pages and was written in typical Ribbentrop style. Its scope and nature showed that it had been issued with Hitler's permission. It main points were as follows: 'The Czech question must be resolved to our satisfaction before the autumn, and although we would prefer other methods, we must be ready for war. I do not agree with those who claim that France and Britain will intervene. The lightning speed of our actions will make any such attempt on their part futile. If, however, they do decide to intervene in the dispute, I have to say that the German army has never been stronger or better prepared since 1914 and will emerge from the war as the victors.'

This was followed by detailed instructions concerning Germany's action. Action against Czechoslovakia would begin 'before 20 September'. Von Putlitz added that Schulenberg, the German ambassador in Moscow, had reported that Moscow was in no position to come to Czechoslovakia's assistance. His message reinforced Hitler's opinion.

There were grounds for supposing that in the opinion of the Reichswehr, and especially the Intelligence Department of the German General Staff, war was inevitable and that in this respect Hitler sided with Ribbentrop, Himmler and

[Joseph] Goebbels. There was a serious difference of view between Ribbentrop and Goering.

The Reichswehr thought they would lose the war, but they understood that it was impossible to oppose the Führer's decision. Those who attempted to inject a note of caution were told that the Reichswehr had twice before advised Hitler against action (in the Rhineland and in Austria) and had been proved wrong on both occasions,

The German Secret Service (Abwehr) under Admiral Canaris posted a number of its representatives to embassies and foreign missions and established in Holland their principal base for operations against France and Britain.

They had already been highly active in Holland. Indeed, two German intelligence officers, Piepenbrock and Maurer, told von Putlitz that they had agents throughout the country, that they had saturated the hotels and restaurants with their agents, and they boasted that they could get hold of any documents they wanted. (Colonel Hans Piepenbrock later came to our notice as Admiral Canaris's principal assistant.)

All this information on the German plans for Czechoslovakia and preparation for war was passed on to the Foreign Office, the Home Office, SIS and the DMI [director of military intelligence].

On 13 September 1938 we reported that there had been changes in the disposition of German units and that the second part of the German plan—secret mobilisation—would get to the stage [of initiation] by 25 September; that the button would simply need to be pressed on any date thereafter to activate the German forces for the invasion of Czechoslovakia. The invasion was regarded as inevitable, and it was assumed that Great Britain would be unable to prevent it. This fact and additional information from this and other sources gave us a clear, if hypothetical, picture of the line Hitler would take during the Munich crisis later that month.

It seemed to the officers of B Branch that all else aside, the nature and far-reaching significance of the information reaching us in August and September and the subsequent crisis provided solid grounds for significantly expanding the counter-espionage staff.

But when the crisis passed without any clear sign of the broad-scale reorganisation of our department, which was needed if we were to deal with the clear danger that Hitler's aggressive policies would continue to produce, Section B prepared a further memorandum summarising all the information received from von Putlitz and other sources.

We naturally had to go to great lengths to conceal the identity of von Putlitz and the other Germans—some in official positions, others simply private individuals—who had provided the rest of our information.

The report presented a picture of Hitler based on facts we had received indirectly from some of his closest friends in the Nazi Party. It described how his tactics in matters of statecraft were the same as those he had previously deployed in less important issues: 'He would confuse his enemies by a feint in one place and a serious thrust in another, accompanied by simultaneous offers of peace. When he had got them where he wanted, then, without giving them any time to collect their thoughts, he would launch a strong attack, pressed home with lightning speed.'

Goebbels was quoted as saying that this was an excellent description of the Hitler of today. Goebbels also said that the only chance of influencing Hitler was to tell him no to his face and to match his threats with effective counter-threats. Anything short of this just made him even more determined to destroy his enemy.

His comrades in arms found it funny that other countries had still to realise that this was Hitler's modus operandi.

The same source reported that Hitler was very fond of joking about the 'umbrella pacifism' of the once impressive British Empire, on which the sun never set, that he used to refer to [Prime Minister] Chamberlain in schoolboy obscenities.

One of these reports (which Sir Alexander Cadogen minuted had proved correct) stated that the Nazis thought that Neville Chamberlain had become too popular in Germany and that it was undesirable [for the press] to be constantly singing his praises.

The Propaganda Ministry therefore suggested that everything possible be done to portray him as a figure of fun while at the same time stressing that the British opposition was a pro-war party bent on destroying the Munich Pact.

The source suggested that the Nazis never took Munich seriously; they planned to manoeuvre Britain into being the first to breach it.

Our report suggested that if these facts could be relied on, Hitler could be expected to present ever greater demands, all the more so if he was convinced (as he undoubtedly was) that Great Britain was in decline and lacked the will and strength to defend its empire.

We concluded with the comment that this information raised the question of whether, in addition to the paramount need for rearmament, further steps should not be taken to develop our intelligence system and to make a thorough review of security measures.

Lord Halifax saw the report at the end of 1938 and told us he had read parts of it out to Mr Chamberlain. We therefore anticipated that further steps would be taken to improve the organisation of our department, but nothing of substance was done before the outbreak of war.

We were, however, told that Hitler's coarse comments about the prime minister had left their mark (we had in fact included them in the hope that this would indeed be the case), and these facts, read in conjunction with our report as a whole, had made a significant contribution towards the reshaping of Chamberlain's policy, including the announcement of conscription at the beginning of 1939.

[D.] Propaganda

In his book Colonel Nikolai outlined the propaganda concepts he had developed as a result of his experiences in the last war and expressed the view that an intelligence service needed to be involved in propaganda as well.

In *Mein Kampf* and in his speeches, Hitler, who had been powerfully affected by Britain's effective propaganda in the 1914–18 war, demonstrated the enormous value he attached to these techniques. His propaganda apparatus played a major part in his campaign for power and continued to make an important contribution as he orchestrated German activities on a broader scale.

Taken as a whole, this very broad theme was felt to be outside the remit of our department, but from time to time certain aspects of it required our attention.

Propaganda in Nazi Germany was the domain of Goebbels and his Propaganda Ministry. It naturally followed that German journalists in the UK were obliged to play their part in the effort.

As noted above, propaganda in the UK, whose aim was to bring about an improvement in UK-German relations, was handled by the AO.

However, the campaign went beyond Bohle's organisation. It involved the entire Party apparatus in Germany, not just the Ministry but also Ribbentrop's *Dienstellen* in London and Berlin, the Rosenberg Bureau, the Hitler Youth and other auxiliary organisations, all of whom came together in an intensive propaganda effort, inspired and motivated by a common purpose.

A regular flow of intelligence on this effort reached MI5 as the by-product of investigations into espionage, plans for sabotage in the event of war and other activities inimical to the interests of the state.

At the end of 1937, B Branch put together a summary of information on German propaganda in the UK, which it circulated to the principal government departments in the UK and those organisations in the Dominions with whom we correspond.

In circulating it to the Dominions we pointed out that our writ did not run to investigating the activities of British subjects who, consciously or unconsciously, facilitated the objectives of German propaganda; the propaganda itself was of interest to us, since there were some grounds for thinking that the efforts to mould British public opinion with the aim of influencing our foreign policy had a single source, the Nazi Party leadership in Germany.

We knew that Goebbels and Bohle of the AO took credit for influencing British public opinion by various methods, including some of those mentioned in the summary. We drew attention to the possibility that if they took too optimistic a view of the results of their efforts, the Nazi Party and Hitler might be misled into making wrong policy moves based on false assumptions.

It was pointed out that since there had been no direct investigation into this propaganda activity, our assumptions about it might not be complete and comprehensive, but it was appropriate to assemble all the information we had into a single summary, given that the entire Nazi machine had a single objective. In trying to understand that objective, it was necessary to bear in mind that Hitler and the other Nazi leaders attached a high, perhaps exaggerated value to propaganda and its effects. All of their propaganda efforts were directed to bringing the British to take a favourable view of Germany and to understand that the British point of view did not come into the picture.

The inescapable conclusion is that the aim was in part to promote, under the banner of anti-Bolshevism, the foreign policy idea propounded by Hitler in *Mein Kampf*—namely, to bring about an alliance or mutual understanding with Britain, which would leave Germany a free hand to act in other directions.

When Ribbentrop arrived in London as ambassador, he stated clearly that he hoped to develop Anglo-German friendship actively, using methods rather than different from those of traditional diplomacy. These would include the use of a private office [*Dienstelle*], like the one he had had in Berlin, to allow him to play the same role as he had in German foreign policy. Ribbentrop's office was in direct touch with Hitler's Reichskanzlei [Chancellery] and had played an important part in the negotiations that Ribbentrop had conducted leading up to the German-Italian Anti-Comintern Pact (with its secret clauses) and, later, the German-Italian-Austrian Anti-Comintern Pact (which also contained such clauses).

Ribbentrop housed a significant part of the *Dienstelle* in London, and its senior staff commuted regularly between London and Berlin.

Their job, in essence, was to influence the broadest possible range of British public opinion in a pro-German direction. The *Dienstelle* thus included individuals with connections in royal as well as diplomatic, political and industrial circles; religious and political institutions also came within its sphere of operations.

It supported, and in some instances actively collaborated with, societies such as the Anglo-German Friendship Society, the Anglo-German Circle, the Anglo-German Fellowship, the Link and the Anglo-German Fraternity.

The AO pursued similar aims via the Anglo-German Information Service, which was under the ultimate control of the Landsgruppe and the Party and was responsible for educational exchanges. We had information suggesting that German students and teachers had been offered opportunities to lecture on political or quasi-political topics in Britain, subject to their lectures being pre-cleared by senior Nazi officials. The service distributed a large volume of pamphlets and other propaganda material. It was 100 percent controlled by the AO.

Although we had no clear and direct evidence, Mosley's BUF and the smaller National Socialist organisations that had recently broken away from it were known to be getting German subsidies, presumably in part to support a pro-German propaganda effort. Evidently satisfied with the results that they felt they had achieved in the UK, the Germans planned to set up a similar organisation in the Dominions. Although this would be principally a matter for Goebbels as the responsible minister, there were grounds for thinking that these organisations in the Dominions and the Colonies would be under the general supervision of Bohle's AO.

Given that the ultimate goal of the propaganda campaign run by Hitler, Goebbels, Rosenberg and Ribbentrop was to expand Germany's territory on the Continent, one assumes they derived some satisfaction from the fact that sums amounting to hundreds of thousands of pounds were raised for this purpose from British sources (including firms such as Unilever, Dunlop Rubber and ICI) by capitalising on the overwhelming desire of the British to maintain peace, as well as on British business self-interest.

It is worth stressing that propaganda of this nature in many differing forms was being targeted at individuals in all walks of life and at all levels of society even after Ribbentrop had declared within the privacy of his embassy that the objective was to bring about the downfall of the British Empire.

1 [2]. German Espionage, 1933–34

The main reason we had a better picture of German intelligence in the Second World War was that before the war began in 1939, German intelligence and its agents communicated by mail and courier rather than by radio. The first specific indication of a new approach came when the Hamburg Abteilung supplied its agent Owens with a transmitter in January 1939, to be used if war came. As pointed out earlier in the First World War, special Home Office warrants for mail opening and postal censorship had provided the most important sources of information, since they allowed us to intercept the messages of German agents in Britain.

In the period under review, clandestine mail opening continued to produce useful results, but did no more than provide a trail to agents in Britain and their controllers in Germany or neighbouring countries, rather than yielding the sort of clear and comprehensive evidence on which we might build an overall picture of the German organisation.

It may be noted that in the First World War we found out very little about the German organisation, and MI5's book on the German police system cited above indicates that such information as we did get came to light only after the partial occupation of Germany at the end of the war. Even then, it was sketchy. We were able to ascertain that there was a distinction between the intelligence organisation, or Nachrichtendienst, and the counter-intelligence organisation, or Abwehrstelle. It also showed that the German intelligence service had close ties to the police.

We now know that as a result of the conditions created at the end of the First World War, the Intelligence Department (Nachrichtenabteilung) ceased to function and its intelligence work eventually became the responsibility of the Abwehrstelle, even though the Abwehrstelle was nominally a counter-intelligence operation.

Before and during World War I, the German Admiralty had close ties in the intelligence area with the central police departments in Hamburg and Berlin; the Abwehrstelle in Hamburg, which had earlier dealt with intelligence against the British Empire and the USA, continued in this role in the 1933–39 period.

Investigation of cases that came to notice in this latter period yielded no detailed intelligence on the Hamburg organisation beyond the fact that it had an outstation in Cologne, which also operated against Britain.

Our knowledge of the staff in Hamburg and Cologne was confined to the cover names they used in correspondence and a few personal descriptions provided by some of their agents from their recruitment interviews.

This essentially was the only information we had that was related to agents who came to Britain. We therefore looked to SIS to penetrate the German organisation and to procure intelligence from inside agents on its size, its methods and its staffing, but this proved fruitless.

Over this period, we brought to light thirty cases of individuals who had worked as agents or at whom the Germans had made a pass. Twenty-one of these were British subjects, many of whom made no attempt to collect intelligence of value to the Germans but simply passed on items of little significance in a bid to get maximum reward for minimum effort. In fact, most of these British subjects received no training at all, and the way they were recruited suggests that the Abwehrstelle was ham-fisted.

The problem was not the quantity but the quality of the Abwehrstelle's agents, but we cannot say for certain whether the weight of an indifferent number of agents actually served as a cover to shield the existence of a few high-grade assets.

Half of the British individuals involved were not of the brightest and were simply in no position to procure intelligence of any value. Among the more suitable people whom the Germans recruited or attempted to recruit were four ex-officers, four businessmen and four members of the armed forces (officers and ORs [other ranks]); most of them reported the approach to the authorities immediately or shortly afterwards.

One of the ways the Germans recruited was by replying to small ads in the newspapers, especially those placed by job-seeking ex-officers, businessmen and specialists with technical knowledge. The Germans also placed advertisements in British papers themselves, offering jobs for commercial and technical specialists. From 1936 on, the Hamburg Abwehrstelle stepped up its efforts considerably, and twenty-six of the thirty known cases came to notice between 1936 and the outbreak of war.

In three cases that came to our attention in this period, Germans acted as agent recruiters, and in these cases the addresses of Germans (one in England, one in Scotland and one in Eire) were used as mail drops, via which the German Secret Service received messages from their agents in the USA and France. All three were run by the Hamburg Abwehrstelle. The latter, however, concerned that incoming mail was liable to be opened, never used these drops to communicate with their agents and often used couriers on German merchant ships instead; they seem not to have realised, however, that mail dispatched by their agents was just as susceptible to interception.

Eleven of the thirty agents told us about the German approach; nine were exposed by mail intercepts, five were denounced by private individuals whose suspicions had been aroused, one was reported by an immigration officer and one was denounced by an anonymous informant; the other two were uncovered by accident.

Experience showed that while opening mail produced definite results, it did not give us enough to actually 'land the fish'; the networks were too extensive.

Investigations revealed that personal contact was the method favoured to recruit agents, but only in one case did such a contact actually lead us to uncover an agent.

Of the eleven agents who reported that they had been recruited by the Germans (had they not done so, we would probably never have got on to them), six were recruited via a personal contact. We cannot know for certain how many others did not report that they had been recruited and who thus remained undetected.

Although in all the circumstances this can be no more than a tentative conclusion, there are nonetheless grounds for believing that when the war began, the Germans had no more than a handful of agents in the UK who were actually sending them information.

Three PO [Post Office] boxes in different women's names yielded far more interesting information on the German set-up, although they did not have a direct bearing on espionage in the UK.

One of the women, a Mrs Duncombe in London, received intelligence collected in France, while a Mrs Jordan was used as a mail drop in a case under investigation in the USA and widely reported in the press at the time.

The central figure in the case was one Rumrich. His brother was arrested in Prague at the same time and found to be in possession of the address of a Mrs Brandy in Dublin; this was the third mail drop.

Clandestine reading of her correspondence showed that she was receiving accurate and therefore dangerous intelligence messages from a French merchant navy officer. How the messages were passed on was not discovered, but they were probably carried by couriers on ships plying between Eire and Hamburg. As a result of these investigations, we passed information to the French, and it was discovered that the messages came from a French merchant navy officer named Aubert. He was arrested at the end of 1938 and shot.

These three cases also demonstrated that part of the German tradecraft was to use mail drops in countries other than those they were targeting; they were possibly getting intelligence on British overseas territories in the same way.

Although no specific information on this point came to our attention, some

German 'agents' did report to us that they had been supplied with addresses in neutral countries.

Some of the agents who disclosed their recruitment to us at the outset or soon after the fact were tasked to work against the Germans under our control and did so for periods ranging from six months to three years.

Running double agents in peacetime presented major difficulties, since it was almost impossible to feed them with intelligence that was harmless and, at the same time, would satisfy the German appetite.

Much basic information and even sometimes information of greater importance was available in the UK simply for the asking.

The Germans had ready access to important information on our heavy industry, our scientific research and our overall military potential; this included not only maps, railway routes and data on public utilities, docks and bridges but also a wealth of detailed industrial statistics accessible to the many Germans involved in business in the UK.

The focal point for all this was the German Chamber of Commerce in London, which had been set up by the Nazis and which they described as a 'bastion' of their Party. Although this initiative did not involve secret material per se, the opportunities available to the Germans were so broad that it had to be assumed that while much of the information they gathered could be classified as no more than commercial intelligence, the information also cast a valuable light on branches of British industry of military relevance, and it further had to be assumed that this intelligence, collected systematically and regularly, was being communicated to the appropriate quarters in Germany.

There were also examples of close German ties to our aircraft industry, and the fact that they kept a careful eye on machine-tool manufacturing gave them almost unlimited scope to obtain a wide range of data on the capacity of individual plants and on overall aircraft, tank, lorry and munitions production.

The scale of the German organisation that dealt with the war industry and industrial mobilisation is described in Appendix A to the 'Report on the German Intelligence Service' compiled by our department in August 1942.

The report highlights the relationship between the Military Economy Staff (Wehrwirtschaftsstab; WWS) of the German High Command and the Economic Department of the Abwehr and describes in broad terms their areas of mutual interest, one consequence of which was an undertaking given by German industrialists (who had special relationships with the international cartels) to the Führer that they would collaborate in all aspects of the interface between the German military machine and German industry.

The basis of a modern great power's military machine is its heavy industry and overall technological development; it thus clearly follows that it was of primary importance to the WWS to be able to obtain vital intelligence.

In this respect, the Western democracies were at a disadvantage compared to a country like Russia, which could and did go to extraordinary lengths to protect its security. The German system also lent itself more readily than the British one to the implementation of very comprehensive security measures.

Even had our Service been larger than it was before the war, it would still not have been possible to guarantee security in the face of the efforts of the WWS, with all the overt and covert sources it had at its disposal in the UK. The most we could do was to expose the secret agents employed by the AO and the Abwehr, as well as the WWS.

Up to 1941 we had practically no intelligence on the Abwehr of operational value, and we had to rely on the results of investigations into individual Germans who we felt might be in a good position to procure high-level intelligence.

In 1938, as stated in the final paragraph of Appendix A to the above-mentioned report, the Abwehr (as we learned from von Putlitz, whom we considered a trustworthy source) was ordered to set up shop in the UK.

Indications that the cement industry was a target of special interest led us to investigate Germans employed in it, especially the staff of the Concrete Pump Company, Ltd, which was owned by a German and his son; the latter had been born in the UK but was nevertheless liable to conscription in Germany. Their business gave them access to information on the dimensions, purpose and location of a number of aerodromes and secret naval installations, as well as numerous defence plants around the country. Our investigations gave grounds for concern about many other areas of trade and industry.

Other information was obtained from an unwitting source in the German Foreign Ministry, who provided intelligence of great significance on the negotiations between Germany and Russia in 1939; he also told us, unknowingly, that office equipment distributors were an important source of intelligence for the Germans.

Based on all the information at our disposal at the start of the war, while it could be assumed that the Abwehr employed a large number of agents of very poor quality and of little or no value, it was capable of major successes, as in the cases in France and the USA that came to light via the UK mail drops. Nor could there be any assurance that the Abwehr did not also have well-placed agents in the UK who were in touch with Germany via third countries and whom we failed to uncover.

The potential for overt acquisition of information of vital importance on our military potential, on aircraft production and on our munitions plants was so vast that security investigations could only scratch the surface. We had nonetheless to investigate many individuals about whom there were grounds for suspicion and also to examine particular areas where secrecy was critical, e.g. new aircraft construction methods, DF [direction finding] and similar highly important areas.

B Branch's investigations were thus not confined strictly to espionage but also covered the wider area of general prevention. Many of these investigations required them to co-operate and research laboratories, especially those related to aircraft. Section D officers brought to light many alarming cases of glaring lapses of security.

2 [3]. The Prevention Division

In addition to the report and memoranda referred to in Chapter III, Part 2/1, in 1936 and subsequent years, we sent the Foreign and Home Offices numerous papers on the Nazi Party organisation (AO).

In 1936, B Branch wrote a report that its head passed to the PUS at the FO [Foreign Office], suggesting that the development of the one-party nation-state in Germany and Italy (for which there were both recent and historical precedents), together with the existence and activities of the AO and the FAE, required us to clarify and define our position on the issues of British sovereignty and citizenship. The report described the German concept of total war, which encompassed air raids without warning not only against the enemy's armed forces but also against the civil population. It was pointed out that both the organisations mentioned were part of a machine operated by their governments for the waging of total war, and the possibility was raised that both organisations might be used for sabotage. Attention was also drawn to their efforts to bring into their orbit persons of German and Italian nationality who also had British citizenship. The aim of the report was to raise the question of introducing legislation to ban these Party organisations on British territory.

But it proved impossible to reach any consensus on what should be done. When the general question was put to the Cabinet in 1936, the prime minister asked the home and foreign secretaries to defer it until such time as circumstances were more favourable for taking action. We expressed the view that given the pace of German rearmament, it would probably become even more difficult to take action as time went by. The foreign secretary reverted to the issue in October 1936, but the Cabinet again deferred a decision.

As a result of our representations, the PUS of the FO, the [PUS of the] Home Office and the director of the Security Service drafted a joint memorandum in April 1937 for presentation to the Cabinet, proposing that the German and Italian governments be given friendly off-the-record advice that they should take steps via their London embassies to close down the Nazi and Fascist Party branches that had been set up in the UK. The Cabinet discussed the matter again in July 1937 and decided that while it could not be deferred sine die and needed to be kept under constant review, given the difficulty then being experienced in reaching agreement on matters relating to Spain, no firm measures could be taken at present. In September 1937, Sir Robert Vansittart raised the matter again in the light of developments in the interim—in particular, that the Congress of Germans Living Abroad met in Stuttgart in August. He reverted to the topic yet again in July 1938, when, after a meeting with the director of the Security Service, he wrote to Lord Halifax and Sir Samuel Hoare referring to a request from the French foreign minister to know 'what practical steps HMG intended to take to limit the activities of the Nazi organisation [AO] in Great Britain'.

Over the same period, we continued to circulate reports based on information obtained from the clandestine reading of Nazi Party mail on various questions, in particular, as a consequence of an edict that required [German] civil servants to join the Nazi Party, the 'Gleichschaltung' of members of the German Embassy in London. Given the German government's position that German subjects could retain their nationality even though they acquired British citizenship, if that was deemed of benefit to Germany, steps were taken to restrict the enlistment of such persons in the armed forces.

For want of an established policy, we were able to take preventive measures only as a result of investigations on a case-by-case basis. These included measures to allow Germans to be refused entry to the UK and measures to bar doubtful individuals—Germans or dual nationals—from employment in aircraft, munitions or ancillary plants.

One of the most important cases in which a German was refused entry was that of Otto Ludwig, who aroused a custom officer's suspicions when he arrived in the UK on 10 April 1937.

Following inquiries, he was expelled under the provisions of the OSA, examination of papers in his possession having shown that he had come to the UK on behalf of an organisation called the Bureau of Political Intelligence and that three German journalists in London—Nidda, Krome and Edenhofer—had, as they themselves admitted, been supplying him with political intelligence information of a semi-secret nature. This case led to a more thorough investigation of the German press corps in the UK. The British press had already commented on their number, and on making inquiries, we found instances where even small-circulation German papers maintained more than one accredited correspondent in London.

We drew this to the attention of the FO, and on 4 May 1937 a meeting took place—with Sir Vernon Kell and Captain Liddell in attendance—under the chairmanship of Sir Robert Vansittart. He opened the meeting by stating that in his opinion the question was closely linked with the more important issue of the German and Italian organisations on British territory. The foreign secretary regarded the matter as one of internal security and thus the domain of the home secretary, Sir John Simon, and it was for the latter to raise it with the Cabinet. Sir John had said he was prepared to do so on condition that the foreign secretary agreed to present this as one of the main thrusts of his foreign policy vis-à-vis Germany. We thus had a situation in which the foreign secretary was prepared to back the home secretary, and vice versa, but neither was keen to take the initiative in raising the matter with the Cabinet.

As regards the journalists, Sir Robert considered that although we were not yet in a position to take action on the overall issue of the Nazi and Fascist organisations, every opportunity must be taken to respond appropriately as specific cases came to notice. He had reviewed the papers in the Ludwig case and was of the view that Nidda, Krome and Edenhofer should be asked to leave the country. The same should apply—albeit not in any rush—with any other German journalist identified as engaging in undesirable activities.

Another meeting on the German press corps (with Sir Vernon and Captain Liddell again in attendance) was held at the Home Office on 21 June 1937. The home secretary stated that a distinction must be made between journalists connected with the Ludwig case and others who had been identified as undesirable elements. The overall issue of cutting back on the large number of German journalists was a matter for the foreign secretary, and he did not wish to take steps that might generate banner headlines at a time when [Foreign Minister] von Neurath was due in London. As regards the general question of the Nazi and Fascist organisations, he wished to review the matter in greater detail.

At the end of August 1937 we submitted a further report to the FO on the German press corps. Attached was a list of seventy individuals we had drawn up in April, and we pointed out that this number had now increased to ninety, although it was possible that a small number of these were not actually employed by various arms of the Nazi government. When this figure had been reported in the UK press, the Nazi doyen of the press corps had said that there were no more than thirty German journalists in the UK.

German Nazi organisations had an obvious interest in procuring political intelligence in the UK, and it is conceivable that their operations were not fully co-ordinated. They included the Party's Foreign Press Bureau, the Propaganda Ministry in Berlin (which was connected to the Johansen bureau in Hamburg), the AO, the Ribbentrop *Dienstelle*, the Foreign Ministry, the Foreign Policy Department (Aussenpolitische Amt), which was linked with the anti-Comintern organisation, the Defence Ministry and the Ministry of Aviation.

The reason behind this state of affairs is probably to be found in the fact that the German army had advised against the reoccupation of the Rhineland in 1936, while the Party had predicted that there would be no serious repercussions. Hitler took the Party's advice, which proved correct. It is probably fair to conclude that as a result, both the army and a whole gamut of German government departments and official bodies felt it essential to have first-hand access to accurate and detailed intelligence on British public opinion.

We also know that alongside his ambassadorial role, Ribbentrop used his *Dienstelle* to procure intelligence, on which he based the advice he gave Hitler.

Our report pointed out—by reference to the part Ribbentrop had played in [negotiating] the German-Japanese Treaty and by reference to his special interest in Austria and southeast Europe—that the propaganda campaign he was waging in the UK in a bid to develop good relations with Germany meant that he must have access to a wide range of diverse and well-informed sources. There was information to indicate that Ribbentrop had a personal interest in the information bureau that Ludwig was supposed to set up in London.

In our opinion there were two differing schools of thought in the Defence Ministry (Reichswehrministerium) on political issues, and it was quite conceivable that each side had its own agents in the German press corps.

Two German journalists who came to notice had been recommended for expulsion. Another whom it was also proposed to expel had used unacceptable methods to obtain information on air matters.

We indicated that considerations of high policy aside, the situation was troubling from our more parochial vantage point. We had an ambassador who went way beyond his ambassadorial brief (engaging in intrigue in both countries and running a propaganda campaign in the country to which he was accredited). We had a large number of German entities represented in the UK, each of which sheltered agents of various kinds.

The task of uncovering individuals engaged in espionage had (all the more, given the political situation) become too large for our small organisation to handle.

We were diverted by having to track the activities of so many journalists, nor was it feasible to keep track of all of them; it had also become impossible to determine which were bona fide and which were not.

Through 1937 and 1938 the Home Office and the Foreign Office discussed expelling more of the journalists. As a start, six were asked to leave on account of incompatible activity, but it was decided that taking more extensive steps would not be worthwhile. Although the German government declared that it officially recognized only thirty-one journalists, it was assumed that as long as the various German government and Party departments maintained their own foreign affairs bureaus, they would go on trying to obtain intelligence via their representatives abroad. The FO was of the view that if we were to expel the agents they had here now, we would not achieve our objective, or would at best achieve very little, since they would find ways to send in replacements. It was further suggested that many of the German journalists were in fact filing objective reports, which did much to counter the false impressions of British weakness and decadence that had been created in Germany.

We learned from a reliable source that the expulsion of the German journalists had led to a quarrel between Goering and Himmler and that Himmler had decided as a result to use other covers for his agents. (Taken together with other even more reliable intelligence available to us, this may to some degree serve to confirm the impression that Ludwig was an agent of the SD.)

In response to our representations, Lord Halifax told the German chargé d'affaires in April 1939 that it had been decided to ask three leading members of the AO in Britain to leave the country in the near future—namely, Herr Karlowa, *Landesgruppenleiter* of the Nazi Party in the UK, Herr Himmelmann, its *Organisationsleiter,* and Frau Johanna Wolff, head of the Women's Section of the Deutsche Arbeitsfront in the UK.

We received extremely reliable reports that the action taken against Karlowa as the Nazi Party's leader in the UK made a profound impression on the Nazi leadership and made them realise that we appreciated the importance of his position here and that his removal was the first step in breaking up the Party's organisation.

[Note: according to a report dated 23 May 1939, the Foreign Office had received the following information. 'Munich party circles are currently very concerned that the (action by the) British prime minister might embolden other, less powerful states to break up the Nazi organisations in their territories. Boettinger has said it was 'perfectly clear that if war comes, the Nazi organisations abroad will play an important role and will be entrusted with some very dangerous tasks. The brunt of the burden will be borne by Nazi groups in the so-called neutral countries. It is surprising how slow these democracies have been to wake up to the real significance of having these *gleichgeschalten* (co-ordinated) political organisations in their midst. Boettinger concluded by saying that in Dr Kordt's view, this would not be the last expulsion of Germans from Britain and that further surprises could be expected in the future.]

In April 1939 we submitted a report on German propaganda to the deputy DMI based on thorough surveillance of mail being sent to an address in Germany. We indicated that the Germans were attempting in various different ways to develop direct personal contacts between members of HM [His Majesty's] forces and their propaganda organisations. We suggested there should be a discussion of whether the attention of service personnel should be drawn to the danger, and [we suggested] the undesirability of correspondence with these organisations. The persons nominated as 'pen pals' in Germany were bound to be ardent supporters of the Nazi regime, and any hints about British public opinion or any information on the army or navy that might be mentioned in letters, totally unintentionally, would of course be passed on to those responsible for the conduct of Nazi foreign policy. The DDMI agreed that it was desirable to circularise commanding officers on the matter.

After our review of all the information on the AO in London and its role in implementing Hitler's objectives, Section B suggested to the [Military Intelligence] Directorate that preparations be made for Party members in Britain to be arrested in case of war. In the light of the threatening build-up to the Munich crisis in September 1938, the director-general [DG] of the Service had been authorised by the home secretary to arrange for the names of all members of the Nazi Party and ancillary organisations to be passed to the police. Telegrams ordering their arrest and the arrest of individuals suspected of spying for Germany were prepared and held ready for dispatch the moment authorisation was given. These so-called Lisbon telegrams were finally sent out when war was declared in September 1939.

3 [4]. Liaison with the Authorities in Eire

In April 1938 the governments of Great Britain and Eire signed an agreement providing, inter alia, for withdrawal of British garrisons from Irish ports. On 31

August 1938 (at a time of steadily increasing German aggression, which culminated in Munich), Mr Walshe of the Department of External Affairs in Eire raised with the Dominions secretary the question of liaison on counter-intelligence matters and stated that he would very much like to see representatives of our counter-intelligence organisation. His approach was a result of a discussion of information on defence plans communicated by HMG to the Irish authorities; Mr de Valera had evidently been moved by what he saw as a gesture of trust and immediately asked Mr Walshe to get in touch with the authorities here.

On the DG's instructions, Captain Liddell then met Mr Walshe and Mr Dulanty. Mr Walshe explained that his government was concerned about the NSDAP group in Dublin, which it felt might lead to an infringement of Irish sovereignty. Captain Liddell met with Mr Walshe again in London on 10 September 1938 and, in response to a request from Mr Walshe via the Dominions secretary, handed him a copy of our memorandum on the NSDAP, as well as B Branch's memorandum.

The latter memorandum began by emphasising that it contained proposals for the structure of a counter-intelligence operation based on our own experience here (Captain Liddell had already said that this had led to the creation of a typically British organisation, which had evolved gradually with various additions at different stages of its development). The memorandum expressed the view that it was probably most appropriate for a counter-intelligence service to come under the Ministry of Defence and that its senior officer should have direct access to the minister in case of need. The success or failure of the organisation would depend in large measure on the personality of its senior officer; consummate tact was a prerequisite in order to enlist the co-operation and assistance of the police and government departments. Experience has also shown that such an organisation needed to be in a position to

a. monitor the arrivals and departures of foreigners;
b. maintain surveillance on them while they were in the country; and
c. intercept mail, cable and telephone communications.

The memorandum expressed our readiness to place at the disposal of an Irish (counter-intelligence) organisation information obtained by the Security Service on suspicious foreigners. It further stated that it stood to reason that the powers of the Irish organisation should be based on the provisions of our OSA of 1911–21 and our aliens legislation of 1914–19.

The Irish defence minister appointed Colonel Liam Archer to head the counter-intelligence organisation, and during September 1938 Archer had a number of meetings with Security Service officers. His organisation had to start from scratch under conditions of the greatest secrecy and without experience, staff or resources. It was also subject to the vagaries of Irish politics, a feature of which was a difference in views on this question inside the Irish government itself. From its creation and up to the start of the war, it was in fairly regular correspondence with the Security Service via the high commissioner's bag. This correspondence was confined in the main to German-related matters. The value of the connection depended on the good relations that developed between the counter-intelligence officers on either side of the Irish Sea.

4 [5]. Liaison with the US Authorities

Chapter III, Part 2/2/Para. 4, mentioned the case whose central figure was Gunther Gustav Rumrich, a member of a 'spy group' in the USA. In 1937, in the course of general inquiries into German espionage in the UK, Lieutenant Colonel Hinchley Cooke intercepted mail en route to an address in Hamburg used by the Abwehrstelle there. It was also discovered that a Mrs Jessie Jordan, whose address was used by the Abwehrstelle as a mail drop in Scotland, was receiving letters from the USA, which she forwarded to Hamburg. One of these letters described a plot to attack a US officer in order to lay hands on important documents in his possession. As soon as this came to our attention, we reported it to Colonel Lee, the US military attaché in London. He cabled the salient facts to the US authorities, and the investigation that ensued led to the indictment of a number of Abwehr officers in Germany who had organised the 'spy group' and to the conviction of a number of individuals in the USA. There was much press coverage at the time.

In March 1938, Captain Liddell visited the USA and met with a number of officials of the War Department and the State Department's Political Relations Section, and also with Mr Hoover and the FBI officers who had handled the Rumrich case. Mr Dunn of the State Department said that he hoped there could be an exchange of information on the activities of the German and Italian (Nazi and Fascist) Parties overseas. He explained that the US government had made it clear to the German and Italian ambassadors that it would not tolerate organised Party groups that, in its view, clearly infringed sovereignty. Captain Liddell was able to tell Mr Dunn that notwithstanding the German ambassador's assurance that no such organisations existed in the USA, he was in a position to say with confidence that Nazi groups did indeed exist, albeit covertly.

It became clear to Captain Liddell in his talks with the various officials that the scope of the FBI's operations was being gradually extended and that it was quietly investigating Soviet agents, although that was not within its official remit.

Captain Liddell also visited Ottawa, where he discussed various general topics with the commissioner of the RCMP, who was in close touch with Mr Hoover over their common interest in matters such as German and Italian activity. But as the commissioner explained, by mutual agreement their exchanges focussed more on criminal than on political issues.

From subsequent talks in the USA with a staff officer of G-2 and Mr Turrow, Captain Liddell learned that Rumrich had confessed that the mail drops had been located in Britain so that, if worse came to worst and the operation was blown, the finger would point to Britons. It was agreed to exchange detailed information on the UK (where Mrs Jordan had been arrested) and US aspects of this case. Mr Turrow told Captain Liddell that Eric Pfeiffer of German intelligence made a practice of selling to the Japanese for considerable amounts of money intelligence procured by the Germans in the USA.

Upon his return to London in April 1938, Captain Liddell discussed these matters in depth with Colonel Lee, the US military attaché, and Mr Herschel Johnson, the chargé d'affaires. It was made clear that the State Department wanted to retain control over liaison issues, but communication on the current case could be maintained with Colonel Lee. Captain Liddell handed Mr Johnson a copy of our memorandum on the NSDAP and drew his attention to the fact that the German espionage case in the USA had revealed that the entire Party and state structure had been mobilised in support of agents whose assignment was to procure intelligence on US secrets and military capability on a massive scale.

In October 1938, Colonel Lee told the Security Service that in the light of recent events, he was more than ever convinced that our two countries should work closely together on German intelligence activities. He asked us for a general outline of what a new US counter-intelligence organisation might look like. We gave him a broad description of our organisation along the same lines as in our talk with Eire mentioned above. We went on to emphasise the importance of good relations with the armed forces and with industry to safeguard blueprints of new inventions and of equipment being manufactured in government and private munitions plants. We also stressed the need for officers to make on-site security visits. Colonel Lee studied the whole question thoroughly and sent papers to the War Department in Washington, but we understand that the latter took no action. He had emphasised the need for a counter-intelligence service to be free of any political taint and said that there were some grounds for thinking that a move was being made to enlist public support in the USA by popularising the FBI. He expressed the view that a good counter-intelligence organisation could do without this sort of 'popularizing'; on the contrary, its work should remain secret.

However, in typically American fashion, it was the FBI that was to play the leading role in counter-intelligence, and liaison with the FBI was boosted when the USA entered the war.

Part 3. Italian and Japanese Aggression

1. The Italian SIS and the Italian National Fascist Party

Until Italy went to war with Abyssinia in 1935, the Security Service had no grounds for investigating the Italian Fascist intelligence service or the Party organisation on British territory.

But the tension that followed the imposition of League of Nations sanctions, including the dispatch of major units of the British fleet to the eastern Mediterranean, required us to take steps to get a better picture of the issues.

The only information available was a general review of the Italian system very broadly defined, compiled several years previously by Section V of the SIS. There were no later data.

We thus pressed Section V for detailed information on the Italian intelligence service and its place in the Italian military machine, but they were unable to come up with anything of value.

At the same time, we opened an investigation into the local branches of the FAE, and we shared the information obtained with the representatives of the Dominions and the Colonies, as well as with the authorities in the Middle East with whom we liaised.

A message from Egypt at an earlier time of tension had shown that the RAF [Royal Air Force] in the Middle East had fired a large number of Italian civilian employees of British aerodromes. Highly reliable information came to hand showing that this time around, if war came, the National Fascist Party leadership intended to use the Party organisation to sabotage British aerodromes and aircraft in the Mediterranean region.

SIS also received information from an independent source that specific plans were in place to use the Italian Fascist militia in Greece to impede mobilisation of the Greek army should Greece and Italy find themselves at war as a result of the proposed closure of the Suez Canal to Italian shipping. The report said that the plans envisaged sabotage of Greek railways and bridges; the Fascists had apparently been told that war would begin without any prior breaking of diplomatic relations.

Such inquiries as we were able to make in this period, given the paucity of the Service's resources, produced no indications whatever of any serious Italian intelligence activity in Britain. Information at our disposal showed that the Italian consuls and Fascist organisations had collected some rough intelligence on troop and material movements to the Near East from the UK. However, our overall conclusion was that the Italians had got most of this information via official channels with the help of the Party organisation. A careful watch was therefore kept on the organisation, and the results of these inquiries were collated in our 1936 dossier 'The Organisation and Activity of the Italian Fascist Party in the UK, the Dominions and the Colonies'.

The issue of the possible use of these Italian organisations for sabotage was reviewed again in 1936 in our 'Memorandum on the Potential for Sabotage Activity by Organisations Set Up in British Territories by the German and Italian Governments'.

The JIC's subsequent directive that MI5 should keep this issue under review also referred to the FAE. One of its most important elements was the Italian Overseas Youth Organisation (Giovani Italiani all'Estero). Many Italian children on British territory were British subjects by birth, but the FAE made every effort to preserve their 'Italian essence' (*Italianita*). One of their methods was [to hold] summer camps in Italy, where large numbers of children from Italian communities around the world came together to be fed Italian patriotic propaganda, to be put through military training and to be generally imbued with a spirit of militarism.

Although we were aware that all this activity merited our attention, since it could have adverse consequences in case of war, we were equally well aware (as was Mussolini, by some accounts) that there was very little evidence indeed that the Italian people were anything like as militaristic as the Germans.

Additional comments on the role of the FAE were prepared in 1937.

Investigations, which continued right up to the outbreak of war in September 1939, produced no material evidence of Italian espionage in the UK. There were a few minor cases in the Middle East, and there were various indications of Italian intrigues and propaganda in the Middle East aimed at boosting Italian, and diminishing British, prestige.

In summary, we could say that in the sense that we had no inside information to enable us to make a clear assessment of the problem from a pure intelligence point of view, the result of our investigations of the Italian service and the FAE was not satisfactory. But at the same time, while we felt obliged to devote part of our scarce resources to investigate the problem, it was perfectly understandable that we should tend not to take seriously the military (or espionage) threat the Italians represented. It was recognized that if war came, the threat would be greatest in the Middle East, and officers of our services in Cairo were urged to develop their intelligence sources and to take other counter-intelligence measures.

2. The Japanese

After the expiry of the Anglo-Japanese Entente, we received information that the Japanese were concentrating their efforts on procuring intelligence on the British navy. In the years leading up to Second World War, Japanese naval intelligence undoubtedly obtained a great deal of information from their officers' frequent and officially sanctioned visits to British yards.

In 1936 a naval officer named Colin retired at his own request and went to work for Vickers. He was discovered to be in contact with the Japanese naval attaché in London, who paid him for information; he was sent for trial under the OSA and pleaded guilty to lesser offences (possession of documents).

In 1932 the Japanese hired Lord Sempill as a technical consultant with a special emphasis on aviation. Although there are some doubts (as there are bound to be in such cases) as to whether Sempill passed on to them information he should have known was secret, there is no doubt that his role as a technical consultant was a conflict of interest. He remained under observation for several years.

In 1923 they hired a former RAF officer, Frederick Joseph Rutland, as a technical consultant on air force matters. The Security Service kept him under observation for some considerable time. The surveillance was not without its problems, and on one occasion he confronted the people who were trailing him, but in the face of their cover story he had to admit he was mistaken! The case provided a good illustration of Japanese methods, since from 1933 onwards they used him against the USA rather than Britain. If it came to war between Japan and the USA, they planned to use an [espionage] organisation he was to set up in America and the Pacific Basin. This was the brainchild of Ota, the Japanese naval attaché in London, but the plans came to our notice as a result of our interception of the attaché's dispatches to Tokyo and our clandestine opening of Rutland's mail. Ota tried to reinforce the security of his diplomatic ciphers by also using a simple plain-language code in which various words were camouflaged before encryption—e.g. Japan was referred to as Denmark.

The intercepts showed Ota telling Tokyo the cover he had provided Rutland in the form of a business in the West End of London, with its headquarters in California and branches in Vancouver and various Pacific ports.

Rutland's assignment was to obtain intelligence of military value on the west coast of the USA and in the Pacific Basin; if war came, the organisation would be beefed up. SIS handled the case first but was unable to provide a satisfactory analysis of the information obtained. This was done by the Security Service in the light of the fuller information at its disposal. When the Japanese attacked the USA in 1941, Rutland, who was then in the UK, was arrested and interned for having dealings with the enemy. The value of the case lay in the light it shed on the Japanese use of a citizen of one Western country to spy on another.

From time to time we received quite a few reports indicating that Japanese intelligence was active throughout the western Pacific, especially in Singapore and the Dutch East Indies, but we got little corroboration beyond claims that Japanese officers disguised as fishermen were taking depth soundings and surveying the whole area.

DSOs [Defence Security Officers] were established in Singapore in 1936 and in Hong Kong in 1937 to counter this threat, but with little in the way of concrete results. In fact, we were unable to establish a satisfactory counter-Japanese intelligence organisation in either place (nor were we able to do so via our liaison with the Australians). General security measures were introduced, and the Overseas Defence Committee reviewed measures for the security of the garrison in Singapore. In March 1933 an inter-departmental conference in London had reviewed the question of the entry into, and residence of aliens in, Malaya—with particular reference to the defence of Singapore.

It had been decided that everything possible should be done to reduce the size of the Japanese community in Malaya and that we should plan to expel all persons who were, or were suspected of being, dangerous, and an approach was made to the governor on the matter. It was noted that it was particularly important to expel people who were or were likely to be important in any Japanese intelligence effort in the region. Deportation orders for suspects were to be prepared in advance, ready for immediate use.

Part 4. Personnel

As noted in Chapter III, Part 1, there was a radical change in our staffing in 1931, when Captain Liddell, Captain Miller and others were transferred from Scotland Yard to the Security Service. Captain Liddell became deputy to Mr Harker, the head of Section B, which, until around 1935, dealt mainly with Communism and the USSR. In 1934 the staff was somewhat expanded; Section D was established to deal with plant security. It had one officer from the Admiralty, one from the War Office and one from the Air Ministry, each responsible for his own area.

At the same time, B Branch, which had begun to deal in 1934 with matters relating to the Fascist movement and the Nazi Party, saw some increase in its staff. This was further expanded to some degree for operations against German espionage and Communism.

There were no noteworthy changes until the summer of 1939, when some six new operational staff were added. The Admiralty and the War Office had agreed to train a small number of officers through participation in the work of the Security Service with the aim of using them in due course for liaison or security-related intelligence matters. The War Office side of things was a fiasco, since various COs [commanding officers] seconded totally unsuitable officers, whom they were doubtless glad to be rid of. The Admiralty made a better job of things, since it seconded reserve officers, who turned out to be both suitable for the work and able to make a useful contribution in wartime. Nothing further was heard of the officers seconded by the War Office after they finished their training course.

Nothing whatsoever was done to train officers who might be needed for expansion of the Security Service itself.

Chapter IV
Changes Related to the Second World War, the First Phase

There are naturally considerable differences in the rights of the Security Service in time of peace and in wartime, and the situation in the Second World War was in sharp contrast to that in 1914–18. In the latter period the interrogation of spies and those suspected of espionage was undertaken by the police, since Basil Thomson, deputy commissioner of the police, dealt personally with a large number of cases. In the inter-war years there were few spies, and there were long intervals between their capture, and it was accepted that the cases would be handled by the police from as early a stage as possible, with MI5 officers functioning as consultants, using the special information and data available to them.

In the Second World War the situation changed completely with the establishment of Camp 020, where interrogations were conducted by Security Service officers in circumstances that will be described in more detail below, although we can note here that this set-up provided important additional means of acquiring information, through monitoring the conversations of known spies or suspects and through the fact that the operation was run by Security Service officers rather than the police. A similar radical change was achieved through the establishment of the London Reception Centre, where, if there was any reason to suspect them, travellers arriving in the UK were held for a limited period of time and questioned. These two establishments gave the Security Service powers of a completely different nature than they had had hitherto in carrying out their tasks. The powers of the Service enabled it to catch individual spies while also obtaining extensive documentary material for the London Reception Centre's Information Index. In turn, the efforts were facilitated by questioning based on the index and on intelligence data gathered from more extensive and detailed interrogation in Camp 020. In turn, this data, combined with intercepts and British control of captured enemy agents, created the opportunity for the Service to build a proper understanding of the organisation.

[page missing]

88A, Para. 3, gave a person authorised by the secretary of state power to enter and search premises.

The limited powers arising from Orders 80A and 88A were, as indicated above, granted to a number of officers, including SLOs [security liaison officers] in the regions. Other powers granted to certain officers are noted in Article 7/4 of the Aliens Act of 1943, the act dealing with travellers arriving from British and foreign territories, and Article 15A of the Aliens Act of 1920. Two officers of the Service were authorised to give directions to the police.

[Chapter] V
Activity of a Consultative Nature

Although a number of officers were authorised to act in accordance with various regulations, as noted in the preceding paragraph, it was generally accepted that wherever possible, members of the Security Service should refrain from exercising these powers, other than in emergencies, and that wherever the circumstances permitted, recommendations for the necessary action were to be made to the police and other government departments. The reason for this lay in the fact that it was desirable that members of the Service should appear publicly as rarely as possible; it was also thought that there were advantages to obtaining the co-operation of the police in all cases where executive functions such as search and arrest were involved. In relation to persons detailed in Camp 020 or the London Reception Centre, one cannot over-estimate the advantages that followed from the employment of executive functions, and the procedures followed in this case resulted in the accumulation of extensive intelligence material, especially of a documentary nature. This would not, of course, have been obtained if the methods of the last war had been used.

As regards the most important preventive measures, such as the internment of foreigners and the holding of British subjects under the Detention Rules, the Security Service has no executive authority and can only advise in these areas. If action is initiated on the recommendation of the Security Service, the home secretary utilises the Consultative Committees appointed to investigate each individual case.

As regards liaison with other government departments, the functions of the Security Service are almost entirely confined to tendering advice or passing on information.

In the First World War, the Security Service did very little in the area of deception. In the present war the scope of its work in this field has become far more extensive and comprehensive, based on a far-reaching concept of control and co-operation implemented by the Service departments, the Home Defence Executive and the Security Service through the medium of the XX Committee and the X Council. The latter, which comprises for the most part intelligence chiefs and the senior home defence officers, took its policy guidance from the XX Committee. The functions of this committee were not clearly defined, but its chairman, a member of the Security Service, ran its affairs with the principal objective of gathering intelligence data by gaining the co-operation and goodwill of the Service departments in order to supply military information to enemy agents run under British control. This narrow aim gave rise to the secondary but far more significant task of helping in the active deception of the enemy as regards our own strategic plans. This was in addition to the more passive role of utilising our counter-intelligence structure to prevent the enemy from acquiring political-economic strategic and tactical intelligence data.

The arm of the Security Service tasked with deception measures was Section B1(a), which worked by running agents sent into the UK by the enemy, using them after they were captured to supply disinformation mixed in with a large amount of correct, though unimportant, information.

An effort like this can be successful in an area such as the UK only if the enemy's network is 100 percent under control, and that we were successful is attributable to the fact that we did indeed have total, or virtually total, control. In other words, we can say that the enemy had no important or good penetration agents that we did not know about. Admittedly, there may have been some minor agents, such as sailors picking up rumours in pubs, who remained unknown to us, but this had no bearing on our basic control of the operation. The record shows that even if the Germans had indeed had such agents at critical moments, they would not have been able to alert their master to the real intentions concealed behind our larger-scale operations. Control over the network of German agents allowed B1(a) to deceive the Abwehr on the decisive issues at the time of the Normandy landings and in other major operations. At the time of the landing in Sicily this was done through an agent who had been turned and by a stratagem that brought the enemy to believe that a British air force officer washed up on the Spanish coast was carrying important dispatches.

A detailed description of the complex system created for this purpose will be given in a later chapter. The facts are mentioned here briefly to show that the organisation of a counter-intelligence system needs to be adapted to serve both operational and legal ends.

Experience has shown that the structure developed for these operational ends can be successful only if closely linked to the structure concerned with detection of enemy espionage and the gathering of general intelligence data on the way the enemy's intelligence is organised. The fact that the Security Service has to carry out these two different kinds of function—legal and operational—in wartime brings one to the conclusion that if it reports only to the Home Office, its operational functions will be impaired.

The dominant factor, and one that was almost lost sight of, was the position of the UK, looked at in its proper perspective, as the most important military base for an attack by the Western Allies on Germany. In this sense, it was in the combat zone throughout the entire war. Despite this, however, the basic principles of the law remained in force, and they determined the actions of the Security Service.

[Chapter] VI
Liaison with Other Departments and Authorities in the UK with the Dominions and the Colonies and with the Allies

We have seen above that in carrying out its functions the Security Service liaises closely with the Home Office and the operational staffs. There is also liaison with the Home Office and the Service departments on the question of undesirable elements in the armed forces and on issues relating to propaganda and counter-sabotage activity. While these were the most important links, it was also necessary to liaise in various cases with the Foreign Office, the secretaries of state for the Dominions and the Colonies, the Ministry of Economic Warfare, the Censorship and the police, the relative importance of each of which was as follows.

In the First World War the Censorship played an important part in uncovering quite a number of German spies, many of whom used mail and cable to transmit information from the UK to the Continent.

In the current war the Censorship has succeeded in spotting microdot communications passing mainly between the Western and Eastern Hemispheres and also a series of letters containing secret writing, emanating from a group of commercial organisations and from the Russian secret police in the Western Hemisphere. The Censorship has also yielded extensive information of a general intelligence nature.

It has led to the detention of only one spy in the UK, but its work has been of value for the Security Service by forcing spies to avoid using the mail.

Relations with the police have always been regarded as one of the most important aspects of the work of the Security Service. As noted above, the police have a specific role in relation to espionage and sabotage activity; in such cases they often carry out the executive functions. The police are an important source of information in relation to almost all aspects of the Service's work. Up to the Second World War, relations with the police were maintained via direct exchange of memoranda, but in 1940, as the threat of invasion loomed, SLOs were appointed to each of the twelve areas into which the UK was divided, and these officers served as a filter between Head Office departments and the police, with responsibility for maintaining good relations; they were remarkably successful. They also played a useful role in maintaining good relations with local military commands and, even more important, in serving as intermediaries on security matters between those commands and the police.

Depending on the circumstances, these contacts could relate both to the detection and to the prevention of espionage; details can be found in the general description of the history of the Security Service, which follows later, and also in the departmental reports, which have been separately prepared.

Liaison with the Dominions and the Colonies were organised through a structure involving a department known as Overseas Control, involving security officers in a number of important points, the number of which varied from time to time, and via military, police and other authorities in all five Dominions and almost all the Colonies, Protectorates and Mandated Territories, including some of the smallest, such as Mauritius and the Falkland Islands.

Relations with intelligence centres such as Section V of SIS are of particular interest, and we should note the surprising and, given the circumstances, generally satisfactory state of co-operation with the security organisation in Eire. Many of these contacts were established during the First World War and were maintained throughout the inter-war years, although communications with most of the smaller islands was intermittent and sometimes ceased altogether. The system distributed to all areas, except the smallest islands, important information such as documents on the NSDAP and the opportunity for espionage available to German businesses and organisations by virtue of their location, as well as information in the form of the 'Bulletin for Overseas Territories', publication of which was halted in July 1944.

In 1930 the deputy head of the Security Service visited India, Colombo, Singapore, Hong Kong, Shanghai and Ottawa on a trip aimed at establishing and developing liaisons with the Dominions and the Colonies, but no plans were worked out for systematic maintenance of these liaisons.

Liaison with the Allies was usually the job of SIS, although in the First World War, MI5 placed 'Military Control Officers' and 'Military Pass Officers' in Paris, Rome, New York and certain ports (in the case of neutral countries, this was done through MI1[c], as the Secret Intelligence Service was then known).

In the inter-war period, with the agreement of SIS, special ties were maintained with the Deuxième Bureau in Paris and the US Embassy in London. The former ties related mainly to German espionage, the latter to inquiries and information about Communists. However, towards the end of this period the investigations branch passed to the US Embassy information on the Auslandsorganisation and exchanged with them information on suspect Germans. (Underlying this was the aim of co-operation with the Americans on this issue as one of mutual interest, and to do so with an eye to the possibility that Nazi aggression would lead to war, i.e. a war in which good relations with America would be in the national interest.) This understanding continued after the outbreak of war until the FBI attached its own officers to the US Embassy for liaison with the Security Service. The liaison covered Communist matters as well as issues relating to counter-intelligence against the enemy.

As the various Allied governments re-established themselves in London after their countries were occupied by the German armies, liaison on security matters was established by B Division and later maintained by E Division. This liaison extended to cases involving their own subjects against whom there were suspicions in the UK emanating either from us or from their own governments. There was also liaison with Allied counter-intelligence services in London in connection with interrogations at the London Reception Centre, in which they were sometimes interested or were in a position to provide assistance in, in matters relating to their own subjects. SIS also liaised with the Allied intelligence services in London on matters of mutual interest outside the UK.

[Chapter] VII
Functional Links with SIS

As indicated above, the functions of the Security Service can be summarized as: the detection and prevention of espionage, sabotage and illegal Fifth Column activity; acquisition of intelligence data; organisation and development of measures designed to deceive and confuse the enemy; the transmittal of intelligence data to the relevant British authorities and the offering of advice on matters of security to government departments and other bodies; and liaison on these matters with the Dominions and the Colonies, as well as the Allies. We have also seen that from the outset the organisation set up to deal with these matters has had three natural components: (1) a branch or division dealing with investigations, including the gathering of intelligence information through agents and via the interception of enemy communications, including investigations of organisations in the UK who may be working in the interests of an enemy or potential enemy, (2) a division with responsibility for preventive measures and measures of security and control, (3) an internal administration division, incorporating the Registry, whose job is the registration of intelligence information in a way that allows it to be utilised in conjunction with fresh data as these are received. We have also demonstrated that looked at another way, the functions of the Security Service are both operational and legal.

This review, however, has been confined to only a part of the structure: that for gathering and utilising secret intelligence data—that is, data obtained by secret means, as distinct from overt information—within British territorial limits. It should be noted that, rising out of the Security Service's roles, secret intelligence data has to be obtained from overt sources, without which secret information in itself may offer little or no practical value. Put another way, the review has been limited to the structure of the Security Service itself, but this does not represent the entirety of the system employed to obtain secret intelligence information. The other element [of the system] is known as the Secret Intelligence Service, whose remit is to obtain from other countries the secret intelligence data needed by a number of government departments—in particular, the Foreign Office and the military authorities—relating to the political, economic and strategic resources and activities of other countries and of international organisations such as the Comintern.

In order to understand the functional connection between the Security Service and SIS, we need to describe briefly how the latter is structured. In summary, it consists of 'circulating sections', each of which does its job of passing on the appropriate information to the relevant government department. Among these sections, V is responsible for the flow of information to the Security Service and, under normal conditions, is the sole channel of communication between the Service and SIS. SIS obtains its information from its representatives overseas, some of whom are designated as Passport Control Officers. The PCOs are also part of the counter-espionage apparatus, on which the Security Service relies in peacetime as well as in war, in the sense that by utilising information about persons suspected of espionage, they can alert the appropriate authorities to prevent spies, enemy agents or agents of the Comintern from reaching British territory or, during wartime, areas abroad where British forces are operating. Their routine functions require liaison with the police and military security authorities of their host country. Since their roles are similar to those of the Security Service, they inevitably receive from the Service information on matters of common interest. However, this common interest requires delicate handling, since it presupposes some degree of mutuality of interest in foreign policy matters between the UK and the host country. The work of the PCOs is naturally linked with the task of obtaining intelligence information either by collecting it from visa applicants or by the use of secret agents. Communications from SIS representatives abroad go to Section V as the circulating section. Under an agreement whereby MI5's Registry retains a record of all counter-intelligence data available to the British government, all this information also goes to the Security Service in all cases where it relates to counter-intelligence issues of sufficient significance to justify its being retained in the archives for future use. The SIS also has other functions that relate to the gathering of counter-intelligence information, since it has responsibility for the organisation and management of the services known as RSS (Radio Security Service), RIS (Radio Intelligence Service) and GC & CS (Government Code and Cypher School), which handle the interception of the wireless and cable traffic of an actual or potential enemy, including diplomatic and military communications, as well as communications of a nature likely to be of interest to the Security Service. They also intercept, as necessary, the post and telephone communications of foreign embassies and missions in British territories. Through these various routes they obtain a mass of information, some of which is passed to the Security Service if it facilitates their objectives.

Most of this information is entered by Section V in the SIS Registry, although this has always had a very small staff. In the past it has been recognized that since it did not have the capacity to do the work of making the file card entries, the Security Service Registry would handle this. The [SIS] Registry had a staff of only twenty before the war; it grew to forty between 1939 and 1944. By contrast, before the war the Security Service Registry had a staff of eighty, whereas by 1941 it had grown to almost four hundred.

However, in 1941 it was decided that the entire responsibility for card-indexing overseas names and addresses should rest with SIS and that the Security Service Registry should no longer add them to its index, with the exception of cases that had a special, and more than local, significance. This decision brought about a radical change in the functional relationships between the two services. Since the SIS Registry staff was not commensurately increased, it was unable to ensure that all the material was entered in its card index and could not organise it systematically for registration in a way that would have enabled data to be easily retrieved. Section V, however, put together a completely separate card index for intercepted German intelligence (Abwehr, SIPO and SD) radio transmissions. This change somewhat blurred MI5's declaration at the end of the last war that its Central Registry was the repository for all counter-intelligence information at the British government's disposal. At the same time and on the basis of this change, Section V declared more definitely than hitherto that counter-intelligence issues outside the British three-mile limit were not a matter for the Security Service and that it was for Section V alone to manage and handle the card indexing. This would seem to imply that Section V was responsible for processing all counter-intelligence information relating to matters outside British territory and for the measures to be taken in this connection. Section V maintained that this is what it was doing, but in practice it was unable to process the information, since it was understaffed. The only work SIS could do with this information (given these constraints) was to gather further information and, to a limited extent, pass messages to (1) the Security Service if a spy or a suspected spy was entering British territory or if the intelligence information was directly linked to some case on British territory in which the Security Service had an active interest and (2) the Foreign Office (although this led to complications too confused to be discussed here).

After this, if not as a consequence of this, relations between B Division and Section V deteriorated, and there followed a period of considerable difficulties, exacerbated by the incomplete state of SIS's archives. Even if they had been complete, problems would have been inevitable, given the need for both Registries to handle inquiries in the exceedingly large number of instances in which one service or the other wanted to run a 'check'. If the 'check' revealed information in the other Registry or in both, the sections concerned in both services needed to co-operate to facilitate access to all of the information bearing on the person or matter that was the subject of the inquiry.

In a nutshell, the situation is that as Section V has developed over recent years, it has come to occupy a position completely different from that of SIS's other circulating sections. It declared that its duty was to process and enter into the card index intelligence material relating to the area beyond the three-mile limit and that it considered it had the right not to give information to the Security Service, notwithstanding the fact that in other cases it was the job of the circulating section to pass secret intelligence data to the appropriate department, which could then compare them with information obtained from other sources. As a result, material obtained from secret sources and having a bearing on counter-intelligence, whether in relation to individual spies or to Communist agents, was divided into two, hindering co-ordination and comparison and creating more opportunities for errors and omissions than there would have been had the work of entering the data in the card index and comparison of all the information available been carried out within one organisation.

However, the Security Service did receive information directly from RSS, RIS and GC & CS. The committees dealing with their product, which were chaired by a Security Service officer, handled the co-ordination and kept the Security Service informed of the valuable results obtained from interception of Abwehr, SIPO and SD radio communications. RSS, RIS and GC & CS worked together in the production of important papers based on study and textual analysis of intercepts. This work, together with the information obtained by the Security Service from interrogations, from double agents and from other sources helped build a very full and detailed picture of the German organisations, their work methods and their agents. All of this was recorded in a series of reports prepared by various organisations interested in these matters and passed on to those it might concern. In turn, where useful, this information was made available to SHAEF [Supreme Headquarters Allied Expeditionary Force] for counter-intelligence use.

Further details of the functional links between SIS and the Security Service are to be found below in other chapters and in certain of the section reports. These relationships have been touched on in general terms since they are very much bound up with the functions of the Security Service and since they represent a difficult problem that is still under discussion and so far unresolved.

[Chapter] VIII
Functional Links with Military Intelligence Staffs in London and in the Combat Zone

Secret intelligence data obtained from intercepts of enemy intelligence communications, i.e. counter-intelligence information, were circulated directly by GC & CS and the other constituents of SIS to the heads of military, naval and air intelligence if they were of operational interest. In the same way, all information obtained from Security Service sources is also passed to them. In this connection there is a direct link between a number of the intelligence departments, such as the MI14, which receives radio intercept material, and the department dealing with POW interrogations (MI19), which can sometimes produce secret intelligence data as well as operational information.

When British and Allied forces are fighting overseas, there is inevitably a link between the activity of the enemy's intelligence directed against these forces and its activity directed at the enemy's bases on British territory. The activity of hostile agents and the system controlling them is directed by a centralised structure, even when this activity covers different areas of operation. In this sense, in the same way that the strategic direction of the war is described as integral, counter-intelligence can also be regarded as one integrated effort, regardless of whether it is being carried out by the Security Service, Section V or the intelligence staffs in the combat zones. As noted above, this information is placed at the disposal of SHAEF; by a decision of the director of the Security Service a large number of his officers were assigned or posted to work at SHAEF, and an organisation styled the War Room was set up for co-ordination purposes.

During operations in the Mediterranean in the Second World War, counter-intelligence work was the job of SIME [Security Intelligence Middle East] in co-operation with Section V and the Security Service, while during the Burma campaign the Security Service played just a small part, except for work of a consultative nature and assistance by trained officers; counter-intelligence was run by the Theatre HQ and the Indian authorities. This whole question will be examined in greater detail in the chapter dealing with the Second World War.

[Chapter] IX
The Scope of the Security Service

The Service's scope encompasses counter-espionage work directed against spying inimical to British interests conducted by any power in the world. It has also been extended to cover revolutionary movements such as international Communism and Fascist movements with international ramifications. Both of these extremist movements are often described as 'subversive', a term that gives rise to difficulties, given the false impression it can create.

No statute lays down that the Security Service is charged with the task of working on these revolutionary movements because they are, or were, a weapon or potential tool for Germany, Italy or Russia in their pursuit of a 'power politics', used to facilitate their military operations or for subversive work, let alone because, like revolutionary movements within our country, they are directed against the Constitution. No decision has been taken to include the investigation of these movements within its remit in the same way as it investigates revolutionary movements within our country. It was only when firm grounds emerged for thinking that Sir Oswald Mosley's visit to Italy was linked with an understanding that Mussolini would provide his movement with significant financing that the government decided that the Service should undertake a careful investigation of the activity of the BUF. This was initiated only in 1934.

The fact that Communism and Fascism turned out to be a tool of potential or actual enemies naturally led to their inclusion in the remit of the Service. Ever since its establishment as MO5 under the supervision of the War Office in 1909, the Service has paid serious attention only to counter-measures against German intelligence, Russian intelligence and the Comintern; the last, as noted earlier, should be viewed not just as an international organisation, which it is in theory, but also as, in reality, a tool of the Soviet government. Active work was also undertaken, though to a far lesser extent, to investigate Japanese and Italian organisations, including the Partito Nazionale Fascistsi.

Since 1909 no power other than those that were German satellites in the two world wars has waged or even threatened war against our country. No instances of serious or organised espionage on the part of these satellites or any other power came to notice, and there was thus no case for developing the [intelligence] organisations in order to counter them. However, after 1931, when the Service was tasked with taking a detailed look at Communist movements in the UK, and the connections in this regard with other British territories, and a study of the general linkage of international Communism to those issues, the Service in fact began, without any defined remit, to shift in the direction of investigating other movements and organisations in which anti-constitutional tendencies might arise.

The Service thus collected information, sometimes quite superficial, on such movements as the Trotskyites, the anarchists, the Scottish and Welsh nationalists, the Jehovah's Witnesses, pacifist movements and others. In so doing, it was a guiding principle that while serious attempts to penetrate such movements were not always necessary, the Service needed at least to have some general information on them in case one or another were to come to represent a serious threat. The Trotskyites, for example, might become involved in strikes in wartime, and the Home Office might then need to be in a position to evaluate their significance. The Service has more opportunities to get to know such movements arising out of its work on the international movements, and in a way that gives it more access than the Special Branch has, let alone other police departments.

The Service deals with these less important issues whenever it can, even though, strictly speaking, they are not among the tasks for which the Service was originally established. There were, however, in rare instances more important questions, the investigation of which was entrusted to the Service as a special measure. One example was the investigation into the Maundy Gregory case, and [there were] certain other investigations of a more delicate nature that were carried out on the prime minister's instructions in connection with Edward VIII's abdication. These questions concerned the Constitution and matters of supreme authority and were far removed from any question of the defence of the realm against penetration by some external enemy or even insurrection on the part of the king's subjects. They were related to the internal integrity of the realm, and the Service was tasked with conducting inquiries because no other appropriate machinery existed for this purpose.

Moreover, the director of the Service, Sir Vernon Kell, enjoyed the respect and confidence of the authorities. As long as the Service retains this position of trust, it is probable that it will be used in such rare special cases, a fact which provides substantial support for the requirement that its officers must always be selected with special care and that they must avoid all political affiliations so as not to create any grounds for doubting its impartiality. If the Security Service did not exist, it would be necessary to create for this purpose a special organisation reporting to the prime minister or the home secretary, depending on the circumstances, as was done, for example, at the time of the Cato Street conspiracy.

In conclusion, the functions of the Security Service are divided naturally into (1) the detection of espionage, or investigation, (2) preventive measures, or ensuring security, (3) collection of intelligence data, including maintenance of file records, and (4) active disinformation against the enemy.

The first three are closely inter-connected, and from the outset the organisation was structured to deal with them, being split into three divisions—namely, Investigative, Counter-Espionage and Administrative Divisions—with the last responsible for the recording and registration of information.

The differing conditions that define the work of the Service in peace and in war, and the complexities created by the growth of Communism, on the one hand, and the rise of Nazism and Fascism, on the other, together with the closely related concept of the 'Fifth Column', meant that in the inter-war period these functions came to overlap. A further confusion arose from the complications related to the functional relationships between the Security Service and SIS's Section V and from the lack of good information relating to German intelligence services from penetration agents before the war.

The main work (i.e. the active work required to carry out the four functions or duties identified above) of these organisations, taken together, can naturally be split into the following component parts:

1. recruitment of penetration agents in foreign states.
2. recruitment of penetration agents on British territory.
3. detection of enemy agents (here and henceforward the word 'enemy' also includes 'potential enemy') on British territory. This includes the entire process from the first steps in discovery, by whatever means, up to the point when the case is ready and is handed over to the DPP [director of public prosecutions].
4. interrogation of captured enemy agents.
5. interception of communications between enemy agents and the enemy's intelligence service.
6. processing documentary information relating to enemy intelligence obtained by seizure in wartime, by interception or via penetration agents.
7. taking measures to obtain case-related information from any available source, whether official or secret.
8. logging all information so obtained so that it can be readily utilised by counter-intelligence and security officers.
9. processing and compiling information on both individual enemy agents and persons suspected of espionage, as well as their organisations, so as to facilitate the creation of a co-ordinated action plan to counter enemy intelligence.
10. training, recommendations and advice for other departments and organisations (including, inter alia, public- and private-sector arms producers) on legal and administrative measures designed to impede and, where feasible, to prevent espionage and to sabotage Fifth Column activity, as well as on utilisation of the resultant 'control' mechanisms.
11. development of disinformation measures in consultation with other intelligence services.
12. employment and development of a very wide range of technical skills to facilitate the general tasks of the Security Service.
13. ensuring that the organisation's internal administration facilitates the smooth operation of its other areas.
14. general direction and co-ordination of the work of the whole apparatus responsible for the detection and investigation of espionage, preventive security measures, intelligence gathering and disinformation.

PART II

Kim Philby's SIS Documents

K im Philby is responsible for the bulk of this book, having maintained a
constant flow of secrets to Russia throughout and after the war, concentrating on information that would ensure the powerlessness of the
British Secret Intelligence Service to neutralise the NKVD across the globe.
Although Philby's data often appears quite technical, it was precisely the kind of
information that Moscow required to identify, counter and penetrate its principal
opponent in an age when the CIA did not exist and the SIS 'robber barons' of
Broadway were perceived to be the biggest obstacle to Stalin's ambitions. Charac-
teristically concise, Philby selected his documents with care, knowing exactly
which files would be of greatest value, and his choices can be seen to have compromised the identity and work of practically every SIS officer of importance and
to have disclosed the organisation's priorities, methodology and future plans. In
total, the collection amounts to the most damningly comprehensive betrayal of
any intelligence agency at any time; it effectively neutralised the work of hundreds of personnel based at headquarters and at local stations overseas and allowed the Soviets to anticipate hostile operations and prepare suitable counter-
measures. Code-named SÖNCHEN and later STANLEY, Philby proved to be an
assiduous spy for the NKVD, compromising both current and future SIS
operations.

6   *Colonel Vivian's Briefing, 1943*

Translated from the English on 1 December 1943, a report from SÖNCHEN dated
10 May 1943, describing a briefing given to SIS's Section V on 6 March 1943 by
Colonel Valentine Vivian on the subject of Communist penetration of British secret organisations, about which he [Vivian] had spoken to him privately the previous Saturday: 'He added little of significance to what he had already told me,
but the following details may be of some interest.'

He began with a brief review of Communist revolutionary movements and warned again the general tendency in the UK to whitewash the USSR. As he put it, the Anglo-Soviet alliance notwithstanding, the Russians had demonstrated their guilt by having espionage organisations here working against the British armed forces.

Vivian's tone was, for the most part, one of indignation and surprise; he thought it curious that Russia should be spying on one of its allies. According to Vivian, one of the most surprising successes in British penetration of Russian secret organisations was the case of Johann de Graf. Frank Foley (now VX) met de Graf in a Berlin beer garden soon after de Graf had learned that his wife was being badly treated in Russia. This in itself had been enough to turn de Graf against the Communists. (This was around 1932 or 1933.) Foley managed to get alongside de Graf and convinced him to work for the British. Shortly thereafter de Graf travelled to Britain ostensibly on behalf of the AM Movement (an anti-war organisation). In fact, he was playing back to the British everything he did. De Graf travelled to Britain under the name of Dinkelmeir. His cover was as a wine merchant.

De Graf met Vivian and spent the weekend with him in the country. He is now in Canada.

Another case touched on briefly by Vivian was that of HARRY Christian Pieck. According to information received, Pieck spent £20,000 in Geneva wining and dining various members of the cipher staffs of the British and other missions. He then recruited King from the Cipher Section of the Foreign Office and used him right up to the moment King was arrested.

Turning to the present, Vivian said that the British authorities had stumbled by sheer chance upon an extremely serious Soviet espionage organisation when a series of forged petrol coupons came to the attention of the police. They traced these to a clandestine print shop run by one Green in London, where they found a number of photographs of secret papers. According to Vivian, this organisation was run by the Fourth Department of the Russian General Staff.

Vivian made only vague allusions to radio traffic. He did say that urgent material was transmitted to Russia by radio and that this 'probably gave Brigadier (Sir Richard) Gambier-Parry [of Section VIII] a headache'.

I personally conclude from this that Vivian is convinced that these transmissions are from an illegal set, not one of those which the Soviet Embassy or Military Mission have been authorised to use. Be that as it may, it seems that the British have not yet succeeded in breaking this traffic.

Reverting to the past, Vivian noted that at some point around 1935, Bletchley Park (GC & CS) had broken a Russian cipher. He indicated, although I am not entirely sure of this, that this cipher was not characteristic of Russian transmissions from here. However, the same cipher, or at least one very similar, had been used for transmissions from several other places, such as China, Belgrade, Sofia, etc. According to him, these transmissions occurred during the most interesting period of the Spanish Civil War, and the fact that they were being monitored and read had become known to the Russians as a result of a 'stupid error by the Post Office'. He did not elaborate, although he noted that the cipher was very high-grade.

Coming back again to the present, Vivian cited the case of a clerk, an NCO in Eastern Command, who had recently been caught red-handed copying official documents for the Russians. According to him, the man's desk was opened in a routine spot check ordered by his CO [commanding officer] and copies of these documents were found. Vivian went on to say that the Russian had shown great interest in Bletchley Park. When talking to me privately, he gave me the impression that Bletchley Park had already been penetrated. His briefing of Section V did not go that far. There was some feeling that the Russians, being very interested in Bletchley Park, might have made contact with some of the younger people on its staff with the aim of utilising them at some future point. Vivian said, however, that there was no reason to think that they had been successful in doing so.

Vivian said that the type of people in whom the Russians took an interest were those who belonged to university Communist clubs and societies, subscribed to *Labour Monthly,* and so on. He mentioned Abby Lazarus, who had an excellent memory and an aptitude for that sort of thing, as someone who might be involved in recruiting Bletchley people.

Vivian said that, in addition to the Green organisation, which worked for the Fourth Directorate of the Russian General Staff, Hollis at MI5 had come across clear evidence of an attempt to restructure the AM organisation, rebuilding its lines of communication to be similar to those it had maintained via Johann de Graf. It was not clear whether he was talking about the case of the NCO referred to earlier, the interest of LAZARUS in Bletchley, or something else entirely. I assume it was not in fact the latter; if it had been, I am sure he would have told us more about it.

Vivian said that the Russians had known about Operation TORCH in advance, repeating what he had already told me—namely, that the Russians had had accurate intelligence on the codes, beaches, medical supplies, etc., for the operation long before it was launched. In his words, senior officers involved had gone straight from their desks at the War Office to clandestine rendezvous with Communists. Frank Foley then asked where those officers were now. Vivian replied that they were still in their jobs. 'We did not want to make a big thing of it,' he added. This reply of course leads one to assume that the authorities know who these officers are, although I cannot vouch for the accuracy of what Vivian said.

There then followed a more general discussion related mainly to Communists' loyalty to their Party, a factor thought to be of critical importance. Vivian, Foley and [Felix] Cowgill stressed that such intense loyalty to a party was a most unusual phenomenon. Vivian also mentioned the very high standard of Communist tradecraft and referred in particular to the fact that underground Communist operators are allowed to know only the bare minimum about their organisation so that if one of them is caught, there is not much he can tell anyone. He also mentioned that Green had been forbidden by his controllers to forge petrol coupons and that his organisation had been found out only because he disobeyed orders.

When Vivian had concluded, Cowgill said—and this is the most important part of my report—that as a result of Green's being found out, CSS [SIS chief] had insisted on attaching one more officer to Section V whose sole responsibility would be to investigate Communist espionage. Up till now, this had been the job of Mills, but he had not been asked to do anything beyond producing material on Communist activity from already available sources; he was not authorised to do anything about it (as he was supposed to be concentrating his attention on the activities of the Axis powers). Peter BROWN had been tasked to take a more active interest in the Communist files, but so far he had focussed only on the political aspects of the job, specifically Yugoslavia. The new man is to deal with the intelligence aspects. Cowgill added that in view of the extreme delicacy of this issue, CSS had laid down that papers on Communist activity were to have extremely limited circulation.

It is perhaps very significant that two days after this meeting, Peter Brown telephoned me and asked if I could find the time to get together. I will see him Wednesday. If he wants to do the new job, I intend to press for him to be appointed, since we get on well and I am quite sure that he will pass on to me everything of real interest.

Milne, about whom I have already spoken to you, reacted extremely favourably to Vivian's remarks. He was frankly astonished by the whole thing. He told me that SIS had a representative in Russia and that long before there was talk about our 'gallant allies', the diplomatic bags of the 'gallant allies' of Great Britain had no immunity at all as far as the British were concerned!

In fact, Vivian's moral indignation had no effect on him whatever, and he may even have been rather pleased by the Communists' obvious success.

He told me he would not take part in any intensified campaign against the Communists. His reaction convinced me that he would take a favourable view of a very gradual introduction to the work, and I would like to have permission to make an approach. The advantages would be (a) having a double cover and (b) concentrating attention in particular on RSS and GC & CS, where, since he has a lot to do with intercepted material, he is much better placed than I to follow attempts to break Russian communications and codes.

7   ISOS, March 1943

Information on the Organisation of British Wireless Intelligence
ISOS [intercepted hand ciphers]:
Intercepted Services Oliver Strachey

According to intelligence from agents and documentary material, the British military radio intelligence service is intercepting the following German traffic:

1. Operational orders of the German High Command (a) from the HQ of the Luftwaffe Group in the Caucasus; (b) from the operations section of the IV staff of the Luftwaffe to the commander of the Caucasus Group of the Luftwaffe and Luftwaffe HQ in the Crimea; (c) from the Luftwaffe mission in Romania to Goering's field HQ; (d) from the Luftwaffe HQ in Italy to the Luftwaffe Fleet Air Arm Commander in Varna; (e) orders from Goering's field HQ; (f) orders from the HQ of the Naval Commander Crimea to the heads of Crimea military harbours; (g) orders from the Wehrmacht Southern Group to the C in C [commander in chief] German navy.

2. ABWEHR directives.

3. Diplomatic traffic: in particular we have recently received via agents the following British intercepts of cables between ambassadors and their foreign ministries:

   from Sofia to Berlin
   from Ankara to London
   from London to Madrid
   from London to Lisbon
   from Kuibishyev to Ankara
   from Bucharest to Tokyo

4. The British service is intercepting almost 100 percent of MAX traffic, which originates from areas along the line from the north from Leningrad through the Caucasus to Rostov and Kerch, from Novosibirsk to Batumi from Georgia, Azerbaijan, Armenia, from Iran, Baghdad and Basra, as well as Kuibyshev, Astrakhan and the western side of the Caspian Sea.

5. MORITZ traffic. This covers the whole sphere of British influence in the Middle East. The reports come from Egypt, Libya, Palestine, Syria, Cairo, Iran and Iraq. The MORITZ traffic closely resembles MAX traffic.

6. IBIS traffic. These messages evidently originate from Turkey, in all likelihood from Istanbul. Most of them, however, relate to Syria and Palestine.

7. ANKER traffic. This is transmitted from Ankara. It relates to the USSR and Britain in the Middle East.

According to agent reports from London, in order to cover all the areas from which enemy traffic might originate, British intelligence has distributed its intercept stations as follows:

Traffic Relating to Africa and Italy

Luftwaffe traffic—30 positions (the Luftwaffe mostly uses a universal aviation
   key)
Wehrmacht administration—16 positions
Traffic relating to convoys between Italy and Greece—4 positions
Traffic of armoured units in Africa and the Afrika Korps—1 position
   Making 51 positions in all.

Traffic from the Eastern Front (USSR)

Luftwaffe (GAF [German air force]) traffic—31 positions
OKW traffic—7
Military traffic—2
German intercept-station traffic—6
Army and Luftwaffe co-ordination—1
Eastern Germany—4
Movements of German armed forces in Germany and Russia—2
Army movements—2
   Making 55 positions in all.

Traffic from Germany and Central Europe

Servicing of armies deployed in eastern and southeastern Europe—3 positions
[Nazi] SS—11
Railroad services—5
Army services—3
   Making 22 positions in all.

French and German Traffic

Servicing of Luftwaffe (GAF)—28 positions
Luftwaffe (GAF) test transmissions—5
   Making 33 positions in all.

Norway

Servicing of Luftwaffe (GAF)—9
Servicing of army—4
   Making 13 positions in all.

In all, there are 174 intercept positions; 47 are held in reserve, with 20 DF
[direction-finding] stations deployed to home in on new transmission points.
Minor changes are introduced to the intercept positions weekly.

Deployment of Fixed Wireless Positions

Great Britain (War Office Y Group): Chicksands—99; Harpenden—30; V—3;
Sandridge—1; Denmark Hill—7; Cupar—1; Wymondham—17; a total of 246.
Abroad: Alexandria—20; Heliopolis—5; 8th Army—5; Sarafand—5; Malta—2;
Gibraltar—10; a total of 51.

According to agent reports, a joint radio committee has been set up at the
Royal Signals School in Barnet to deal with the interception and deciphering of

German wireless traffic. The committee meets weekly to discuss ISOS policy. It comprises representatives of Section V of SIS (Counter-Intelligence Overseas), MI5 (Military Counter-Intelligence), the RSS (which is part of Section VII of SIS), and GC & CS. The attendees vary, but the following are usually present:

From Section V of SIS: Major Cowgill and Major Ferguson
From MI5: Captain Guy Liddell, Dick White and H.L.A. Hart
From RSS: Colonel Maltby and Major Morton Evans
From GC & CS: Dennys Page and Palmer

The committee's permanent secretary is Captain Trevor-Roper. The committee is authorised to discuss all matters related to radio interception. Major Cowgill is responsible for product collation.

ISOS has two sections:

1. The technical (or operational) section, which is concerned with intercepts and decoding
2. The intelligence section, which collates all incoming intercept material and re-lays it to the appropriate departments

We understand that the permanent secretary, Captain Trevor-Roper, does not get on with Cowgill. There is frequent acrimony between Section V and the other committee members. Section V controls the ISOS intelligence function, guards the ISOS product jealously and usually objects to its being distributed to anyone at all. As an example, as we already know, Section V recently broke the Abwehr's machine cipher but did not give the Americans the full picture, passing on to them only part of the Abwehr traffic relating to Europe.

There is a similar attitude even as regards British intelligence organisations, especially MI5.

The committee had its thirty-fifth meeting on 22 October 1942 according to intelligence at our disposal (information from 'P'). Present were Captain Guy Liddell (in the chair), Colonel Maltby, Major Ferguson, Dick White, Mr Hart, Dennys Page, Major Morton Evans, Major Frost and Captain Trevor-Roper. The meeting discussed the comparative significance and interest of the various German intelligence communications links. Evans (RSS) stated that the committee now had to review and prioritise the entire list of such, since there were a large number of transmitters used by the German service in Stettin and Warsaw which were not of interest and which could be dropped. He went on to say that the members of the committee had to understand that complete intercept coverage could be laid on only for the most important links that were on the priority list.

In a discussion of the fact that interesting information of relevance to the Russians was transmitted via circuit 7 / 23 (between Sofia and Vienna), which handles MAX TRAFFIC, Liddell asked, 'Could the Russians organise the interception and decoding of the traffic over this circuit?' Major Ferguson, Page and

Major Evans replied that 'no technical radio or cryptographic intelligence has been passed on to the Russians'. The representatives of RSS and GC & CS stated that passing the necessary technical information to the Russians so that they could set up interception would not impede British ability to read other German circuits.

Major Ferguson replied: 'The primary aim of SIS is to do this as a trade, hoping that we could force the Russians to give us intelligence in exchange.' This reply was, we understand, sharply criticised by the other committee members. In its conclusion the committee expressed the hope that it would be possible to hand over to us the Sofia-Vienna line, and it apparently minuted its disagreement with the decision of SIS Section V.

8   *Breaking Soviet Ciphers*

Intelligence

Intelligence from STANLEY on the steps being taken by the GC & CS to break Soviet ciphers. STANLEY does not know the details but is aware that:

1. GC & CS is currently preparing measures to break all Soviet ciphers—diplomatic, military, naval, etc.
2. GC & CS assumes that Soviet ciphers are machine generated.
3. So far the British have not been able to break any Soviet five-letter ciphers.
4. s[TANLEY] cannot answer the other questions since he is not in the picture.
[5.] GC & CS has already put together a large group of specialists and technical personnel to work on Soviet ciphers.
[6.] At the British GC & CS over one hundred women are already employed solely on preparing decrypts for British government departments.

9   *SIS Sources for Strategic Appreciations*

[Redacted] source submitted by BOB [Boris Krotov]

Intelligence on Sources Used by the British to Appreciate the German Army and German Strategic Plans

1. Intercepts

a. Operational materials. This is the only good source. Intelligence is extracted from it on German orders for operations and troop movements.

b. Abwehr traffic—the best source of operational intelligence information.
c. Diplomatic cables—useful for clarifying rumours but of no military significance.
d. Police traffic—useful for appraisal of SS orders relating to their military operations and sometimes casting an indirect light on German army operations.

Censorship

Commercial cables provide no intelligence whatsoever. Postal censorship provides valuable input on German civilian morale but very rarely sheds any light on the military situation.

2. Agents' Reports

Practically none of the agents in the SIS network provide reliable reports; in some cases it is clear from what they send in that they are professional agents. The best agents are those who are run not just by SIS but also by other General Staffs; e.g. good intelligence on coastal defences and rail movements comes from agents run by both the British and the Belgian General Staffs.

The best intelligence on France comes from officers of the Deuxième Bureau of the Vichy government working against Germany; it is received either directly or indirectly via their links with the Swiss General Staff.

The Poles have an extensive intelligence organisation in France and to some extent in Spain and Poland; in fact, they often get intelligence from most countries in Europe. On the whole, the intelligence they provide is more detailed than that received by SIS. In particular, the Poles provide first-class intelligence on troop movements through Poland.

The British also have two or three good agents in the Baltic States, the best of whom is Colonel Saarsen, apparently an Estonian.

The British do not have agents reporting from inside Germany, although they have one or two commercial travellers who make periodic trips through Germany and collect intelligence, though their reports are not of operational value.

SIS has been strongly criticised for its inaction in the inter-war years and in particular for not creating an intelligence network inside Germany and for its inability to exploit anti-Hitler sentiment in Austria to recruit agents.

The British do not have agents in the Protectorate, although they have received good intelligence from the Czech organisation that existed prior to Heydrich's appointment to Czechoslovakia. Nor do they have agents in the USSR.

10   C's Directive, September 1944

Directive of CSS [Sir Stewart] Menzies Dated 26 September 1944 on the Work of Sections V and IX of SIS

Sections V and IX

Further to my recent briefing on co-ordinating the work of Section IX and the resources of Section V this directive will have effect from the dates indicated in Para. 7.

1. The direction and management of Sections V and IX will remain, as at present, under the immediate control of DD/SP [SIS director of security]. Lieutenant Colonel Cowgill will be responsible to DD/SP for the work of Section V. After the final handover from the head of Section IX, Mr Philby will be responsible to DD/SP for its work.

2. In carrying out their functions, Sections V and IX will, as now, liaise directly with all the sections that generate intelligence relating to their work (e.g. the P sections, GC & CS, RSS, Censorship, etc.) and with departments such as MI5 and IPI [Indian Political Intelligence], which are customers as well as intelligence suppliers.

3. In the interests of more efficient management, a small administrative section is to be set up under Major Adams (VP [Section V, Sub-Section P]), who from the date designated in Para. 7 will use the symbol SP/SD. This section will be responsible to Sections V and IX for the allocation and support of staff (including officers and secretaries) in terms of accommodation, supplies, communications and finance and to DD/SP for supplying whatever detailed information he may require for resolving various administrative and housekeeping issues (the foregoing does not of course detract from the higher-level responsibilities of DD/Admin., DD/F, CSC, head of Codes, etc.).

4. In the overseas system the work of Section IX should not be confined to Section V personnel stationed abroad. Although the training and techniques of Section V officers make them the best suited for Section IX operations, nevertheless only individual Section V officers occupying posts appropriate for the task are to be employed for this purpose. It will also be necessary in agreement with Section I and Section P to select suitable support staff in other categories and to use them for Section IX work after appropriate training or instruction.

5. Our people abroad are still engaged for the most part on assignments directly related to the war, but I would nevertheless hope that without impeding such assignments all legal opportunities will be exploited to expand the work of

Section IX along the lines of its primary mission, the exception being situations where I issue general or special warnings in the interests of preventing exposure.

6. Sections V and IX will work very closely with one another, with Sections I and V/LWM. However, in order to eliminate the possible leakage of highly secret intelligence it might be necessary to restrict the exchange of certain materials to those with a direct need to know.

7. Mr Philby will give up his responsibility for Section V from 1 October 1944. In the following six weeks he will familiarise himself to the maximum extent possible with the background and current intelligence relating to his new responsibility and will gradually pick up the work of Section IX while at the same time establishing the necessary connections outside SIS and while also agreeing with DD/SP, V, Mr Curry and SP/SD on the resources needed to ensure that Section IX has the officers and secretarial staff it requires.

Mr Philby should thus be in a position to assume executive authority for Section IX by 15 November 1944, at which date Mr Curry will return to his own service.

Major Adams will take up his new position and adopt his new symbol from 1 October, at which point he must be in a position to discuss the administrative consequences of this directive.

8. A detailed directive defining in more detail the duties of Sections V and IX, the staff required for the latter, the main reasons for the urgency of this measure and a progress report to me by DD/SP will follow from DD/SP, and regional controllers can familiarise themselves with it on request to him.

11   Report from Philby, December 1944

Information from STANLEY

Cowgill, Vivian, Curry, Milne, Steptoe, O'Brian and Philby attended a meeting on 18 August in the counter-intelligence department of SIS to discuss the development of anti-Communist work in the time ahead and the co-operation of Section V in this area.

The general view was that at the present time the main job of Section V was the destruction of the German military and political intelligence services and that it was therefore unable to divert much in the way of resources for anti-Communist work. It was, however, recognized that given the growing interest of the Foreign Office in investigating the Communist movement, Section V should do something towards this end.

It was suggested that officers of Section V attached to the military staffs in Italy and France might be used for this purpose. Philby argued against this and suggested that certain Section V officers should be recalled from other military staffs and first trained for this work.

Agreeing with this, the meeting decided to recall Captain Dawson from Rome to be trained in anti-Communist work. Dawson is studying at the Jesuit College in the Vatican, where he has two years to go before he completes his studies. The idea is that he could get close to the innermost workings of a Catholic organisation working against the Communist Party and the USSR and provide the SIS with intelligence obtained by the Jesuits.

It was also decided that Steadman, who has been appointed Section V representative in Vienna, should also be trained in anti-Communist work and that all heads of station should in future receive instruction in this field before taking up their posts.

Vivian said that Section IX had received valuable intelligence from Section M of the Deuxième Bureau in Algiers. This section carries out anti-Communist work, and its operations are carefully concealed from members of the National Liberation Committee, certain of whom are Communists, since if the work were discovered, the section could have a serious problem, and its present head, Commandant Paillole, might have to resign.

Asked whether there were communications between Moscow and the National Committee of the [British Communist] Party, Vivian replied that at the present time SIS was breaking 'some Russian version of ISOS'. Some cables had been deciphered, but their contents were difficult to understand; they did, however, indicate that the Party had a directing centre.

NOTES BY *REZIDENTURA:* The source has been tasked:

1. To clarify which Russian ISOS traffic is being broken by GC & CS
2. To provide personal data on Dawson and all officers designated for anti-Communist work

12   *Philby's Memo to C, November 1944*

TOP SECRET

CSS

The attached excellent, albeit somewhat lengthy memorandum by Curry—which exemplifies his best features, perception and diligence—has brought me 'to a crossroads' as regards SIS attitude to the problem.

When I requested your agreement to the creation of Section IX, I envisaged its work in extremely broad terms. I assumed that its functions should include the making of critical analyses, and the collating of the incidental intelligence we have received over the past five or six years, and the professional handling of any cases coming to our notice involving Communists or people concerned in Soviet espionage; I also concluded that the time had come to organise, in the SIS system, a detachment of specialists who, at the appropriate time, could create units abroad that would help heighten our awareness and make precise and effective use of such intelligence as came our way. I approached this issue on the assumption that foreign intelligence would be obtained by Section IX only when it was directly required for the war effort—above all, in the run-up to the cessation of hostilities. However, recent events and especially the position described in Curry's memorandum have led me to wonder whether we should not in fact be looking at the problem as an integral part of the military situation, intelligence on which might be of real significance for the foreign secretary and the prime minister in determining policy and which should at a minimum provide reliable and useful background even before hostilities cease and far in advance of the peace negotiations.

This means that we have to take specific steps, now especially in certain countries, initially in the area of intelligence production; if we do not, it will be too late.

This is the issue that requires your attention and your guidance. I urge you to read Curry's memorandum. I believe that when you have done so, you will be convinced that there is no time to be lost.

It seems to me that Loxley should be asked to review and consider the memorandum and perhaps to discuss with Sir Alexander Cadogan the question of whether SIS should not begin, with all due care, to look at the organisational issues so that when the time comes we can be sufficiently well informed; this would enable us to be alert to potentially inappropriate actions and help the foreign secretary to build a general idea of the factors that may be encountered during or after the cessation of hostilities.

DD/SP 13 November 1944

13   Section IX Personnel

Letter no. 4 of 16 July 1945

Herewith CVs from STANLEY on the officers of SIS's Section IX:

1. Assistant head of section Lieutenant Colonel Rodney O. Dennys. Dennys joined SIS in 1938. He was Section V's head of station in The Hague and worked in Section V after the evacuation from Holland. At the end of 1941 he was posted as Section V's head of station to Cairo, where he ran counter-intelligence across the entire Middle East. He has SIS's symbol 89700. He was recalled to London at the beginning of 1944 and began to prepare for the post of counter-intelligence department representative in the Far East. Health reasons prevented him taking up the job, and he remained in Section V. He was transferred to Section IX at the beginning of this year.

2. John O. Ivens is IXa. A fruit merchant by profession. Joined SIS's Section V in December 1941. At the beginning of 1942 he was posted as assistant head of the counter-intelligence department in Madrid. At the end of 1944 he was re-called to London. Since there were no openings in Section V, he went to work in Section IX. He is of Levantine extraction. His family have been merchants for many years. He will leave SIS at the end of July 1945 and return to his business. SIS intends to use him in the future to carry out certain assignments, taking advantage of his legal cover. His current job is dealing with the Western Hemisphere (*sic!*).

3. Major Charles de Salis is IXb. A teacher by profession. Began work in Section V in the middle of 1942. In mid-1943 he was posted to Lisbon as head of Section V. Recalled to London in December 1944 to work in Section IX. Looks after western Europe. Around August 1945 he will be posted to Paris as head of station for Section IX.

4. Miss Priscilla Welles. IXb1. A teacher by profession. Used to work in Censorship and was transferred to Section IX at the beginning of 1944. She works for Curry. She does not plan to stay in SIS for the long term; she wants to go back to teaching. She works as the assistant to IXb and deals with Holland, Belgium, France, Spain and Portugal.

5. Lieutenant Sir Colville R. Barclay. IXb2. Assistant to IXb looking after Italy and Switzerland. When IXa leaves for France, Barclay will be in charge of all the western European work.

6. Captain John D. Evans. IXc1. Evans is not a permanent member of Section IX. His regular job is assistant to Commander Kenneth Cohen, Controller, Western Europe. He was attached to Section IX for training in anti-Communist work. He has worked as an intelligence officer in Czechoslovakia, Yugoslavia and Bari. Evans may soon be sent to Germany, where he will specialise in Section IX work while still reporting to Cohen. He presently looks after Finland, Austria, Czechoslovakia, Scandinavia and Finland.

7. Richard Comyns-Carr. IXd. Worked at the BBC before the war. Joined MI5 in 1940 and worked in the Spanish Section until 1942, when he joined SIS's counter-intelligence department, where he looked after Spain and Portugal. Began working in Section IX in 1944. Looks after Poland, Hungary and the Baltic States.

8. Captain Kemp. IXd1. A teacher by profession. Joined Section V in 1944 and was soon transferred to Section IX, where he looks after Greece and Bulgaria.

9. Major Anthony K. Milne. IXe. Brother of I.I. Milne, head of Section V. A journalist before the war. Joined the Intelligence Corps in 1940. Posted to Cairo, where he became involved in intelligence work via the 'old boy network'. Transferred to BLOCKADE [Ministry of Economic Warfare]. Ran the propaganda side throughout the Libyan campaign. Accepted into Section IX in May 1944. Looks after the Middle East.

10. Mrs Archer. IX. Has worked at SIS with Vivian for more than twenty years. Deals with ISK [intercepted-machine-cipher] matters and all intelligence relating to the central organisation apparatus, etc., of the NKVD and the now dissolved Comintern.

11. Robert Carew-Hunt. IX. Worked for GCHQ for less than a year, mainly on Italian and Romanian ciphers. At the end of 1941, joined Section V, where he handled all intelligence reaching SIS on the Abwehr, SIPO [German Security Police] and SD [Nazi Security Service]. Began work in Section IX in the second half of 1944. Deals with all intelligence reaching SIS on the NKVD and various national Communist Parties.

14   Commander Dunderdale's SLC, July 1945

S3 Letter no. 4 of 16 July 1945

There follows information from STANLEY on Dunderdale's organisation. Dunderdale is SIS's Controller, Special Liaison (SLC).

His section has two sub-sections—Atlantic and non-Atlantic—the former dealing with certain types of intelligence relating to the USSR. The latter handles liaison with, for instance, Donovan's organisation [US Office of Strategic Services], Polish intelligence, certain sections of French intelligence, etc. As far as STANLEY can establish, there is no organisational connection between the two sections. It would be very easy to separate them and put each under its own head.

The Atlantic section gets intelligence on the USSR from the following sources:

a.   decrypting of radio telegraph traffic;
b.   radio telegraph messages en clair;
c.   radio-telephone intercepts; and
d.   sundry overt sources such as the Soviet press.

As far as (a) is concerned, the transmissions are intercepted and broken by the Poles. The latter have intercept stations in Stanmore and Scotland. The latter [station] operates under cover, ostensibly as part of a larger military radio installation. The Polish code-breaking bureaus are in Boxmoor.

The traffic referred to in (b) is read by a system run by Heal, an officer of SIS's Section X. He is responsible for telephones, telegrams, liaison with the Post Office, telegraph companies, etc. It is thus assumed that Heal uses his connections with them to obtain the material. All the traffic concerned is en clair. It is passed over by Heal to GCHQ and goes for review to Hastings, who then passes it to Dunderdale.

As far as (c) is concerned, these reports are received by a branch of Dunderdale's organisation. This is located in Roehampton in a house named FIRBANKS or something similar.

The person in charge of these radio-telephone intercepts is one Bunakov, who, in STANLEY's opinion, is a White Guard. He is a cripple. He intercepts conversations from as far away as Kizel, the Tannu Ola Mountains and Tashkent.

The intelligence received from all these sources is passed to Dunderdale at his main office on the first floor of the Alliance Building in Caxton Street near Broadway.

The principal offices of the Atlantic sub-section are as follows:

Department A run by Mr Shelley. He is responsible for communications between Head Office and all the production units listed above. He briefs them and supervises distribution of the intelligence in Head Office.

Department B run by McKibbin (a British subject, though with a lot of Finn in his blood). This department analyses reports on labour, wages, cost of living, social conditions, taxation, financing, oil, coal and timber.

Department C, under Rikovsky, is the military section dealing in the main with problems relating to the Red Army and the following branches of industry: chemicals, rubber, medium-machine building, railways. It also follows the NKVD.

Department D, under Narkevich, is the naval section. It also deals with power stations, agriculture, bread supplies, livestock, export and import, the building industry and reconstruction issues.

Department E, under General Baranov, is the aviation section, which also covers metals, machine tools, heavy-machine building, coke production, etc.

It can be seen from the above that the sub-sections are divided mainly along the lines of the areas of the armed forces that they target. Economic reporting is distributed more or less arbitrarily, depending on each department's workload.

The departments subject incoming intelligence to detailed analysis. Names of individuals, the number and names of factories, and details of army, navy and air force units are entered into a card index so that, when needed, the intelligence required can easily be retrieved for any given period. After enough intelligence has been assembled to allow the officer dealing with it to compile a coherent report, the material is analysed, collated and presented in a way that the user departments such as BLOCKADE and the Foreign Office can easily assimilate. After a report is compiled, it is given first not to the user department but to the relevant SIS section. For instance, a political report goes to Section I, an economic report to Section VI, etc. The section has the discretion to decide whether or not a particular report will or will not be forwarded to a user department.

It should be stressed that, if read in isolation, the majority of the reports obtained by these means do not make much sense. The best product is obtained when a whole series of reports can be looked at together and a coherent summary produced.

Dunderdale avoids this approach with energy. He claims that the barriers erected around the USSR are so watertight that the old methods, i.e. agents, are virtually impossible to use. Moreover, the strict controls existing inside the country make rapid detection of agents virtually certain. It will thus be necessary for SIS to rely on techniques like this to obtain intelligence that an agent network can no longer provide.

He claims that the French have come to the same conclusion and are applying the same principles to their work. In fact, Dunderdale went to Paris on 4 July to discuss with the French the possibilities for co-operation in producing and exchanging such intelligence. These questions are dealt with for the French by Rochard and de la Marky.

STANLEY does not know whether it is correct but Dunderdale claims that texts transmitted inside the USSR on the Baudot [teletype] system are now being intercepted. STANLEY does not know what this system is, but Dunderdale told him that it involves transmitting six texts simultaneously. Dunderdale has two assistants: Major Allen, based at Roehampton, and Squadron Leader Macdonald. The latter is Dunderdale's deputy and runs the sections in his absence.

15   *Memo on Penetrating Russia*

Penetrating Russia for Intelligence Production

SIS may be tasked for this soon after the cessation of hostilities in Germany. This paper attempts to anticipate and resolve certain problems.

The original of this memorandum from SPS [Rodney Dennys, secretary of the SIS Planning Department] was first passed to XS/F [Lord Farrar] and then to V1/C [Robert Smith] for comment. To make it easier to read, their comments are noted against each paragraph.

Part I

1. Long-Range Plan

If we want to achieve any sort of success, our plan must be designed for the long term.

The contemporary young Russian official, brought up in and, in many instances, born into the Party, has no historical basis for comparison and thus no international experience, either, to help him form his own views. These views are thus inevitably those of the Party, as are his knowledge and his opinions (including an inherent distrust of foreigners), and these in turn are based on the Party's policy.

British officials and business representatives who have to come into contact with Russians need to bear this in mind, as indeed do we in planning clandestine penetration of Russia.

Comment by XS / F:
Agreed. No comment.
Comment by V1 / C:
Ditto.

2. The Need to Ensure Security

The suspicion of every step we take is evident even from our current experience [in the USSR]. Even though the objective of the Barclay mission was an open and frank exchange of intelligence and its work was strictly confined to co-operation on matters of mutual interest, it took eighteen months for the mission to get anywhere.

It thus follows that our security needs to be perfect. To achieve perfection the cover needs to be natural. To a Russian there is nothing more natural than a British subject engaged on the sort of trade, industrial and financial matters that they see as the very essence of the imperialist bourgeoisie.

Comments by XS / F:

I agree up to and including the word 'perfect'!

Unfortunately, the Russians are particularly suspicious of us when it comes to matters of private-sector trade. Their foreign trade monopoly system means that real business is never done with non-Russian visitors. In the past, foreign business visitors to Russia were seldom granted visas if they spoke Russian, and those who did get there were handed over to Intourist, who worked with the GPU secret police to orchestrate their trip down to the very last detail. The Soviet government understands very well that responsible and genuine British circles now know that new business deals with the Soviets can be done only by going through the appropriate Soviet trade organisation in London or in whichever other Western capital they handle the trade in question. All orders are reviewed by an inter-departmental committee in Moscow, with the Finance Commissariat having the final say. Sometimes there is a request for several British specialists, but since HMG takes a dim view of technical assistance agreements, the number of these concluded between British firms and the USSR is very small. After a comprehensive discussion with the Committee of Imperial Defence, HMG set its face against such agreements because the Soviet Government has developed, and has insisted upon signing, a standardised form of agreement that requires the British counter-party to allow Soviet trainees in the UK full access to all its factories, services and workers' organisations. Although conditions have improved, it remains doubtful whether the security organisations and the Home Office would agree, even now, to British firms accepting such conditions. As a consequence, those British specialists who do travel to the USSR tend to be not very highly qualified and thus do not have the opportunity to mix with well-informed people.

The Board of Trade currently has information on certain private businesses which have permission to have staff permanently based in the USSR.

Comments by V I / C:

A clear obstacle to the Barclay mission's work is that it is open to all sorts of idle and prying eyes. It lacks cover. This state of affairs will continue until there is a steady flow of British travellers to the country and until the mere sight of a foreigner ceases to be a rare event. As the Russians have now regained self-confidence and the Party is no longer frightened of internal complications, their earlier fears, suspicions and precautions will probably wane.

Many British industrial concerns would gladly place all their technical knowledge at the Russians' disposal if they were able to get equal access to the latest Russian scientific and technical discoveries.

(With reference to XS / F's comments about the low level of qualification of British specialists sent to the USSR—this is past history!)

Responsible British businesses who have come to work well with the Russians rarely, if indeed ever, consult the Board of Trade or any other government departments except on purely official questions. First, because they know their business inside out. Second, they fear that information will leak to their competitors.

The firm of Farrow, Gaine and Kohl has already requested permission to have a permanent representative in Moscow, since it and the Russians are co-owners of the Russian Wood Agency. They have designated for this post Colonel James Martin, who worked as a manager in their Russian department before the war. He later applied to us. He accompanied [Lord] Beaverbrook and [Harold] Macmillan to Moscow. He then became representative of the Ministry of Transport in Archangel. He is now at a loose end somewhere in the UK. He should have been seconded to us for training while he was still in the army. It is now too late.

3. The Plan

We should thus use trade and finance as our primary channel. HMG will play a greater role in the trade and finances of the USSR than could have been anticipated several years ago. We thus have at our disposal two distinct and totally satisfactory covers:

a) official cover—government finance and economic missions, commercial attachés and junior commercial representatives in consulates
b) natural cover—businessmen, industrialists, specialists, engineers, chemists, etc., or trained intelligence personnel accompanying them on their visits to the USSR

Comments by XS / F:

I fear most of these comments will be negative, since I find that the plan proposed fails to take sufficiently into account the principles and practices of the foreign trade monopoly, that sacred cow of the Soviet government, which they show no sign whatever of abandoning. This virtually excludes the possibility of 'natural cover' in this field. As far as official cover is concerned, trade relations are the area in which the two countries have been furthest apart, meaning that the commercial counsellors' section has always been the first target of Soviet suspicion, and I fear this will continue to be the case. For example, other than at breakfast time, when the line was simply disconnected, the commercial Section telephones were monitored constantly. All the counsellor's visitors were followed, and 'approaches' were made to his typist and to her successor.

Comments by V1 / C:

Here XS/F is missing the wood for the trees. At the present time, for a number of practical reasons, the principles and practices of a foreign trade monopoly are just as much of a sacred cow for HMG as they are for the Russians, since Treasury control of foreign exchange and the Board of Trade's control over the issue of import and export licences will continue long after other wartime restrictions have been lifted.

'Natural cover' has served us well in Russia in the past—indeed, right up to the Metropolitan Vickers affair,* which was due entirely to our own carelessness. There are already positive signs that under certain circumstances the Russians will welcome direct negotiations with the British. 'Official cover' is another matter and will continue to be a delicate and complex question until such time as travellers are able to move freely between our two countries. In the meanwhile, 'official cover' remains too obvious and too unreliable.

I agree with XS/F's comments up to point (a).

4. The First Stage

Each agent and each operational officer must be briefed that they are not to try to obtain nor to accept any secret intelligence other than political and economic intelligence, strictly defined. In this first stage the NKVD will undoubtedly seek to offer military, air or naval intelligence to visitors to Russia, using agents provocateurs for this (and for indeed other purposes) in order to satisfy themselves that British visitors really are solely concerned with trade. It is therefore of vital importance that visitors confine their interest exclusively to matters of trade and finance.

In order to lull the Russians into a sufficient sense of security in this regard, the first or commercial stage will need to last at least three years.

Comment by XS / F and V1 / C:

Agreed.

5. The Second Stage

Over the next two years the situation will need to be carefully evaluated. The experience gained over the first two years of Stage 1 can be used to formulate a

---

*In 1933 a group of engineers working on a power station construction project for Metropolitan Vickers were convicted of espionage at a trial in Moscow. Upon conviction they were deported.

policy for direct intervention—political and military—in the XB [counter-intelligence] and XK [anti-Communist] areas.

Comment by XS / F and V1 / C:

Agreed.

6. Section V (Counter-Intelligence) and
Section IX (Anti-Communist) and Intercepts

We do not propose to expand in this paper on the work of these two SIS sections and merely suggest that over Stage 1 no attempts should be made to penetrate within Russia the GPU, the NKVD, or the now dissolved Comintern or any successor organisation.

The scope for this sort of work outside Russia is broad enough and intercepts will also play an extremely important part in this matter.

Comments by XS / F:

Agreed.

Intercepts (particularly internal): In the immediate future we shall have to rely primarily on intercepts. Considerable success was achieved during the war in scanning, selection and collating techniques, and our military experience must be adapted immediately for use in peacetime.

One of the most important elements is to understand and carefully note the requirements of client departments and to teach them to advise us of any changes in their needs immediately. The secret of successful management is to eliminate work on valueless material at the earliest possible stage of the processing cycle. I know, however, that the relevant departments are well aware of this.

Comment by V1 / C:

Totally agree.

Part II

Assuming that the arguments advanced in Part I are accepted, we set out below a brief review of the mechanism through which the work will be implemented.

7. London as a Clearing House for the USSR's international trade

The behaviour of the Russian trade mission and other signs suggest that the USSR intends to turn London into the clearinghouse for its international trade.

Comment by XS / F:

Agreed. But judging from past experience, the Soviet government will be able to conduct its business in London only by using several organisations in parallel. These organisations sometimes show signs of being jealous of one another, which can create openings for us.

Comment by V1 / C:

XS / F is quite right to point this out. I shall revert to it later.

1. [8.] Definition of Political and Economic Intelligence

We need to draw a clear distinction between political and economic intelligence, on the one hand, and commercial intelligence, on the other; the latter is not one of our functions and must be carefully avoided. This may be quite difficult, since many agents used in Stage 1 will be trained to approach things from a commercial point of view.

Political and economic intelligence can be defined as follows:

a. International economic policy
b. Plans, whether financial or commercial, which might affect the economic interests and plans of the Commonwealth, i.e. gold mining, purchase and sale of oil and wheat, long-range plans for the production of consumer goods, etc.
c. Secret chemical inventions in the area of agriculture and industrial production
d. Economic plans relating to the Far East

Comment by XS/F:
Agree in principle, but in practice economic and commercial intelligence are closely intertwined.

Comment by V1/C:
XS/F has completely missed the point. 'Economic intelligence' should be undertaken only in cases directly affecting the UK and its relationships as a state to the governments and arms of government of other countries. 'Commercial intelligence' is a matter affecting the wallets of private individuals and the interaction of these private interests when they come into conflict or competition with one another.

9. Producing Political and Economic Intelligence Through Official Cover

The post of commercial counsellor in Moscow comes to mind as cover for our head of station; under him would be the commercial attachés and commercial consultants or representatives in the consulates. Some of these should be SIS officers who have been fully trained for their cover jobs. Individuals heading British government missions, whether scientific and cultural, economic, industrial, agricultural or financial, should, when appropriate, be properly briefed by us, or SIS officers should be attached to those missions.

Comment by XS/F:
See my comment on Para. 3a. Moreover, before the war we were allowed to maintain consulates only in Moscow and Leningrad.

Comment by V1/C:
We can be confident that after the war reciprocal ties will grow and broaden.

10. Producing Political and Economic Intelligence via Natural Cover

This can be effected in the course of the normal development of foreign trade with the USSR or when we are so tasked by HMG or directly on a normal commercial basis.

Appendix 1 list the sectors of industry and the firms that will be motivated to develop trade relations with the USSR quite quickly, either with the encouragement of HMG or by their own commercial interests.

The heads of missions can also be inducted in suitable cases. They may be used either as conscious or as unwitting agents. SIS officers or ex-officers who have returned to business life should be included in such commercial missions, with the knowledge of the head of mission, where this is possible, or without his being aware, on the pretext that the Board of Trade has recommended their inclusion in order to look out for British government interests generally.

Comments by XS / F:

See comment on Para 2.

None of the industries listed would be able to open an office in the USSR without the permission of the Soviet government. Before the war this used to be refused point-blank, and this will probably be the case after the war, given the Soviet government's clear intention to conduct its foreign trade via London. Timber offices already operate in London. The fur trade there competes with the Russians, and from a commercial viewpoint there are no grounds for it to be handled via Moscow. A large proportion of Soviet flax is sold via Riga and is marketed as Latvian. Orders for machine tools are placed exclusively through the Soviet trade mission in London and financed via ECGD [Export Credit Guarantee Department].

As for insurance, all Russian insurance matters are handled by the (Russian) Black Sea and Baltic Insurance Company in London, while in tourism the Thomas Cook travel agency is not even allowed to issue direct tickets to Russia; travellers have to purchase supplementary tickets in Berlin. Its competitor Intourist, however, does have an office in London.

Mr Bruce Ottley knows everything there is to know about the ballet, and as far as I am aware, he takes the view that it offers little scope for us.

Workers' organisations may, when the opportunity arises, be useful in specific initiatives, but they are very much a two-edged sword, which we play with at our peril.

Comments by V1 / X:

XS / F is way behind the times! I have already mentioned the Russian Wood Agency. The Hudson's Bay Company has a great deal to teach the Russians about treating, curing and marketing furs. Soviet flax was only sold via Riga when Latvia was still independent. Malcolm and Company has in fact used Riga as a base for its technical organisation, which the Russians need.

11. The Advantages of the Plan

The plan envisages gradual but extensive penetration with complete security.

The plan does not require substantial expenditure of government funds.

All those identified for penetration purposes, whether officers or agents, have natural pretexts to meet one another.

HMG will not have to answer Russian claims that SIS is undertaking espionage in Russia. Even if suspicion falls on one or other mission or individual, HMG will be able to get out of it by saying that it cannot always control private commercial intelligence activity.

Comments by XS / F:

This plan may indeed not expose HMG to the risk of being criticised for behaviour incompatible with diplomatic norms but will generate bitter complaints from our most important industrialists that by mixing extraneous issues with their business affairs we have ruined extremely important business opportunities.

Comments by V1 / C:

XS / F exaggerates. As long as we stay out of 'commercial espionage', we have nothing to fear. If, however, we do fall into that trap, his comments will have a great deal of validity.

12. Head Office Organisation

The issue of cover in London is as important as that of cover abroad, and it is vital that we create a centre to which all stations and officers can cable or mail their reports or which they can visit in person without arousing any suspicion.

The most natural cover for this sort of activity would be the Commercial Department of the Foreign Office. The head of this department, provided he was suitable and had the appropriate knowledge, would have completely natural reasons to liaise with all official and other missions travelling to Russia, could evaluate each mission on its merits and decide whether or not members of a particular mission should be used as fully conscious or unwitting agents or whether an SIS officer should be attached to a mission as a Board of Trade representative.

We do not intend to elaborate in this paper on details of organisational structure; these can be worked out later if the principles advanced herein are accepted.

Comments by XS / F:

As far as I know there is no Commercial Department in the Foreign Office. There may be an Economics Department, but we need to bear in mind the distinction between commerce and economics drawn in Para. 8 of the draft. The head of the Economics Department would not know the major British industrialists anything like as well as the Overseas Trade Department or the Board of Trade, which are in constant touch with them.

Comment by V1 / C:

We spoke. Give him an SIS number!

Final comments by XS / F:

In the final analysis I would suggest that at the right moment we give the appropriate Soviet authorities sight, via some premeditated 'cock-up' on our part, of some of our reports, on condition that they (a) are correct and (b) contain no hint of the methods by which they were obtained. The experience of the Barclay mission is undoubtedly a good omen in support of this opinion.

Appendix [1]

Industries and Firms of Interest

1. The Timber Industry

In the immediate future, imports from the USSR are the only way to meet the British demand for timber. The matter is so urgent that negotiations are apparently due to start very soon.

Note: We should bear in mind 36000 [SIS head of station, Stockholm), who is tied into this.

2. The Fur Trade

Having accumulated large fur inventories during the war, the Hudson's Bay Company is apprehensive about Russian competition. The USSR has a large stockpile, too, and will compete with Hudson's Bay unless the latter fairly quickly agrees to talks on market sharing or worldwide distribution of Russian furs. In all likelihood, these talks will begin soon.

3. The Flax Industry

Certain types of flax can be bought only in Russia. Malcolm and Company, which has Russian speakers on its staff, will probably begin negotiations soon.

4. Industrial Plant

Industrial plant is one of the items in the long-term Anglo-Russian credit programme and also requires the presence of British missions (Vickers et al.) in Russia.

5. Insurance

Price Forbes Reinsurance Ltd will have a lot of dealings with the USSR.

Note: C.F.E. Duvier is a director of this firm. He speaks Russian and worked in our organisation from October 1939 to June 1945.

6. Travel Agents

Cook's

Note: VC was Cook's representative in Moscow.

7. The Russian Ballet

8. Workers' Organisations

Exchanges of visits by workers' groups, factory workers, etc.

XS/F:

Reports Received from Private Individuals. Pursuing your idea, I assume that the people selected by us will live and circulate in some new circle in which the traditional differences between the policies and methods of the USSR and ourselves do not exist. I myself am unclear what sort of circle that might be; pure research, music and sport come to mind. We have many interests in common in these areas and have the chance to create ties of personal friendship that might prove useful reinsurance in the case of mistakes or a general deterioration in relations. The people chosen should be young and should not be biased about Russia or indeed Great Britain.

VI / C:

I also agree. If people like SCE had worked in Russia in peacetime as they worked in China during the war, under our direct control, they could have begun by inviting Russian opticians and technicians to their laboratories and factories in the UK, knowing full well that the Russians would respond similarly.

The same can be said about music, ballet, the theatre, etc. Sport too; in this regard, a start needs to be made now on preparing the ground with the Football Association so that they are ready to go into action whenever the right time comes.

Travel is a sure thing. The Sir Henry Lunn firm is already approaching the Russian trade mission about organising travel on a very large scale. Once we have introduced it into the apple, the worm will soon grow fat!

We might add to the list:

Sir Henry Lunn Ltd. I hope to be able to pass to you in a few days a copy of the letter they are sending to the trade mission

H.A. Brassert and Company is currently developing a large-scale plan for the Donbass mines, based on an annual production of a hundred million tons—about one half the total British production.

Lambert Brothers Ltd is in active negotiations with the trade mission and the Russian Oil Products Company.

Johnson Mathey and Company has entered into preliminary talks with the mission about processing and distribution of Russian platinum and other precious metals.

Harland and Wolff, Belfast. Plan to get into talks with the Russians soon about freight-carrying icebreakers for use in Russian Arctic waters.

Hudson's Bay Company. The chairman, Ashley Cooper, is on his way across the Atlantic for talks with the Canadian government about Russia.

See also comments on Para. 10.

16   Colonel Vivian's Reply to the Memo

Penetrating the USSR for Intelligence

I have read the attached paper carefully. I will try to resist the temptation to comment on it in detail and will confine myself to an examination of the plan as a whole.

As such I completely disagree with it.

In my opinion it flies in the face of the fundamental policy of the Foreign Office and SIS.

A few commonsense constraints aside, the Foreign Office has allowed me considerable latitude in relation to XK [anti-Communist] work and Soviet official links with us, but only insofar as we steer completely clear of doing anything whatever in the USSR itself.

Though the USSR is a special case, this is really no more than a reaffirmation of SIS's general line that no SIS station acts against its host country.

Policy aside, common sense and twenty-five years' bitter experience should suffice to lay to rest once and for all the forlorn hope that any organisation in Russia, whatever form it may take, will provide us with the opportunities we need.

The optimism that permeates the comments of V1/C (Robert Smith) is to my mind totally misplaced, especially his view (page 2 comments of V1/C on Part 1, Para. 2) that 'suspicions and precautions will probably wane'. In my view, this assertion is utterly groundless.

The USSR has to date been governed by a dictatorship and is what the Americans quite rightly term 'a super-police state', and there will be no relaxation whatever of the twenty-four-hour surveillance of all foreign officials and businessmen, whether officially sponsored or there on their own affairs.

Indeed, surveillance is likely to be all the more rigorous because the Russians will be expecting us to behave as they do; I would wager a large sum that their trade missions and individual representatives in the UK or in other countries are used for espionage. They will thus assume we do likewise. Nor am I anywhere near as optimistic as V1/C in his comments on Part 1, Para. 3, and I suggest it would be sensible to accept the point made by XS/F (Lord Farrar, former PWE [Political Warfare Executive] officer). 'Natural cover' might have been possible up to the time of the Metropolitan Vickers case and even afterwards. But that was the SPETSOV period, when the Russians were striving to get first-hand knowledge of modern industrial methods and not only were prepared to pay a high price for American and British knowhow but actually paid it. But there can be no assurance whatever that having now proved that they can stand on their own two feet, they would welcome the arrival in Soviet Russia of a whole crowd of specialists or businessmen just to get their hands on knowhow which they might need at some future point. It is far more likely that they will seek to get the information they need to modernise their industrial methods via Soviet representatives sent out to the countries where the knowledge is available.

I am equally convinced that Part 1, Para. 4 (First Stage), is nothing more than a forlorn hope, since I just do not believe that we will be able to 'lull the Russians into a sufficient sense of their own security' in thirty years, let alone three.

I completely agree with Para. 6 of Part 1. The significant words are 'in Russia', and I consider this paragraph applicable not just to V [counter-intelligence] or XK operations but to the work of SIS as a whole.

My considered opinion from all this is that trying to work on the inside will get us nowhere, and that we need to set up our organisations on the Russian perimeter. We will find out far more in London, the Baltic States, Finland, Poland, Germany, Czechoslovakia, Austria, Turkey and Persia about a whole range of Russian matters in the XM [Russian citizens], XN, XP [political], XS [economic], as well as XB [Soviet agents] and XK areas both inside and outside Russia than we could if our organisation was in Russia itself.

Of course, we need a first-class head of station there under official cover who can keep us fully informed on all these subjects in Russia, based on intelligence reaching the embassy or [coming] from British businessmen, and who can assess and check the credibility of intelligence we obtain from outside. But in my mind we would be wasting money, taking an unjustifiable risk and kidding ourselves if we were to require our head of station to obtain, directly in the USSR, secret intelligence of any kind now or even many years ahead.

Vivian

17   *SIS Symbols, 23 July 1947*

Symbols

SIS = SIS
CSS = Chief, SIS
VCSS = Vice Chief, SIS
ACSS = Assistant Chief, SIS
DD/Navy/Army/Air = Deputy Director
DD/SP = Deputy Director, Security
DD/Admin. = Deputy Director, Administration
DD/F = Deputy Director, Finance
CSO/A = Chief of Staff, Administration
CSO/T = Chief of Staff, Training
SLC = Controller, Special Liaison
CSC = Controller, Secret Communications
CNA = Controller, Northern Area
CWE = Controller, Western Europe
CFE = Controller, Far East
CMed = Controller, Mediterranean
CPA/CSS = Principal PA/CSS
PA/CSS = Personal Assistant/CSS
PSO/CSS = Personal Secretary/CSS
RCS = Radio counter-intelligence
RIS = Radio intelligence
B = SIS Censorship Department
N = Press Department
RP = Coding Section
CR = Central Registry
X = Telegraph and telephone communications
MI5 = Counter-intelligence
GCCS = GCHQ
DD/C = DD of GCCS

NID = Admiralty Naval Intelligence
KID = Colonial intelligence
SOE = Special Operations Executive
MID = War Office Agent, Intelligence Section
ISOS = Radio Intercept Service (dealing with intelligence intercepts)
ISK = Radio Intercept Service (dealing with hand ciphers)
PWE = Political Warfare Executive
LCS = London Controlling Section
FORD = FO Research Department
DMO = Operational Section, First Department of Anglo Indian Army HQ
DSM = French counter-intelligence
SIM = Italian military intelligence
SPS = Indian political intelligence
G2 = US Army Intelligence Section
XB = Counter-intelligence information
XS = Economic intelligence
XP = Political intelligence
XXX = Material extracted from diplomatic bags
WP = US State Department
YP = US Embassy, London

18   SIS Internal Country Codes Used Up to the Second Half of 1946

06000 = Uruguay
07000 = Brazil
12000 = Germany (old symbol)
14000 = Romania
17000 = Egypt
18000 = Turkey
19000 = Denmark
21000 = Finland
22000 = Atlantic islands
22500 = Czechoslovakia
22600 = Yugoslavia (old symbol)
23000 = Spain
24000 = Portugal
27400 = Algeria (old symbol)
31000 = Latvia (old symbol)
32000 = Italy
35000 = Yugoslavia (new symbol)
36000 = Sweden
38000 = Poland (old symbol)
41000 = Greece
42000 = Switzerland

43000 = Estonia (old symbol)
44000 = Austria
48000 = USA
49000 = Malta
51000 = Gibraltar (presumed)
52000 = North Africa
53000 = Abyssinia
56000 = Tangiers
57000 = Lubigo (Angola)
58000 = East Africa
59000 = West Africa
60000 = Burma (presumed)
[illegible line]
72000 = Colombia
74000 = Honduras
75000 = Argentina
76000 = Chile
77000 = China (presumed)
78000 = Japan (presumed)
79000 = Venezuela
81000 = Aden
82000 = Iraq
83000 = Iran
86000 = Middle East (HQ)
87000 = Lebanon
88000 = Palestine
89000 = Middle East
92000 = Italy (new)
95000 = USSR
99000 = Wartime SIS agents in Norway, Denmark, Holland, Belgium, France, Spain and Portugal

A = Communism
B = Soviet intelligence agents
C = USSR
D = Soviet intelligence organisations
E = Communist Parties
F = Soviet government
G = Soviet officials
H = C[ommunist] P[arty] members
I = Soviet intelligence
K = On Soviet territory
L = In Soviet missions
M = Soviet citizens
N = Poles
XK = Communist activity
IX = Polish intelligence

19   Report on SIS Reorganisation, July 1945

Agent's Report, Source: STANLEY, 6 July 1945

A committee set up by the chief of SIS on the reorganisation of the British intelligence system began work in June this year. By 6 July it had already met eight times.

Although its remit was to look into the whole reorganisation issue in great detail (down to appointing officers even to the more junior positions), the committee has so far concentrated only on the general basis of the future organisation of British intelligence. A preliminary report on this has already been submitted to CSS.

The committee comprises: Chairman—Menzies, CSS. Deputy chairman—Maurice Jeffes. Permanent members: Colonel Cordeaux, Dick Ellis and Philby.

Ad hoc members (who attend for specific issues): Brigadier Gambier-Parry; Captain Edward Hastings and David Footman.

Menzies attended only the first meeting. Thereafter he was represented by [Christopher] Arnold-Foster.

This rather odd situation came about because the 'Old Guard' of SIS realised that Arnold-Foster would use the committee as a platform to attack the Service's old ways and its senior people. It was therefore decided that he should not serve as a member of the committee but should have the right to attend as the director's representative, thus making him immune from criticism.

Comments on the Committee's Work and Composition

Jeffes, the deputy chairman, is head of the Passport Control Department. He liaises closely with SIS, although he is not a member of the Service. He reports directly to the Foreign Office. Passport Control is financed on the open vote and has a legitimate role within government. In most cases, however, it provides cover for SIS officers, hence Jeffes's close ties to the Service and probably the reason why Menzies nominated him as the deputy chairman.

Cordeaux is a colonel in the Royal Marines. He has been in SIS since 1942 as deputy director for naval matters. At the end of 1942 or early in 1943 he became Controller, Northern Area, i.e. head of Section P, which deals with Holland, Norway, Sweden, Denmark and Finland. He was recently asked to examine the possibilities for intelligence gathering in Poland as the first step in penetrating the USSR and the countries under its influence for intelligence purposes. There were two reasons for Cordeaux's appointment to the committee. First, he is the most capable of the regional controllers; second, he is totally honest and has no personal agenda, since he will leave SIS at the end of the war.

Dick Ellis has been an SIS officer for twenty-four years. For many years he was responsible for intelligence production in western Europe. He spent several years during the war as deputy to Sir William Stephenson (the US head of station), an assignment he was given as a result of the animosity between him and Dansey. When the latter returned to the UK from Switzerland in 1940, he was made assistant chief with broad responsibilities for intelligence production in western Europe, thus putting Ellis out of a job.

Ellis returned to the UK in 1944 and was appointed Controller, Production. His job included the use of legal and natural cover (journalists, businessmen, etc.) for intelligence gathering. His role was regarded as extremely secret even within SIS. Ellis was appointed to the committee for his experience and his objectivity (he does not intend to leave SIS).

Gambier-Parry heads Section VIII. He is credited with the creation of an extensive communications network and a large number of workshops producing technical equipment. He was appointed for his considerable organisational skills and his technical knowledge.

Hastings runs the civilian side of GC & CS. At the outbreak of the war he was posted to Washington as GC & CS liaison officer with the US army and navy departments, which, as you know, have a monopoly on government cryptography. At the end of 1943 or early in 1944 he returned to the UK. At the beginning of 1945 he was appointed to replace Commander Denniston on the latter's retirement as head of the civil side of GC & CS. Hastings was appointed to the committee for his knowledge of the school's organisational side (plans, methods), which plays an important part in British intelligence, as well as for his business-like approach and his resourcefulness.

The qualities behind Footman's appointment were his level-headedness, his common sense and his bias toward objectivity.

The committee's secretaries are Major Denny and Colonel Rodney Dennys. The former was selected because he has considerable experience as secretary to the planning committees. Dennys is deputy head of Section IX and was selected on Philby's recommendation. He is a first-class draftsman.

The secretaries are not supposed to join in the committee's discussions, but in practice sometimes they do so.

Jeffes is a weak chairman. His opinion carries no weight, and he lacks the ability to grasp a new train of thought.

De facto, the committee is chaired by Arnold-Foster and Hastings. The former is the dominant figure, since he has the ear of CSS. Hastings is a flexible, decisive and independent thinker and has considerable influence over the committee's decisions.

Gambier-Parry is strong-minded and has much to say on all technical and administrative issues, but in discussions of intelligence handling and production he is almost totally ignored and has little to contribute.

Ellis makes a sensible and balanced contribution.

Although what Footman has to say is also usually sound, his personality is such that his comments often come across as destructive rather than constructive.

Cordeaux has strong views on secondary issues such as training, but for the most part he has nothing to say.

Philby sticks to a moderate line. He has decided that his best approach will be to hear the committee's point of view first and then support whichever line seems to offer the most effective results, mindful above all of avoiding even the slightest risk to his own position. He avoids mistakes and never argues with anyone.

The following are the main general principles adopted by the committee, which form the basis for the preliminary report to CSS.

There should be one person—CSS—at the head of the organisation with a deputy (DCSS) who, like the chief, is to be witting on all secret matters.

In the absence of CSS, DCSS has the right to give orders on all issues to do with intelligence handling, on all operational and administrative matters and on policy issues. He can represent CSS vis-à-vis other departments, foreign intelligence services, etc. He is a deputy in the fullest sense.

Directly below CSS and DCSS will be four directors—for production, for operations, for administration and for technical services. These four officers will be the only ones with direct access to CSS and DCSS and will be the sole channels for reporting to them on their respective divisions. The directors may have personal assistants.

The Director, Production, will run the division concerned with evaluating, collating and distributing to user departments such as the Foreign Office, the War Office, the Security Service, etc., all material obtained by British intelligence.

The division will have political, military, naval and counter-intelligence sections, the details of which have yet to be worked out.

As well as dividing the organisation functionally, thought is also being given to overlaying a regional structure so that, for example, the French counter-intelligence section can be aware of what is going on in French issues in the military, economic or political sections.

The director of production will also have under him the Registry responsible for the filing and collation of all intelligence.

The report stresses that the present SIS central filing system is out of date and that the Service needs to create something on the lines of the Security Service's Registry. It also emphasised the need for the Director, Production, to be an officer of real calibre with leadership qualities. The present structure of the sections, which work in completely different fields and completely independently of one another, has been unanimously rejected. The committee emphasised that it was essential to bring order and discipline into the distribution of intelligence so as to maximise its effectiveness.

The Director, Operations, will run the Operational Division. The work will be divided into four regions: (1) western Europe; (2) northern Europe; (3) the Middle East and the Balkans; and (4) the Far East and the Western Hemisphere.

The committee looked closely at whether from an operational viewpoint the work should be divided by the nature of the underlying targets (in which case the USSR and countries adjacent to it, such as Poland, would fall within one region) or by the location of the bases used for penetrating the USSR.

The committee decided that the latter was a better approach, since penetration was the cornerstone of the effort. Penetration of the USSR from Stockholm was a different problem from penetration from Tehran, for example, and should thus be tasked to another operational section. The committee took as given that penetration of the USSR from other countries was the most important challenge facing British intelligence. In fact, the sole purpose of the operational regionalisation is to facilitate penetration of the USSR from the north, south, east and west.

The Director, Operations, will have reporting to him four controllers, each responsible for one of the above regions, and a fifth in charge on a worldwide basis of the work of agents based in the UK and operating under natural cover. In turn, each controller will have sub-regional controllers corresponding to the present P sections. The term 'sub-regional controller' has not yet been finally adopted, although the job descriptions are in place. Thus the Controller, Western Europe, will have reporting to him sub-regional controllers in Italy, Spain, France, etc.

The committee attached great importance to close co-operation between the Production and Operational Divisions, not just between their directors but at lower levels as well. Thus the head of the Political Section should work closely with the regional controllers, and likewise the staff of the Political Section should work on France with the sub-regional controller in France. There needs, moreover, to be close contact between officers of the Production and Operational Divisions and their representatives abroad. This will be achieved by frequent inter-divisional transfers as resources and time permit. It is worth noting that the committee placed particular emphasis on the need for the Director, Operations, to really manage; i.e. he has to move away from the present situation in which each regional controller hoards his own available resources, whether they be people, money, supplies, etc. The director must ensure the most efficient allocation of resources between regions.

The Director, Administration, will be responsible for administration and finance. The committee highlighted that because of Menzies's weakness, the present deputy director (Finance), Commander Sykes, had throughout the entire war been a law unto himself, even though his job was in theory no more than to keep the books. For instance, he refused to sanction funds requested on the personal authorisation of a regional controller simply because he, Sykes, disagreed with the expenses budgeted for the proposed operations.

The Director, Administration, will also be responsible for the hiring of staff, promotions and appointments, accommodations, transport, and the sorting and distribution of paperwork. He will also look after the administrative files, which will thus be kept separate from those on intelligence matters.

At present our Registry is a complex tangle of administrative and intelligence files in which it is extremely difficult, if not impossible, to find what one needs.

The Director, Technical, will have under him two main sub-departments: communications and codes, and technical research and production. The former's role is self-explanatory. The second will be concerned with research and production of scientific inventions of interest to SIS, e.g. microfilms, secret inks, pocket radio transmitters (if they exist), etc. Details about the technical department are still being worked out but will obviously be, of the most part, dealt with by Gambier-Parry.

The foregoing represents the primary plan that, as recommended by the committee, will provide the framework for all of SIS's work.

A large number of questions remain unresolved in relation to minor matters, but the committee is confident that they can be accommodated within this framework. Examples of these include:

a. Removing operational and investigative functions from the Fifth Counter-Intelligence Section (up till now, as you know, the fifth section has had its own representatives abroad independently of the P sections)

b. Removing operational and investigative functions from the B sections (Boyle, as you know, has responsibility for removal of material from foreign diplomatic mail and as well for circulation of intelligence data)

There remains, however, one fundamental question—namely, the merger of SIS and GC & CS. The committee will be discussing this in the near future with GC & CS representatives. The review may take several weeks. In the final analysis, the committee's decision may be influenced by an extraneous factor—namely, Findlater Stewart's inquiry into MI5, which could have a bearing on the definition of the functions and duties of the counter-intelligence sections of SIS and GC & CS.

20   *Colonel Vivian's Memo, September 1944*

Sections I, IX, V, VK
22850, CMed., CNA, CWE, CFE

Reasons

1. This memorandum provides a general picture of the XK [anti-Communist] situation in SIS both at home and abroad and sets out the reasons that have

prompted me to seek your advice on the best methods of organising our work in this area overseas.

The problem is extremely broad and complex. It therefore seems to me to be both impractical and undesirable to discuss it in a formal meeting. It can, nonetheless, be readily divided into convenient component parts, which can be sufficiently clearly defined and which are independent enough of one another that in each instance one would need to have only a very few officers involved in the discussion and formulation of advice.

As far as I can see, these component parts might be:

i. Head Office Organisation
ii. Overseas Organisation

Each of these can, in turn, be sub-divided.

i. Head Office Organisation

The final shape of a Head Office organisation can be resolved only by CSS himself, and he has already stated that he is not yet ready to express a view. There are nonetheless certain questions that can conveniently be examined now and those that need discussion to enable us to take appropriate steps at home and abroad. They include:

a. Bearing in mind that VL/WM will retire at the end of, or soon after, the war ends, should we not control or co-ordinate the work of Section I, the Russian Section of SPS-a, Section IX and Section V (or the work of Section IX in Section V) in some way that goes beyond mutual liaison and co-operation?
b. Knowing that the present head of Section IX will be leaving SIS after the end of the war in Europe, should we not designate his successor now and begin to work with him immediately to avoid any interruptions in the work?
c. At the present time Section IX does not have enough people to handle the heavy load of investigative and collation work needed to enable PCO and SIS officers to handle operational tasks abroad appropriately or to allow Section IX to sort its way properly through the raw material when compiling the periodic reports frequently called for by the Foreign Office and others. This situation is exacerbated by the truly chaotic situation with the XK files in CR [Central Registry] and CR's inability—given its present level of staffing and management—to deal efficiently with XK files in the time ahead.

We need, as a matter of urgency, to set up a section on the lines of [illegible], staffed with experts and analysts, and a small but responsive section similar to [VC?].

Can Section V detach a part of V/L and VO1 for this purpose? If so, when can they put it at our disposal, and is there a need to get this confirmed by CSS?

The staffing of Section IX as a whole needs discussing and then resolving, with an eye in particular to the handling of top-secret material within the section and the changes needed to rectify the shortcomings of CR.

Could this be dealt with now, since it is important to begin the next phase with the appropriate organisation in place, at least in embryonic form?

ii. Overseas Organisation

The overseas organisation can conveniently be divided as follows:

a. Existing SIS stations abroad, which can in turn be divided into:
    1. Western Hemisphere stations
    2. Iberian Peninsula stations
    3. North Africa and Middle East stations
    4. Sweden
b. Enemy-occupied, recently liberated or soon to be liberated countries. These can be arranged by region as follows:
    1. France and Belgium
    2. Italy
    3. Balkans and Greece
    4. Holland, Norway, Finland and Denmark
    5. Austria and Czechoslovakia
    6. Poland
c. Operational regions (outside Europe)
    1. China
    2. Dutch East Indies
    3. French Indo-China
d. Enemy countries
    1. Germany
    2. Japan

2. The issues raised in Para. 2 above (Head Office Organisation) are best resolved in an unofficial meeting of SPS, I, V, IX and DD/SP. The review of each of the country groups listed in Para. 3 might perhaps be of a more official nature, using the planning staff. In each given case, it will be sufficient to have present the officers mentioned above, plus the relevant target controller, and the officers or staff members dealing with these targets.

We need to tackle first the Balkans (especially Yugoslavia and Greece), Italy, France, Belgium, Holland, Norway, Austria, Czechoslovakia and Poland. The Foreign Office also has a particular interest in Spain, South America, the USA and China.

Prior to any meetings dealing with the countries in the Mediterranean region and the Middle East, the attached report of Mr Steptoe on XK problems, and his advice, needs to be studied and taken into account, and he should attend himself.

Mr Steptoe should also be present for discussion of XK issues relating to China and Japan; the Dutch East Indies and French Indo-China can for the moment be left to one side.

3. A personal but important issue needs to be settled. With CSS's agreement the work of Section IX has now been co-ordinated with the Section V set-up. It

might be thought to follow that XK work abroad will be the monopoly of Section V offices overseas. Is it not desirable to make it clearly understood that any appropriate SIS officers who may now be transferred, whether from Broadway or from Ryder Street, are obliged to act in accordance with the instructions of the directives of the XK section (whatever shape it may take), and also of Section I, transmitted through ordinary SIS channels?

This has a bearing on issues of selection, training and appointments, but is, I think, desirable, too, in the interests of economy and flexibility.

DD/SP, 6 September 1944

21   *The XK Problem in SIS, 6 September 1944*

1. Head Office Organisation

Section IX was set up in May 1943 as an independent mobile section under supervision of DD/SP with the general aim of handling 'intelligence relating to clandestine, subversive or espionage activity of the Comintern or any other organisations linked with it or with the government of the USSR'. In more detailed directives approved by CSS the responsibilities of the head of section are defined as follows:

a. To study and collate all intelligence on this issue received by SIS from the time Communism became a target of primary interest in a global context and in particular [intelligence on] individual countries.
b. To process, and as necessary recommend, steps to be taken in relation to current intelligence on this question.
c. To propose, as considered necessary, the infiltration of agents to increase the intelligence available to us.
d. To co-operate closely with the Section F of MI5 and V/LWM of SIS (which deals with the more overt manifestations of the left wing, including Communism).
e. To compile periodic reports on the Communist movement in a global context and in individual countries in response to specific taking requirements.

Before the war XK [Communist activity] was looked after exclusively by Section V in conjunction with Section I.

In June 1944, as a consequence of a memorandum by DD/SP submitted to CSS on the organisation of XK work in SIS, CSS recognized that, while he was not yet ready to express a view on what form of organisation would be desirable, he 'does not approve of a permanent division between the work of Sections V and IX,' and he concurred in the proposal that we should now proceed 'to unite Section IX and the Section V set-up'. (Note: This statement was formally requested in connection with the overall difficulties experienced by DD/SP in selecting overseas SIS officers for training and in giving sufficiently authoritative instructions on general and special matters to SIS officers in countries from which intelligence was required.)

    f. Other sections of SIS involved in certain aspects of this subject are:
        i. Section I (the political side)
        ii. The Russian Section, headed by [redacted] (whose functions are not precisely defined)
        iii. V/LWM (left-wing movements, overt activities)

We thus have five separate sections dealing, in one way or another, with these issues, only two of which (V and IX) are controlled or co-ordinated by the same supervisor below the level of CSS. Only one of these sections, namely IX, has its functions precisely defined.

[2.] Requirements

In October 1943, DD/SP was instructed by the Foreign Office, 'provided strict secrecy is maintained and provided nothing is undertaken within the USSR itself', to obtain intelligence on 'what the Soviet government is doing abroad via ancillary organisations like the Communist Party and what special game they are plotting' in certain countries.

The FO added that 'in our opinion it is no more than a sensible precaution to find out as much as possible about their aims and activities, and you will not put yourselves at too much risk if you do this via foreign Communist Parties outside the USSR.

While agreeing that Communist plans relating to Spain, South America, the USA and China were of especial interest, the FO in the same letter emphasised in particular the Communist problem in the Balkans (especially in Yugoslavia and Greece), in Italy and in enemy-occupied countries, especially France, noting that in all of these countries the FO considers the issue to be 'Extremely timely'.

As regards the pace of the effort, the FO expressed the view, almost a year ago, that there were good reasons to view the acquisition and verification of intelligence on the clandestine activities and goals of the Communist organisations to be an immediate task for SIS, and not just something of value for the future, and further that the creation of an agent network to produce this intelligence should not be put off until the cessation of hostilities or the Peace Conference.

In addition to the FO, MI5 is another client that, in order to protect its own narrow interests in this issue, wishes to receive intelligence on Communist activists, their methods and their operations in all parts of the world.

Other clients do not indicate a direct interest in XK work, other than the Admiralty, which has specifically asked SIS to look into any evidence of Communist influence in the navies of the largest Latin American republics and to keep them informed.

2. [3.] Section IX's Achievements

It must be borne in mind that Communism has not been a current SIS target since 1939. We have gradually lost practically all our special agents who were at one time particularly effective, and in addition the war has deprived us of our links with various official sources from which we used to get valuable intelligence. We have, nonetheless, obtained a certain amount of information from the Censorship submissions (WWs) and from collateral sources; but prior to 1943, when Section IX was created, we did not even have a section that processed this collateral intelligence, and our knowledge of this target was virtually nil.

In the subsequent fifteen months, Section IX has become significantly better informed through determined investigative work, and we have been able to build up a picture of the direction in which organised Communism is moving at the present time and its ties with the Soviet government.

We have trained or partly trained certain officers of Section V who have been assigned for work abroad. We are attempting to stimulate the production of whatever intelligence we can glean from overseas on special questions arising from information that has come our way at random. We have arranged to obtain information from certain of our Allies, having given them assurances of non-disclosure. We have issued several general directives for SIS officers outside the UK, defining the kinds of intelligence that we require and setting out the conditions under which promising channels of information may be utilised.

As a whole, however, our briefing of SIS officers has been more admonitory, restraining, or at best explanatory in nature than stimulative, since we were constrained by the fact that our officers overseas lacked sufficient basic knowledge of the issue to prevent them from causing diplomatic complications or even being exploited by pro- or anti-Soviet interests.

It should also be noted that Section I's questionnaires (which request specific information from the recipients) are beginning to include requests for intelligence on various questions about Communism related to the USSR. These are evidently being dispatched via the P sections to overseas officers, who may be able to provide the required intelligence because they are 'on the ground' but who have had no training at all on this task.

One PCO (in Rome) has been properly trained to conduct XK work abroad, but instructions from Section V forbid him to take active steps of any nature in this area for at least six months.

I am extremely distressed to hear this, all the more since Sir Noel Charles and Mr Hopkinson have both expressed great interest in intelligence received on this theme, and the FO itself, in its briefing on the issue of Communism in Italy, expressed the hope that the Rome PCO would soon be in a position to supply intelligence on this target.

Another officer (Mr Sedcole) has been appropriately trained for work as a 'floater' agent for Section IX in the Middle East and is now attached to S9700 for this purpose. He has a potentially valuable link with a Czech intelligence officer, which we hope will be maintained by periodic meetings in Bari. However, Sedcole has been designated a member of the SIS group earmarked for Hungary, and his work in the Middle East has to be viewed as a temporary assignment.

Finally, 22850 (Mr Steptoe) is fully trained for this purpose and has completed a major swing through the Middle East region to train selected representatives in SIS's requirements, to determine the prospects for productive work on the XK subject and to recommend measures for use of the routes that have begun to suggest themselves to us.

22850's very clear report is attached and will be reviewed separately.

4. Sources

SIS has acquired absolutely no new sources for the production of XK intelligence. We are left with the handful of old sources in Palestine who did not disappear in the war, our somewhat shaky liaison with the Poles, a more reliable and valuable link with the Czechs, and a very promising though as yet short-lived connection with Section M of the Deuxième Bureau in North Africa (on the topic of Communism in Metropolitan France); this will last only until the Deuxième Bureau is transferred back to Paris. But no measures have been taken to implement the policy laid down by the FO in its 1943 letter, a policy that is also reflected in Section I's questionnaire.

5. Reasons for the Stagnation

This state of stagnation is without doubt a temporary manifestation brought about by the fact that SIS officers abroad, whether run from Broadway or from Ryder Street, are completely overwhelmed by tasks directly related to the war. But the root causes are also to be found in (a) the abnormal situation at Head Office, (b) the extreme delicacy of this issue from a diplomatic point of view and the limitations we feel obliged to impose as a result, (c) the handful of SIS officers who know enough about the target to provide competent intelligence without putting their foot in it in the process of producing it, and (d) the manifest futility of training for this purpose officers who will not be staying in SIS after the end of the war.

The fact remains that we have not taken effective steps to get our house in order, either at home or overseas, or to grapple appropriately with solving a problem that will almost certainly be one of the most important tasks of the future SIS.

[6.] The Relative Urgency of the Problem

There is a general view among SIS officers at HO [Head Office], who have not studied the issue in any detail, that the XK problem is just another of the tasks to be planned for in the distant future and not one of pressing urgency. For this reason there is a perfectly natural tendency to put off any practical steps towards implementing our plan abroad until the ending of military operations in Europe relieves us of certain current responsibilities.

We may be compelled willy-nilly to accept this point of view, but I must insist that the critical moment when HMG will need to have detailed, high-quality inside information is already almost upon us—i.e. the moment when local governments will begin to be restored in the liberated countries, when resistance movements with a heavily Communist flavour may exert a decisive influence out of proportion to their real national significance, and when underground groups supported or directed from Moscow and run by covert or overt Soviet organisations abroad may lead to the creation of governments totally unrepresentative of the wishes of the majority or may even provoke civil war and postpone indefinitely the restoration of law and order.

It is precisely at this stage that our Foreign Office and armed forces need regular and reliable intelligence; it may even be that we have already missed the opportunity to shed light, successfully, on this vital stage in history. We must, therefore, realise that we have to make, at a minimum, certain decisive efforts to save the situation by the urgent creation of an organisation overseas. If we delay further, it may take years before we can successfully meet HMG's requirements.

2 September 1944

22   *Report on the Mediterranean Inspection, August 1944*

22850's Report on His Trip Through the Mediterranean Region in Connection with the XK Problem

1. AIM—The purpose of the trip was, in essence, to provide basic training in XK issues, to assess the situation on the XK front in all the stations visited, to study the opportunities for development of XK work and to present a comprehensive report on these matters for Head Office review upon my return.

2. LINE TO TAKE—This can be summarized as follows:

a. In training on XK matters special attention must be paid to the extreme delicacy of the task of penetrating the XK, bearing in mind the risk of diplomatic complications.

b. Officers' attention must be drawn to the fact that, generally speaking, requirements in XK cases fall into the following three categories, in diminishing order of sensitivity:

i. XK movements and organisations that are already being used or may be used in the interests of Soviet national policy

ii. Clandestine movements and organisations that damage our interests or are intended for that end, irrespective of whether they are linked to the USSR

iii. XK organisations whose aim is to penetrate our own intelligence services

Intelligence operations against (i) and (ii) need to be conducted with extreme care, whereas (iii) may be regarded as conventional counter-intelligence work; it may be pointed out in this connection that if we were to fail to take steps to protect our interests in this area, we would be bound to forfeit the respect of the Russians!

c. Officers' attention must be drawn to the dissolution of the Comintern in May 1943. It must be stressed in particular that one of the most important intelligence questions is whether there continues to exist in Moscow a central directing organisation that controls the activity of national Communist Parties and thus brings them and their policy into line with Soviet foreign policy. Officers must be told that it can be deduced that such a central directing organisation does indeed exist, and that the production of evidence on the basis of which their deduction might be elaborated or corroborated is a matter of the utmost importance. Officers must also be advised that in investigating these matters and also in penetrating the personal organisational and clandestine activities of XK, the watchword should be *Festina lente*—'Make haste slowly!' and that they should not pursue lines of inquiry which might create an obvious risk for SIS or leave the impression that SIS are taking an interest in, or attempting to penetrate, Soviet national movements or Parties. Finally, officers need to be made aware that they should not investigate possible penetration routes without prior Head Office approval.

3. METHODS—The principles cited above were clearly and fully explained to all the officers with whom I met, and I left a summary of these instructions at most of the stations to prevent future misunderstandings. In addition, all officers were taken through the 'Memorandum on the Structure of the GRU and the OGPU/NKVD' and were required to read a previously prepared memorandum on the Communists' revolutionary programme, the Comintern, the Brazilian Revolution of 1936 and the Green, Springhall, Uren and Pieck cases. I augmented these case papers with comments from my personal report as head of station for the Far East, when I had to deal with Communist activity in that region, in particular the Noulens case, and with matters relating to the staffing and activity of the Comintern's Far Eastern Bureau. I also attempted (perhaps not that successfully) to interest the officers in the ideological outlook of the Communists and the factors that, in all probability, will guide Soviet post-war policies. Finally, on the chief's instruction, I put particular stress on producing as much detailed intelligence as possible on the personality profiles of Soviet officials and their connections so that the present unsatisfactory level of our knowledge about particular individuals may to some extent be improved.

In all stations the officers made notes of our conversations and on the cases I had written up, and before I left the station, steps were taken to ensure the safe custody of these notes. Stations were visited in the following order: Cairo, Tehran, Baghdad, Jerusalem, Beirut, (a side trip), Constantinople, Beirut, Cairo, Algiers, Naples, Rome and Bari. I also saw HM's envoy in Tehran, Sir Noel Charles, Mr Hopkinson in Naples and Mr Caccia in Rome. I sketched out for them the purpose of my trip in accordance with my briefing. Sir Noel Charles and Mr Hopkinson expressed some satisfaction that steps were being taken to look into XK issues, especially in Italy, and also voiced the hope that in the future SIS would be able to provide them with more intelligence on the subject.

4. THE XK PROBLEM IN THE MEDITERRANEAN REGION

Before making a detailed review of the XK problem in relation to the various stations I visited, I believe it necessary to attempt a sketch, albeit incomplete, of Soviet policy in the region generally. Without this it will be difficult to identify the factors that, in my view, are essential for a correct evaluation of that policy.

I will begin with the eastern Mediterranean. I believe it may be said with confidence that the Allied occupation of Persia has given Russia a potential base there on which it can build either an aggressive or a passive policy, as the mood takes it. In all probability either policy will be directed by other, broader considerations. For instance, when the present conflict ends, will the Soviets direct their energy towards internal reconstruction, and will they subordinate their expansionist notions, which are a natural concomitant of their military successes, to such a reconstruction and to the development of the vast potential resources inside their country? On the other hand, having overcome the danger from Germany, might the Soviets, with a shrewd eye on the weakening of the political and economic life of their neighbours in the Middle East, not try to shape this to their own ends and to influence these aspects of the future national life of these countries? In the realm of 'power politics', will the possibility of a post-war anti-Soviet bloc have any bearing on Soviet policy? In the case of the Middle East, such a bloc might manifest itself in the creation of a Muslim Union within the region as a response to some ideological propaganda; might not Soviet Russia itself respond to the existence of such a bloc by taking advantage of the political and economic inequality that prevails between the people of some of the Middle Eastern territories (e.g. in Persia, Egypt and Palestine), to keep them in a state of discontent and thus prevent the implementation of whatever long-term policy HMG may have in mind? Educated young people in all these areas, as well as the representatives of the vast landless class, might prove fertile ground for cultivation of the seeds of discontent.

Finally, is the Soviet activity, which we have seen manifested in their vast missions in Egypt, Algeria and Italy, a sign of a long-term policy of enveloping the entire Mediterranean, or is it simply evidence of Moscow's natural concern to see that if the Free French representatives concentrated in Algeria and the present Bonomi government in Italy do indeed emerge as something approaching responsible governments, they will carry a vivid Communist birthmark?

From the point of view of XK, the most important area is Palestine. The situation there is made more complex by the fact that national development has been held back by the existence of a marked contrast between Arab interests and the developed political and economic collectivism of the immigrants and the Jewish refugees who have settled there. It is complicated still further by the question of Arab unity, which we will evidently support, and the lack of confidence in both the British and the Russians on the issue of Palestinian Zionism. I believe it is impossible to tell to what extent Soviet Russia intends to take advantage of these complications. Its ties with Zionism are evidently confined to cultural links and are unofficial connections with the Jewish War Fund, or V League. The nature of this connection can change in an instant with any change in the league itself or in the make-up of its leadership, its relationship with us and our Palestine-Jewish policy.

It is also fair to suggest that the Soviets are hardly well disposed to the idea of Arab union, since from their point of view, such a union will be influenced much more by its conservative, landowner, merchant leadership than by the countries' younger and more progressive elements.

5. THE XK PROBLEMS IN THE VARIOUS STATIONS VISITED

a. Cairo—Factual evidence of Soviet activity in Cairo in particular or Egypt in general is hard to come by, although there is a general feeling that the Soviets are conducting a low-key propaganda effort aimed at putting Russia 'on the map', since the population for the most part know almost nothing about the Soviet political system and the economic transformation of the USSR.

I believe the main reason for the lack of intelligence is the way officers have hitherto been briefed on XK issues. To this we must add the almost complete ignorance of Russia, particularly Communist ideology and past policies, about which officers have only the haziest notions. Our officers, therefore, found it almost impossible to provide any sort of assessment of the nature, scale and ramifications of the XK problem, especially in its XP [political intelligence] form. As I understand it, however, this latter aspect is regarded in Cairo more as a function of 17000, but since this officer was not amongst the heads of stations with whom I spoke on XK issues, I cannot gauge either the nature or the volume of the intelligence on XK to which he has access.

This is a convenient point at which to note that a similar lack of knowledge of XK questions was apparent in almost all the stations I visited, for similar reasons. I nonetheless hope, and to some extent believe, that my preliminary briefings on XK will stimulate interest in this problem and that our officers now have a general idea on the basis on which to operate and will be able to evaluate correctly any intelligence they succeed in acquiring.

As regards the XB [counter-intelligence] aspects of XK, I am fully satisfied by the way it is handled by the officers of 89700's station and in other places in the Middle East. After my briefings on the Soviet intelligence system we may look forward to receiving more precise intelligence on what particular individuals are up to, especially those connected with the NKVD.

It came out in my conversations with 89700 that a certain amount of XK intelligence is obtained by SIME through its own agents and that similar information comes via the SLUs [Special Liaison Units]. Whereas the distribution of intelligence obtained by SIME does not give rise to any problems, the passing on of material by the SLUs directly to SIME, BGS(i) and PIC has in the past caused some confusion.

This has now been sorted out, 89700 having taken the necessary steps to see to it that w.e.f. [with effect from] 5 April the direct distribution of XK material by the SLU will cease and that thereafter all XK material will be sent to 89700, who will be personally responsible for its distribution.

89700 also considers it very important that SIS, and not MI5, should be responsible for the investigation, processing and distribution of XK materials in the territories where SIS is operational; in his view, these are the Balkans, Turkey, Persia, Iraq, Lebanon and possibly Palestine. I suggest that this question merits attention, since I doubt that SIME is capable of handling intelligence of the sort mentioned in Para. 2(c) I and II of my 'Lines to Take'.

89700 also told me what he had heard from Dennett, who now works for X2 in the Middle East; he claims that Washington is beginning to focus on XK issues in the Mediterranean, although he personally has been given categorical orders not to get involved. It would be interesting to find out more about the extent of the American interest in the problem and in particular the lines along which they are working, and I suggest that 48000 be asked to make discreet inquiries.

I had a long talk in Cairo with the previous 83900, who has been assigned to Head Office for training in XK work. His comments on XK work in Tehran are contained in notes on the station files. I formed the view that although the previous 83900 knows the structure of the GRU [Soviet Military Intelligence Service] and OGPU/NKVD well, and knows what to watch for abroad in this connection, his knowledge of broader XK issues, especially the XP aspect, is limited, and I feel that unless his knowledge improves through the training proposed for him, he will be of limited value to other officers in the Middle East, who will naturally look to him for leadership and advice.

b. Tehran—In my view, this is our most important station in the Middle East after Jerusalem, and one of those in which it is absolutely essential to have a head who is as well trained as possible.

The present head of station, 83000, was recruited in the Middle East and has not had intelligence training. He is, however, getting to know a lot about SIS's operating methods from practical experience. As he put it, he has had to operate by 'trial and error'. My sense is that his lack of training, together with the strict instructions that he has had about XK work in the past, has blunted his interest in the matter. His relationships with ZP are excellent. I understood from 89000 that he will be replaced this coming October by 88900. The latter is an extremely capable individual, and if he does the job as well in Tehran as he did in Jerusalem, the station will be well and appropriately staffed. It should, however, be borne in mind that 88900 has not had SIS training either, and in XK matters his knowledge is limited to a general, though acute, interest in XK and to what he managed to glean from my briefings.

Acquisition of XK intelligence in Persia is a difficult job, and in the absence of another agent like the Czech—our former 83900—I doubt that anything of value will come our way in the near future. The Russian diplomatic community lives in almost total isolation and appears in public only on official occasions, and when they do, their behaviour is strictly controlled; any attempts to go beyond arms'-length contact would be bound to fail. To begin with, even seeking to build first-hand personality profiles of the people who are instrumental in implementing Russian policies and activity is impossible.

Local sources, especially Persians and Armenians, should we decide to engage them, need to be selected with the greatest care, since they are unreliable. In the case of Armenians in particular, they are often pro-Russian as well. Agents in Tehran's Czech community also need careful handling, since the community contains both pro-Russian and anti-Russian elements, between whom there is considerable friction. The only possible Czech agent is the engineer Titer, information on whom is in HO files. It is possible that agents of value may also be found in the Polish community, but our former agent 83900 told me that he had never had any luck with them on XK matters. It is, however, possible that 83900 will be able to get a line on suitable Polish agents through his friendship with Colonel Rudmetsky, the Polish military attaché in Tehran. The OSS [US Office of Strategic Services] has a representative in Tehran, but I gather that SIS does not have a close relationship with him, and it is doubtful whether he has intelligence on XK at his disposal, since General Connolly has laid down as a matter of principle that in view of the close US-Russian relationship, there are to be no intelligence operations against the USSR.

From time to time SIS receives some XK intelligence in Tehran, but it is invariably confused, and where individuals are concerned, the first names are usually missing, which is of course a key omission. An incident that happened when I was in Tehran emphasises the point. SIME sent us a preliminary list of Soviet officials in Persia. Of the seventy-five names, in only thirty-six cases were their jobs shown. In nineteen cases we were given initials only, and in no instance did we get the full name.

The XB position is more satisfactory. I was told that an understanding had been reached to keep in close touch in the field, as a result of which all movements of Soviet official and unofficial personnel from the Tehran zone to the British zone in this country and also to Iraq and Egypt are communicated by the

VM in Tehran to the VM in Baghdad and to the SIS head of station in Tehran before permission for the journey is given.

The prospects for producing good intelligence on XK are thus not spectacular, and our head of station will need to make a very strenuous effort, since the Soviets are extremely active. They maintain their own well-equipped hospital, where the majority of patients are Persians and Armenians of all classes. Their propaganda offices are extremely well stocked with reading material and photographs. In particular, reading material in various languages is available gratis upon request. These offices are well patronised.

Although there is no Communist Party in Persia, Tudeh, the only party of significance in the country, is said to be completely imbued with Soviet doctrines and is totally in sympathy with Soviet ideals. It has a reasonably good attitude towards the British, but despite being the leading party in Persia, it has not received support from official British sources.

When I was in Tehran, I was told that the Soviets were augmenting their existing consulate representation in Meshed and Naushahr and that a new consulate is to be opened in Quazin, to be headed by Bespalov, a former secretary in the consulate in Tehran.

The Irano-Soviet Cultural Association recently opened a Russian-language centre for beginners and for more advanced students.

There is also evidence that Soviet representatives are secretly supporting workers' organisations in the textile industry in Isfahan, as well as oil industry workers in the Persian Gulf. There is said to be a strong movement among the Azerbaijanis to form autonomous Soviet republics.

c. Baghdad—The XK situation in Baghdad does not need comment. When I arrived there our former 82000 was ready to hand over to 82000, but as the latter fell ill when he arrived at the station, I was unable to have any detailed discussions with him. So my talks went no further than the conversation I had with 82900. This officer was recruited in the Middle East and has not had intelligence training. However, he is very keen indeed on the work and is a clever and well-read individual who knows a lot about XK. My understanding from 890009 [*sic*] is that he is to be transferred to Jerusalem to replace 88900 following the latter's posting to Tehran.

I gather that in the past the relationship between the previous 82000 and the embassy staff was far from good. The Oriental secretary apparently has a dim view of SIS, shared to a lesser degree by the counsellor, who apparently has left-ist leanings. As a result of this, and possibly other factors too, for the Oriental secretary's office to be providing the cover for ISLD [Inter-Services Liaison Department] may be rather unreliable.

The attitude of the head of public relations towards our station in Baghdad is also somewhat troubling.

Stuart Perowne is ideologically a Communist sympathiser. His direct aim is reputed to be to sabotage the SIS station in Baghdad, on the grounds that its use of writing and paid Iranian agents is incompatible, in his opinion, with his work as a public relations officer. According to 82900, Perowne tried to penetrate SIS through one of the radio operators attached to our station. 82900 wrote 89000 a detailed report on this. For cover purposes, Perowne attached to him one Philip, the local head of SOE: the latter is alleged to be very 'Red' and is a member of the Holborn branch of the Labour Party. Philip lives with one Seton Lloyd, the British advisor to the director of the Historical Monuments Institute of the Iranian government. Lloyd is said to be ideologically sympathetic to Communism.

I think it expedient to keep a close eye on what their people get up to in relation to SIS.

The Iranian Communist Party is illegal and has been officially banned. It is claimed to have some twelve thousand members, but there are signs that the government, apprehensive about generating unfavourable comment, is turning a blind eye to the Party's activities. Their main centres are in Baghdad, Basra and Mosul. They are said to have ties to the Communist Party in Syria and Lebanon. Kamel Chadarchi is said to have petitioned the prime minister for permission to operate a group or party under the name 'The Society of Popular Reform'. This request has not so far been granted and is unlikely to be, since in the government's view, if the Communists were legalised, they would seek to gain control over all of the movements whose aim is to improve labour conditions in Iran, which would inevitably lead to collective representation of workers' interests, something the government is seeking to avoid. It is possible that the [Irano-Soviet] Cultural Association subsists on Communist funds. Intelligence in April 1944 suggested the growth of Communist tendencies among the office and workshop staff of the Iranian State Railways. It also suggested that Communist principles were proving increasingly attractive to educated Iranian white-collar workers. It is claimed that the Arabs, who have been disappointed in their Iraqi-Sunni policy and who are now in power, are looking ever more intently towards Russia in the hopes of achieving their 'new destiny'.

Some Communist literature published in Arabic is in circulation. The best example is *Red Army,* which also covers social conditions in Russia. It is well produced, with few typos, and is thought to be shipped in from Cairo, since it would be impossible to print something like this in Baghdad.

The Communist newspaper *El Qaeda* (The Foundation) circulates widely in northern Iran, especially among the Kurds, both clandestinely and openly. It is thought to be printed in Mosul.

SIS work on local cases is limited mainly to the XB aspects of XK; close liaison with 'Izmir' is maintained to this end.

For the reasons above, I was not able to get any specific suggestions for further progress in XK, but 82000 and 82900 promised to pay more attention to this subject and to send any suggestions they had under this heading to HO for review.

Following my talk with 82900, I attach a note I wrote on my return to Cairo for 89700.

d. Jerusalem—I rate Jerusalem as the most important station in the Middle East as regards XK. Comparatively speaking, and especially from a Soviet point of view, its geographical [position] gives it convenient communications with Cairo to the south, Lebanon and Syria to the north and, across its territory, Turkey; there are air links with Tehran via Baghdad. It is well placed for the centres of Jewish activity in Haifa and Tel Aviv, and Jerusalem itself has several Russian Orthodox churches, in which the Soviet Embassy in Cairo is taking a growing interest. The activities of the Arab Communists are concentrated in Jerusalem, and the recent visit there of Mr Sultanov was in all likelihood not without significance in this connection, since he is a scientist, speaks fluent Arabic and is a Muslim.

However, the XK situation in Palestine is complicated and needs careful study in order to make sense of it and draw the correct picture. The Palestine Communist Party is illegal, but the government does not interfere with it. There is known to be a direct tie between the V League and the Soviets, and it is claimed that in May Sultanov had contacts with representatives of the Arab Communists in the person of Abdullah Bandak and Radwan Hilou.

The Zionists are flirting with the Soviets and making every effort to gain recognition for their movement. The Arab Muslims are switching their attention to social improvements but probably still regard the USSR with suspicion, given the latter's attitude toward religion. The restoration of the Patriachate has done a lot to calm the Orthodox Christians, who are no longer quite as terrified that the church properties in Jerusalem might be put under Soviet control.

This might be a convenient point to try to summarize the XK position in relation to (a) the Jews and (b) the Arabs. (a) The Jewish position vis-à-vis Russia incorporates two separate points of view, that of the individual Jew and that of the Zionist Party as a whole. Although he himself may be an ideological supporter of Communism, the individual Jew always criticises the individual Jewish Communist on the grounds that the latter's position on Zionism is incorrect in relation to the Jewish-Arab question, the essence of which is that Zionism must control Palestine as a Jewish state. The Jewish Communist, on the other hand, reckons the Zionist point of view to be narrow and reactionary. (b) The official Zionist point of view, in a nutshell, is that Zionism must find allies wherever it can and, consequently, that the party must be prepared to flirt with whomever it wishes—Great Britain, America, the USSR, Poland, Czechoslovakia, etc. The Party has gone a long way with the USSR and is probably ready to go even further with the aim of obtaining Soviet recognition and support, but . . .

It will be clear, I believe, from the above incomplete review that the XK situation in Palestine merits serious attention. Our own station is dealing appropriately with the XB aspect of the problem in conjunction with the Palestine police and SIME. The fact that 88000 knows the region well is a big advantage, but, as he himself admits, he has next to no experience in XK work and depends heavily on material he receives from non-SIS sources for intelligence on the subject. Putting together a new SIS-led agent network will be difficult, especially if recruiting among Poles living in Jerusalem and elsewhere in Palestine is excluded.

88000 promised, however, to pay urgent attention to this issue and will forward his proposals to HO for consideration.

e. Lebanon and Syria—The XK situation in Lebanon has a number of interesting features, and I am grateful to 87000 for his very interesting analysis, which is summarized below:

1. The Syrian CP [Communist Party]
2. The Lebanese CP
3. The Eastern Churches and the Armenians
4. The French: Even in the early stages of the war, when the Communists in France were fiercely pursued, those in the Levant states enjoyed a surprising degree of immunity under the French Mandate. This benevolent attitude continues. As far as the Syrian Party is concerned, this may be explained by local political factors, since the Syrian Party is hostile to the National Bloc. This does not apply to Lebanon, however, because the Lebanese Party came out with a strong call for Lebanese independence during the events of November 1943 and has maintained that position ever since.

There is a reliable report that Nikola Shaul, a leading member of the Lebanese Party and the local TASS representative, communicates with the Soviet Embassy in Ankara via the French delegate's diplomatic bag. It should be noted that the French *délégué générale* recently told the Syrian and Lebanese governments that the Soviet government was examining the possibility of recognizing the independence of these two states and appointing diplomatic representatives. The two governments welcomed the idea but let it be known that they would prefer to conduct talks on the matter independently and not via the French. (It came to notice by chance that Mikhailov, a secretary at the Soviet Embassy in Ankara, recently visited Beirut without making contact with the French *délégué*, the local authorities or even the local Communist Parties; he concentrated exclusively on local residents who were Russian or former Russian nationals.)

Local French propaganda is trying to strengthen the ties between the USSR and the French National Committee. A recent editorial in *L'Orient*, a French-language paper that is 'inspired' by the French but not officially controlled by them, praises the local Communist Party and attacks the bourgeoisie in a way that not even the Communist mouthpiece *Saut al Sharq* has ever done. The editorial was almost certainly instigated by the French.

The next day the editorial was followed by another one praising the Soviet system in the USSR. *Saut al Sharq*, the Arabic-language mouthpiece of the Syrian and Lebanese Communist Parties, contains little that is specifically Communist. It is, generally speaking, a very good newspaper, as a result of which it has a high circulation by local standards. It is almost certainly subsidised, but from which source or sources has not yet been established. It may be partly supported by the local Communist Parties, but they do not have substantial funds at their disposal. They are not even able to buy themselves a seat in the elections either in Syria or in Lebanon and are thus unrepresented in either assembly.

At first sight it is quite difficult to reconcile the conciliatory French attitude towards Soviet pretensions in the Levant with the French desire to be the primary player there. The reasons may be either that the French Committee of National Liberation does not take Soviet ambitions in the Levant seriously and thus does not rate the Soviet Union as a potential rival or that it sees current Soviet support as something more important than any future considerations which might affect French prestige in the Levant. There is evidence that many local French officials do not share in the slightest the official French enthusiasm for the Soviet Union. However, even they probably prefer the possibility of Soviet influence to the reality of British influence, and the prospect of a serious counter-weight to British influence is so attractive to them that it blinds them to the reality of the situation.

6. THE COMMUNISTS AND ORGANISED LABOUR—Labour organisation in the Levant is rudimentary. It comprises:

a. Guilds, i.e. organisations of qualified and semi-qualified workers in a particular trade—e.g. printers, shoemakers, etc. Each trade is organised separately and there are only very loose ties between the various guilds. The guilds include both employers and workers, since most of the trades concerned are of an artisan nature, such that the employer works at his trade with the worker helping him.

b. Special committees set up from time to time in large businesses to present demands to management or petitions to the government or to organise strikes, etc.

A strong Communist influence has recently been perceptible in both the above types of organisation. This influence has, however, taken the form of 'inspiring' these organisations so as to make them more effective in defending their members' interests; it has been established that there has been nothing whatever in the way of political agitation.

c. In Lebanon the Communist Party has specifically stated to the government that it has no destructive plans and simply wishes to improve workers' living conditions. It appears that in Syria there is very definitely a hidden subversive current of Communist activity, but there are no signs of it in the craft guilds.

The structure of the Communist Parties in the Levant States is believed to be as follows: a three-man Central Committee is elected by the Party Congress, which meets periodically. The Central Committee elects a General Secretariat, which we understand consists of the following members: Khaled Bikdash; Farajalla Hilu; Nikola Shawa [sic], the local TASS correspondent; Artin Medoyan, reckoned to be the Party's 'brains'; Quadul Qudhoj and Tabit.

The Party's policy is implemented by an Executive Secretariat working under the direction of the Central Committee. According to the head of the Party in Aleppo, its membership among Muslims is increasing steadily, and they are delighted at Soviet political and military achievements, which have in large measure contributed to the growth of Communism in Syria. Communist pamphlets have been widely circulated. In this connection it is not without interest that Shawa receives press material and propaganda from the Soviet Embassy in Ankara through the French delegates' diplomatic bag. It was learned in February 1943 that the Party was receiving funds for propaganda from Soviet sources in Iran, and Bikdash has also stated that prior to the dissolution of the Comintern, there was a significant degree of co-operation between the Parties in the Levant and the Palestine Communist Party; this no longer exists.

I was very struck in Beirut by the interest shown in XK intelligence by 87000 and local staff, and as a result of the further interest which I believe was stimulated by my briefings, I hope that a still greater quantity of XK intelligence will be obtained and that proposals will come forward for expanding our penetration.

d. Turkey—in Istanbul I saw very little intelligence on XK activity in Turkey, and what there was, was of far too general a nature, serving to prove no more than that the Turkish Communist Party really does exist, that as a result of the repressive measures taken by the Turkish authorities there has been little or no overt Party activity, that the main centres of clandestine activity are Istanbul and Smyrna, and that there is no intelligence to prove the existence or a link, direct or indirect, with Moscow, although an indirect connection is believed to be maintained via Greece and the Balkans. The local Soviet Embassy is extremely careful in everything it does, and there is no evidence which might confirm that any of its officials are actively connected to the local CP.

On the other hand the SIS station has received evidence of the existence of a Soviet intelligence organisation operating in Turkey (see the report of 18770, no. XB473 of 24 March 1943). The main points in this report were discussed in detail with 22500 and his supervisor, both XB officers, but we were unable to add anything to it or to go any further in identifying the individuals mentioned in the original report, since it was no longer possible to contact the sources via the Turkish WB (see my cable QXQ/395, undated, from Constantinople).

I suggest that the insignificant amount of intelligence available at the SIS station can be explained, in the main, by the fact that its officers (especially the XB officers) are preoccupied with more important and urgent issues related to 12-Land [Germany] activity in Turkey and the Balkans. However, all the XB officers are keenly interested in the XK problem as a result of their briefings, and I hope that henceforward XK issues will receive greater attention, especially in Turkey itself.

22500 informed me that he had put forward proposals for closer high-level collaboration with the Soviets in the Balkan region and that he hopes that such collaboration, while admittedly presenting the Soviets with opportunities for penetrating our own organisation, will afford us the same opportunities to penetrate the NKVD organisation and give us a better insight into their structure and tradecraft.

On the advice of 22500, I discussed the XK question with 85900, and I attach his suggestion for operations in countries 18 and 91. They deserve close attention, although I am not convinced that his advice that our agents should claim to be working for Country 12 is totally correct.

I did not visit Izmir or Ankara. I had the opportunity to meet 41280, with whom I discussed in the most general terms the XK position in Greece. Although I have no doubts about 41280's overall honesty and his genuine support of the Allied cause, I cannot escape the impression that he is something of a propagandist for Greek interests in general and that his knowledge of XK activity within EAM [the Greek resistance organisation] is not based on first-hand intelligence or on first-class sources. But I may be completely wrong.

In my view, operations in the XK area carried out from Constantinople are the station's most important task in the future and even today, when Turkey has broken off diplomatic relations with Germany, a fact which in and of itself may serve to reduce the time spent by XV on tracking German activities in the country, despite the fact that in all probability Germany has prepared the ground effectively by creating a 'stay-behind' organisation.

The decisiveness of Russian policy in the Balkans is of major significance, and we cannot exclude the possibility that it is aimed at the creation of a Soviet-Balkan federation, based on the fact that the nationalist movements in the Balkans are so strong and that the Balkan peoples are so deeply imbued with nationalism in contrast to internationalism. Soviet Russia has had to deal with similar factors in earlier years with the Cossacks, the Turkmens, the Uzbeks, the Georgians and the Armenians, i.e. the peoples who are now content with their situation and who are moving forward in autonomous republics within the [Soviet] Union and with their own representatives in centres of power.

Russia already controls the most important sectors of the resistance movement in Yugoslavia; it also exerts a measure of control over the movement in Greece, and it is possible that the Bulgarian CP, which Moscow has always rated as the most effective Party outside the USSR, is the main driving force behind the anti-Fascist movement in Bulgaria.

Romania will be an easy victim of Soviet psychological warfare as soon as the time is ripe. Russia can always count on the inherent hostility of the Balkan peoples towards the Axis dictatorship and on the outstanding victories of its forces on the battlefield. Russian activity in the Balkans should be monitored from Constantinople and Bari.

23 Report on the Western Mediterranean Inspection, August 1944

It remains to review the position of XK work in the western Mediterranean stations.

Algiers—The transfer of AFHQ [Allied Forces Headquarters] to Italy, and with it Station 92000 and its XB organisation, will inevitably mean the end of XB work in North Africa unless 27400's organisation, which I gather is to remain in Algiers, can carry the extra load.

This would be a pity, since despite the small amount of XK intelligence received in Algiers, things were under way and might have developed further, especially as regards source 'Matters' from the Austrian Liberation Movement, together with the possible use of Algiers by Spanish Communists from South America to establish contact with the Party itself in Spain.

As I understand it, the XB aspect of Station 92700 is to be undertaken by the PCO, and I therefore discussed the XK issues with him in some detail. I have no doubt he will give them as much attention as he can. But the intelligence that he will be able to provide will be strictly limited both in nature and in volume. We cannot expect him to tackle the XP aspect of XK, which in this region might be of greater significance than the pure XB aspect.

Naples—As I understand it, Naples is the HQ of 92000, and I gather he will return there after first making contact with his officers in Rome. Since the station has only just been set up, it was difficult for me to get even an approximate idea of its opportunities for work on the XK line or about the directions in which such work might be developed. I did, however, provide briefings on XK issues to the XB officers who were present.

I also met Sir Noel Charles and explained to him the aim and intention of my Mediterranean trip. I explained to him that Mr Loxley was aware of it and the reasons behind it and that, as far as I was aware, the trip had the support and blessing of ZP. I went on to give Sir Noel a general picture of what I had been able to establish about XK activity in the Middle East and to outline some of the conclusions I had drawn. He showed interest and expressed the hope that we would be able to build an effective organisation for XK work in Italy, since it was of the utmost importance to him and he had almost no detailed intelligence. I took the opportunity to explain the instructions I had been given by the chief, and he completely understood the necessity of not acting precipitously, bearing in mind the extreme sensitivity of the task and the need to avoid diplomatic complications at all costs. He promised his support in all the efforts we might make to meet his special needs, and underlined that he would be dependent on SIS to a significant extent for the production of inside intelligence on XK matters.

Rome—I visited Rome with 92700 and had long and detailed talks with 32900, 32700/DV and 44902/Aa on the subject of XK activity in Italy.

32900, who works with 32700/A although he has not had SIS training, has a good understanding of the XK issue in Italy. This was achieved through his handling of 'MAC'. I did not meet this agent; 92700 and I decided it would not be prudent. As I understand it, he has a direct line to Togliatti and through him an indirect one to Tughatti, Reali and Seccia Maria, who make up the Communist triumvirate in southern Italy. It appears that Tedeschi is not as powerful a figure as he was, and has been transferred to the comparatively unimportant post of editor of the Communist paper *Unita*. He apparently no longer participates in the councils where Italian CP policy is decided and is thus not a source from whom we will be able to obtain current high-level inside information. In 92700's opinion, production of this sort of information will become even more difficult as a result of the reinforcement of Party discipline on which Togliatti recently insisted.

32900 is of the view that one of Togliatti's main tasks is to bring about Badoglio's return to power.

The Communist Party apparently does not reckon Bonomi to be an appropriate head of government. In 32900's view, the Party's policy is, in essence, to proceed carefully on all issues and to strengthen its position to an extent that will make it a force to be reckoned with, if not the ultimate leading force, in all future political events in Italy.

It was clear to me from what 32900 said that relations in the past with certain members of the Italian CP were really close and that our links with our own agents in northern Italy were in some cases placed at their disposal. Apparently (at least, insofar as I understand it), the military authorities in Italy began to object to the closeness of the relationships, and as a result, they were allowed to lapse. As 32900 put it, the Communists now look to OSS to give them the same assistance, which the latter provides gladly, doing in fact all they can to win the favour of Communist circles.

While I was in Bari, 32000 also mentioned the attitude of the Army High Commander in Italy on the question of mutual relations with the Communists and complained that Communists he had recruited in Tunis and brought over to Italy, as well as Communists put at his disposal by the Italian CP for work in northern Italy, were used exclusively to obtain military and operational intelligence and not to produce political intelligence that might be of value to SIS in penetrating Soviet national institutions and the Party. I refrain from further comment, since I know nothing of the background to this matter.

32900 has nothing beyond supposition as to the way in which the leadership of the Italian CP maintains contact with Moscow or the channels via which funds or subsidies reach the Party. He promised to bear these two topics in mind.

In my talk with 32700/V, I was struck by his keen interest in XK questions.

His background is well known to HO, and although he has not had SIS training, I feel that with it he could become one of the best officers in this field for the long term. It was for this reason that I supported 92700's suggestion to recall this officer and send him to the UK for training. I understand that this was turned down on the grounds that near-term CE [counter-espionage] work will continue to have priority over plans for the future. Although I understand this point of view, I would like to note that 32700/V is only one of twelve officers in SCI [Special Counter-Intelligence], and bearing in mind his interest in XK matters and his exceptional connections in the Vatican, I suggest that the decision is wrong, and I would like the matter to be reviewed.

I believe there may have been a small misunderstanding in connection with the suggestion that 32700/V be recalled and used henceforward exclusively for work on the XK line. There were two reasons for suggesting his recall: first, so that he could be trained, and second, to minimise the chances of his being 'outed' as an intelligence officer. Although it is certainly true that his present cover is not doubted by students in the various Vatican circles in which he moves, he nevertheless admits that older, more senior people and professors treat him with a certain reserve. He has no reason to believe that this reserve is entirely attributed to suspicions. He thinks the fact that he intended to enter the Jesuit Order, and later changed his mind also has something to do with it. Furthermore, there was never any intention that 32700/V should try at the present time to find sources in the Vatican that he would use specifically to obtain XK intelligence.

The thought was that in conversations and in other roundabout ways, he would try to establish the Vatican point of view on XK activities in Italy and the Balkans. The fact that Vatican circles are an excellent (albeit in some respects also prejudiced) 'sounding board' can hardly be seriously doubted, and as Soviet activity increases in Europe and the Balkans, the Vatican's desire to obtain the fullest possible intelligence on it will increase in proportion. Information on XK matters in Germany itself is already reaching Vatican circles. 32700/V was told as much by one of his Vatican contacts, although nothing was said as to what the reports contained. He acted correctly in not pressing to find this out.

There are several potential sources in the Vatican: Vatican diplomatic circles, which maintain normal diplomatic ties, supported by the State Secretariat, and an array of second-level 'lay officials', most of them Italian. These people may not be that well informed, and are probably zealots, but they are thought to be reliable enough for the production of good and fresh intelligence on the opinions and intentions of Vatican diplomats.

32700/V states that his chances of penetrating these two circles are slim, and in my view he should not even try. This is a matter for conventional diplomatic channels. The Vatican circles that he might be able to penetrate are those of the Catholic Church in Rome at the national and regional levels. He can maintain relationships with the students of the national colleges, with the Propagation of the Faith courses for students who do not have a national college, with the Eastern Institute run by Cardinal Tisser, which deals with all issues concerning the Eastern Rite churches, and with the Russicum, a special institute run by the Jesuits under the control of the Eastern Institute. But we would be especially interested in connections that might be established in the various Uniate communities of the Greek and Russian Orthodox churches in Rome, which include Armenians, Syrians, Georgians, Ruthenians, etc. But if he is to operate successfully, 32700/V must have far more training in XK work than I was able to give him in my briefings. This can be done only in the UK and, in the final analysis, would undoubtedly more than compensate for the loss which would result from withdrawing this officer from direct CE work.

While in Rome I also had a long talk with Mr Hopkinson, to whom I explained the purpose of my trip and the conclusions I had reached. He showed great interest in XK issues and stressed the need to pay particular attention to this subject in Italy. He agreed with my view that we should appoint an XK officer as soon as possible to the Western European Region, and expressed the hope that I would return in that capacity.

Bari—I went from Rome to Bari, where I had long talks with 92000, 32000 and the SCI officers 35600 and 32300. I briefed the latter on XK matters. The main focus of my talks with 92000 and 32000 was a detailed discussion of the conclusions I had reached and the general thrust of my report and advice. 32000 explained to me in detail his connections with certain members of the Italian CP, the reasons they had been recruited, the missions they had been given, and the way he had run them. Since up till now they have been used to obtain purely military and operational intelligence, I do not believe such connections have done us any harm at all.

I returned to the UK by air via Algiers and Casablanca and drew up this report the day I got back, 28 July. Before reviewing my conclusions and the proposals based on them I would like to express my gratitude for the help given me by all the stations in carrying out my tasks and to note the interest expressed by all XB and other officers whom I met in the general subject of XK.

Conclusion—The fact remains that only a few of the officers I met have anything more than the most general idea of the XK problem, whether in its historical context or in its present stages of development, or the factors that are most likely to have a bearing on its future complexion.

Of the two aspects of the problem, it is easier to tackle XB, and I have no doubt that all the officers whom I met are competent enough to carry out this work properly, the more so since there was very great interest in studying the structure and mechanism of the GRU and the NKVD and the illustrative case files that I had taken with me. I am confident, moreover, that the interest in this aspect of XK will not lessen and that valuable intelligence will be forthcoming on a regular basis on the activities of Russians and non-Russians attempting to penetrate our intelligence service.

I am less confident whether our officers (with certain exceptions) can cope with the XP aspect of XK; this is of even greater concern since, as I understand it, ZP now regards such intelligence as of primary importance. In the first place, many of those with whom I spoke had not had intelligence training in the UK. I accept that getting hold of agents is extremely difficult and that local recruitments in the areas run by 92000 and 89000 were unavoidable in the past and will have to continue in the future.

I also appreciate that for a whole range of reasons local training by on-the-job experience [is] the best we will be able to do. It is also equally clear to me that the production of military and other operational intelligence had to take first place as long as the Mediterranean was an active combat zone, and as a result, less emphasis was placed on XP, and XK was not regarded as a matter of great importance or urgency. But I venture to assert that the situation has now changed markedly and requires officers who can be assigned to XK work; to do so they need to be sent first to Head Office for training and, even more important, to enable a general assessment to be made of their ability to handle the work's generally accepted sensitivity.

There is one more important consideration. If XK work is to be a long-term project and if our plans are made accordingly, the officers selected for it will need to be drawn from those who intend to make SIS their career. This is the only way we will be able to achieve continuity in our efforts and, no less important, to my mind, a constantly developing picture of XK in all its aspects. In this context I have been greatly struck by the fragmentary nature of the available intelligence on XK cases and on the head-of-station inability to pull this intelligence together into an overall conception of XK activity either as a whole or even just in relation to the regions for which they are directly responsible.

There are many factors behind this state of affairs. Above all, there is the directive covering all matters of XK activity—to work slowly, to do nothing without prior agreement and direction—guidance that I was obliged to reinforce in my 'Line to Take'.

This has affected the work adversely, since officers have the impression that XK 'can wait'. The result has been fragmentary intelligence and sporadic efforts to bring various pieces into some sort of order, if only to be able to sketch the local picture.

Another factor is a lack of knowledge by our junior officers of the historical underpinnings of XK and of its ideology. For most of them, the function and activities of the old Comintern were a closed book. When the Comintern's role in Brazil and China was explained to them, it came as a revelation, and they were astonished to learn about the Communists' revolutionary programme. But I fail to see how, without this understanding, they will be able to cope with assignments like those arising from Para. 2(c) of my 'Lines to Take'.

It was part of my task to teach them the basic principles needed for this understanding, and although I hope I was successful, I would prefer the results of my trip to be evaluated by the overall interest in [the] XK problem that I was able to arouse in our officers.

But arousing interest is not enough. The main thing is to reinforce it, to develop it and to guide it along lines that are capable of achieving successful results, notwithstanding the difficulties and disappointments that are inevitable in working on XK. In London we need an unremitting effort on the part of all concerned to produce the intelligence required by XK officers, since definitive resolution of this problem is a task in which XK officers in London have an equally important part to play.

Proposals

With this in mind, an XK officer (ex 83900) has been appointed in the Middle East, and taking account of the comments I made at the end of the paragraph dealing with the XK problem in Cairo (Para. 5a), I suggest that this has been a successful appointment. I therefore recommend the appointment of a similar officer in the western Mediterranean with minimum delay.

I discussed this appointment with 92000, who agreed with me on the following job description. The XK officer should join 92000's staff and work under his supervision. He should be responsible for all XK work in the western Mediterranean and for collecting information on XK issues. He should also liaise with the representatives of ZP in Italy on these issues, given their direct interest in them.

There should be the closest possible links between the XK officers in these two areas, even including reciprocal visits as and when required, and both officers need to be in a position to travel freely within their areas.

There needs to be a direct link between the XK officers on 92000's staff and the XK officers at HO so that he can be fully aware of HO's views and the intelligence available on XK questions at the earliest stage of his inquiries. This will enable him to maintain a meaningful liaison with the ZP representatives in Italy and to direct officers working on XK.

The XK officers need as support one secretary-typist drawn from the Head Office pool. Since there will not be a great deal of wireless communication in the early stage of the work, separate ciphers and a staff of cipher clerks will not be needed.

92000 agrees in principle with the above and has authorised me to tell CSS (which I assume DD/SP will do) that if such a post is created and if I am selected for it, I am acceptable to 92000 and that CSS does not need to specially request 92000's agreement.

If I am appointed, 92000 suggests that I should be attached to him as a civilian officer.

Before concluding this report, there are two matters that I would like to emphasise: first, I consider it essential, given the long-term nature of inquiries into XK investigations, that the officers who are to deal with XK should be drawn from those who intend to be career SIS officers and that they should all have thorough training in all aspects of XK at Head Office, such training to include a detailed study of its aspects.

My trip has convinced me that the demarcation line between XK and XP is so blurred as to be virtually non-existent. So, second, I must insist that if circumstances permit, the XK officer at Head Office should make a trip round the Mediterranean to assess the situation himself, since what is happening there on the XK front cannot, in my view, be divorced from the overall XK problem that will manifest itself in Europe in an acute form after hostilities cease.

18 August 1944

22850

Appendix
21 June 1944

The following comments are based on a talk I had with 82900 when I visited his SIS Station.

1. I suggest that from an XB point of view and in connection with the XK problem as a whole, it would be worth looking into the individuals named below to establish their activity and their connection.

M. Korostovsev (see SIME report on Syria no. ECE/74 of 14 June). This man is, I gather, the TASS correspondent in Cairo. He is also an archaeologist and Egyptologist of some standing.

His connections with one Girshman may be of some interest. I was told that Girshman is not an Egyptologist of any distinction, as much as he pretends to the contrary. In 1940–41, Vichy sent him to Afghanistan to a 'dig' in the area near Kabul. Girshman's head office was in the French diplomatic mission. Considerable friction developed between him and the French ambassador, which led to him being expelled by the Afghan government. While in Kabul, he travelled to a small village in Persia called Sousa or Shousti, where, according to his wife, he made contact with the Russians. Madame Girshman claims that this encounter was entirely accidental, but 82900 does not believe this to be the case and told me that when she was telling him this, Madame Girshman was far from convincing. From Shousti, Girshman travelled to Cairo, where I understood he now lives. He is employed at the French Institute of Archaeology, a body which I do not believe it would be an exaggeration to say has always served as a cover for political activity. It is, of course, possible that this political activity consists of no more than pro-Vichy propaganda, but in view of his known contact with the Russians, it might be an indication that he is working as an NKVD agent.

The institute also employs, as a librarian, an Armenian named Arpog

Mikhitaryan, previously secretary to the director of the Egyptian Museum in Brussels. When Belgium was overrun, he managed to get out, though how and via what route we do not know. However, we do know for certain that by ideological conviction Mikhitaryan is a Communist supporter and that he constantly travels out of Cairo to other parts of the country and abroad; he has been unable to provide a sensible explanation for these trips. Nor do we know where he gets the money to pay for them. But since he is not a first-rate Egyptologist, he would hardly be given sums of that size to carry out research in the area.

We need to look into the connections between these three individuals and one Gerdseloff, a Russian Jew of independent means and a good Egyptologist. He currently works at the former German Institute at 21/13 Amiz (?) Street. He is politically unreliable and shows concern over his post-war future. He also travels a good deal around Egypt, and if he is not already working for the NKVD, he must be considered a potential candidate for recruitment for the reasons given above.

2. The foregoing is not enough to allow any precise conclusions to be drawn as to what these individuals may be up to. But it would be interesting from an XB viewpoint to establish whether any of them, and, if so, who, has contact with one Fairman, who I gather works at 17000. Fairman is, of course, an outstanding Egyptologist, and I assume that he has used Mikhitaryan and Gerdseloff without knowing their background. It is, however, possible that the individuals mentioned may attempt to penetrate our organisation via Fairman, who is, of course, known in Egyptian circles as a man engaged in work of a secret nature for the British authorities. I leave it, of course, to your judgment whether to tell 17000 all or some of this. I am unable to do so, but I am sure a friendly warning to Fairman on 17000's part would be appropriate.

24   The Structure of SIS

Cohen is DP.

Controllers	WR [Western Region]: Commander Patrick Whinney
	NR [Northern Region]: Harry Carr
	Eastern Mediterranean: Colonel John Teague
	Commander William H. Bremner
	Americas: Rex Miller
	Special: Ellis

Miller spent the entire war as head of station in Buenos Aires.
Head of Intelligence Department, John Morley; assistant, Annabel Leach.

P2 Europe (Italy, Spain, Portugal, North Africa, Switzerland). Head, Desmond Bristow.

P3, headed by Peter Bide; assistant, Phillip Wyatt.

P6 and 7: heads, Christopher Phillpotts and Wood (Scandinavia, Poland, Czechoslovakia, Finland and the Moscow station).

P8, headed by Malcolm Munthe.

P5 deals with the Balkans; Leonard Harris; assistant, Wilhemind Payne Sparrow. Reporting to the Controller, FE [Far East], is P9, led by Barff; the Controller, Americas, supervises P8, whose head is Reginald Hoare.

SIS has the following stations abroad:

1. The Hague, Brussels, Paris, Toulouse, Madrid, Barcelona, Gibraltar (where the HoS [head of station] also represents MI5), Lisbon, Tangiers, Casablanca, Rome, Milan, Trieste, Caserta, Bari, Zurich, Vienna, Klagenfurt, Bar Salzuflen, Hamburg, Hanover, Berlin and the Ruhr.
2. Stockholm, Oslo, Copenhagen, Helsinki, Prague, Moscow, Warsaw.
3. Budapest, Bucharest, Belgrade, Athens, Salonika, Florina (a sub-state of Salonika), Istanbul, Tehran, Abhaz, Baghdad, Beirut, Damascus, Jerusalem, Cairo, Tripoli. SIS plans to open a station in Addis Ababa shortly.
4. Singapore, Batavia, Honor, Hong Kong, Nanking. SIS plans also to open stations in Shanghai, Tientsin, Bangkok, Seoul and Tokyo.

Ellis (CPR) has Bedford working for him in London. He will also soon get an assistant from the Information Department, Charles Dennis Dundas, [and] two staff officers, Geoffrey Paulson and Rodney Dennys, junior to the controllers but senior to the leader sections heads of the Intelligence Department.

Requirements:
Headed by Wing Commander Easton; two symbols, DR and ACSS. DR means Head of Information Department.

Eight sections report to DP:
R1 (Political); R2 (Air); R3 (Naval); R4 (Military); R5 (Espionage and Sabotage); R6 (Economic); R7 (Science); and R8 (Co-ordination). Number of staff varies from 1 in R3 to about 20 in R5.
Head of Section R1: [illegible]; R2: Squadron Leader Hugo; R3: Commander George Birley; R4: Lieutenant C. Priest; R5: Harold A.R. Philby; R6: Rear Admiral Limpenny; R7: Commander [illegible] (temporary); R8: [illegible].

ACSS also has staff officers assisting him. These are: R1—George Pinney, Charles Dennis Dundas, Francis Head, Richard F. Comyns-Carr, Enthoven, Miskin. R4—Major Skinner. R5—Anthony K. Milne, F. Witty, A.M.M. Makins, Mrs H.M. Montgomery, Michael Morton, Robert O. Slocum, Charles Ransome, Peter Fairbairn, Geoffrey Hinton, Smith-Wright, Whitestone, Evans, Robert Carew-Hunt, Mrs Jane Archer, I. de Jong, Kenneth Worke, Robert Smith.

The officers in R2 and R4 are not officers of SIS but regular service officers seconded to SIS and paid by their respective ministries. They may be recalled from SIS at any time, although in practice it is assumed that they will serve there for about two years. The aim is to have within SIS a cadre of experienced people from the army and air force able to explain to SIS the requirements of their service and also to explain to their service SIS's difficulties, constraints and potential opportunities.

The only section not involved in intelligence procurement is R5. Government departments are usually responsible for procuring intelligence of relevance to them. For instance, the Service ministries collect military intelligence. There is thus no sense in R4's duplicating this work. However, there is no government department responsible for the procurement of intelligence on espionage and subversion, so this work is done by R5. As a result, Section R5 has a larger staff.

R8 is a new section whose functions have not yet been fully defined. They include, however, responsibility for collating all important intelligence from other sections coming in day to day and summarising it for SIS's senior directing staff. R8 is also responsible for collecting and co-ordinating all negative and positive evaluations of SIS's intelligence from its client ministries in order to maintain an up-to-the-minute picture of how they rate SIS's product. R8 is also responsible for prioritising ministries' requirements—e.g. R8 may be requested to determine the relative importance of a War Office requirement for intelligence on the movements of the Russian army in the Caucasus as against a Foreign Office requirement for political intelligence on China. Where R8 is unsure about relative priorities, it will ask the relevant R section for its view. Any disputes are referred to ACSS. R8 is also responsible for liaison between the Intelligence Directorate and the London Signals Intelligence Centre. It should be noted that certain R sections, particularly R5, have direct contacts with LSIC.

R7 is also a new section, which is in the early stages of formation. The old Science Section, headed by Dr R.V. Jones, will soon be transferred back to Air Ministry Control and will sever its ties with SIS.

In addition to the above-mentioned R sections, there is another small section reporting to ACSS, known as TUBE ALLOYS Liaison, headed by Lieutenant Commander Eric Welsh. Its job is to give advice, and to promote the production of intelligence, on the advances being made by the countries in the area of atomic energy. Welsh has offices in the Ministry of Supply Building in Shell-Mex House, and in SIS's Broadway HQ.

Administration Directorate

This is headed by Captain Frank Slocum DO/Admin.; he is responsible for SIS's administration policies, supervises the administrative machinery, and chairs the Selection Committee and also the Permanent Committee for Registry and Archives. He also manages organisational development, administrative inspection of overseas stations and runs the W Department, which handles the production of forged papers. His PA [personal assistant] is Miss M. Porter Hargreaves.

'A' is Commander B.A.P. Davis, who is deputy to DO/Admin. He is responsible for management training, as well as dealing with secret seaborne operations. He runs Section A (see below), is secretary to the new Selection Council and chairs the S Council for Selection of Technical Staff.

A1 is Captain H.P. Taylor, whose responsibility is the training of SIS's operational personnel, as well as liaison with universities, with the Ministry of Labour and other organisations from which candidates for recruitment to SIS might come; he also liaises with the Civil Service Selection Board and is in charge of compiling personal dossiers, for vetting, for medical examinations of new recruits and for running language proficiency exams.

A2, Major G.D. Hiles, is responsible for officers' entitlements, for granting sick and family emergency leave, retirements and dismissals, for formally establishing causes of [officers'] deaths, for issuing references and service records, pensions and emoluments, for organising training courses, for organising medical, dental and optical services, and for accommodating staff in London in case of need.

A3, Major L.D.J. Wallerstein, is responsible for officers' postings, filling vacant positions, questions of salary, documentation of officers' marriages, payment of travel expenses, naturalisation, and the granting of ex gratia payments and rewards.

A4, Commander Pearse; responsibilities include expense advances, messing allowances and expenses, living allowances, funds for equipment and clothing, including clothing coupons, compensation for loss of effects, and drawing up the Administration Directorate's annual budget.

A5, Captain F.A. Quinn, is responsible for recruiting of support staff, their training and enrolment, financial aid, transfers, regular and early retirement, processing of marriages, payment of pension and gratuities (the support staff include porters, guards, messengers, lift attendants, etc). The problems of the Passport Control staff—passports, statistical monitoring—are handled by Miss Middleton. Other matters handled include drawing up the organisational structure, financial issues, salary scales, head count, control of ID cards, maintenance of files on station and section personnel, compiling regular staff lists, and running the daily staff movements register.

A6 is run by Lieutenant Colonel F.W. Niall, who is responsible for developing post-war conditions of service, preparing background papers to be used for advice on recruitment, and maintaining the staff lists by rank, as well as acting as secretary of the A Advisory Selection Board (which deals with senior appointments). He is also a member of the C Advisory Selection Board. He has also a number of Head Office staff administrative functions and handles liaison with the controllers for advice on Germany and Austria.

Q1 and Q2 are technical sections.

Q3, Mr W. Holland; responsible for motor vehicle policy, maintenance of SIS vehicles, providing and training staff for vehicle maintenance overseas, running the motor pool and its staff.

Q4, Mr L.H. Thomson; document copying, printing and distribution sections. Photocopying. Section W, run by Miss K.J. Andersen, is responsible for preparing agents' papers, such as false passports, ID cards, etc. Mr T. Woodfield, as PRA, runs the Registry and Archives.

The Administrative Directorate is now under the joint directors for finance and administration. The director is Musson.

25   The Reorganisation of SIS

Information from STANLEY Dated 6 January 1947

The directorate of SIS has decided to implement a fundamental reorganisation. It will be put into effect in the near future. The basic organisational structure of SIS will be as follows:

The position of head of the Intelligence Directorate will be abolished and his functions transferred to VCSS [vice chief of SIS]. The latter will be responsible to CSS for SIS's intelligence and sabotage operations. 'Intelligence' means the procurement of intelligence information. 'Sabotage' refers to those elements of SOE's operations that will be allowed to continue.

Reporting to VCSS will be three chief controllers [CCs]:

1. Europe—Commander Kenneth Cohen
2. Mediterranean—Colonel John Teague
3. Pacific—Mr C.H. Ellis

The CC Europe will have under him three controllers:

1. Northern Region—Mr Henry L. Carr
2. Western Region—Commander Patrick Whinney
3. Eastern Region—Mr S.A.V. King

The Controller, Northern Region, will oversee the Scandinavian and Baltic countries, Poland and Czechoslovakia.

The Controller, Western Region, will handle Belgium, Holland, France, Italy, Spain, Portugal and French North Africa.

The Controller, Eastern Region, will supervise Germany, Austria and

Switzerland. (C's directive does not say so, but he must assume that it follows from this that Controller, Eastern Region, will also look after Yugoslavia, Hungary, Romania, Bulgaria and the Soviet Union.)

The Chief Controller, Mediterranean, does not have controllers reporting to him, but has a deputy. Lieutenant Colonel Richard Brooman-White has been appointed to this post.

Under the Chief Controller, Pacific Region, will be two controllers, Commander William H. Bremner for the Far East and Rex T. Miller for the Western Hemisphere. Reporting to the controllers will be the heads of the P sections, who are responsible for intelligence work and the operations of the stations. For the most part the heads of the P sections will remain unchanged. SIS's directorate has appointed a principal staff officer as assistant to VCSS in the conduct of intelligence and sabotage operations. He will be Robin Brook, who used to work in SOE and now has a senior post at the Bank of England. He is a close friend of [Hugh] Dalton, the Chancellor of the Exchequer. Though working in SIS, Brook will retain his Bank of England position.

The so-called Controller, Production Research, will also report to VCSS. The position is temporarily held by Ellis. The CPR is responsible for recruiting and working with agents in the UK. When such agents go abroad, they will not maintain contact with SIS's stations. They will be used solely as travelling agents and will be drawn from among businessmen, commercial travellers and others who have good reason to go abroad on business for a short period of time.

The special liaison controller, Commander Dunderdale, will also report to VCSS. His main job at the moment is to maintain contact with US intelligence.

To enable VCSS to manage the intelligence and sabotage operations efficiently, responsibility for other areas of SIS's work will be assumed by ACSS [assistant chief of SIS]. In addition to the Information Department, he will run the Training and Development and the War Planning Departments.

26   Telegrams from SIS's Moscow Station, July 1942

[In July 1942, Colonel Fedotov, then the head of the NKVD's Second Directorate, responsible for internal security, was supplied by Major Fitin of the First Directorate with copies of SIS telegrams sent to London, where they were copied by Philby, together with two cables from London addressed to George Berry, the head of station in Moscow. Quite apart from compromising individual sources, the content may have been of great assistance to Soviet cryptographers anxious to crack SIS codes.]

1. CXg 458 of 26 May 1942
   'Re Parker, I suggest a basic salary of £400 per annum, free of tax, plus £200 lump sum expense allowance.'
2. CXg 459 of 22 May 1942
   'Following is preliminary report of agent 95038/A on the situation in Vladivostok; he received the information from a casual informant. At the present time there are in the port of Vladivostok 22000 [illegible] minelayers and 4 smaller ones. 12 km from the city is a seaplane hangar. In February and March 1942 there were two air-raid defence exercises.'
3. CXg 460 of 23 May 1942
   Information received from agent 95038/A.
   The Fifth Fighter Wing based in Kisel 'has the following types of aircraft:
   1. IL-3 single-seater fighter (dive-bomber) with an M-87 engine. Speed 350 kph? Cockpit? Engine armour-plated. There are three reserve fuel tanks in the wing and fuselage, with a total capacity of 95 litres. Armaments: one Shkas machine-gun with 2000-round magazine and 8 motor-guided cannon that fire anti-tank shells or shrapnel (for attacking ground troops); the cannon can also serve as flamethrowers.
   2. The IL-3, a single-seater fighter (regular and training models). The construction data and weaponry are the same as for the IL-2, the only difference being that it has two, rather than just one, Shkas machine-guns.'
4. CXg 461 of 23 May 1942
   'The PE-2 is a twin-engined dive-bomber, with 2 M-87 engines. Speed 350 kph, armed with one Shkas machine-gun and one Shvak cannon.'
5. CXg 436 of 23 May 1942
   'Following is information from agent 95038/A. The M87 is a water-cooled V-14 aeroengine manufactured at Planks no. 18 and no. 53, which were evacuated from Moscow to Voronegh and Bezymyanka (near Kuibyshev).'
6. CXg 437 of 23 May 1942
   'Korrigal's total salary is £450 per annum O'LEARY gets £139.13.9 per annum, the equivalent of a sergeant's pay, plus 11 shillings a day food allowance and 3 shillings a day for personnel expenses. O'LEARY thus gets a total of around £400 per annum.'
7. CXg 468 of 27 May 1942 (continuation of CXg467)
   'Korrigal is thus at a disadvantage. I propose to pay him £100 per annum for personal expenses.'
8. CXg of 30 May 1942
   'When did you apply to the Soviet Embassy for Parker's visa? When we know the date we will try to chase it up locally.'
9. CXg 474 of 6 June 1942
   'Following from Korrigal. Regular radio communication timetable: 0730 GMT Moscow 1400 Miniform; Moscow 1500, Tehran (link will be maintained from 13 May 1942). The 0915 link via Istanbul was recently stopped because of unfavourable atmospheric conditions. In view of the embassy's wish for a direct link with Archangel, Korrigal suggests setting this up via the British radio station there, daily at 0830 GMT.'
10. CXg 475 of 9 June 1942
    'Following from Korrigal. Advise Archangel of the decision.'

11. CXg 476 of 9 June 1942
'Archangel's call signs are: Vad, Vuk, KFV. Commercial code will be used for communications. Suggests as test frequencies 15052, 14676, 14290 and 11026 khz.
'You will have to use similar frequencies. Begin test transmission with 3 minutes of call signs on the first frequency, then listen for receipt of K on the corresponding frequency. If contact is not established, transmit the call sign on next frequency in the order shown.'

12. CXg 477 of 9 June 1942
'The information given below relates to the beginning of May. It was received from agent 95038/A. Extensive preparations are being made in Pavlodar to receive wounded. Many wounded already arrived there. While before the war all official positions in the town were held by Russians, most have now been taken over by locals, the only exception being the NKVD apparatus. There is an acute shortage of food in the town. It was noted that residents of Yakutiya were now being called up. This is a new development.'

13. CXg 483 of 16 June 1942
'Berry agrees to do the work handled by Lapa while the latter is in Moscow with the ambassador, provided he can have the help of Brimelow, the newly arrived 3rd secretary.'

14. CXg 485 of 17 June 1942
'Information received from agent 95038/A. Young men of the 19–23 age-group were recently called up in Pavlodar.'

15. From London to Berry, CXg 340 of 19 May 1942
'Ask agent 95038/a to indicate the calibre of all guns he has the chance to see, especially anti-tank or anti-aircraft weapons.'

16. From London for Berry, CXg 345 of 23 May 1942
'The Far East Intelligence Centre in Calcutta proposes to recruit some Chinese Communists who used to live in Malaya. We consider it inappropriate to use our official links with the present Chinese Government for these purposes, since that might engender certain frictions. The Calcutta Intelligence Centre, not having diplomatic or other routes, suggests approaching these Chinese with the help of the Russians. We here are not able to talk to the Russians about this and consider that an approval with the help of the Indian Communists is the only way that has a chance of working. Consult the Ambassador and ask whether the SOE Mission in Moscow or Kuibyshev might be of use.'

17. CXg 465 of 26 May 1942
Following is the opinion of the British ambassador to the USSR regarding British intelligence cable CXg 345, sent to Kuibyshev. 23 May 1942:
'The ambassador suggests that the Russians links with the Chinese Communists are quite weak. But he sees no objections to contacting the Russians via the SOE representation in Moscow. Hill is prepared to help if required. The ambassador, Hill and I concluded that for the present the Indian Communists are the most convenient route. If the question goes further than just Communists, the ambassador will set up a meeting of the responsible representatives

with the head of the Chinese secret police, Daley, who is very well informed about Singapore.'

Head of the Directorate NKVD of USSR Senior State Security

27   SIS Plans for Anti-Soviet Operations, June 1944

[This internal memorandum, dated 6 June 1944, sets out SIS's plans for running future operations against the Soviets. Dated June 1944, it supports the hitherto controversial view that long before the war had been won in western Europe, SIS was contemplating anti-Soviet activities, a matter that has been debated by historians, among them Robert Cecil, himself a former SIS staff officer and assistant to the chief, who always denied that such mischievous issues had been raised so early.]

To: 22580
From: 35900

A Plan for Operations Against XK

1. Our main operators against XK must be contacted:
     a. in absolute secrecy as far as XK is concerned; and
     b. in such a way that no one from 12-Land [Germany] nor its allies have any grounds for suspecting any anti-XK activity on our part.
2. The operations have to be of a completely different nature from those we ran against XK before the war, for the following reasons:
     a. Given our present relations with XK, it is virtually impossible to penetrate XK territory.
     b. No other state must have the slightest suspicion that we are working against XK. This relates (in particular) to those countries where before the war our activity in this direction was not a secret.
     c. Given the sensitivity of this matter, it will no longer be possible to utilise émigrés, since they are influenced by the strong position and prestige of XK and they cannot be trusted.
     d. There is no possibility of suborning any overseas personnel of the GRU, the NKVD, the MOPR [International Labor Defense of the Communist International] or the GPU. Although many of their staff wavered before the war, recent events have made them firm supporters of XK.
3. The plan of campaign is divided into two parts, namely: A. Work in Country 18; B. Method of Penetration.
     A. [Work in Country 18]
          a. Through personal friendly ties with XK personnel: In appropriate circumstances this is perfectly feasible, but it will yield better results

if our man is an XK national and can gain their confidence. Since these XK personnel would be exploited unwittingly, contacts of this nature would not give rise to suspicion and would be excellent cover.

b. Through agents: It is possible to recruit such agents, but we would need to take the strictest possible precautions to avoid exposure and blackmail. For this reason our man will need to work through one or two cut-outs, and the agents should not be known to him personally. Moreover, we will need to pretend to the cut-outs that they are working against the people of Country 12.

c. Via 18XB organs: In this case the official link is not recommended in view of the risk of exposure, and we will again need a cut-out in a position to bribe the head of the 18XB Department working against XK. The best cover would be if the cut-out was himself an official of the country.

d. Through XK [trade] organisations: It would be easy to find a man among their staff who would agree to pass us information, since many of them are interested in personal gain and they are easily bribable. As soon as we establish such a connection—and we should note that the man we bribe does not need to have that high an IQ—we could introduce our agent into the local XK organisation. Penetration of higher levels would then be an easy thing to accomplish.

The following additional methods might be used:

a. Procure intelligence from Country 12 nationals: Country 12 has its representatives everywhere to collect intelligence on XK activity. This would not be too difficult, but we would need to craft excellent cover; otherwise, they will [simply] supply us with misleading material.

b. Use our allies who spy on K. They are informed about XK activity not only in Country 18 but also on XK territory, and given our excellent mutual relationships, it might be possible to obtain interesting material in friendly, albeit careful, conversations.

B. Operators in Country 91

We need to begin in Country 18 in order to shift later to Country 91. It will be easier to penetrate here after the present difficulties in communication (between Country 18 and Country 91) have been surmounted, since we must assume that XK reckons that we have grounds for being interested in their activities on this territory, in view of the fact that we are attempting to co-operate with like-minded countries in subversion, intelligence and organising resistance.

Methods of Penetration

a. Through agents we are already running or through new people sent in to link up with them.

b. Exploitation of intelligence procured by 18-XB, which is known to be interested in XK activity in Country 91.

c. Through members of 91-WP and WP/C in Country 18, some of whom are well informed about XK activity in their countries (see 18746).

d. The collection of intelligence on XK activity in Country 91 by all HoS [heads of stations] should be reviewed by all interested sections and be sent to Head Office after processing.

We cannot prejudge how successful any of these approaches might be. The best means of penetration will become clear only after all of them have been tried.

4. To eliminate any sort of suspicion, the head of the section working against XK must have excellent cover.

28   Blueprint for SIS's Post-War Organisation

[This plan was compiled by Patrick Denney, permanent secretary of SIS's Intelligence Planning Bureau.]

The Post-War Organisation of SIS

Foreword

The two main tasks of SIS after the war will be:

1. Deep penetration into the political, economic and military activity of all countries whose intentions represent or may represent a threat to the security of HMG.
2. The protection and maintenance of the security of SIS, such activity inside HMG by joint operations with the Security Service and the penetration of foreign secret organisations and subversive movements that might represent a danger to SIS.

This paper is intended mainly as a review of point 1. The tasks outlined in (2) can be defined later, when a decision is taken about co-operation between [Section] V of SIS and the Security Service.

The paper begins with Part A, 'Penetration'; Part B deals with personnel, and Part C, with the internal organisation of the directing staff. The last two parts presuppose that the conclusions drawn in Part A will be generally accepted.

The reader should bear in mind that this is only a rough sketch, to provide food for thought to those who have the responsibility for planning SIS's post-war organisation. Lengthy studies and a great deal of work will be required to develop a detailed plan for the entire organisation and for each section, such as V, the Economic Section, the Training Section, GC & CS, the Technical Research Section, etc. Papers on some of them already exist or are in the preparatory stage, but it makes no sense to include them in this document until the basic principles have been reviewed in the light of the BLAND Report.

Part A—Penetration

1. This has been drafted in the light of the new conditions created by the Second World War. It is assumed that the FO will be compelled to regard trade, finance and economics as the foundations of our diplomatic relations in the conduct of HMG's post-war foreign policy. The outline we propose is very flexible and can be altered to suit the circumstances of any particular country.

2. Prior to 1940, SIS's weak points were poor security in the PCO operation and the low quality of officers and agents involved in both Z and PCO work. We should also add our inadequate contacts with the Security Service.

3. To overcome these weaknesses it is proposed to use two categories of cover:

a. 'official', i.e. establishments in which salaried members of the FO might work full time; and

b. 'natural'—genuine financial and commercial firms, businessmen, merchants, commercial travellers, archaeologists, scientists, people from the world of education, etc., or SIS personnel who are ostensibly working for them or under their cover.

4. Official Cover: In those countries in which secret intelligence is of major importance, or where the organising 'natural cover' is unlikely to yield high-grade product, it may prove necessary to divide the 'official covers' into two parallel organisations.

PCO: Though this post is almost universally viewed with suspicion, its incumbent can still have an important role to play and in most countries [the post] serves as a cover for the work of Section V of SIS. It has additional value as 'the British SIS', declared to only a few selected individuals, such as, for example, the police and intelligence services of host countries. In this capacity it provides extra protection for other 'official covers' and for organising 'natural covers'.

Other 'official covers' need to be highly realistic and above suspicion. They should be selected to suit either particular local conditions or the people who are to operate under them. This means that in any country where active trade relationships with the British government create opportunities for the commercial secretary (or the trade attaché) to develop a broad range of contacts, this is the post we should use to cover our own organisation's work. The job will in fact be for the most part that of a commercial secretary. It is suggested that we use only genuine commercial secretaries for it after they have had an appropriate SIS training course. Equally, our head of station might be an SIS officer with a certain amount of training in commercial matters, posted as assistant secretary, commercial.

Likewise, under different circumstances we can use press attaché or second or third secretary posts, manned by SIS officers with the requisite training. In certain circumstances it may be possible to use British government overseas missions to cover for witting or unwitting agents; alternatively, a member of SIS might be included in the mission.

5. Natural Covers: This area offers unlimited opportunities, if properly exploited, with the additional advantage that it saves us money.

Major firms and banks have their own intelligence set-ups in most countries, which can be 'tapped at source'; in rare cases we can also get intelligence from them in London. 'Tapping at source' requires that we cultivate and recruit a manager or director of one of the firms working in the country concerned—in most cases, the individual with the need to be paid, provided he is totally confident that his security will be fully safeguarded, both in the country where he works and vis-à-vis his London superiors. Examples include banks, oil companies, travel agencies, shipping companies and, in some countries, community service organisations.

Another category would include archaeologists, scientists, the British Council, teachers and lecturers, and tourists.

[Those in] the first category probably have some sort of intelligence involvement already. The second represents fertile soil for recruiting agents.

6. Security

a. Official Covers: As noted above, the PCO organisation requires no security measures over and above those we have had in place for a number of years. Others need special security precautions. For instance, no one in the relevant country must know that X in job Y is an SIS officer apart from the Head of Mission—the ambassador or envoy—or the PCO (if the latter is a Section V officer).

b. Natural Covers: Special precautions need to be taken in regard to individuals operating in this capacity. It is essential that, as a rule, agents or officers working under 'natural covers' should not be known to any British officials whatever in the country in which they operate. Exceptions to this rule may be made in certain countries, but these must be limited to ambassadors, envoys, trade attachés and PCOs, but even then only with the written agreement of the 'natural cover' operator.

'Natural covers' in London are just as important. It will, therefore, be necessary to set up an international firm or finance company with which SIS representatives or agents can deal and to which they can send reports without giving rise to gossip or suspicion. Setting up an internal structure for this purpose does not present any insuperable problems.

7. Communications: These present no difficulties for representatives working under official covers. Nor should they be an issue for 'natural cover' representatives in countries where the trade attaché or assistant trade attaché is an SIS officer and knows the identity of the 'natural cover' representative. In other cases, however, where the 'natural cover' representative wishes to remain incognito or where there is no official SIS representative, the trade attaché needs to be briefed by the appropriate FO department about receiving cipher telegrams and

passing them on to the above-mentioned business address (see 6 (b), Para. 2) without asking questions. This should be done in such a way as not to arouse suspicion, even on the part of the trade attaché or, of course, anyone else; in fact, this sort of thing has been done quite often before, in normal diplomatic work, when important international financial or commercial agreements have been under negotiation.

Conclusions: It may be noted that this organisation plan is appropriate for many penetration permutations. All these can be brought into action in any country with operations conducted by a combination of both approaches or by any one of them on its own. If this draft is approved, a detailed plan, and the question of selecting and training appropriate personnel, will be reviewed in a special paper.

Part B—Personnel

We currently require of anyone that we engage that:

1. He must be well trained.
2. He must have some sort of identity of his own (be independent).
3. He must match his cover.
4. He must have some financial means of his own.
5. He must have total presence of mind.

Up to 1939 very few SIS people met these requirements, and we have to recognize that in fact not many of the SIS officers who have served during the war are suitable for post-war employment. In the immediate post-war period, or even during the time it takes to negotiate a full peace treaty, many of these officers will prove useful, but we have to face the fact that if we intend to turn SIS into a well-organised and effective mechanism, able to do its job on a significantly reduced budget over the next three–four years, we will need to have a root-and-branch review of the entire staff.

Even a cursory glance at Appendix 1, 'Internal Organisation', will show straightaway that an organisation with a Head Office structure comprising forty-eight officers can function only if it is nimble and efficient and allows senior and junior people to work closely together.

How are we to find the real intelligence officer, and, having found him, how do we keep him?

The answers lie in:

1. our selection procedures; and
2. conditions of service.

Part B—I: Selection of Members of SIS

1. Officers: Although it can be argued that SIS should be staffed by people selected from the widest possible range of backgrounds, we are also able to divide them into two main groups:

Group A—twenty–thirty-year-olds for training from scratch
Group B—thirty–forty-five-year-olds who have already had considerable experience and training in the political, technical or business worlds, which might be useful for SIS

SIS's main job in peacetime is politico-economic espionage and counter-intelligence. In both cases, both of the above officer groups can be used, though in different ways.

Take counter-intelligence work first. Given its close connections with the Security Service, the people chosen to be retained for this work will mainly be from Group B, either as PCOs or for work in the SIS Head Office structure.

Some of those selected in Group A can be used by giving them on-the-job training, as junior officers either in the PCO section or in Head Office.

Most new recruits for intelligence work will belong to Group A. They need to be the same type of individuals currently being recruited into the FO, i.e. people who can hold down a diplomatic post if and when the need arises.

The ideal recruiting method is through the usual FO channels, in the normal way. In the process, SIS representatives need to be allowed to review the files of all FO candidates and make note of any who seem suited to intelligence work. Nothing whatever must be said to these people about SIS work until they have served at least one year in the mainstream FO, but their progress will need to be carefully monitored. If at the end of the period the Selection Commission has not changed its mind and still considers someone to be suited for the duties of an SIS officer, it will be necessary for an approach to be made.

If the individual agrees, he will be transferred to SIS for a short induction course, including some time as a junior member of staff in the Head Office Intelligence Department. The process will generally take six–nine months. The next logical step would be to return the trainee to the FO for an overseas posting of one year as a junior (third) secretary, handling the day-to-day responsibilities of the job and steering well clear of the intelligence side, other than to keep his eyes and ears open. I would go so far as to suggest he should not make contact with SIS officers in the country to which he is posted, since the main aim of the one-year posting is rather to get him accustomed to the diplomatic routine and adapt to his surroundings.

At the end of this period he will already have spent three years in government service, and the confidential reports on him, together with his own written observations, will prove whether he will make a good SIS officer and, in light of his turn of mind, which section he would be best suited for. Then, after the individual has had further practical experience in London, the directorate would be in a position to decide the next phase of his career, which might involve intelligence or counter-intelligence work in Head Office or a posting abroad as a junior officer in a station or as support for a PCO in counter-intelligence.

Thereafter his career would evolve naturally, depending upon his abilities and personal qualities.

Part B—II: Conditions of Service

A great deal has already been written on this extremely important theme, and we can assume that the conditions of active service and post-retirement pensions will be examined with vigour. It is, therefore, inappropriate to offer any advice on the matter in this paper.

It should, however, be noted that:

1. Salaries should be graded and should not be less than those of the corresponding FO grades.
2. There need to be genuine opportunities for promotion, which must be based on merit; time in grade should be of secondary importance.
3. The one-month's-notice provision must be eliminated and sensible terms of employment introduced.
4. Pensions should be introduced, on a par with those of the FO.
5. We should not skimp on expenses.

If we do all this, there is a reasonable hope that SIS will be able to recruit people with the qualities needed for its work.

For people working under 'natural covers' and not part of SIS permanent staff:

1. Salary as such is not necessary. Those invited to undertake this sort of work are, in most cases, not in it for the money.
2. However, expenses specifically incurred on SIS work should be reimbursed very generously.
3. Upon recruitment, people working under 'natural cover' should sign a special secret contract setting out the need to observe security rules.
4. The category and level of development of people selected for work under 'natural cover', and also the quality of their work, will depend entirely on the abilities and personal qualities of the economic controller and his assistant. He can create a worldwide intelligence organisation of extremely high quality if he is determined enough, and for an insignificant cost in terms of public expenditure.

Part C—SIS Head Office

The Appendix contains a rough outline of the post-war structure of the SIS Head Office. It is intended to respond to SIS's post-war mission. This question has been the subject of the most thorough study in light of the position described in the attached paper. The structure has been developed in draft and may not match the conclusion reached by the Bland Committee.

The assumption is that one can create a highly qualified head office structure made up of a maximum of thirteen senior officers (grades 1 and 2) and thirty-six ordinary staff members (grades 3 and 4), subject to the latter being appropriately trained.

What follows should be read with the annexed outline in mind.

1. The position of deputy director of SIS should be abolished.
2. All matters relating to intelligence work, planning and administration should be incorporated into the remit of the Planning-Intelligence Department.
3. The distributing sections should be eliminated.
4. We should co-operate directly with the Security Service in the area of the Controller, Counter-Intelligence, in the work of the Counter-Intelligence Section and in the Subversive Movements Section.
5. We and the Security Service should set up a Central Joint Registry.
6. The Controller, Economic, should handle issues relating to the organisation and incorporation of 'natural covers'.
7. Abolishing the deputy director position is obviously the first essential step. We do not need to rehearse the arguments in its favour, since whatever limited value the position may have today will vanish completely with the cessation of hostilities.

There will be places for the deputy directors in the future structure, but the responsibility they may have had in the past will be transferred with advantage to the proposed new Planning-Intelligence Department.

In addition to the issues of planning and the management of intelligence work, the proposed new Planning-Intelligence Department will need to take on the administrative functions now handled by the Planning-Intelligence Bureau and the deputy director and also deal with financing and recruiting issues. If this department is properly set up, and if the scope of its activity is not seriously restricted, it will enable CSS to be freed from a large number of the minor day-to-day decisions that clog his workload.

Eliminating the distributing sections is a step that will allow those who produce the intelligence, i.e. the regional controllers and their operational staff, to interface directly with their regular client—the ministries—and will allow the latter to explain their requirements directly to those responsible for fieldwork. (See the attached explanatory note.) To a large extent, a decision on this depends on the attitude of the ministries, which would need to introduce immediately a number of distributing (information) sections of their own. The advantage of such a step, both for SIS and for the ministries, are clear.

4. Direct and close co-operation with the Security Service is an issue of substance even today. Its significance will increase enormously in line with the growth in a whole range of subversive activities that will characterise post-war Europe for the next ten years. We will need to take steps to ensure that this co-operation is maximised, both at the level of the Controller, Counter-Intelligence, and in the work of the Counter-Intelligence Section and the Subversive Movements Section.

5. The issue of the Registry is inextricably bound up with all of this. It is quite obvious that by setting up a joint, highly professional Central Registry that combines the file records of SIS and the Security Service, we would create a common basis for these organisations and thus strengthen every aspect of co-

operation. It would also eliminate a huge amount of duplication in our work and would have the additional benefit of saving money.

6. Security is a vital factor in organising 'natural cover' and requires the creation of an independent 'cover' section in SIS London. This should be under the management of the Controller, Economic Issues, or his chief assistant. All contacts with SIS collaborators and agents working under 'natural cover' should be handled exclusively by this section. Neither the regional controllers nor any SIS officers will be permitted to have any communication with anyone working in the 'natural covers' section. This will need to be completely compartmentalised, receiving its directives or presenting its reports to the Controller, Economics, or his deputy, either directly or via special lines of communication.

This paper does not examine items relating to the work of younger members of staff doing on-the-job training or the requirements for secretarial staff. These will be reviewed later as the detailed organisation plan is worked out. Nor does this paper examine issues relating to the organisation of overseas stations or the number of officers required either for 'natural' or for 'official' cover operations, since the Planning-Intelligence Department will need to work out a specific plan for each country to match the requirements of the client ministries for intelligence.

29   *Symbols of SIS's Senior Personnel*

CSS Director	Brigadier General Menzies
VCSS Vice Director SIS	Colonel Dansey
DD/Navy	Arnold Foster
DD/Army	Brigadier General Beddington
DD/Air	Wing Commander Payne
DD/SP Security	Colonel Valentine Vivian
DD/Admin.	Wing Commander Peak
SLC Controller Special Communications	Lieutenant Commander Dunderdale
CSC [Controller] Secret Communications	Brigadier General Richard Gambier-Parry
CNA Northern [Controller, Northern Area]	Colonel John Cordeaux
CWE [Controller] Western Europe	Kenneth Cohen
Section I Political Intelligence	Major Woollcombe
Section II Air Intelligence	Squadron Leader Winterbotham
Section IIB Air Ministry Liaison	Squadron Leader Sofiano
Section III Naval Intelligence	Captain Russell
Section IV Military Intelligence	Colonel Hatton Hall
Section V Overseas Counter-Intelligence	Lieutenant Colonel Cowgill

Section VI Economic Intelligence	Rear Admiral Limpenny
B SIS representation in Censorship	David Boyle
	Responsible for safekeeping and distribution of documents extracted from diplomatic bags and censorship of personal correspondence of SIS officers sent by diplomatic bag.
CSO(T) [Controller] i/c Agent Training	Major Peters
O Seaborne Infiltration of agents	Captain Slocum
P.14 Head of agent training in codes and ciphers	Campbell
PA/CSS	Robin Cecil
PSO/CSS	Pers. Sec. Lieutenant Colonel Koch de Gouyrand
CFE	Gibbs
C/Med.	General Marshall-Cornwall

30   *SIS's Internal Structure, March 1946*

Information from STANLEY by Letter no. 1 of 8 March 1946.

The Structure of SIS Following Its Reorganisation

The reorganisation of SIS is now advanced sufficiently to enable some light to be shed on its structure. The changes that have been made may not be final. Much will depend on SIS's budget, of which more will be known in April. It is presumed that it will be significantly cut back.

Brigadier Menzies remains the director (CSS). There are rumours that he will be replaced but so far no confirmation.

Major General Sinclair has been appointed deputy director (VCSS); he was formerly DMI [director of military intelligence] at the War Office. He deputises and assists in all aspects of SIS's work—namely, the procurement of intelligence, its evaluation and distribution, administration, finance, communications, and so on. In theory, CSS determines policy, and VCSS sees to its implementation. In fact, Sinclair is proving very active. He also plays a significant role in directing SIS's work. VCSS has five directorates reporting to him, headed respectively by the director of intelligence, the director of information, the director of finance and administration, and the director of training and development. These directorates cover almost all of SIS's activities.

There are a few exceptions, which will be noted below.

Intelligence Directorate

The director is Commander Kenneth Cohen, whose symbol is DP and whose deputies are all the controllers. Lieutenant Colonel Geoffrey E.M. Paulson and Colonel Rodney O. Dennys serve as his assistants.

Paulson assists him in the execution of intelligence operations—e.g. procurement of political, military and scientific intelligence. Dennys assists on the counter-intelligence side—e.g. operations against foreign services and political movements categorised as subversive.

The director of intelligence is responsible for the organisation and management of all SIS's stations. As his title indicates, he is also responsible for the procurement of intelligence by secret means.

All the stations engaged in counter-intelligence are also being transferred into the Intelligence Directorate, and from this point on, SIS's overseas stations will combine intelligence and counter-intelligence functions.

The DP has five controllers reporting to him, namely:

CWE [Controller, Western Europe]—Commander Patrick Whinney
Controller, Eastern Med.—Colonel John Teague
Controller, Northern Area—Mr Harry Carr
Controller, Far East and America—Mr Dick Ellis
Controller, Production Research—also Dick Ellis

(Ellis recently reached retirement age. It is not known whether or not he will actually retire. His future is undetermined. He may be persuaded to stay. If so, he will probably give up the CFEA job and retain only the CPR responsibility.)

The controllers head intelligence sections, each of which has a defined area of responsibility.

Under CWE are:

P1—Holland, Belgium, France, Luxembourg; head, Mr Morley.
P2—Italy, Switzerland, West Africa, Iberian Peninsula; head, Major Desmond A. Bristow.
P3—Germany and Austria; head, Lieutenant Commander MacKenzie.

The CEM runs the following section:

P4—Middle East; head, Captain Folkes
P5—Balkans, including Hungary; head, Mr Leonard Harris.

The sections reporting to CNE are:

P6—USSR, Poland, Czechoslovakia; head not yet appointed.
P7—Scandinavia and Finland; head, Mr Christopher Phillpotts.

The CFE A runs:

P8—North and South America; head, Mr Reginald Hoare.
P9—Far East; head not yet appointed.

The controller of production research runs P10. This does not have responsibility for a specific territory but handles the recruiting of agents in the UK for use in operations overseas.

As a general rule, intelligence sections run the stations. The controllers deal with fundamental issues of policy, organisation, personnel, etc.

Intelligence Directorate

This is headed by Wing Commander Easton, director of intelligence, who came to SIS from the Air Ministry. His deputies are Footman and Philby. His assistant is Lieutenant Colonel I.I. Milne.

Easton is responsible for ensuring that SIS is aware of the intelligence requirements of the various government departments, that the intelligence sections are fully informed of these requirements, and that incoming intelligence is properly evaluated and passed on rapidly to interested government departments. The Intelligence Directorate has replaced the old circulatory sections.

Easton is also the assistant to CSS (VCSS). He is thus third in the SIS hierarchy. He has under him eight sections, each responsible for handling a specific type of intelligence. They are:

R1—Political Intelligence; head, Mr David Footman.
R2—Air Intelligence; head not yet appointed.
R3—Naval Intelligence; head, Commander Geoffrey Birley.
R4—Military Intelligence; head, Colonel Priest.
R5—Counter-Intelligence; head, H.A.R. Philby.
R6—Economic Intelligence; head, Admiral Limpenny (temporary).
R7—Scientific Intelligence; head not yet appointed.
R8—Co-ordination Section; head, Squadron Leader John Perkins.

The Co-ordination Section is the only new department of the Intelligence Directorate. There was no equivalent in the old 'SIS'. Its job is to co-ordinate the requirements for intelligence with the agent opportunities for procuring it. Thus it has the very important task of comparing the value of intelligence procured with the price of procuring it, a comparison that it is required to make across every region and on every issue.

The intelligence sections are still at a formative stage. Some of them are expanding. Most, because of the need to cut back on costs, are being reduced. It is assumed that by year end, the largest section will be R5, which will have a staff of fifteen, and the smallest, R3, which will employ only one person.

Special Communications Directorate

This is headed by Brigadier Gambier-Parry as DSC. He will have a deputy, probably Colonel Maltby. It will have two sub-directorates, namely:

1. Consisting of:

SC1—RT [Radio Telefony] Communications
SC2—Graphic Communications
SC3—Communications via travelling agents
SC4—Codes
SC5—Special Operations Communications

2. Headed by the controller of communications development and consisting of:

SC6—Development
SC 7—Equipment Procurement
SC8—Production

This directorate is in effect the former Section VIII. It will be responsible for all forms of SIS communications (RT, secret writing, couriers, mail, etc.) and for running a sub-section specialising in the development and adaptation for SIS's needs of new inventions in the realm of communications.

Finance and Administration Directorate

This is headed by Mr Musson. He has just taken up his job. He was in the RFC [Royal Flying Corps] during the First World War and has previously been a Treasury official.

As of February, Musson had two deputies: one, Percy S. Sykes (DD/F), for finance, and the other, Captain Frank Slocum, RN (DD/A), for admin. matters.

Sykes and Slocum have been in SIS for a long time and have under them their own teams dealing with accounting, hiring, maintenance and similar matters.

As per a CSS directive, with effect from 1 March 1946, Commander Percy S. Sykes will give up the job of deputy director of the Finance Directorate and will from that date act as advisor on financial policy (AFP) to CSS. In this role Sykes will carry out at CSS's directions certain financial functions for which CSS is directly responsible. The post of DD/F will thereupon cease to exist.

The Finance Directorate is being transferred under the direct control of D/F & A. The various appointments and allocations of responsibility among the directorate's sections will come into effect from 1 March 1946. D/F & A will designate the chief accountant of Passport Control.

The Finance Directorate has three sections:

F1—Chief Inspector's Section, headed by C.C. Govett. Its functions cover (a) auditing all SIS's expenditures at home and abroad; (b) checking financial accounts and expenditures; (c) monitoring the reporting system and keeping an eye on all financial matters.
FIA is run by Todde, who is responsible for auditing UK expenditures and the general ledger.
FIB, run by Commander R. Pearse and Mr Brown Hovelt, audits overseas expenses.

FIC, under McGillivray, deals with SIS staff income-tax issues.

F2, the Chief Accountants Section, is run by Lieutenant Commander R.K. Waters and is responsible for (a) payroll; (b) SIS's Sterling and forex [foreign exchange] operations; (c) the Bought Ledger, including purchases, rent, etc.; (d) remittances to SIS's heads of stations.

F2A, run by Bridges, maintains the UK payroll, and F2B, under Hebble, runs the overseas payroll.

F2C, under Captain Thomas, handles the payroll for those SIS staff who are members of the armed forces.

F2D, run by Tegart, deals with salary scales and payments.

F3, the Chief Accountants Section [*sic*, but see above for F2], is headed by Emett.

The section is responsible for:

a. Authorizing purchase and sale of surplus equipment
b. The Bought Ledger
c. Stock control and inventory management
d. All aspects of insurance, other than health and unemployment

All financial matters of significance that need the Finance Directorate's authorisation are passed directly to D / F & A for approval.

All other papers are sent to the relevant FD section and pass via the usual channels to the directorate in Room 423, from which they go to the appropriate officer for execution.

Training and Development Directorate

The DTD is Colonel John William Munn, a former SOE officer. In 1941–42 he ran SOE's special training schools, which were concentrated in Beaulieu, Hampshire. From 1943 he looked after SOE's technical equipment area. Munn's directorate is in a very embryonic state.

General Comments

1. A small group from SOE is presently being merged into SIS. It was initially intended to create a sixth directorate for special operations, but this has now been rejected. Instead, the SOE sub-sections are to be divided up between the existing directorates. It is not clear what these SOE officers are intended to do, but their main job would seem to be:

evaluation of intelligence relating to the development overseas of subversive techniques;
ensuring that British techniques are kept on a par with those of its competitors;
collecting of intelligence about friendly overseas countries which can be used for subversive purposes in case of war (they are not allowed to have contacts with foreigners in this category in normal peacetime conditions);
to continue the propaganda work in which they have been engaged up till now in the Middle East and only in the Middle East.

2. Colonel Vivian has now been appointed ASP (advisor on security policy). His main job is to give advice on security matters to any officers in need of it. He is also to be consulted on all matters relating to SIS's collaboration with that. In addition, he runs the investigation of past cases of enemy penetration of SIS. He has reporting to him two former officers of the section, Major Mills and Captain Blake-Budden.

3. The Intelligence, Information, Finance and Administration Directorates and ASR are at Broadway. Located at 14 Ryder Street are the Training and Development Directorate, the SOE group (temporarily) and what is left of Section Y, which will cease to exist at the end of March. Some Section Y personnel will transfer to R5; others will go to various other directorates. The Special Communications Directorate remains at Whaddon Hall, which is near Bletchley.

4. The grading system for SIS officers has been completely changed. There are now five levels: directors, deputy directors, senior officers, officers and junior officers. There are five directors—Cohen, Easton, Musson, Gambier-Parry and Munn—and nine deputy directors, Harry Carr, Patrick Whinney, John Teague, Dick Ellis, David Footman, Kim Philby, Eric Maltby, Percy Sykes and Frank Slocum. These various categories are further sub-divided so that an officer can get an increase in salary without the need to be promoted. For example, on joining SIS a junior officer will get £600 pay, whereas after four years' service and while still a junior officer, he will earn £750.

5. It is hoped to introduce a pension scheme comparable to that of the Civil Service. However (taken together with the new pay scales for permanent staff), it is clearly a complex problem, since nothing specific has yet emerged, although CSS and his assistants have been working at it for many months.

6. At the present time, SIS is still going through its reorganisation process, and there may thus be further charges to come, but the basic structure will remain as outlined above.

GCHQ continues as before to report to CSS, although it is an independent establishment. It is, however, proposed to make certain changes in GCHQ's functions in the time ahead.

PART III

John Cairncross's Documents

John Cairncross was one of the most intelligent men of his generation; his cerebral prowess was demonstrated when he gained the top marks in both the Home and Foreign Office Civil Service examinations in 1936, a unique accomplishment. He was also a Marxist and supplied secrets to his Soviet contact from almost the moment he entered the Foreign Office. Always a difficult colleague, socially insecure and notoriously awkward to deal with, he moved to the Cabinet Office to serve as Lord Hankey's private secretary and later in the war was called up for the army, only to be posted to the Government Code and Cypher School at Bletchley Park. Here he was of enormous assistance to the NKVD, removing thousands of ULTRA intercepts from the closely guarded compound to deliver them to Anatolii Gorsky at clandestine meetings held in London pubs.

Cairncross found working at Bletchley Park to be a strain and arranged a transfer to Section V of the SIS, the counter-intelligence branch, then based in St Albans. He commuted by train from his flat in London and became acquainted with Kim Philby, although it was many years before he learned that they were both serving the same master in Moscow.

Initially code-named MOLIERE and then LISZT, Cairncross was undoubtedly the source of the copy of Lord Hankey's report on MI5 and the SIS, which was written by the minister without portfolio at Prime Minister Neville Chamberlain's request to establish whether the agencies were ready to cope with spies, saboteurs, Fifth Columnists and the challenge of fighting the enemy on the Continent. Prepared in conditions of great secrecy in March 1940 and retained to this day by the current Cabinet secretary, this remarkable document remains classified and has never been released to the Public Record Office.

Soon after Cairncross joined SIS, his NKVD code name was changed to EDWARD, as can be seen from one of the messages he sent in November 1944. What make the content so remarkable are the frequent references to Philby, who had been appointed to head Section IX, the anti-Soviet branch, which Cairncross evidently believed would be of great interest to the NKVD, never suspecting that Philby, too, was holding regular meetings with Soviet contacts.

31   *Lord Hankey's Inquiry into SIS and MI5, 1940*

Copy to Mr Gladwyn Jebb
11 March 1940
TOP SECRET

I have today sent to the prime minister my first report on the Secret Service with copies to the foreign secretary and the Service ministers.

I am also sending a copy to Gladwyn Jebb for the files. I look to him to ensure that in due course all those concerned will be advised of its conclusions.

I hope that you will find it possible to put into effect my recommendation for monthly meetings under your chairmanship. I attach some importance to these meetings as an integral element of the Secret Service.

I regret that I cannot include a copy of my report, since my copying and re-printing capability is very limited, and I have only my working draft left. But you will be able to get the foreign secretary's copy or arrange to have it duplicated—whichever is most convenient.

I would like to take the opportunity to thank Gladwyn Jebb, who I would like to think will co-operate with me on the second part of my inquiry concerning the work of MI5 (internal security).

Signed: Hankey

To Sir Alexander Cadogan
Copies sent to: The Foreign Secretary
                The First Lord of the Admiralty
                The War Minister
                The Air Minister
                Mr Gladwyn Jebb (without report)

11 March 1940
TOP SECRET

I include herewith a copy of my first report on the Secret Service (intelligence), which describes the various organisations under the command of Colonel Menzies.

The report took longer than I had expected, because the organisation has grown significantly since I last had any dealings with it.

In reading my report you will note that even while my inquiries were under way, significant steps were taken to strengthen the Secret Service. I make below certain additional recommendations. I believe that Sir Alexander Cadogan's private secretary, Mr Gladwyn Jebb, who was of great assistance to me during my inquiries, will be able to bring these recommendations to the attention of all those concerned.

There are a few areas of Secret Service work, among them cryptography, on which I was unable to include any details or even to express my views on paper. But in none of these areas was my opinion in any way negative.

I have now begun the second part of my inquiry—i.e. a study of internal security (MI5)—and will deliver my report in due course.

Signed: Hankey

To the Prime Minister The Rt Hon. Neville Chamberlain
Similar letters were sent to: The First Lord of the Admiralty
The Minister of Aviation
The Minister of War
Mr Gladwyn Jebb

11 March 1940
TOP SECRET

Attached please find a copy of my letter to the Prime Minister on my report about the Secret Service, a copy of which I enclose.

Signed: Hankey

To the Foreign Secretary, Viscount Halifax
TOP SECRET

The Secret Services Inquiry Conducted by the Minister Without Portfolio
First Report

1. Preface
2. Secret (Foreign) Intelligence Services
3. Secret Service
4. Dissemination of Information
5. Radio Communications (Section VIII)
6. Activity in Enemy Countries

7. Activity in Neutral Countries
8. Finances
9. The Spirit of the Secret Service

The Secret Services Inquiry Conducted by
the Minister Without Portfolio
First Report

1. Preface

1. In December 1939, the prime minister, the foreign secretary and the three Service ministers asked me to carry out an inquiry into the activity of the secret intelligence services. I was greatly helped by Mr H. Brittain of the Treasury and by Mr Gladwyn Jebb of the Foreign Office. The latter also acted as secretary to the inquiry. I also benefited from the close co-operation of Colonel S.G. Menzies, DSO, MC, recently appointed chief of the Secret Service, and also with the directors of intelligence of the Admiralty, the War Office and the Air Ministry, with the director of economic warfare intelligence, and with Sir Campbell Stuart.
2. My starting assumption was that given that we were at war, the most useful way to proceed was that where all those concerned agreed that some particular change was needed, such changes would be put into effect immediately, without waiting for the conclusion of this report. It will therefore be noted that the report cites several reorganisation measures that have already been implemented and thus does not contain much in the way of proposals.
3. The Secret Services were created in 1909 following a review by a sub-committee of the Committee of Imperial Defence. The proposal was signed by:

Lord Haldane (chairman)
Mr Mackenna
Mr H.I. Gladstone
Mr Sidney Buxton
Lord Esher
Lord Hardinge of Penhurst
Sir George Murray
Sir Edward Henry
Admiral Battle
Generals Ewart and A.I. Murray

Their proposal: 'To create a secret service office to conduct espionage and to act as a screen between foreign spies and government officials.'
4. It was soon realised, however, that this work breaks down into two main areas—namely, foreign intelligence and internal security (MI5).

These are still the basic areas of secret intelligence. Not only has activity increased sharply within these areas, but with experience and scientific progress, and also as a result of wartime experience and technical development, clusters of other secret and semi-secret services have gradually built up around them. They deal with cryptography; radio interception; radio direction finding; and the detection of illegal radio stations, radio beacons and other possible means of leaking secret information—for example, with the help of infra-red rays—and also with cable interceptions, with the maintenance of foreign radio services and with subversion and propaganda in enemy countries.

This inquiry would be incomplete if it did not describe the relations between the two initial secret intelligence organisations and these junior organisations from the intelligence point of view as well as from that of technical co-operation.

5. Our initial concern was with work in the area of foreign intelligence. After only a few weeks I realised that the scope of this inquiry had to be expanded. This is why this first report is concerned with the foreign intelligence service in relation to its internal organisation as well as its external relations. The inquiry was helped by the fact that Colonel Menzies had only just been appointed to the late Admiral Sir Hugh Sinclair's post as chief of the Secret Service and that he himself was in the process of reorganising work in connection with the conditions of the current war.

2. Secret (Foreign) Intelligence Services

6. The secret foreign intelligence services consist of two basic organisations, namely: cryptography and work on interceptions; the Secret Service.

The first type of work (Government Code and Cypher School, subsequently GC & CS), however, is funded not out of the intelligence budget per se but on the Foreign Office vote. On a strict interpretation of our remit, we could have left GC & CS out of the scope of this report. But since it is one of the main sources of secret information, this would have made no sense. It was known that due to the successful and patient work of a very capable staff GC & CS became one of our most reliable sources of wartime intelligence.

7. The close link between these two branches of foreign intelligence is further emphasised by the fact that even though they are separate organisations, they work under Colonel Menzies, who is also responsible for co-operation between them as well as for liaison with the Foreign Office and the intelligence services of the Service ministries, the Ministry of Economic Warfare and other government departments.

8. The GC & GS obtains its deciphering product from British telegraph companies and intercepted radio dispatches. The expense of maintaining its two stations of the GC & GS and for building a third are carried on the Foreign Office vote. At the beginning of my inquiry I visited the 'war station' of the GC & GS. Because of the extreme confidentiality of this area of secret intelligence, it is not

appropriate for me to commit anything about the current work of this organisation to paper or even to express an opinion about its current state, although I am prepared to give verbal explanations during a secret off-the-record meeting. Suffice it to say that I do not propose any changes except in relation to intercepts as mentioned in Paragraph 44.

9. I recommend that all individuals who are aware of the existence of this report take the greatest care to refer to it only in places where they can be absolutely sure that confidentiality will be preserved. It is not to be mentioned in Cabinet minutes or any other circulated documents.

3. Secret Service

10. The Secret Service works under the direction of the Foreign Office. Officially, it is funded by the Treasury. Although Parliament votes on these credits, the use of these funds is not subject to the normal parliamentary oversight. The chief of the Secret Service (CSS) works under the immediate direction of the permanent under-secretary of the Foreign Office, to whom he is accountable for the expenses of the various services that report to him. CSS is responsible for drawing up a budget for all normal and foreseeable expenses. Wartime experience has shown that there may be cases where the Secret Service is asked to plan and implement large-scale measures, which may require funds over and above the budget.

11. When such unbudgeted operations were such a scale that the Foreign Office and the Treasury wished to seek ministerial guidance, which a busy minister like the foreign secretary was unable to provide, I was asked to look into the matter and make a ministerial decision in consultation with the other ministers and ministries.

12. It seems to me that a similar procedure could be used in the future, although in some cases it may be better to put a specific question before a minister other than the minister without portfolio. In any case, the minister who handles the matter must do so in close co-operation with the Foreign Office and preferably through the foreign secretary's Private Office.

13. At present, the majority of the Secret Service's activities are conducted at the war station outside London, not far from the GC & GS and also not far from the Political Warfare.

14. The following are the basic areas of Secret Service activity: Collection of information on other countries, partly in London, partly at the war station. Distribution of information, partly in London, partly at the war station. Activities in enemy and/or neutral countries, partly in London, partly at the war station. Radio communications, partly in London, partly at the war station.

Moreover, on a smaller scale, work of great importance is being done about which it is better not to confide anything to paper. I personally visited almost all of the above-mentioned branches mentioned in London and outside the city.

15. The direction and control of the entire organisation is carried out by Colonel Menzies from the headquarters in London. At the beginning of my inquiry, when Colonel Menzies had only just been appointed CSS, it was obvious that he was greatly overburdened with work at the war station as well as at headquarters. He has now implemented considerable decentralisation, including the following appointments:

1. Colonel Vivian, who, besides being head of the war station, also acts as deputy to the head (Menzies)—in my opinion, a position for which he is remarkably well qualified.
2. Lieutenant Colonel A.M. Craig, RM [Royal Marines], former assistant director of naval intelligence and a well-trusted officer, has been appointed liaison officer between the Secret Service and the Admiralty.
3. Mr Claude Dansey took over the direction of several departments that hitherto reported directly to Colonel Menzies and acts as a kind of 'under-secretary'.

16. The policy of the Secret Service lies entirely in the hands of its head, who reports to the Foreign Office. In determining policy, he obviously takes into account the requirements of the directors of navy, army and air intelligence and of economic warfare intelligence.

17. In spite of this, I came to the conclusion that it might be of use to arrange regular meetings between the directors of these services mentioned above and the CSS on whom they depend so much for secret intelligence. Such meetings might take place monthly to discuss policy and to exchange views on requirements, possible improvements, the work of the nine SIS departments, communications, the training of intelligence agents, etc.

18. With the approval of all those concerned, we also agreed that there should be monthly meetings between:

the permanent under-secretary of the Foreign Office (in the chair)
the director of naval intelligence
the director of military intelligence
the director of air intelligence
the director of economic warfare intelligence
the CSS
the private secretary to the permanent under-secretary of the Foreign Office
    (as secretary).

Note: My initial thought was that these meetings might take place within the framework of the Joint Intelligence Committee. However, Colonel Menzies stressed that since its inception the Service had been an organisation that regarded secrecy as of paramount importance and had therefore always carefully avoided government body standing such as the Defence Committee and the Chiefs of Staff Joint Planning Committee have, and that he preferred the proposed meetings to be held unofficially.

I concurred.

19. Requirements are the starting point for intelligence collection. At the beginning of the inquiry I was concerned whether the Secret Service was fully aware of what government departments needed by way of intelligence; good communications are the prerequisite for such awareness.

20. It turned out, however, that the Foreign Office, the Ministry of Economic Warfare (whose head of intelligence is a former Secret Service officer) and Military Intelligence (which possesses no fewer than eight serving officers currently attached to the Secret Service, including two recent appointments) are fully satisfied on this point. As the object of this inquiry, the director of naval intelligence was less satisfied, but the subsequent attachment of Lieutenant Colonel Craig (cf. Paragraph 15/II) to the Secret Service and the temporary posting of an RN [Royal Navy] officer have already improved the position, and it is now hoped that the Admiralty and the Secret Service will be able to develop new approaches to planning and implementation of operational tasks. Based on the reaction from the service director of air intelligence to the regular questionnaires, [he] was satisfied that his requirements are well understood, although he does not receive as much technical intelligence as he would like. More about this in Paragraph 28.

At present, the Air Staff has minimal representation within the Secret Service.

Colonel Menzies would welcome the appointment of several RAF [Royal Air Force] staff officers, if and when possible, but Air Commodore Bass has just retired as director of air intelligence and would prefer to leave this question to the discretion of his successor.

21. I suggest that the director of air intelligence and Colonel Menzies take into consideration the feasibility and desirability of seconding additional personnel from the Air Staff [to the Secret Service] as suitable officers become available.

22. I now turn to how specific intelligence needed by government departments is best obtained. General and political intelligence is by and large considered very satisfactory, and the Foreign Office and the Ministry of Economic Warfare in particular are content with the quantity and quality of political intelligence.

23. In regard to technical questions, however, the situation is less satisfactory. None of the three Service intelligence departments receives all the technical intelligence it needs.

24. The Admiralty, for example, would like to receive timely intelligence on the movements of enemy vessels through the Danish Narrows.

However, SIS advised me that to provide this would be an operation of great difficulty, if indeed it was even feasible in wartime, given the apprehension of the Danish government.

For example, I was told that the Danes had completely destroyed the German coastal observation service in the Narrows at the beginning of the war. In Norway, opportunities for land-based ship watching are greater, and an interesting and new method of obtaining intelligence is under development.

25. Similarly, intelligence about movements through the Kiel Canal and about the location of German capital ships in their home ports has also been difficult to obtain, but from time to time shore-based data is reinforced by Air Intelligence data.

26. The Secret Service was of great assistance to Naval Intelligence by providing it with intelligence about vessels in neutral ports, but there are few data on the Russian navy, and Italy has disappeared from the map completely.

27. The director of military intelligence stressed the importance of more precise data on the present and future production of enemy factories and plants and levels of supplies, ammunition and military equipment. In particular, the great importance of photographic copies of documents or other positive proof was stressed, not only as concerns enemy countries but also for neutral countries such as Italy, Russia and Japan.

28. The director of air intelligence would like to receive more intelligence on the number of aeroplanes currently on German airfields and also about their types, wing markings, etc. At first sight it might seem that this would be easy to obtain, but I was informed that the Germans keep a close watch in order to prevent outsiders' access to airfields. Generally speaking, however, Air Intelligence is well informed about the German air force movements from a source that cannot be revealed here.

The director of air intelligence told me that the last information he received from the Secret Service on German production dates from the beginning of 1937. At that time, a very valuable document was also received that described plans for an expansion of the German air force. He added that they had very little information at present about production of the latest model of the Messerschmidt fighter.

29. The Secret Service stressed that a certain amount of detailed intelligence is already being received but that it will take years to develop regular and reliable sources for obtaining intelligence of this nature. The resources available before the war were insufficient, and it is extremely difficult to set up the necessary networks in wartime. It must also be realised that it will take a long time to rebuild the networks in Poland, Czechoslovakia and even Holland, where the Venlo incident badly damaged the organisation. Similarly, a new network in Finland will take time to construct.

30. I do not think one could take issue with Colonel Menzies' explanations, and all the Service intelligence directors understand his position. Strengthening the links between the Secret Service and the other services will lead to a closer mutual understanding between them and will help to improve this aspect of their work.

31. The director of economic warfare intelligence, while also fully satisfied with the political intelligence he needs for his work, asked for more concrete information, e.g. copies of documents on the Customs revenue of certain neutral states, trade statistics, and so on. He acknowledged that this kind of intelligence had

been obtained in several countries, notably Romania, and that there had also been some success elsewhere. However, he would like more. He reckoned that the reason such intelligence was scarce was that Secret Service officers and agents abroad were not fully aware of exactly what was needed.

32. Colonel Menzies told me that work on meeting the Ministry of Economic Warfare's requirements had begun only quite recently and had not yet been fully developed. But some good progress was being made, and he has already managed to obtain some of the intelligence required. (Major Morton has just recently advised me of a relative improvement in the quantity as well as the quality of commercial intelligence data received by him from the Secret Service. I think that there is no need for further concern on this question.)

33. Various people have suggested that those who are in charge of intelligence work abroad, i.e. Passport Control Officers in countries bordering on Germany, were not sufficiently informed about the requirements of the ministerial intelligence departments, especially in the technical area. It goes without saying that it would be very difficult to find men for these posts who would be competent enough to cater for all three services, but one way to improve matters would be to give the relevant officers a special training course.

34. This is one of the questions that could be discussed in the meetings under the chairmanship of the permanent under-secretary of the Foreign Office mentioned in Paragraph 18.

35. There are different opinions among various government departments about the best form in which Secret Service intelligence reports should be disseminated. Some consider that the most useful reports are those based on specific items of intelligence (raw data), which can be summarized by the ministerial intelligence department and supplemented by information that they have received from other sources.

Others consider that reports are more useful if they are first summarized and collated by the Secret Service. All those concerned seem to agree that the political reports compiled by Mr Woollcombe, including his 'analyses', are very valuable. It is this form that the Foreign Office, the Ministry of Economic Warfare and Naval Intelligence prefer. On the other hand, the Military and Air Intelligence services stated that they preferred to receive intelligence without 'analyses' attached. In my view, it is impossible to lay down one rigid formula. As far as political and general intelligence is concerned, some analysis is desirable. As a former Naval Intelligence officer, I can understand how in cases of technical intelligence—i.e. in answers to a questionnaire, information should be precise and without commentary.

This is one of the questions that could be discussed in the meetings under the chairmanship of Sir Alexander Cadogan mentioned in Paragraph 18.

4. Dissemination of Information

36. However successful the system used for collecting intelligence may be, it will be useless if the information obtained does not reach those responsible for making plans and taking decisions.

37. I did not hear any criticism of the Secret Service in this area. As far as I can tell, intelligence data obtained by the Secret Service and the GC & GS are quickly delivered to all relevant departments concerned.

38. The inevitable difficulties resulting from the existence of parallel organisations in London and at the war station [St Albans] are overcome by reliable communication. In the special circumstances of the war the extra expense this involves is inevitable.

5. Radio Communications (Section VIII)

39. One of the most remarkable developments compared to [what I saw in] my prior acquaintance with the Secret Service is the organisation that has been created to maintain radio communications with stations abroad—for example, at the embassies—as well as with individual agents. For example, this department played an important role in maintaining communications between London and the British missions in Poland during the retreat from Warsaw.

40. This department created remarkable compact sets to meet the special needs of the Secret Service. I recommend that the Service ministers instruct their communications sections to liaise with this department with a view to the possible use of these sets by the Service ministries.

41. As far as I could tell during a short visit to one of the radio stations, a high level of efficiency is maintained by this organisation.

42. The director of naval intelligence told me that the Admiralty is so satisfied with what is being done that they have decided to give direct assistance to the Secret Service by transferring experienced navy radio operators to Section VIII. The director of air intelligence stated that he has also received a considerable amount of valuable intelligence from this department.

43. In the course of the inquiry it became clear that under the special conditions of war it was necessary to make some changes in the system of co-operation between the Services' radio-interception and radio-direction-finding organisations and the Foreign Office's cable-interception service. It has also become apparent that provision has to be made now for including some recently established radio organisations in this system, namely:

1. interception of illegal radio communications, including radio beacons;
2. cable censorship;
3. monitoring German radio broadcasts; and
4. radio direction finding.

44. After consultation and agreement with the departments concerned, I prepared a co-ordination scheme, which I have sent separately to the Treasury, the Foreign Office and the Service ministries. A copy is included for information as Appendix II. It was accepted by all departments concerned and will be implemented soon.

6. Activity in Enemy Countries

45. This section deals with some of the clandestine activity that the government has been compelled to carry out in response to the pressures of the war. This is the most difficult area of Secret Service activity to evaluate. One's first instinct is simply to ignore such operations as inherently distasteful. But since the Germans are heavily and successfully active in sabotage and other underground activities, we must follow suit. For example, sabotage can be a way to cut off or slow down the enemy's supply of vital goods, and this has an effect on prolonging or intensifying the war. We thus have to do all we can to make sure this aspect of the Service is of the necessary calibre.

46. It [This aspect of the Secret Service] is the part of Department IX, whose primary role is propaganda (including deception) and sabotage, not unlike the departments of the German General Staff, which have been engaged in similar activities over many years. As far as sabotage activity on a large scale is concerned, it is too early to express an opinion on the work of this department, since up to now none of the planned large-scale operations have been executed. But a selection of proposed plans from the department files was examined, and it has to be said that they are certainly well put together, accompanied with a wealth of detailed information, maps, photographs, etc. I can also testify that the department showed resourcefulness and initiative when it was asked to draw up plans for particular operations on short notice.

47. I came across one case where information about an important sabotage plan in Yugoslavia leaked. To be fair, however, it has to be said that in this particular case I had been warned beforehand that the nature of the operation concerned meant that if it was not carried out immediately after the preparatory work had been finished, the risk of a leak would greatly increase.

48. Obviously, the selection of agents abroad for this kind of work inevitably involves a high degree of risk, especially when, as in our case, we have not managed to set up a permanent service staffed by people we can rely on. It was difficult enough to build espionage capability after the hostilities began; and it is much more so, it must be said, with sabotage work.

49. Leaving major operations aside, it should be noted that the Secret Service has undertaken useful sabotage work on a smaller scale—for example, on the Danube and on the Polish railways, especially in Galicia, where valuable results were achieved and connections between Germany, Romania and Russia were disrupted to a considerable extent.

50. In the first month of the war, a few difficulties and some friction arose between the General Staff's MI(R) Department, which was engaged in similar activity, and the Secret Service. But by the beginning of the present inquiry, it had been agreed in principle that MI(R) (consisting of ten officers), would deal mainly with research and planning while the Secret Service would take over immediate sabotage work in enemy countries. [It was agreed,] however, that if there was a possibility of British troops being required to operate in collaboration with local authorities, it would be better to assign such sabotage operations to MI(R). The question of the destruction of Romanian oil wells may serve as a good example, with which War Cabinet members will be familiar. That operation could be carried out only in collaboration with the Romanian government. British specialists would be sent out to participate in this work, and responsibility for it would lie with MI(R). Similarly, several operations planned in case of a German attack on Belgium or Holland, in which British forces would participate on the invitation of the Belgian or Dutch government, would also be carried out under the direction of MI(R). On the other hand, operations in countries under enemy occupation or in Russia as a potential belligerent would normally fall in the Secret Service's sphere of activity.

51. To me, this division of labour seems logical and sound, provided close cooperation between the two departments is maintained. However, individual minor changes in responsibility may occur from time to time to meet wartime circumstances.

I recommend that the CSS and the director of military intelligence ensure the closest possible co-operation between the heads of these departments. Plans for such co-operation are being discussed at this moment.

52. Moving on to propaganda, I feel that I am on more delicate ground. There is a high risk of overlap between Department IX and the activities of Sir Campbell Stuart, who is responsible for propaganda in enemy countries, as well as those of the Ministry of Information, which is responsible for similar work in neutral countries; in fact, overlap and friction have occurred already.

53. In the case of enemy countries, conflict has been present from the outset. Roughly twelve months before the beginning of the war, when Sir Campbell Stuart's organisation was created, no one except the Secret Service was carrying out any propaganda work in Germany, and that only on a very limited scale. Department IX therefore set up a small propaganda organisation for its own purposes. It was subsequently agreed to transfer the staff involved to Sir Campbell Stuart.

54. At the time it was agreed that Sir Campbell Stuart would be responsible for production of propaganda material while the Secret Service would handle the dissemination in occupied territories of those elements of propaganda material that Sir Campbell Stuart decided were best distributed this way rather than by radio or leaflet dropping.

55. In theory, this division of labour has much to be said for it. If the Secret Ser-

vice has to expand its sabotage work, it needs to have some kind of starting point. It is much easier to get agents to agree to bring propaganda materials into an enemy country than to get them to take part in a sabotage plan or something more deadly. Only through a long period of trial on a relatively safe scale can an individual demonstrate his reliability for more difficult assignments. In short, in the eyes of the Secret Service, [dealing with] relatively innocuous material is indispensable training for more difficult work.

56. Moreover, many technical issues arise. Some material is best smuggled into an occupied country as manuscripts or typescripts to be reproduced locally. It may be desirable for the material to appear to have originated in the country where it is circulated, be that hostile or neutral territory. In such cases, in order to mask its origin, it is important that even the paper and ink are of local manufacture. It is also possible that an agent will agree to smuggle in material of a religious character but will refuse point-blank to take anything that promotes some other ideology, be it Communist, Fascist or whatever.

The Secret Service claims to have great experience in these matters. It believes that the setting up of some new organisation will inevitably lead to serious mistakes. Instead, it seems obvious that to have two government organisations engaged in subversive operations would be a mistake. The Secret Service was created specifically to eliminate this kind of problem.

57. But in practice, the situation is not completely satisfactory. The Secret Service reports that presently seventy–eighty thousand items of propaganda material are smuggled to Germany every month and that three secret presses there print anti-Fascist materials observed to be produced 'somewhere in German-occupied territory'. But the Secret Service has no control over these presses, and Sir Campbell Stuart was far from convinced that the material smuggled in reached its destination. He also wondered if Secret Service organisations were not still producing propaganda material for Germany and German-occupied countries independently. The Service insists that it is necessary to circulate a certain amount of propaganda material in specific regions in order to convince those it wants to use for its work that the Allies will win the war. They claim that, owing to their knowledge of local conditions, it is easier for them than for Stuart to carry out local propaganda, but that they do not aspire to produce propaganda material in enemy countries in a broad political sense. There are weekly meetings to discuss co-operation, but according to Sir Campbell Stuart, they have not been especially successful.

58. As a consequence, Colonel Menzies, Sir Campbell Stuart and I came together to try and achieve co-operation and good mutual relations between the two departments. We came to the conclusion that the liaison was not close enough. It has now been improved.

59. Moreover, measures have been taken to give the weekly meetings a more practical character. It is absolutely necessary for each organisation to know and

understand the needs and difficulties of the other and to make every effort to decide these questions fairly.

60. My recommendations on this issue, which are very preliminary, are as follows:

a. The Secret Service is responsible only for the delivery and distribution of propaganda materials in enemy countries and Russia, but not for the nature of the propaganda materials used in enemy countries. However, it has to know the aims and the nature of the propaganda in order to agree how this material is best delivered.

b. Sir Campbell Stuart's department is responsible for the creation of propaganda materials for enemy countries and Russia, but not for smuggling them into these countries via secret agents. However, the Secret Service must keep him informed as to the means used to deliver the materials.

c. In the interest of maximum understanding and awareness by Sir Campbell Stuart's department and by the Secret Service of each other's opportunities and difficulties and the need to plan jointly, they need, to this aim, to have weekly meetings dedicated mainly to the discussion of existing plans for the distribution of propaganda materials, including any local propaganda that the Secret Service needs in order to support its operations.

d. Colonel Menzies and Sir Campbell Stuart must supervise jointly the delivery of propaganda materials to enemy countries via agents so as to ensure that conflicts are minimised and that the material is delivered and distributed to the areas of Germany and Russia and those targets for which it is intended.

e. Should difficulties arise that they cannot resolve together, they must refer to the minister without portfolio.

I am happy to report that both sides tell me the new agreement is working satisfactorily.

7. Activity in Neutral Countries

61. The extent to which the Secret Service can assist the Ministry of Information in the area of propaganda in neutral countries has been the subject of recent discussions between the foreign secretary and the minister of information, and therefore I will not enter into it here in detail. Generally speaking, in my view co-operation should be organised in the same way as indicated in Paragraph 60.

8. Finances

62. Before war broke out the Secret Service budget for 1939–40 had been set at £700,000; a supplementary estimate increased this to £1,100,000. The preliminary budget for next year is to be £1,600,000.

63. Most of the funds allocated are spent through the Foreign Office, but it would be unwise to confide details of these expenditures to paper. Apart from

the funds used for the work of MI5 (the subject of a further report), the Foreign Office spends the money in two main areas: (a) the normal operating costs of the Secret Service; and (b) special non-recurring expenses, for which ad hoc authorisation is to be granted from time to time.

64. The bulk of the costs incurred under (a) consists of payments to agents for information received from them or for sabotage activity. I was told that these payments are carefully graded according to the importance and usefulness of the agent, and the figures I was given show that pay scales are reasonable. The CSS regularly reviews the roster of agents and decides whether changes are needed in the light of their performance. I have no doubt that CSS will continue to control these expenses in the future.

65. Salaries and expenses of Secret Service staff are also included under (a). As best I can judge, these are not unreasonable.

66. The special tasks mentioned under (b) often require large outlays, and the Foreign Office and the Treasury basically have to rely on CSS to ensure that costs are as far as possible commensurate with benefits. The CSS fully understands the need to control these expenditures carefully.

67. Elimination of overlap between the Secret Service and other organisations—for example, in the area of propaganda—is important from a financial point of view as well as from the point of view of operational efficiency.

68. I am not sure whether the present system of engaging officers on a one-month's-notice basis with no prospect of a pension serves the best interests of the Secret Service or its personnel. But this is not a question that can be easily solved during wartime. In any case, I prefer to postpone the discussion of this issue until the inquiry into the work of MI5, where I expect to encounter a similar problem.

9. The Spirit of the Secret Service

69. I cannot conclude this report without remarking how impressed I have been by the commitment and deep sense of duty that characterises all ranks of the Secret Service.

Signed Hankey
Treasury
11 March 1940

Appendix 1
The Origin and Development of the Secret Intelligence Service

On 10 August 1909, the late Sir Mansfield Cumming was summoned to the DNI [director of naval intelligence] to be told that on the instruction of the Committee of Imperial Defence, a new department would be created to supervise the work of all secret agents reporting to the navy and the War Office.

In October of the same year, the department was divided into a foreign and an internal service, the first under C and the second (as now) under K.

The Secret Service at that time was responsible for:

1. Obtaining intelligence on any movement that might indicate an attack against our country or any hostile action or preparations for such an attack
2. Serving as a screen for the Admiralty and the War Office, on the one hand, and agents, on the other
3. Making inquiries
4. Contacting all paid agents and persons wishing to sell secrets
5. Representing the Admiralty and the War Office
6. Organising a network of agents ready to provide intelligence from behind enemy lines in time of war

The 1919 charter was formulated as follows: 'To provide all government departments with such information as they need that cannot be easily obtained through official channels.'

In the pre-1914 period, political intelligence was not part of the Service's mandate; even work for the War Office was slow to develop, although the files of the War Office from 1905 onwards show that Grierson, Davies, Gleichen, Amis, Holbein, Burnett-Stuart, Robertson and others were persistent in trying to convince the Admiralty of the need to create a naval intelligence division that would work beside an army intelligence development that dated back to Napoleonic times.

It was not until 31 December 1910, when General Sir Macdonogh, at that time Colonel Macdonogh, wrote a classic memorandum on this question (Appendix A) that the wheels slowly began to turn. The crux of the problem was money, since only £6,000 year had been allocated to cover the services of C and K, while the Foreign Office was spending about £60,000 even at that time.

The comment in General Macdonogh's memorandum that 'the essence of an intelligence service is in meticulous organisation under peacetime conditions' is supported by two great authorities on intelligence questions: Colonel Nikolai in Germany and Orlov in Russia. They both reckoned that creating a real, functioning intelligence service would take forty years. The work of the British intelligence pioneers shows how much this could be reduced once having a good intelligence service has been recognized to be a national imperative and as long as its military roots are maintained, a fact that was stressed by Nikolai in all his writings on the subject.

When war broke out in 1914, the Intelligence Department was still amateurish, but with increasing demands from all quarters, it had to take on more and more responsibility. At that time, the Political Intelligence Department, controlled by the Foreign Office in the person of Tyrell, was still functioning. However, as the war continued, separate but interconnected offices were created under the aegis of the Service ministries. Among them there were at least three organisations at GHQ in France, one department of the Admiralty working in

Spain, the Levant office, and two or three others in war theatres further afield. Since at that time it was impossible to control the operations of all these organisations from London, the lack of co-ordination and the inability to verify sources due to the absence of centralised leadership often led to fuzzy and risky decisions. For many such departments the novelty of secret and sometimes alarming intelligence, coupled with their inexperience, made them reluctant to act without multiple consultations with other arms of the government. Fortunately, at home as well as abroad the presence of some outstanding personalities ensured that what these departments did was in the end a success, but the principle was obviously wrong, and steps were taken to unite all secret intelligence services under one unified control and one single roof.

At the beginning of 1916, the Secret Service Office, hitherto known as 'C' Service, was given the cover designation of MI1, thus returning it, in form if not in essence, to the War Office, where it had originated. But even prior to this, the intelligence budget had been channelled to the Foreign Office, so several of the other offices (in particular the Admiralty office in Spain) had to ask for money from 'K', which he had to obtain and disburse without any idea how it was to be spent. In passing, it may be noted that by this time Foreign Office officials had come to appreciate the value and necessity of a service that supplemented its official work so well. Issues such as counter-intelligence, communications, cryptography and an embryonic radio service developed gradually, and intelligence services slowly turned into the indispensable arm of the state so well described after the war by Colonel Nikolai.

The lessons of the war of 1914–18 led to a reorganisation of the Service after 1919, and around 1921 the term SIS (Secret Intelligence Service) began to be used frequently in government reports and in personnel documents. Various government organisations had already adopted the term, especially because they regularly received documents and information from the intelligence services. Around the same time, the secret charter of the Service stipulated the basic principle of centralised control over all military intelligence services, regardless of where they had operated under the different armed service staffs during the war.

The creation of the Passport Control Office, which had not existed prior to 1914–18, made it possible to send representatives of the SIS abroad officially and give them cover, something that had hitherto been difficult and dangerous to obtain. In this regard, British intelligence suffered badly over many years compared to intelligence in countries whose representatives had been fully declared for many years, whether in French, Italian or Japanese Embassies, where they were accredited as military or naval attachés, or as in the case of America and Germany, where they were accredited as first secretaries. It has to be remembered, however, that even in these foreign services the official cover served mainly as a post box, while real intelligence activity was carried on clandestinely by private individuals involved in business or other natural cover work. Except for the head of station in each country, this division of functions is still operative, although in wartime, currency restrictions create great difficulties and sometimes mean that payments to agents abroad, especially in enemy territory, dry up completely. This factor was of no importance in 1914–18. Today it is one of the greatest difficulties facing every intelligence organisation every day.

The Foreign Office has to use the intelligence appropriations at its disposal for a range of activities; exchange-rate movements make accounting difficult. Experiments in cryptography have involved major outlays. There is a danger of losing sight of the fundamental truth, so well put by the NKVD general and defector Walter Krivitsky. Adequate funding is a sine qua non for an effective intelligence service. Failure to understand this essential ingredient of intelligence work has undoubtedly been the reason why, from time to time, intelligence requirements have not been met. But the war will not last forever. Just as it is essential to plan a wartime budget in peacetime, so even while the war continues, we must look ahead and plan for the post-war world. We may assume that whatever form peace takes, there will be vast movements of people all over the world looking for work, better living conditions, better prospects, and so on. The consequence will be our need for very strict counter-intelligence surveillance to identify enemy agents at all border and frontier points. It would also be unwise to assume that there will not be another war. Past experience shows that in the aftermath of war, active operations by an experienced intelligence service is more necessary than ever.

Thus, in discussing the organisation as presently structured, we must also consider its future role carefully. As a starting point, it will be essential to retain a core of experienced officers abroad or at HQ, where their prior experience will allow them to serve as effective 'filters' of incoming intelligence.

Today's Secret Service consists of:

a. Political, navy, army, air and economic (a new but important factor in both war and peace) military-intelligence-gathering stations overseas.
b. Counter-intelligence stations overseas.
c. Communications stations.
d. Receiving stations in the UK to handle incoming radio communications and also transmit urgent, press or other messages that the government wishes to transmit abroad by secure channels. The Foreign Office and the Ministry of Information have saved millions of pounds by using these SIS facilities.
e. Cryptography schools with a large number of trained cipher specialists working on (1) improving the security of British secret communications and (2) deciphering and analysis of other countries' secret messages.
f. A counter-intelligence centre in the UK where incoming intelligence is received, registered and passed on to the Security Service (MI5).
g. A department, similar to the German staff, that undertakes propaganda (including deception) and sabotage operations, as the German staff has done for many years.
h. A unique register of files on facts and individuals, accumulated by the SIS over thirty years from its reports and investigations.

i. A staff of very experienced officers seconded from the Service ministries, whose experience, intuition and excellent knowledge of the sources enables them to draft reports of considerable value.

j. Finally, it is an organisation controlled by the undivided authority of one chief. An organisation founded in 1909 that has now become one of the indispensable components of the machinery of government.

14 February 1940

Appendix
Memorandum by General Macdonogh, 31 October 1910

DMO

Mr Churchill's sub-commission, which has been discussing the possibility of creating a system of postal censorship at the time of tension or war, has expressed the opinion that since it is impossible to prevent agents of foreign powers from collecting intelligence about our mobilisation and the concentration and dispatch of warships from British ports, it is absolutely indispensable that we, too, create equally good sources of information in order not to fall far behind our opponents in this regard.

At present it seems that our system of Secret Service lags behind that of any similar service of the first-class powers and that if war comes, we will feel this disadvantage keenly. The office is in its infancy, and although great progress is noticeable in comparison to its state when it was created a year ago, much remains to be done before its work can be considered to be satisfactory. If there was a war with Germany, we do not have one single agent who would be of use to us.

The key to solving the problem is that we must take advantage of this period of peace to organise carefully for the future. This relates to all divisions of the intelligence service, but in particular the Secret Service, since recruiting reliable agents is a gradual process, and it takes a prolonged period of work with them to establish the mutual confidence between an agent and his controller that is indispensable. It must also be remembered that an organisation which obtains valuable intelligence in peacetime may be absolutely useless during war, when vigilance is intensified and communications are a hundred times more difficult.

The question of obtaining intelligence via Secret Service agents in wartime has been discussed several times over the past twenty-two years, but so far little or nothing has been done. The main reason has always been lack of funds, but now, after the office has been formed and we have established closer links with the Foreign Office, this is less of a problem, and it seems likely that if a well-argued scheme were submitted to the Foreign Office, we would succeed in obtaining funds for our operations. Initially, we would have to move carefully, but if we are successful, we may be able to expand them.

This document is the property of His Britannic Majesty's Government.
To be kept under lock and key.
Special care is to be taken to ensure that the secrecy of this document is preserved.

The Secret Service Inquiry Conducted by the Minister Without Portfolio
Second Report Concerning Counter-Intelligence (MI5)

1. Introduction

1. The present inquiry is the continuation of my earlier inquiry, the report on which was submitted on 11 March. Again I had the pleasure to work with Mr G. Brittain from the Treasury and Mr Gladwyn Jebb from the Foreign Office, both of whom gave me all possible assistance. Mr K.A. Hankey, my private secretary, took part in the inquiry in the capacity of secretary.

2. MI5 developed under the continuous leadership of Major General Sir Vernon Kell, who held the post of director for thirty-one years. He is also commandant of the War Office Police—a unit staffed by ex-soldiers and created in August 1925 on the recommendation of the Committee of Imperial Defence to provide for the security of military installations. It does not provide security for naval or air force installations; the Admiralty and the Air Ministry organise this themselves.

3. I began my inquiry by studying MI5's work methods and organisation. I then proceeded to canvass opinions about MI5 from the government departments, organisations and officials primarily concerned with domestic counter-intelligence—for example, the Services, the Home Office, Scotland Yard, the director of public prosecutions and the Central Advisory Committee on Internment Matters. Sir Vernon and his staff gave me every possible assistance. In addition, the following people appeared before me or were approached by me for consultation on various aspects of the inquiry: Brigadier General Sir Eric Holt-Wilson, deputy director; Lieutenant Colonel O.A. Harker, assistant director (Investigations); Lieutenant Colonel K. Butler, assistant to the director; Lieutenant Colonel H.I. Allen, assistant to the director, Section GS; Sir Alexander Maxwell, permanent under-secretary of the Home Office; Mr F.A. Newsam, assis-

tant under-secretary of the Home Office; Sir Edward Hale Tindal Atkinson, director of public prosecutions; Rear Admiral J.H. Godfrey, director of naval intelligence; Major General F.G. Beaumont-Nesbitt, director of military intelligence; Air Commodore A.P. Boyle, director of air intelligence; Mr Norman Birkett, chairman of the Central Advisory Committee on Internment Cases; Air Vice Marshal Sir Philip Game; Sir Norman Kendal, assistant commissioner of New Scotland Yard; Mr Albert Canning.

4. I visited MI5's headquarters in Wormwood Scrubs together with Mr Brittain on 27 March. As well as giving a detailed review of the Registry, which is the core of their organisation, we had the chance to meet MI5's senior staff and discuss their work with them

2. History

5. MI5 was established in 1909 as described in the third section of my first report. For a few weeks, SIS and MI5, as they were then called, formed one department, but then it was decided that their respective objectives had little in common, and they were separated.

6. It is said that from the reign of Charles II until MI5 was formed, not one spy was caught in the UK. But by 1909 there was enough evidence of German espionage to make it essential to conduct proper inquiries. So, when Captain, now Major General, Sir Vernon Kell began his work, he was building an entirely new activity. When war broke out in 1914, the new department more than acquitted itself; twenty-one out of twenty-two leading German agents were arrested (one of the twenty-two was in Hull at the beginning of the war and fled on a steamer), and the work of German intelligence in England was paralysed.

7. Besides combating espionage, MI5 liaised with the Home Office in an advisory capacity in implementing the measures recommended before the war by the Imperial Committee of Defence for the handling of enemy aliens in the UK in wartime. After war broke out in 1914, many such aliens were arrested; the peak number of 32,458 was reached on 28 October 1915. Over the war as a whole, thirty-one known enemy agents were taken out of action, of whom fourteen were executed. MI5's operations steadily expanded. Besides working against espionage, incitement and sabotage, it began to employ techniques such as impersonating arrested enemy agents and feeding the Germans with substantially correct but harmless facts, occasionally mixed with false information, all calculated to deceive. During the last war I myself drove around in a car bought by MI5 and lived on a salary paid by the Germans for such fictitious services. Later, there were problems with the Treasury over the use of German payments, but that is a different story. One might also mention counter-sabotage work. Sometimes double agents went as far as to carry out carefully organised petty sabotage in our country. This did not cause us any harm, but it was enough to satisfy the Germans that their agents were satisfactorily active in the UK and

that they therefore did not need to take any new initiatives. [It was good] for the enemy to be content with the activity of its agents in our country and not to try to open up new channels that might be more dangerous and more difficult for us to detect. By the end of the war MI5 had earned a good reputation.

8. After the war, it [MI5] was considerably scaled down, and for the next ten years it continued to work more or less on pre-war lines. In the relatively calm international atmosphere of that period, Sir Vernon Kell took the imaginative step of creating the IP Club as a means of keeping in touch with former and serving MI5 officers. The club operated continuously until the beginning of the Second World War and played a useful role in expanding MI5 to meet wartime needs.

9. In 1931 the functions of MI5 were significantly expanded. Until then its activities—officially at least—had been confined to counter-espionage, counter-sabotage, and CI [counter-intelligence] work in the Services, at naval dockyards, at arsenals, at airfields and at industrial and other businesses (both public- and private-sector) of national defence significance, as well as with the communications on which they rely. However, in the period following the First World War, Communism had made itself felt across Britain and had become a potential danger to the Services as well as to the country as a whole. For a while, there was something of a lack of co-ordination and a risk of overlap between Special Branch, which monitored the Communist Party in the community, and MI5, which dealt with the purely military aspects.

10. As the result of an inquiry conducted by Sir Warren Fisher, in collaboration with Sir Robert Vansittart, Sir John Anderson (former permanent under-secretary of the Home Office) and myself, in 1931 the responsibility monitoring all aspects of Communist Party activity in Great Britain was transferred from Scotland Yard to MI5, which at about that time was re-named MO5. From then on, this monitoring was gradually expanded and came to include in due course not just organisations on the extreme left (Communists, Peace Pledge Unionists and others) but also those of the right (Fascists and Nazis).

11. It may be asked whether it is right that an organisation whose remit was originally counter-espionage should now cover such a wide area or whether in principle these political organisations, such as those above, should be put under observation in a country where freedom of association lies at the heart of our system of government. However, as mentioned above, the decision to transfer these functions to MI5 was taken after due and careful consideration. On the question of principle, suffice to say that the political movements mentioned above are mostly of foreign origin, are sometimes supported by foreign money, and often participate in initiatives aimed at destroying our free institutions, while organisations like the Peace Pledge Union, even though founded and directed by individuals of unimpeachable character, can fall under the control or influence of experienced extremists and be duped into becoming the instrument of forces that are less well intentioned.

12. It must be said that MI5's scope is not limited to internal counter-

intelligence but has gradually extended to cover the empire and British garrisons overseas. Liaison with the Colonies and the Protectorates is maintained via the Colonial Office, and CI measures are included in the Overseas Defence Committee's planning. Additionally, however, the assistant director visited a number of Colonies a few years ago with the aim of strengthening CI measures. Contact with India is maintained via Indian Political Intelligence (IPI), which, though located in London, is a branch of the government of India. It deals with Indian revolutionaries abroad and with illegal arms shipments to India. It is housed in the same building as MI5 and has a very small staff and budget. Contact with the Dominions is maintained via the Dominions Office, but no attempt is made to influence their policies.

3. Status

13. Like the SIS, MI5 is funded on the basis of the secret vote, which is not subject to debate in Parliament nor to scrutiny by the Public Accounts Committee. As with the SIS, MI5 accounts are submitted to the Treasury via the Foreign Office, which also acts as a conduit for operational and secret vote funds and has formal responsibility for their use. However, this is where the similarity ends. On the one hand, SIS is in the business of carrying out important tasks in obtaining intelligence for the Foreign Office, which is therefore particularly interested in its organisation, efficiency and even its work methods.

MI5, on the other hand, is of only marginal benefit to the Foreign Office. Its responsibilities bring it into much closer contact with the Service ministries and the Home Office. In other words, the department (Foreign Office) that is responsible for MI5 and disburses its funds is not the department primarily interested in its organisation, efficiency and work methods and does not pretend to exercise any form of supervision over its activities.

14. This anomalous situation has its roots in the origins of MI5, set out above in Section 2, and in particular in the fact that in 1909 the Committee of Imperial Defence did not realise the extent to which the functions of MI5 differ from those of an intelligence service.

15. From its early days MI5 was in fact, externally at least, connected with the Intelligence Section of the General Staff at the War Office, where it initially originated, hence its original name, 'MI5'. But the name was adopted primarily in order to 'cover' or 'mask' activities that were to be kept as secret as long as possible. Since the Admiralty and the Air Ministry are in fact as interested in MI5 as the War Office is, the claim that MI5 forms 'a part of the War Office' was not justifiable.

16. This situation is really somewhat anomalous, and the fact that MI5 has achieved its current standing under such circumstances, without provoking friction or ill feelings, demonstrates the tact and goodwill of the relevant government departments as well as of the senior officers of MI5.

17. I have thought hard about whether its status should be changed. At the present time, it is somewhat isolated; it reminds one rather of something of a lost child, and the situation is not made any better by the fact that it is presently located in Wormwood Scrubs, although in the present circumstances there presumably is no alternative. MI5's view, as expressed by its director and several of his principal subordinates, is that they must in the end be put under the supervision of a minister in a central position who does not have departmental responsibility. As specialists, they rightly assert that they know more about MI5 than any other department. They have the opportunity to submit their views for the consideration by the appropriate department, but they stress that if their advice is rejected, they do not have any other recourse. If a matter of concern to them ever comes before the War Cabinet (or—in peacetime—the normal Cabinet), they do not have anyone to represent their point of view. They object to supervision by the Home Office because they feel that much of their work is closely connected to other ministries, among them the Service ministries, the Ministry of Supply, the Ministry of Information, etc., not to mention the Colonies, Mandate Territories, and Protectorates and their links with the Dominions and with India. They think it would be inappropriate for them to fall within the remit of any one ministry. I have been aware for twenty-five years of General Kell's wish for his department to be attached to the Committee of Imperial Defence, so that it would come under the authority of the prime minister. However, as the secretary of the Committee of Imperial Defence, I have always realised that it would be wrong to burden the small secretariat of its Advisory Committee with such a large subordinate department. I learned that this is also the opinion of my successor. When reporting to me, Sir Vernon Kell urged that MI5 should be attached to the Ministry for Defence Co-ordination. However, a couple of days later the latter was dissolved.

18. Overall, I have come to the conclusion that matters should be left as they are. As mentioned before, MI5 is paid for out of the secret vote and is not subject to parliamentary oversight. If it is attached to some government ministry, there is a danger that this advantage will be lost. MI5 is essentially an inter-ministerial, advisory and non-executive body. The responsibility for decisions and actions lies with the government ministry that it is working for on any particular issue. I do not find MI5 to be as powerless to present its views properly as its representatives tend to assert. It is not only permitted but also obliged to present its views to the responsible ministries, and afterwards it is free to send copies to other ministries for which a particular question may be of concern, even if only indirectly. For example, if the director of MI5 feels that Home Office policies or decisions are insufficient to ensure adequate CI efforts for wartime conditions, he has the right to make representations to the Home Office and send copies to the Service organisations. Likewise, if the latter feel that armed forces are at risk because CI measures for the defence of the country against espionage, sabotage and other kinds of hostile or other subversive ac-

tivity are inadequate, they have not only the right but the duty to take this matter up with the Home Office, and the question will then be settled through the machinery of government.

19. (First recommendation:) For the above-mentioned reasons, I recommend that the status of MI5 be left as it is in time of peace. In war, however, care should be taken to ensure that the opinions of the departments concerned with CI are fully co-ordinated. This should be done by setting up a special committee, as recommended in Paragraph 28.

20. (Second recommendation:) In addition, I recommend that one of the members of the War Cabinet who has no departmental duties be given the function of a 'court of appeal' or referee to resolve any disagreements that may arise between government departments on CI issues and that are significant enough to justify an appeal to the War Cabinet. The same minister could be consulted by the director of MI5 on those questions that cause problems or present difficulties.

4. Functions

21. Briefly, the functions of MI5 consist in providing a centre for collecting all intelligence data on espionage, sabotage and other subversive and illegal activity. It has to obtain as much intelligence as possible and give as much theoretical and practical support as possible to the appropriate government departments so as to prevent and detect such activities, whether directed against the state as a whole or against the Services in particular. Thus, MI5 is an advisory agency and not responsible for policy.

5. Organisation

22. The organisation of MI5, described in some detail in the Appendix, is intended to perform the above-mentioned functions, which can be summarized as 'prevention and cure'. Roughly speaking, 'prevention' is part of the brief of the deputy director, while 'cure' is in the purview of the Investigations Department. The organisation looks as follows:

Director
Deputy Director

| Assistant Director | Deputy Director | Assistant Director |
| (Section GS) | (for investigation) | (for organisation) |

23. The deputy director gives theoretical and practical support to the appropriate government departments in putting in place the right legislative and administrative measures to prevent espionage, sabotage and other illegal and subversive activities. He is also deputy commandant of the War Department constabulary.

24. The assistant director (Section GS) helps departments to implement measures to prevent similar activities directed against the Services, whether from within or without. Together with the deputy director, he is responsible for the majority of MI5's core initial functions.

25. The deputy director (for investigation) is responsible for providing theoretical and practical support to the Services as well as to the Home Office and Scotland Yard in the investigation of suspected violations of the law in the above-mentioned areas and for providing the legal authorities with material to enable them to decide whether or not those responsible should be charged and, if so, for providing evidence.

26. None of the witnesses criticised MI5's organisation, but one did express the opinion that MI5, now located in Wormwood Scrubs, was not in sufficiently close contact on policy issues with the relevant departments—that there has been not a single meeting on the question of CI in which all departments concerned have taken part. Like the other witnesses, he agreed that contact through liaison officers is excellent and that, in addition, the director of MI5 and his deputy director often held individual meetings with senior officials from the departments concerned. Nevertheless, as he saw it, MI5 is 'too cut off' from policy issues. In his view, it would be of great advantage to create some kind of oversight, similar to [that provided by] the committee that was created for the work of SIS under the chairmanship of the permanent under-secretary of the Foreign Office as a result of my first inquiry.

28. I am not in favour of creating a new committee at a time when everyone is so busy. However, assuming that it would meet about once a month, I tend to think that the implementation of this suggestion would close a real gap. Therefore I recommend setting up a committee (Third recommendation) composed of the following:

an independent chairman (maybe someone from the Foreign Office),
the permanent under-secretary of the Home Office,
the director of naval intelligence
the director of military intelligence,
the director of air intelligence,
the director of MI5, plus a secretary, from the War Cabinet,

to meet regularly (at least once a month) to discuss issues of interest to all departments principally concerned with CI, with the aim of assisting the director of CI. The committee must have the right to invite representatives of other departments when needed, and its members must have the right to send deputies when they cannot attend themselves.

6. Vetting

29. In its work against subversion and illegal acts such as those mentioned above in Paragraph 21, MI5's role is in part to co-operate with the government departments engaged in preparing legislation, orders in council, decrees, etc., and in part to assist departments in their implementation. A very important part of the latter [role] is the vetting of job applications by people with unsatisfactory papers seeking employment in government institutions or in businesses that handle confidential or secret government work. Roughly the same applies to the vetting of exit permits, military passes, recommendations of the Passport Control Office in response to visa inquiries in relation to British subjects and Home Office inquiries in relation to foreigners. The work of the Aliens Tribunals, which were created by the Home Office and had to review the cases of 73,353 Germans and Austrians, led to a major increase of the workload and a very significant expansion of MI5. The Registry, where the cards and files are kept, for example, has been almost quadrupled in size since the beginning of the war and will have to be further expanded as the war continues.

30. Under these circumstances it may come as no surprise that the representatives of some government departments responded when pressed that sometimes MI5 is slow in responding to inquiries—a weakness which, by the way, is in no way exclusive to MI5. When vetting inquiries come in, any one of MI5's staff may be required to trawl through the files; depending on the inquiry's source, it is entirely possible that one and the same person—be he an enemy alien, a suspected enemy agent, a Communist or an individual against whom criminal proceedings are contemplated—may be the subject of simultaneous multiple inquiries. This difficulty can be overcome by introducing duplicate files, but this would be rather difficult at the current stage in the development of MI5, at the height of a war and when the whole of MI5 is under great stress. Sir Norman Birkett as well as representatives of the Metropolitan Police, after stating that MI5 worked slowly and was clearly overburdened at the beginning of the war, explained that as far as his tribunal was concerned, this [problem] had already been eliminated. In fact, he declared that MI5 may be running ahead of the tribunal in preparing cases to be reviewed. Nevertheless, it appears that the director of MI5 might examine the issue of how responses to inquiries could be accelerated, and I recommend (Fourth recommendation) that he make every effort to do so.

31. Overall, the government departments concerned were satisfied with the quality of MI5's responses to vetting inquiries. Sometimes the information they received was rather vague, which is perhaps not surprising given the volume. There seemed to be a general impression that by the very nature of their work, MI5 officers tend to be unduly suspicious. This may well be the case, but it may be justifiable, since MI5 is purely an advisory body and decision making rests with government.

7. Counter-Espionage

32. Throughout the inquiry, there was repeated criticism, though never expressed in so many words by any one of the witnesses, that not enough spies had been arrested at the outbreak of war. As mentioned above in Paragraph 6, at the beginning of the 1914–18 war, twenty-two leading German agents were arrested, and the German espionage network was significantly damaged. It could be asked why nothing similar was done in September 1939 and why, with such a large number of enemy aliens in the country, no one was brought to trial for espionage.

33. MI5's answer is that conditions have completely changed. In 1914 we were dealing with a specialised 'spy organisation', which did not exist in 1939. We are fighting a 'total war' against a 'totalitarian state', i.e. a state all of whose resources both national and individual are dedicated to the war. An example of this, as I learned from MI5's experts, is the law on military service, which applies not just to German citizens but also to Germans who have been naturalised as British citizens. Totalitarian concepts affect German intelligence work no less than any other aspect of Germany's national life. All the resources of German industry—German railways and shipping lines and, maybe most important, the information collected via ordinary commercial transactions by German export-import businesses—must now be reckoned part of the war effort. The problem we faced at the beginning of the war was made even more complicated by the fact that there was a highly organised Nazi Party branch in the UK which had achieved a high level of centralised control over a very large part of the German colony in England. MI5's memorandum goes on:

The solution of our CI problem was approached on three basic lines:

a. We eliminated the foreign organisation of the Nazi Party. We had a list of some thirteen hundred members of this organisation, over one thousand of whom left the country at the beginning of war; the remaining two hundred sixty were interned as appropriate.

b. We also took action on a list of some fifty individuals who were suspected of links with German intelligence. Some of them were British subjects, some refugees.

c. We further undertook an immediate screening of foreigners seeking asylum in the UK. In the first instance, this was handled by the regional advisory committee set up by the Home Office, but MI5's records were used to compile reports for the main tribunal in London. Out of twelve thousand persons so reviewed, there was compromising evidence on the files for some two hundred of them, and in approximately fifty out of one hundred cases, the individuals were interned or placed under restrictive orders based on MI5 evidence. MI5 continues to work with the regional committees, who plan to ask for information on another twenty-two thousand individuals.

34. Further investigations led to the arrest of sixty-nine people on the basis of Section 18B of the Defence of the Realm Regulations and of two hundred

seventy-four enemy aliens on the basis of the royal prerogative, although some of these were later released as the result of further inquiries. This put a huge workload on MI5. Two hundred fifty enemy aliens were interrogated at length, and the advisory committees were sent reports on more than six hundred cases.

35. It is clear from all this that we are facing a completely different situation from that in 1918. The individuals arrested in 1914 were known spies, whereas today they are no more than active members of organisations that are considered to be dangerous. As MI5's memorandum says: 'However, while in 1914 we could congratulate ourselves on having dealt a shattering blow to German intelligence, we now must admit that although we have undoubtedly put an end to the activities of a large number of dangerous individuals, MI5 is a long way from being able to say that it has met its obligations, given the all-embracing nature of the German intelligence organisation, which is working through the mechanism of a totalitarian state.'

36. Finally, CI emphasises the difficulties caused in Great Britain by the Communist Party and the organisations that it subsidises and also by the British Union of Fascists and its affiliates. Neither was a factor in the 1914–18 war. They now present considerable difficulty, since both are working actively in the interests of the enemy.

37. In this connection it should be mentioned that the director of public prosecutions, Sir Edward Tindal Atkinson, has commented favourably on MI5's work in preparing the material on which he bases his recommendations as to whether to proceed with prosecutions. MI5's practice is to consult him at an early stage of an inquiry and to keep him fully informed throughout, [and] he has highlighted the special thoroughness of their work in the fixed stages of an inquiry before the case is heard in court. Although to date only one case has resulted from a unilateral initiative by MI5, the appropriate authorities are currently reviewing many other such cases.

38. The representatives of Scotland Yard, including the Special Branch, confirmed what I had been told by MI5 officers about their close links with MI5. However, they asked to be informed at the earliest possible stage of any investigation that might lead to an arrest. According to them, there might be some cases where they already possess evidence that could accelerate a case and eliminate the necessity for further inquiries by MI5. Moreover, getting information on a case at the outset can make their job easier if an arrest is eventually necessary.

39. (Ninth recommendation:) To avoid duplication I recommend that as a rule, MI5 should contact Scotland Yard at an early stage of any investigation likely to lead to an arrest.

8. Aliens Tribunals

40. In Paragraph 29 above I mentioned the great pressure put on MI5 since the beginning of the war by their work for the Aliens Tribunals set up by the Home Office.

41. Mr Norman Birkett (the tribunal chairman) had no direct personal contact with MI5, only with the lawyers responsible for submitting cases for review, on whom he commented favourably. However, he cited a few 'gross mistakes and pathological stupidities' committed at the beginning of the war, when individual enemy aliens were interned on the advice of MI5. Their advice in itself was not necessarily wrong but in some cases was 'terribly unjust'. Some individuals were detained for months, although subsequent investigation showed that there was no evidence against them. In some cases totally innocent and well-intentioned people were subjected to terrifying, dreadful ordeals that affected their relatives, their dependents, their financial position, their business and their prospects merely because it was established that they had joined the German National Socialist Workers' Party [NSDAP] or the German Work Front [DAF] under pressure. Mr Birkett agreed that in the tense circumstances prevailing at the beginning of the war, with the possibility of raids by air and sea, interning these people may have been the right thing to do. Nor did he argue with the view that in the light of recent events in Norway, membership in the NSDAP or the DAF is a factor to which MI5 may rightly have ascribed significance, although he stressed that the individuals concerned, as prominent members of the community, were hardly likely to become spies or saboteurs. But he remarked that if MI5 itself could have questioned these people earlier, they would have been freed much more quickly and their excessive ordeals avoided.

42. In reply to this criticism it may be argued that MI5 was terribly overburdened in the early days of the war. The waves of refugees who poured into the UK over the previous few years from Germany, Austria, Czechoslovakia and Poland created a problem that was almost overwhelming until MI5's organisation was expanded to cope with the additional work. Mr Birkett, speaking as a man who sees the problem from both sides, clearly realises that MI5 carries out its work in conditions of great difficulty and says that its work now is 'thorough, bold and efficient'.

43. For my part I have no hesitation in saying that when war was declared, MI5 had no option but to do what it could to defend national security, and the Home Office had to accept that *Salus populi suprema lex* (The well-being of the people is the highest law). Some hardship was inevitable, but 'bad cases make bad law'.

44. When I asked about preparations against the eventuality that a new power (e.g. Italy) would enter the war, I was pleased to learn that all necessary preparations, including gathering material, have been made. So the necessary internments can be carried out, I recommend (Sixth recommendation) that MI5 review each case as quickly as circumstances allow in order to ensure that those

enemy aliens about whom there are no grounds for suspicion can be speedily released.

9. Work at Ports and Airports

45. Paragraphs 12–16 of Appendix I provide a short report on the Field Security Police [FSP], a unit maintained by the War Office for CI work in army units at home and abroad. MI5's Section GS, which has close links with this unit, provides an element of oversight.

46. Forty-three UK ports have a Field Security Police section, usually with twelve men, and an officer. There are also sections at some airports. Field Security Police works under the direction of MI5. It has maintained 'stop' lists and co-operates closely with and gives advice to—from a CI viewpoint—immigration officers, who have the ultimate responsibility for admitting people into the country.

47. Although representatives of the Home Office and MI5 assured me that currently there is little tension between the Field Security Police and MI5, it was admitted that in the past there had been some friction, and I am not sure that it will not recur. I was struck by the dissatisfaction on this front expressed by Air Marshal Sir Philip Game and other witnesses from New Scotland Yard, who, when addressing other issues, had not expressed any bias against MI5 and indeed had spoken warmly of their close relations with it. They stressed that before the war the ports had been staffed by immigration and Custom officers and officers of the Special Branch, who had always co-operated closely in passenger interviews. They did not understand why the Field Security Police was now involved. They stressed that the FSP has the Special Branch 'stop' lists, in which the branch would be glad to include names reported by MI5.

48. However, MI5 says that the immigration teams in some ports are somewhat understaffed and cannot handle the responsibilities exercised by Field Security Police officers; this does not apply to Liverpool, however, where there are enough Special Branch officers to carry out the work. They also claim that, generally speaking, immigration officers and police lack the 'CI nose'. In peacetime, the immigration officers have overall responsibility for determining that a traveller's papers are in order. That does not necessarily ensure that MI5's concerns are dealt with, since enemy agents go to great lengths to ensure that their papers are in order. Moreover, immigration officers do not have MI5's links with Passport Control Officers abroad, which enable it to provide the Service with much valuable information on individuals.

49. They [in CI] also state that the Field Security Police officers carry out certain duties for which neither immigration officers nor the police are suitably trained. For example, they process the crews of cargo vessels leaving the UK in order to ensure that the crew that leaves is the same as the one that arrived, and that the ship is not carrying any unticketed passengers. Likewise, while local

military authorities in port cities are responsible for implementing the regulations governing neutral ports, under which foreign merchant ships are guarded to ensure that their crews do not disembark in the UK, MI5 officers are responsible for the co-ordination of these measures. However, this forms only a small part of the Field Security Police officers' work. In addition, they are responsible for collecting intelligence by using linguists on their staff to interview captains, crew and stewards of foreign vessels. They have obtained valuable information of interest not only to the Admiralty but also to other government departments, as well as local intelligence agencies and the police. This information is collated by MI5 and passed on as needed to the appropriate government departments. The Field Security Police also represents the special interests of the Services. For example, a naval officer recently instructed FSP units in certain ports to search several neutral ships for suspicious persons. They are responsible for checking crews and their documents; existing British Merchant Navy papers are unsatisfactory from a security viewpoint, leaving a loophole for enemy intelligence. Another responsibility is prevention of any sabotage attempts while crews of foreign ships are on shore leave, crews that do not fall under the provisions of the Neutral Ports Regulations, and they exchange information with their opposite numbers in the British Expeditionary Force.

50. I do not believe that any attempt should be made to pull the Field Security Police units out of the ports, but I recommend (Sixth recommendation) that the Home Office review this issue jointly with CI with a view to reducing the potential for friction.

10. Finance

51. The expenses of MI5 are currently met from several sources:

   a. In 1939–40, £93,000 was channelled via the Foreign Office on the secret vote. In 1940–41, ca. £170,000 will be required.
   b. The Home Office allocates a grant of £10,850 yearly out of its share of the secret vote; of this, £1,035 is allocated for special payments to the chief constables.
   c. The officers of Section GS are paid by the War Office, although the cost of their subordinate staff is met by MI5 out of the monies received under point (a).
   d. The War Office also meets the cost of the Field Security Police.

52. I have no comments on points (c) and (d).

53. I doubt that the Home Office grant under point (b) is of any use. Initially it was intended as reimbursement for that element of MI5's work which is of particular concern to the Home Office, but under the present circumstances it is not clear that it bears any relation to the actual costs incurred, and it is impossible and unnecessary to try to seek to apply this funding to any specific compo-

nent of MI5's overheads. In my opinion, thought might be given (Seventh recommendation) to whether it would not be better to do away with this grant and simply add the amount to MI5's subvention via the Foreign Office.

54. It is evident from (a) that the expenses of MI5 have recently increased greatly as a direct consequence of the war. Of the £170,000, ca. £130,000 is needed for salaries, the staff having tripled since last August; this is hardly surprising given MI5's heavy responsibilities for work against enemy agents and CI measures generally. However, much of this work will not be permanent and will not even continue until the end of the war, and the number of staff will undoubtedly begin to fall when the vetting of enemy aliens passes its peak. For now, however, it is necessary, if unfortunate delays are to be avoided, to provide for whatever staff MI5 needs. Although I was unable to check the duties of the staff in detail from top to bottom, I formed the general impression that MI5 is not overstaffed; indeed, in the short term, further staff increases may be necessary in the best interests of the Service.

55. The growing amount of intelligence gathered by MI5 has created immense problems in regard to registration and recordkeeping. The director has already sought advice on the adoption of a system, and it has been agreed that experts from the Treasury will provide what help they can in order to minimize the increase in clerical staff.

56. As in the case of SIS, I was given some salary details, and bearing in mind that none of its officers are eligible for a pension (a point on which I will comment below), the salaries seem reasonable.

57. However, in this connection one point needs to be mentioned. Mainly to avoid disclosure to the Inland Revenue, salaries in SIS and MI5 have always been paid without deduction of income tax. This means that at a time like the present, the staff of these bodies escape any direct taxation that would flow to the Exchequer to help meet the country's new war needs. It would probably be unwise to do anything that would have the effect of reducing current salaries, although I am in favour of normalising the situation at some future point. (Eighth recommendation:) Meanwhile, I welcome the suggestion made by Sir Vernon Kell and supported by Colonel Menzies to make a special appeal to the staff of both bodies to lend money to the government through purchase of national savings certificates and war loans. This would, of course, be voluntary, but it could be suggested to staff that they aim to set aside savings in an amount comparable to the additional income tax burden imposed on incomes similar to theirs since the beginning of the war.

58. Pensions. The directors of both organisations expressed the view that it would be desirable to try to provide for those members of the staff who leave after a long period of service. At present there is nothing of the kind, except for a very small fund set up only three years ago in MI5, from which small grants can be made. Something similar to the Civil Service Pension Scheme would most likely be unsuitable for these organisations, for whom the flexibility of being able to dismiss

employees when necessary is important. At the same time, the nature of their work means that officers should have an inducement to remain in service for as long as they remain effective. I do not propose delaying this report in order to examine kinds of pensions that would be most suitable—e.g. something on the lines of the Universities' Superannuation Scheme, retirement gratuities or some other system. I recommend (Ninth recommendation) that the Treasury be asked to examine, with both directors, the ways their concerns might best be addressed.

11. Conclusions

59. I was not asked to evaluate the state of CI in the UK, but I cannot express my view on the efficiency of MI5 without touching on this broader issue.
60. It would be risky to assume that putting a few spies on trial means that there no longer is a German espionage network here, although, given that both in Britain and in France there is a Parliament permanently in session that demands information on all aspects of our military policies, and an uncensored, unguided and indiscreet press, one may legitimately ask why a potential enemy actually needs espionage until he actually launches his attack. Similarly, although no major case of sabotage has been discovered in our country so far, it would be wrong to assume that one will never happen, since, as we have seen in Poland and Norway, the Germans tend to bring their sabotage and espionage operations to a head only when they launch a major operation.
61. During the course of my inquiries, the representatives of the Services did not hide their fear that, in a large-scale enemy attack, we might be faced with the kind of dangerous sabotage (e.g. destruction of communications, pinpointing of HQ locations, etc.) that was seen during the land battles in Europe. In fact, the representatives of MI5 expressed themselves as strongly on this issue as the representatives of the Services did, laying particular stress on the difficult conditions under which they have to work because of the large numbers of enemy aliens, refugees, Jews, etc., that have found refuge in Britain over the past few years, not to mention the Communists, Fascists, Nazi sympathisers, members of the 'Peace Pledge Alliance' and various other unreliable elements in the country. It is not that they have any reason to think that the majority of these people are dangerous, but the scope of their surveillance responsibilities has become much greater in comparison to what they were in the last war. This is compounded by a totalitarian ideology under which it is standard practice to threaten not only people who escaped from Germany but also their relatives who stayed behind. I considered it my duty to report the opinions I heard to the home secretary, and he has now submitted a memorandum on the policies of his department on this issue to the War Cabinet (W.P. (G)/40/115).
62. The work of MI5, just like the work of government departments, can be judged only by its results, and its success will be evident only when the critical point is reached. For British CI, this point is still to come.

63. Subject to this caveat, and based on the evidence briefly summarised above, I have no reason to believe that the quality of our CI effort is below the high level that all agree MI5 achieved in 1914–18.

64. I must, however, repeat that the present situation is entirely different. We cannot be sure that, when the critical moment comes, we will not come under attack by traitors in our rear, directed by some organisation that we may not have succeeded in uncovering in time. I hope, therefore, that everyone concerned will attach appropriate weight to all precautionary measures that MI5 may recommend. We simply cannot take any risks, and any injustices that might be caused by these measures are minor compared to safeguarding the security of the state.

65. At the same time, I am not wholly convinced that MI5 has sufficient staff even now, especially in the Investigations Department. It is not up to me to make detailed recommendations on this question, since we can rely on Colonel Harker to say what his requirements are. I would simply stress that any request of this nature should (Eleventh recommendation) be considered very carefully. The risk that MI5's machinery may turn out to be too small to deal with an unexpected crisis is so grave that we cannot ignore it, and yet it is very easily avoided.

Treasury

11 May 1940

Appendix I
The Work and Organisation of Counter-Intelligence

The Deputy Director

1. The deputy director and the Service's senior regular officer, Brigadier General Sir Eric Holt-Wilson, has been a member of MI5 since 1912. He is responsible for the overall organisation and supervision of MI5's preventive policies, measures and responsibilities and also of the type of police matters concerning the civilian population, including foreigners. He is in charge of providing advice and suggestions from a CI point of view on British laws, defence regulations, orders in council and departmental instructions for the implementation of CI policies and administrative measures. He is responsible for co-ordination of and consultation on analogous CI tasks throughout the British Empire. To this end he maintains contact with no fewer than fifty Colonial and overseas counter-intelligence services and agencies, with whom he exchanges information on CI

measures, usually through the Overseas Committee. Colonial governments are not obliged to take his advice, but when they do—and this happens often—the measures are included in the Colony's defence plan, which is periodically reviewed and sent to London for approval by the Overseas Defence Committee. A few years ago, Brigadier General Holt-Wilson made a long and productive tour through the Colonies. The deputy director also maintains contact with the Dominions though the Dominions Office, but he makes no attempt to influence them. In order to do these jobs, he has to review the relevant overseas CI laws and procedures, which London gets by special agreement with the authorities and which are put into the Foreign Office library. He has one personal assistant.

2. The deputy director represents MI5 at government and inter-departmental committee meetings, including the Committee of Imperial Defence. He is responsible for the preparation and editing of CI and official guidelines, instructions and memoranda on CI operations and responsibilities, including instructions on military CI and CI materials for official purposes and for police intelligence, including identity cards, permits, permissions, etc., for use in the UK and abroad.

3. The deputy director works with the Home Office on matters of entry and exit control. The Home Office has set up a committee under the chairmanship of a member of Parliament and supported by the permanent parliamentary under-secretary to make this work more efficient. The large number of such applications for permission is causing great difficulty, since at present no more than 450 applications a day can be properly checked, whereas some 700 are actually received. Excessive delays lead to complaints from businesses. The situation has been somewhat improved by the decision to consider France and England as one country for entry and exit purposes. However, a British subject wanting to travel beyond French territory must obtain permission in London, and the French government has decided not to respond to such applications without first making inquiries in London.

4. In wartime, the deputy director has dotted-line responsibility to the Home Office to advise the permanent under-secretary on CI questions relating to the armed forces, the police and the control of foreigners. He deals mainly with the permanent under-secretary and his assistant and takes responsibility for certain Home Office matters when required. He has an office in the Home Office, where he spends the middle portion of each day. He is also deputy commandant of the War Office Constabulary.

Assistant Director (Section GS)

5. MI5's Section GS was organised at the beginning of the war and deals mainly but not exclusively with military (in the broadest sense of the word) CI issues. Section GS is engaged mainly in preventive work, consisting generally in imple-

menting the measures put forward by the deputy director's department. When an actual breach of law is involved, the case is passed either to the local police or to the deputy director (Investigations).

6. Colonel H.I. Allen is assistant director of GS, the main tasks of which are set out in the following paragraph.

7. The section is responsible for checking the records ('negative vetting') not only of all officer candidates in the Service but also of anyone whose documentation is prima facie not in order who may be applying for work in the Committee of Imperial Defence, the Service ministries, the Services, naval arsenals, munitions plants and similar factories, munitions inspectorates and many government departments where the work is of a secret and confidential nature—e.g. the Foreign Office, the Ministry for Economic Warfare, the Ministry of Supply, the Ministry of Information (including press and photographic reporters, the Censorship Department, its permanent civil servants, etc.). All foreigners applying for naturalisation or for military work of any kind also have to be vetted. To demonstrate the scale of work involved in the vetting it is worth adding that it also covers persons applying for jobs at the BBC, technical, military and war correspondents, military radio operators, employees of companies working on top-secret orders and companies applying for export licences.

8. Similar 'negative vetting' is undertaken in regard to applications for exit permits, military passes, Passport Control Office recommendations regarding visas, inquiries concerning British subjects and inquiries by the Home Office about foreigners.

9. Overall, the section processes six–seven thousand names a week.

10. Section GS also prepares requests for the declaration of prohibited areas at the request of the Admiralty, the War Office and the Air Ministry and submits them for consideration and advises on the implementation of such declarations. It should be explained that 'prohibited areas' are ones where work of national importance is conducted and where in wartime the authorities need greater powers to limit access and to monitor what goes on. Section GS also deals with the implementation of CI measures in prohibited areas.

11. In addition to assisting the Service ministries (MI5 contains a Navy and Air Section) and the Ministry of Supply with CI information and CI measures within their own organisations, MI5 does a lot to improve CI in industrial companies working on contracts, including fuel oil supply for all three Service ministries. Over the past seven years, such companies have been given assistance and instructions on CI measures through advice, brochures, correspondence and personal visits. MI5 is in touch with thirteen hundred such factories. When a new factory starts production, MI5 is informed by one of the Service ministries, the Ministry of Supply or the Intelligence Section of the Home Office.

12. One of the elements of the CI system is the Field Security Police, which has detachments at all headquarters, at several ports (where MI5 is not represented, the Admiralty deals with these matters itself), in dockyards and at airports.

13. The Field Security Police is run by the War Office, but MI5 is closely involved in the co-ordination of CI, and Section GS is responsible for supervising the police. At the time of my inquiries these arrangements had not been approved by the Treasury, but Mr Brittain was able to accelerate a decision.

14. The work of the Field Security Police in military units includes reporting to Section GS about the units' mood, i.e. everything the officers and other ranks think and talk about in their messes, clubs, shops, barracks, etc.

15. In addition, there is a Special Branch of field counter-intelligence in some ports (again, in ports where Section GS is not, the Admiralty looks after this), as well as in some naval bases and airports. Forty-five seaports have a Field Security Police detachment, usually a staff of twelve men and one officer. Everyone who enters the UK needs a visa, but before granting it the Passport Control Officers abroad require knowledge of the applicant's background. To this end, the Passport Control Officers are supplied with a 'blacklist' compiled by MI5, which is also often asked for advice on individual cases. The Field Security Police officers in the ports work in close co-operation with the immigration officers, who have the final responsibility for and decision on this issue, and advise them from a CI point of view.

16. Representatives of both Section GS and the Home Office informed me that there is very little friction between the Field Security Police officers and immigration officials now, although there has been in the past. One of the sources of potential friction has recently been removed by the decision not to allow the crews of neutral ships to disembark.

17. This, then, is the general brief on Section GS. Its work demands close contacts with other MI5 departments—with the deputy director, much of whose work is done by the section; with the Organisational Department and its Registry, which provides the material for a large part of its work; and with the Investigations Section, which carries out investigations in those cases where suspected violations are discovered while preventive measures are being implemented. The section is in close contact with the Admiralty (usually through the DNI [director of naval intelligence]), the War Office through the DMI and army units, and with the Air Ministry (through the DAI [director of air intelligence] on investigation issues and through the provost-marshal on questions of discipline), but it requires great flexibility in its approach. It is also in touch with the Home Office, the Ministries of Supplies and of Information, Censorship and other areas of government activity as and when necessary. Contact with the police is maintained through the Special Branch.

Deputy Director (Investigations)

18. Up to now we have been concerned with the departments that work mostly, if not exclusively, on preventing or trying to prevent subversive and illegal activities.

19. We now move on to another kind of work—namely, the investigation of violations of laws and regulations that have taken place or are assumed to have taken place despite the work of the prevention agencies.

20. The deputy director (Investigations), Lieutenant Colonel O.A. Harker, is responsible for the direct supervision of B Division, the largest of the three divisions of MI5, consisting of eighteen sections, some of which are under one supervisor for organisational purposes. A detailed description of the functions of each of these sections would demand a wealth of detail, but the following paragraphs attempt to give an overall picture.

21. General investigations of subversive activity and any kind of propaganda in the navy, the army and the air force, as well as at shipyards, arsenals and other defence installations, are part of the brief of B1 and B2. Local investigations are conducted for B1 as required by Section B5a, which also carries out investigations for B18 [which counters] sabotage—cp. below, Paragraph 42. While liaison with the War Office is maintained directly through the staff officer (A) in military units in the UK and abroad, liaison with the Royal Air Force is through its provost-marshal. This looks somewhat lopsided, but since all those concerned agree that it works, I see no reason to change it merely for the sake of theoretical symmetry.

22. B3 deals with communications, the CI and non-technical aspects of wireless and light signals, the cables sent by neutral citizens who have come under suspicion, including journalists, and the use of carrier pigeons. Close contact is maintained with the radio CI agency, MI8, whose headquarters are located in the same building. Lieutenant Colonel Harker spoke highly of its work.

23. Left-wing subversive activity, especially Communist and pacifist activity in India, the Dominions and the Colonies, is the remit of B4, which has two subsections—B4(a) and B4(b). The registration and filing system for this work is very sophisticated and includes not only individuals who have been implicated but also information on places where they have been seen, and their professions and skills. It is made more complex by the large number of foreigners identified as engaged in such activity and the divergences in the spelling of their names, for which purpose special registration methods have been devised. This section, in co-operation with intelligence through B4(b), carefully monitors illegal transfers of arms, false passports and passports that have been obtained illegally.

24. This leads us to the question of the agents employed in some areas of CI work in the UK. The discreet use of agents in Communist, Nazi and Fascist organisations in our country is the brief of B5(b), which works together with B5(a) (external investigations for B1 and B18—cp. below, Paragraph 42) under the personal supervision of Lieutenant Colonel Harker. While there has to be flexibility in the methods used, the approved plan at present is not to buy the services of existing members of such organisations but to employ vetted agents to become members of these organisations and thus gain access to their secrets. The value of this principle was demonstrated by the Woolwich Arsenal case a

couple of years ago. Some of these agents work full-time, others part-time, and some are not paid but work on a voluntary basis.

25. It might be mentioned here that other sections are using agents for objectives such as work among refugees (for which the Czech intelligence service is currently being used in the UK) and monitoring Communist activity in the army.

26. B6 employs approximately twenty special investigators and hopes to build this up to about forty, although it is difficult to find suitable people. Their work consists mainly of surveillance of suspects, and as they say, they need a very light touch, since it is vital that a suspect does not know that he is under observation, and it may be necessary to continue surveillance for several months with no results. For these purposes the police are considered unsuitable.

27. Although the preceding paragraphs spoke of the use of agents by B5 and B6, it should be understood that they work independently of each other.

28. In this war, as in the war of 1914–18, there are double agents who are valuable sources of information, especially in regard to the intelligence data mentioned in the enemy's questionnaires. It would not be expedient to give details of this in a written report (I was told about one case that was almost as amusing as the story with the car mentioned in Paragraph 14 of the main report).

29. The CI authorities in the UK naturally take great interest in the work of the Aliens Tribunals. In fact, the large number of foreign refugees currently at liberty here is possibly the greatest difficulty the Service faces. This area of work is the task of B8.

30. It should be remembered that during the first six months of the war, approximately seventy thousand foreigners were vetted by Home Office tribunals; [they were] divided into three categories, namely:

Category A—interned persons
Category B—persons subject to restrictions (some eight–twelve thousand)
Category C—normal aliens, not subject to any special restrictions, other than the requirement to report periodically to the police

31. MI5 was not represented at the initial tribunals, but the police often consulted it. However, it was represented at the hearings of the Appeals Tribunal in order to put before it the evidence available on individual cases.

32. Categories B and C are being re-reviewed by twelve new tribunals recently appointed by the Home Office.

33. In addition, MI5 is consulted and will continue to be consulted by the chief constables concerned in connection with the courts already created or about to be created to deal with the prohibited areas recently declared in Scotland, north of the Caledonian Canal, and in some ports. This demands very close contact with the chief constables, and it will often be necessary to send MI5 officers to the area. Responsibility for presenting cases for consideration by the court lies with the chief constable, but MI5 is of course obliged to provide him with all ev-

idence that it possesses in relation to dangerous activities by foreigners in the area.

34. B8 also deals with the activities of foreign domestic servants, although the police are responsible for keeping an eye on them. It also monitors the civilian internment camps, for which the War Office is responsible, from a CI point of view. B8 is the busiest section and is currently being reinforced in connection with the additional work on prohibited areas.

35. There is a small unit, B9, which deals with German-Irish activities. It does not employ agents and does not work in Eire but maintains close contact with Colonel Archer, who controls the republic's CI organisation and has so far co-operated effectively. B9 also works in close co-operation with the Eire Section of CI, under Colonel Vivian.

36. MI5 does not monitor the IRA, a responsibility handled by the police.

37. Enemy activity, including propaganda in the Dominions and the Colonies and in the Near and Middle East but not in England, is the brief of B11. It is this section that the Passport Control Office consults for visa and exit permits, except in obviously harmless cases. In the Registry I was told that the average turn-around time for applications was thirty-six hours.

38. The Press, Telegraph and Postal Censorship Departments submit daily summaries to CI as well as copies of many individual letters and telegrams; these are dealt with by B12.

39. Special investigations, and, at the request of the director of public prosecutions, the preparation of cases for review fall within the brief of B13, which is headed by Lieutenant Colonel Hinchley-Cook, a first-class German scholar whose interpretation services I myself have used at several international conferences. He works closely with the director of public prosecutions. No prosecutions for espionage have been mounted since the war began; it is department policy not to initiate proceedings unless there is sufficient evidence to ensure a conviction.

40. Preliminary investigations of cases of suspected German espionage in England are conducted by B10. When a 'prima facie' has been established, it is transferred to B13, Lieutenant Colonel Hinchley-Cook, who, as already mentioned, is responsible for special investigations. B10 deals also with investigations of other German activity and is overloaded with work because of the large number of letters (from members of the public) sent in daily by the police.

41. The work of B10 as well as B16 and B17, which deal with Japanese and Italian activities, is supervised by B15. Recently, both these countries have given little trouble, but the heads of both sections struck me as well aware that they must be prepared to act, especially in relation to Italy, in the near future.

42. The investigation of sabotage is first and foremost the job of the appropriate police force, but the relevant section of MI5's B18 assists by making available to the police any evidence and information available to MI5 as a whole. If necessary, an officer is sent to the area concerned from another section, B5(a), to carry out a local investigation (cf. above, Paragraph 21), and B18 is used mainly for

this objective. In the case of sabotage in Service or government institutions, MI5 does not run the inquiry unless it is invited to do so, but it obviously always gives assistance when needed.

43. Sabotage prevention requires a thorough knowledge of the methods used by Germany, Russia and other countries, and B18 is therefore responsible for the collection, compilation, distribution and utilisation of all information concerning sabotage, regardless of its source. This requires close contact with the Service ministries via Section D of SIS and in particular through D1, D2 and D3 in relation to munitions and arms factories, all Services facilities, railways and other public services—in short, everything on the 'home front' that might present a target for saboteurs. This particularly concerns locations for which the intelligence sections of the Home Office are responsible. There are also links with the merchant navy on questions of sabotage to British merchant vessels and British-chartered neutral ships. This requires contacts with the Dominions and the Colonies and with SIS. B18 is also responsible for the gathering of expert suggestions on possible methods of bacteriological and technical sabotage. However, this has to be handled in co-operation with D1, D2 and D3, since they obtain valuable information of a similar nature through commercial connections.

44. It is a cause of some satisfaction that there has not been a single case of serious sabotage in Great Britain since the beginning of war. The blast at the government explosives' works in Waltham Abbey was reported as sabotage by the press; in reality, as the police have established, it was the result of severe frost. However, what we know about German military thinking indicates the likelihood that serious sabotage attempts will be linked to some major strategic operation, as was the case during the military campaign in Poland.

45. A more recent development, spurred by an evident gap in information on sabotage of relevance to the merchant navy, is the collection and compilation of intelligence on sabotage from all available sources at home and abroad and its distribution to the appropriate departments.

Assistant Director / Organisation

46. Under the assistant director (organisation), Lieutenant Colonel K. Butler, are sections dealing with:

1. Male staff
2. Female staff
3. Internal organisation, communications and teleprinter links
4. Administrative duties related to residential accommodations, offices, equipment, stores, couriers, printing, etc.
5. Receipt and dispatch of documents
6. Foreign Office staff passes
7. Liaison with the War Office / Room 055
8. Safekeeping and circulation of secret documents

9. Ciphers and codes
10. Job applications
11. Registry
12. Finance
13. Seconded military personnel, allowances, travel vouchers
14. Administrative work for overseas counter-intelligence services
15. Technical services
16. Legal section
17. Billeting
18. Transport
19. ARP [air-raid precautions]
20. First aid

47. Apart from finance, which is dealt with in a separate section of my main report, the Registry is the most interesting of the sections, since it is vital for the organisation as a whole

48. Its importance is evident from the following figures:

Number of files	160,000
Number of cards	2,000,000
Incoming correspondence	ca. 200,000 items per annum
Outgoing correspondence	233,028 per annum
Number of messages received during a randomly selected day in March 1940	609

49. Some of the technical difficulties involved in dealing with records and files containing a great number of foreign names have been referred to above, in Paragraph 23.

50. There obviously have been some delays since the beginning of the war, since so many departments have needed access to the same files, in particular personnel files. This difficulty could be overcome by having copy files, but in MI5's present stage of redevelopment this would require a lot of intensive work and a much larger staff.

51. The Registry's staff is entirely female: 52 of them at the start of the war and 188 now. Miss Payton Smith, head of Registry, is to be congratulated for her successful work, especially in view of the growth in volume noted above.

52. Excluding officers, MI5 has a support staff of 445. Of these, 234 are secretaries, 188 are Registry employees, and 23 men work as clerks, photographers and laboratory assistants.

Physical Security Measures

53. My visit did not provide sufficient time to acquaint myself with the details of the physical security measures that are among the duties of this section of MI5, but I gathered that this matter is being given proper attention.

54. The entire female staff, including those in the Registry, work under the su-

pervision of Miss M.I. Dicker, who has been with MI5 for more than twenty-four years. She is responsible for the selection, discipline and general welfare of the staff. She deserves a vote of confidence for the high level of efficiency that is the hallmark of her work.

32　*Message from* EDWARD, *29 November 1944*

TOP SECRET

A circular signed by Menzies about two weeks ago instructed SIS representatives to make attempts to penetrate Soviet organisations but said that all proposals to this end needed to be agreed on in advance with the directorate.

In a previous circular Menzies stated that in implementing his directive, work against Communism was to be undertaken in close co-operation with Section V. The latter's work will be under the direction of Philby (who will have the symbol VN), who will report to Vivian (DD/SP).

He will begin work on 12 October and take over completely from Curry by 15 November.

The circular also stated that XK (anti-Communist) work abroad was not the exclusive preserve of Section V officers and could also be undertaken by officers of any other section if they were suited to it.

33　*Philby's Letter to Peter Loxley, September 1944, with the Curry Memorandum on Soviet Espionage*

TOP SECRET/PERSONAL
DCSS 65/1 of 13 September 1944

My Dear Loxley,

I am not sure whether you are aware that six months ago C [chief of SIS] approved the establishment under my immediate supervision of a small section (Section IX—consisting at present of one officer and a secretary) to make a special study of the illegal activity of the Communist movement in other countries and to investigate cases of Communist or Soviet penetration and espionage.

The underlying thinking can be summarized as follows.

Before the war these functions had been one of my responsibilities as head of Section V.

This was, of course, before the international activity of the Nazi Party and its opportunities in the areas of espionage, sabotage and the establishment of Fifth Column cells relegated to second place work on the activity of the Comintern (and its affiliates) as an international subversive movement potentially targeted against British interests and as a concealed weapon of Soviet national policy. This work had been an important part of the job of my special assistant in our organisation, and we were thus, at that time, well informed.

As the Nazi threat grew with the approach of war we had to concentrate our attention, and to switch our human resources and energy, and also our finances (which at that time were totally inadequate), to tackling German, Italian and Japanese espionage. As a result, in the four years of war—indeed, up to six months ago—we received no intelligence on this issue, paid practically no attention to it and did not process related intelligence that fell into our hands or that came to us in the form of ancillary material obtained in the course of more substantive wartime assignments.

In the meantime, both here and abroad, incidents began to occur and to increase in frequency (some of them are noted in the attached memo), which meant that our policy of turning a blind eye to ideological, subversive and espionage activity by the Communist Party and certain Soviet organisations was fraught with far greater risks than had been the case in the early days of the war.

I was accordingly directed by C to arrange the transfer to SIS of Mr J.C. Curry, a senior MI5 officer, to work under my direction on the tasks referred to in the first paragraph of this letter. Curry has spent several months making himself *au fait*.

He has produced the attached memorandum, which, given the lack of intelligence at our disposal and our overall weakness on the issues in question, is, while far from complete, a good piece of work in its own way.

I think the memorandum will be of substantial assistance in correcting the existing shortcomings as regards the production and collation of intelligence, in studying the aims and the essence of Communist clandestine activity and in revisiting our previous plan, which was to put off the job of putting sources in place to provide intelligence on these matters until after the end of the war or even until after the Peace Conference.

Curry's memorandum makes clear that even a modicum of knowledge of these issues may be urgently needed at a time when we are already late in reorganising ourselves.

I discussed this question with C, who, while noting that there were no pressing tasks to be tackled in these areas, gave his approval in principle to my cautious policy of producing the sort of intelligence on our allies that they are apprehensive about giving to us and by communicating to those of our official representatives in appropriate positions certain information on the key aspects of this very broad theme. Our work will supplement the exploitation of incidental sources such as BJs, the Censorship and extremely sensitive sources of intelligence in countries such as Mexico where there are extensive opportunities for [Communist] activity which bear watching.

C asked me to send you a copy of Curry's memorandum and to inquire whether you are basically in agreement with the policy now to be followed by the intelligence service.

I can assure you that we fully appreciate the extreme delicacy of this question in the current climate, and for this reason, the section that is to tackle it has been placed under my command; as a result, barely a handful of people within our organisation are aware of the nature of its work.

Yours,

13 September 1944

Attachment: Curry Memo

Source 'L'

Memorandum by Head of Section IX of SIS, Curry, on the Operations of Soviet Intelligence in the UK

This memorandum has been prepared on the basis of HOTEL (SIS) and HUT (MI5) files to familiarise SIS's counter-intelligence officers with the operating methods of Soviet intelligence.

[1.] Contents

1. The Communists' Revolutionary Programme
2. The GRU and the NKVD/OGPU
3. The Comintern and the 1935 Brazilian Revolution
4. The Green Case
5. The Case of Springhall and Uren (an MI5 Comment)
6. The Case of Hans Christian Pieck

2. The GRU [Military Intelligence] and the NKVD/OGPU [Foreign Intelligence]

1. The following comments should be viewed as an attempt to analyse briefly but succinctly the structure and function of these arms of the Soviet government.

2. The GRU, Soviet military intelligence, is known in Soviet military circles as the Fourth Directorate. It is reckoned to be the most important component in the Soviet military machine and is staffed by the most competent and politically sophisticated officers. They are not that well paid, but when they retire they get

a range of special privileges. They enjoy unrestricted access to whatever information they need. The directorate has a very well-organised system for secure storage and filing of papers and agents' files.

3. The directorate is responsible for production, detailed collation and dissemination of intelligence of all types obtained both inside the USSR and abroad which may be of interest to the General Staff of the Russian army in case of war.

4. It is assumed, though it has not been confirmed, that the Fourth Directorate does not engage in counter-intelligence.

5. The Fourth Directorate is divided into departments, of which the second and third are of most interest to us. The Second Department processes the material obtained by the Third Department.

6. The duties of the Third Department's agents are:

   a. To obtain the fullest possible intelligence on foreign armed forces as well as all political and economic intelligence that, after detailed processing, might have a bearing on the actions and decisions of the General Staff and the Politburo (it is interesting that the Russians consider it practically impossible to draw a distinction between political and economic intelligence, on the one hand, and military intelligence, on the other) in any country in which the Russian army may find itself engaged.

   b. To create conditions that will facilitate the army's actions—in other words, 'destabilisation operations'.

The Third Department is known to have a special department staffed by skilled forgers, who can turn out false passports, documents and signatures.

7. Agents of the Fourth Directorate are carefully trained abroad or in Moscow before their postings. The schools used are special ones, of a different nature from those of the Party or the NKVD. Training lasts three months. Even if they are Party members, graduates of the school are not allowed to make contact with the local Party organisation when they are posted abroad. Agents trained in the Fourth Directorate schools are usually native Russians or people with Russian citizenship. A Russian will not work in any department that deals with his country of origin.

8. Another important department of the Fourth Directorate deals with Russian officials in contact with foreign states. All Soviet military attachés are trained in this department before posting. It must be noted that military attachés are usually not officers of the Third Department, although their secretaries invariably are.

9. For military espionage abroad the Third Department uses two types of operator: the legal *rezident* and the illegal.

10. Legal *rezidents* are always officers of the Third Department. Overseas they are official representatives of the Soviet government at embassies or missions.

11. The duties of a legal *rezident* include (a) producing as much military intel-

ligence as possible, whether by personal contacts or via Soviet military attachés; and (b) assisting the illegal *resident*. He will service his mail drops and organise code communications between the illegal *resident* and the centre.

12. The legal *resident* may turn for help to the local Communist Party organisation, but this connection is maintained under very heavy cover so as not to compromise the *resident* or the Soviet government.

13. To avoid direct contact with known members of the local Communist Party organisation the legal *resident* uses a cut-out, usually a female secretary whose tasks include handling intelligence, briefing, etc. The same method is used with the illegal; cut-outs for legal and illegal *residents* are recruited locally.

14. There are three types of illegal:

a. *residents* running a network, who are always officers of the Fourth Directorate;
b. rank and file operators, who are mostly the *residents'* assistants—they are usually officers of the Fourth Directorate;
c. agents, usually Austrian, Czech, Hungarian and Romanian émigrés. They have nothing to lose by collaborating with the Fourth Directorate and indeed are often very well paid for their efforts.

16. Illegals and transient agents travel on authentic passports issued by their supposed country of birth; these are obtained, if necessary, with false papers. It is important to note that foreign passports used by Soviet agents sometimes show stamps which indicate that the holder has been in Russia.

17. Cover for illegals: The usual cover is some sort of business. In some cases, a firm is set up specially. Cases have also come to notice where illegals have travelled abroad in the guise of representatives of an already existing firm.

18. The tradecraft of legals and illegals: If a new network needs to be set up, the legal *resident* will get in touch with the appropriate representative of the Communist Party in his host country. This contact is established by agreement between the head of the Fourth Directorate and the Foreign Liaison Section of the Comintern, where consent is invariably given. A Party member designated to get in touch and work with a local *resident* gives up all political activity and is trained as a Fourth Directorate operative. The illegal usually establishes contact with the legal *resident* via a woman whose only job is as a go-between between the illegal and another woman, who has the same role for the legal *resident*. The illegal usually begins his work six months after his arrival by meeting people useful for his work and gaining their confidence. The Party assistant of a legal *resident* recruits agents from among workers in technically important factories. Their reliability is checked out via the local Communist Party branch. It is interesting to note that Fourth Directorate representatives are always skilled photographers and invariably use a Leica for intelligence work.

19. Communications with Moscow: This is handled via the Soviet Embassy or mission. Photographs and messages are sent in sealed packets directly to the Third Department of the Fourth Directorate. The agent himself is never in-

volved in the transmission of his messages and photographs. The Fourth Directorate generally does not use secret inks. When it does, the ingredients are bought in different places. The Fourth Directorate uses the radio, although it is not satisfied with its transmitters.

20. Communication between agents in their host country: The illegal and the legal *rezidents* contact each other via female secretaries as cut-outs, as described above. The illegal never visits the embassy. Other than under pressure of circumstances, the illegal communicates with his agents through letters sent to reliable addresses. The letters are usually collected by a woman. The illegal never services the drops himself. The telephone is only used exceptionally for agent-illegal contact. Use of the post is also forbidden, although in case of real need an agreed code is used. All agents are well trained in avoiding surveillance.

21. Briefing of agents: The Fourth Directorate tasks its people via the embassy or the mission. They have developed a form of questionnaire that it is the Third Department's job to keep regularly updated. The questionnaires are regarded as highly secret and are sent only to the appropriate officers of the Fourth Directorate. The main questionnaire intended for use by desk staff covers a one-year period. It is carefully updated and reviewed after six months and then again three months later so that new inquiries and current work can be incorporated.

22. Financing of the organisation: Payments are made via a British bank in the form of cheques sent out through the embassy or the mission.

23. Destabilisation operations: This is the Third Department's main task. Before the war the greatest effort in this area was in the countries bordering the Soviet Union or in likely enemies, such as Germany and Poland. An attempt, albeit unsuccessful, was made to mount a similar operation against the British army.

[3.] The GUGB [NKVD or OGPU]

24. The GUGB is the main organisation of the Security Service of the Peoples' Commissariat of Internal Affairs [NKVD]; the GUGB headquarters is known as the OGPU.

25. The OPEROD is the operational division of the GUGB and has three sections: (1) INO, the Foreign Section, responsible for sending OGPU agents abroad; (2) a Special Section, which handles counter-intelligence in the USSR; and (3) another Special Section, which handles intelligence and disciplinary measures targeted against official Soviet representatives and Party members.

26. Up to 1937 each of these sections had its own head, but in that year a plan was put forward to put them under the command of a single chief and combine them into one department known as the KRO. It is, however, as yet unknown whether the plan was implemented, but recent reports speak of the existence of the KRO.

27. The First or Passport Section of GUGB has nothing to do with the issue of

passports, whether real or false. It is actually responsible for vetting Soviet citizens being sent abroad, a task that creates a wealth of opportunities for recruiting OGPU agents. The OGPU took a keen interest in Soviet purchasing commissions. It did not appoint its own officers to these groups but instead recruited agents from among the designated members and gave them a short spell of training before their departure.

28. Organisation of OGPU activity abroad: The main thrust of the work is similar to that of the Fourth Directorate. Up to 1934 the OGPU handled the production of political and economic intelligence, surveillance of Soviet and local Party organisations and pursuit of the White Guard formations. In 1934, on Stalin's personal order, the OGPU set up its own organisation to produce clandestine intelligence on the military, naval and air forces of other countries. This organisation was put under the control of INO, not the Fourth Directorate.

29. OGPU agents abroad: Like the legal and illegal *rezidents* of the Fourth Directorate, OGPU agents are divided into official and unofficial (clandestine). They are appointed by INO in Moscow and work under the direction of whichever department of INO looks after the country in which they work. The official OGPU representative enjoys diplomatic privileges and is an official member of the embassy or mission. His duties are established by agreement between INO and the Peoples' Commissariat for Foreign Affairs.

30. Duties of the official representative: He is seldom involved in embassy work; his main job is to create an OGPU network inside the embassy and to maintain surveillance on the official life of the staff of trade missions, where he also recruits agents. His responsibility is to give the maximum possible assistance to the illegal representative, but he is not allowed to maintain direct contact with him. The methods are as described in Para. 3 above. The official representative is also expected to maintain close but not direct contact with the local Communist Party organisation.

31. Duties of the unofficial representative: These are the same as those of the Fourth Directorate illegals, but they control their own organisation and are never run by the local Fourth Directorate illegal.

32. Communications: As with the Fourth Directorate, communications are handled via the official links of the embassy or mission. Secret inks are rarely used, although in some cases they are employed for messages sent via the diplomatic bag. There are radio links, but the equipment is of poor quality. It is also known that equipment may be placed at the disposal of the embassies and missions of neutral countries in case of war. The NKVD uses all means at its disposal to penetrate the diplomatic services of other countries. The NKVD recruits well-educated young people to its work in the hope that they will enter the diplomatic service and work their way up. It is quite obvious that the staffs of most embassies contain someone unknown to the ambassador or head of mission, who in extreme circumstances will collaborate with the NKVD.

33. Liaison between the OGPU and the Fourth Directorate: From 1921 to 1934

the OGPU fought unsuccessfully to gain control of the Fourth Directorate. There are well-defined rules in Moscow to govern their interrelationships, but there has nevertheless been friction, and close co-operation has depended entirely on whether the heads of the OGPU and the Fourth Directorate are on friendly or hostile terms. There is rivalry abroad as well, with each organisation striving to get the other under its influence. Except when there are direct appointments from Moscow, the two do not exchange personnel. Staff seconded from the Party to either organisation are forbidden to meet one another, although in practice this has often proved impossible to enforce.

The OGPU's real power resides in GUGB, and since the latter is influential in the Comintern, it gets free assistance from the Party leadership and individual members. The OGPU has an easier job than the Fourth Directorate when it comes to recruiting. The ratio of Fourth Directorate agents to those of the OGPU varies. In the countries bordering the USSR it is sometimes 20:1.

In 1934, on Stalin's personal order, the OGPU was given control over the Second Department of the Fourth Directorate. Since this was the directorate's most important unit, this meant, in practice, that the OGPU controlled the entire directorate.

In 1935, again on Stalin's personal order, the OGPU set up its own military intelligence organisation. But overall management of military intelligence organisations abroad remained in the hands of the Fourth Directorate, even though the other operatives were controlled by the OGPU.

Following the purge of the army in 1939, the OGPU also underwent a whole series of reorganisations stemming from the mixing of its functions and those of the Fourth Directorate. This situation lasted till 1939 [*sic*], after which some of the staff were transferred to work in counter-intelligence and some to military intelligence. We know that each Red Army unit now has an NKVD representative who reports to the KRO; numbers range from one to two at regiment level to twenty in the army's main staff.

4. The Green Case

1. The case described below is designed to illustrate the methods used by Soviet military intelligence in producing intelligence, and the comments made on the work of the RAZVDEUPR bear careful study.
2. Oliver Charles Green was born in Birmingham in 1904. After primary school, he went into a print works and remained there until 1937. It has been established that by 1933 he was already a CPGB [Communist Party of Great Britain] member. He joined the International Brigade in Spain in 1937 and served there till he was wounded, when he was given the special assignment of profiling the soldiers of the British battalion with emphasis on their political reliability and their leadership potential. Green also worked on the history of the International Brigade.
3. He returned to Birmingham at the beginning of 1938 and a short while later

moved to 293a Edgware Road, NW9, where he again took up printing. In May 1941 he joined the Hendon ARP [Air Raid Precautions] as an ambulance driver.

4. On his return from Spain, Green was approached to undertake secret work under the direction of an individual in London. Since he did not establish contact with known CPGB members and did not have a job allowing him access to classified material, no suspicions arose as to contacts with Soviet intelligence.

5. In 1941, Green was arrested for forging petrol coupons, and a search of his home revealed that he had a darkroom. The police found two rolls of Leica film, which, after development and enlargement, were found to contain photographs of weekly military intelligence summaries—classified documents, though intended for a fairly broad circulation.

6. A notebook belonging to Green was found to contain the address of a British soldier named Eliot stationed in Smedley's Hydro [which was used as a training centre for photo and reconnaissance intelligence] at Matlock. Eliot was known to have been a CPGB member for several years. He too had served with the International Brigade in Spain and had access to the weekly military intelligence summaries from which Green had made partial extracts.

7. Green was imprisoned, and confessed that he worked for Soviet intelligence. He later gave a complete account of his methods.

8. He stated that he had first been approached by an officer in the brigade to spy in France. He agreed. But he was then given the choice of undertaking intelligence work in the UK on behalf of the USSR. He agreed to this too, whereupon he was handed £40 and told to return to the UK and await a letter signed JOHNNY, his signal to go to an agreed rendezvous. He was given detailed instructions how to get there, how to make contact and how to establish the identity of the person he was to meet, and he was briefed on agreed danger signals; he was also given precise instructions for his movements two hours before and two hours after the rendezvous. In the interim he fitted out his flat in Edgware Road, bought the requisite accessories for the Leica, including special lenses for photographing documents, and, although he had no experience, trained himself to be a photographic expert in just nine days.

9. Organisation: Green knew the two leaders of the organisation by sight but not by name (it has been established that they were Russians working at the trade delegation). The actual members of his organisation were all British subjects. Green handed his documents to the man with whom he had been in touch right from the beginning. These documents were extracts from his sub-agents' reports and were handed over as undeveloped film. The meetings were almost invariably out of doors, although on one occasion Green visited the flat of one of his accomplices. The head of the organisation was known to Green as 'the Chief'.

10. 'The Chief', or the legal *rezident*, would get Green's reports, edit them and augment them with material from other sources. He would also brief Green on his intelligence requirements and provide funds, which he handed to Green in

the form of £1 notes. In addition to his expenses, Green was given £500 (which he hid) for use in emergencies, such as if Great Britain were occupied or if the Soviet Embassy moved away. Radio was used more often [to communicate with Moscow] than the diplomatic bag was.

11. Agents: All the agents recruited by Green were British subjects—a soldier, a worker in an aircraft plant, a merchant seaman, a source who had access to an aircraft plant though not working there, a civil servant and a pilot. If someone was suspected to be under surveillance by the counter-intelligence service, they were not recruited (this included all CPGB members). If a CPGB member was thought to be promising material, he would be encouraged to gradually distance himself from Party work and the Party. This was Green's approach. His sub-agents were located in various parts of the country, and he thus needed to travel around extensively. He was forbidden to use his own car for this but ignored the ban, and it was his forgery of petrol coupons that led to his downfall.

12. Meetings: These always took place out of doors. Times were always double-checked, and much care was taken to plan the movements of those involved for two hours before and after a meeting. They avoided establishing any fixed patterns and went to considerable lengths to avoid observation. They also used simple but effective recognition and danger signals. Green stated that he never met more than fifteen agents per month and that in case of need he could see each agent once a fortnight at most. Agents or informants recruited by a group member were not necessarily run by that person.

13. Timeliness of communications: Green himself was responsible for seeing that messages compiled or handled by him were transmitted in a timely way. Much attention was paid to agent training, and the Chief gave Green secret materials to assist in this. Training was ideologically based.

14. Radio equipment and operators: Transmitters were located at various points around the country and used in sequence. There was no difficulty in getting the operators trained. Main-powered transmitters were as yet not used. Transmissions were sent roughly once a fortnight late in the evening or early in the morning, when very few people listen to the radio. The wavelength was changed frequently, and transmissions were sent automatically—the most reliable method when hand-keying is employed (without the help of a Creed machine). Green claimed that the use of high-speed automatic transmissions not only cut down on time on the air but eliminated the risk of the transmissions being picked up by random radio hams; his confidence was misplaced. There were a number of reserve transmitters.

15. Use of undeveloped film: This was used to ensure the security of intelligence, organisational information, etc. Messages were always passed to the 'Chief' on a strip never more than six inches long. The messenger carried a torch so that in an emergency the film could be rapidly spoiled by light. Two copies were always made of all messages. The second was retained until it was

confirmed that the first had reached its destination. Agents' messages were destroyed after being photographed.

16. Objectives of the Green organisation: Its primary aim was to produce political intelligence. After the fall of France, Britain faced two possibilities: a Fascist government, which might declare war on Russia, or the successful occupation of Great Britain by the Germans, which would mean at a minimum the recall of the Soviet Embassy, thus creating a real need for subversion and espionage operations to be directed against the new enemy. If the Soviet Embassy and the RAZVEDUPR's legal *rezident* had to leave the UK, it would be Green's job to run these operations.

Espionage would be conducted in the usual way, but sabotage would be handled by the Communist Party at Green's direction. Five or six months before the German attack on Russia, Green was tasked to obtain information from British intelligence sources on German armaments and the German order of battle. He was also asked to pass on any information he could get on British armaments, but it was stressed to him that intelligence on Germany was the first priority.

Green had no doubt that the Communist Party was not engaged in the same sort of underground work as he was. He was wrong, but it is interesting to note, since his statement apart, there is other evidence that Russian intelligence operated independently of the Communist Party, although it is highly probable that the Party's leading members were involved in the activity.

5. The Case of Springhall and Uren

1. On 28 July 1943, Douglas Frank Springhall was sentenced at the Central Criminal Court to seven years' hard labour for offences against the Official Secrets Act relating to information received from Miss Olive Sheehan, a civil servant in the Air Ministry. Miss Sheehan gave evidence on oath against Springhall. She had been tried somewhat earlier and sentenced to three months' imprisonment.

2. Miss Sheehan had rented a flat together with a ministry colleague, whom we shall call Miss A. Springhall first visited their flat in October 1942. Miss A opened the door. On seeing her he asked whether she was Miss Sheehan, from which we can conclude that he did not know the latter. He did not give his full name but asked them to call him Peter. Springhall came to the flat again that evening and, having found Miss Sheehan at home, showed her his Party card and his credentials. From then on, Springhall visited Miss Sheehan once a fortnight. He told her a little of his own experiences and about Party history and brought her a series of Communist pamphlets, which he discussed with her.

3. After two months of this sort of treatment Springhall asked Sheehan whether she could ever get him documents of interest to the Russians. He added that the

British government was holding back from the Russians intelligence which might help Russia's military efforts. At the time of his approach, Miss Sheehan was not involved in work of a classified nature, but two months later she was transferred to top-secret work in the Air Ministry's research branch. She told Springhall this, and at their next meeting she handed him information on the features of a new and highly secret weapons system, which she had obtained from files passing through her hands. She continued to hand over material up to the point of Springhall's arrest in July 1943, including experimental test results. She told him not only about the nature of the invention but about the place it was being built.

4. Springhall and Miss Sheehan used to talk in the dining room; Miss A was not present. However, she was often in the flat during his visits, and feminine curiosity made her eavesdrop at the carefully shut door. On one occasion she heard a conversation that began with a description of an Air Ministry pass and went on to the subject of the secret invention mentioned above. She was smart enough to realise that Miss Sheehan had no right to do this, and she said as much to her friend, an RAF [Royal Air Force] officer. He advised her to take no action for the time being, since he felt it desirable to obtain confirmation of what Miss A had overheard.

5. At midday on 15 June, Miss A and her friend returned to the flat to find that Miss Sheehan was lying down after a visit to the dentist. Miss A helped Miss Sheehan into bed and asked if there was anything she could do for her. Miss Sheehan replied that Peter was due to arrive and asked Miss A to tell him she was very ill and to hand him a packet. The officer decided to take advantage of the opportunity, opened the packet and found data on the new invention and a list of Air Ministry staff. He made a brief summary of the paper, took a copy of the list and resealed the packet. He and Miss A then left the flat and reported the matter to the Air Ministry. While they were away, Peter arrived at the flat, and the unsuspecting Miss Sheehan handed him the packet.

6. The next day the police searched the Sheehan flat. They established from a photograph that Peter was none other than Springhall. When they entered his own flat, he tried to conceal a piece of paper, which turned out to be the list received from Miss Sheehan. Springhall admitted that he used the name Peter.

7. Among a number of items found when Springhall was arrested was a diary in which he had entered mysterious symbols, addresses, telephone numbers, and so on. A careful examination led to the discovery of a whole series of links with people working in ministries or government departments. Springhall was not always successful in getting information from these sources, but he is known to have received secret documents from an army officer. This officer, Captain Ormond Leyton Uren, was sentenced to seven years' hard labour after a court-martial. Investigations continue into a series of other cases.

8. At the time of his arrest, Springhall was national organiser of the Communist Party and a member of its Central Committee. He was thus a leading Party fig-

ure and significant public figure. It seems very strange that a leading official should engage in espionage and give the counter-intelligence service reason to suspect the entire Party of being similarly involved, although it is also known that the Party was unaware of Springhall's activities. It issued a statement to that effect immediately after his arrest. Although there may be a element of truth in what it said, the counter-intelligence service is aware that the Party undertakes espionage through its own organisation; moreover, the material in which the Party is interested is no different from that sought by Springhall.

9. Interrogations showed that Springhall used different techniques. With Miss Sheehan he played on her desire for a swift end to the war, telling her that this would come about if the Russians had details of the files passing through her hands. It was different with Uren, since he himself expressed the desire to help to a Communist friend who introduced him to Springhall. Uren was a fervent believer in Communism, and all Springhall had to do was to stress his own leading position in the Party and ask what he wanted. Uren was most anxious to do whatever he could to demonstrate to Springhall his total loyalty to the Party and his complete trust in Springhall.

In another case of which we are aware Springhall likewise counted on meeting with the same fanatical degree of trust and asked another contact straight out to pass on secret information. As far as we are aware, however, he received nothing.

10. Both Uren and the person mentioned above were introduced to Springhall by the same acquaintance. It is hard to be sure, but in the final analysis it is quite possible that this person introduced them to Springhall without malice aforethought.

11. Springhall always visited Sheehan at her flat. This did not give rise to any suspicion, since he was a fairly frequent visitor. His meetings with Captain Uren, however, were always on the street. The captain was always in civilian clothes. At each meeting they agreed when and how they would next get together.

12. Middle-class Communist sympathisers, some of whom kept their Party membership secret, were fertile ground for Springhall. Some of his initially unpromising connections turned out to be very important. Some of these were civil servants. Only a few of those who came into contact with Springhall knew of his Communist background.

13. The intelligence obtained by Springhall covered many areas. In one case it related to a new weapon, an invention of undoubted value. (We also possess other confirmation of Springhall's interest in new weapons.) In yet another instance he was mainly concerned with issues that could have direct value only to the enemy. We do not suggest that either Springhall or the CP obtained intelligence in order to pass it on to the enemy. It is more likely that both were so obsessed with spying for its own sake that they could not resist the temptation to obtain secret intelligence from official sources whether or not it had any value for them. Other examples support this conclusion.

In addition the authorities are aware that the CP greatly values any intelligence that relates to the future policy of the government or future military plans, such as, for example, the question of a Second Front. In this connection, it is interesting to note that Springhall made a point of asking Captain Uren if he knew anything of future military plans or the Second Front.

6. Hans Christian Pieck

1. Study of this case reveals the varied tradecraft and wealth of financial resources of the NKVD, one of the Soviet intelligence organisations whose task it is to obtain official secrets of other countries. This case is an example of one of the most serious leaks of information from the Communications Department of the Foreign Office. It ended with the arrest and conviction of an employee of this department under the Official Secrets Act.

2. The case involves Hans Christian Pieck, a Dane of good family and an artist by profession, who came to the notice of the intelligence service in 1930 and again in 1935 as a Communist.

3. In 1929, Pieck visited Moscow and was recruited as a Soviet intelligence agent with the special task of penetrating the British Foreign Office. Pretending to be an artist, he was sent to Geneva. He spent two and a half years there, carefully but with some success creating the image that he was a supporter of British government policy. He gained the confidence of the British vice consul, who subsequently introduced him to a Foreign Office coding clerk. The latter was married to the vice consul's adopted daughter, and through the couple Pieck met a number of other members of the Geneva coding-department staff. Pieck is believed to have spent some £20,000 of OGPU funds on his preparatory work during the two and a half years he was in Geneva.

4. At the beginning of 1935, Pieck recruited an inside agent in the Foreign Office and moved to London, where, through the son-in-law of the British vice consul in Geneva, he got to know an Englishman, with whom he set up a business in Buckingham Gate.

5. Here Pieck set up a darkroom for photographing documents obtained from his agent inside the Foreign Office. Through 1935–36 FO telegrams and documents were regularly photographed. The GPU then obviously became aware of the investigations being undertaken by SIS and ordered Pieck to stop his 'work' and hand over his responsibilities to 'Peter'.

6. Peter worked in the same way as Pieck right up to 1937, when, as part of the purge of Trotskyites, he was recalled to Moscow and evidently shot. Pieck also fell into disfavour for refusing to liquidate a Soviet agent in Switzerland named Reiss, who was nonetheless later shot by another GPU agent.

7. Pieck and Peter were run by the two main Soviet *rezidents* in Europe, one of whom—name unknown—passed them the GPU's instructions, and the other, who used the pseudonym Walter, paid them. Walter was also recalled to Moscow

during the purge but escaped to France and later to the USA. His name was Krivitsky, and he wrote *I Was Stalin's Agent*.

8. In relation to the agent inside the Foreign Office referred to above, it is interesting to note that Pieck invented the story that the agent had a senior position in the FO. He carefully crafted details of the man's personal life, habits and interests. He set up Helen Wilkie in a business in west London. She was the cutout between the agent and Pieck, who had constructed the legend so as to confuse the British authorities; in fact, at a certain point in the investigation of the case, this had exactly the result Pieck had intended.

9. In 1939, Pieck's partner (see Para. 4) told the police that when working with Pieck at 34A Buckingham Gate, he had stumbled across the darkroom and that Pieck's wife had claimed that her husband was getting documents from friends in the FO's Communications Department.

10. The partner stated that one of these friends was a coding clerk, whose name he did not know but whom Pieck met quite often, especially during the Brussels conference, when he was one of two coding clerks attached to the British delegation. Both these men were easily identified; one of them, J.H. King, had been named by Krivitsky in his statement to the British ambassador in Washington as a Soviet agent working in the FO Communications Department.

11. At first sight there was nothing in King's past to cause concern. He was nevertheless immediately sent on sick leave on health grounds and put under observation. His suspicions were not aroused.

12. Observation revealed that King visited Helen Wilkie regularly; she lived at 218 Hamlet Gardens, Ravenscourt Park, W6. This address matched one in Pieck's telephone book, thus establishing that King and Pieck were connected.

13. Searches of Wilkie's flat and her office safe gave us a large number of papers, letters, diaries, and so on, that demonstrated her connection with Pieck, King and other members of the Communications Department staff. Also found in the safe were £1,300 in notes, which she stated belonged to King, and twenty-one copies of Foreign Office documents from the period 1922–24.

14. King subsequently stated that from 1935 to 1937 he received from Pieck and Peter some £2,000 in payment for copies of secret telegrams received from embassies and consulates abroad and decoded in the FO's Communications Department. Cheques found in Wilkie's safe belonged to Pieck and were his personal savings; he was also found to have had a bank credit balance of some £2,000 which was in King's name. Some of this money had been handed to Paul Hardt, alias Peter, whose role in this case was broadly similar to that of King. Hardt left the UK hurriedly, and intense efforts to trace him proved unsuccessful. It appears he, too, was killed (see Para. 6).

15. Pieck's present whereabouts are unknown, and the latest information we have on him dates from 1940. In May of that year he was working as a representative of the Danish Ministry of the Economy at a trade fair in Paris.

The following conclusions can be drawn:

The NKVD has great persistence and skill.

Despite the fact that the police employ effective preventive measures, these are still not sufficient to neutralise or prevent agent penetration, especially if the preparatory work is carried out overseas.

This example demonstrates the danger of complacency in the implementation of disciplinary measures in government organisations and underscores that someone's dissolute personal lifestyle cannot be seen as something distinct from their official life.

April 1944

34   *Peter Loxley's Letter to Colonel Vivian, November 1944*

TOP SECRET AND PERSONAL
Foreign Office
20 October 1943

My Dear Vivian,

Thank you for your letter DCCS 65/1 of 13 October regarding the illegal activity of the Communist movement overseas.

We have no objection to, and indeed see significant benefit in, the organisation you propose on the condition that matters are handled with the necessary care and that you do nothing directly in the USSR (notwithstanding Soviet espionage in our own country). Our view is that we certainly have to know what the Soviet government is doing through auxiliary organisations such as the Communist Parties abroad and what special game they are playing in Mexico, Cuba, etc. Incidentally, Para. 3 of the memorandum enclosed with your letter contains SHVERNIK's suggestion to Sir [Walter] Citrine in Moscow and again at the Southport Congress regarding close co-operation with workers and trade union organisations in Latin America.

We have to assume as a general matter that the NKVD and other Soviet organisations that pursue secret goals and carry out clandestine activity which completely contradicts the declared policy of the USSR but which has the latter's blessing are hardly behaving in a way that is to our advantage.

It seems to us that your task is this—to find out as much as possible about the aims and activity of the NKVD and other Soviet organisations abroad—and that this can be done without any risk whatever by penetrating foreign Communist Parties outside the USSR.

The Russians will simply take us for fools if we do not exploit these opportunities, all the more since it is quite evident that they have an extensive network of agents in England.

There is one omission in the memorandum you enclosed to which we should like to draw your attention. This is principally the Communist problem in the Balkans and other occupied territories. It would be of great benefit to us to have somewhat deeper knowledge of whether the Communist organisations operating in those countries have put their roots down in the local population and the extent to which they support Moscow. This relates at present to Yugoslavia and Greece.

In this connection I enclose a copy of the most recent top-secret and personal cable from the foreign secretary to the prime minister. A similar issue also obtains in France, as was evident in the occupation of Corsica (see Makins's message from Algiers, no. 33 of 27 September, a copy of which I also attach).

I assume that you are in close touch with Hollis at MI5 on all the foregoing. I see him from time to time, and we have spoken on several occasions about Springhall and other issues affecting our country.

We need, of course, to keep a close eye on the British Communist Party, and under no circumstances will the Foreign Office stand in the way if counter-intelligence wishes to take measures against Communist agents in our country.

Sincerely,

Loxley

PART IV

NKVD Reports

Among the many remarkable items declassified and released in Moscow was a batch of files prepared by senior members of the NKVD's Third Department, which was the section responsible for First Chief Directorate operations in England, directly supervising the activities of the *rezident* in London. The evidence suggests that high-grade information came on stream in the later part of 1940, when Anatoli V. Gorsky returned to the Soviet Embassy under diplomatic cover to rebuild the organisation he had been ordered to abandon in February by Lavrenti Beria on the entirely mistaken grounds that the local network had been compromised by MI5. In fact, this suspicion was completely unjustified and little more than a manifestation of the NKVD's lethal paranoia, which not only was prevalent but had accounted for the lives of most professionals with intelligence experience outside the Soviet Union.

Gorsky's two main agents in 1940 were Guy Burgess, who was working for the embryonic Special Operations Executive while simultaneously running a couple of agents for MI5, and Anthony Blunt, who joined MI5's B Division after Dunkirk on the recommendation of Lord Rothschild and gained immediate access to the famed Security Service Registry. Thereafter he seems to have copied whatever files he was requested to, and there can be little doubt that he had a direct hand in copying the four documents contained in the pages that follow.

The first among these documents is a summary of the NKVD's October 1940 interrogation of Aleksandr S. Nelidov, a long-term SIS source who was probably betrayed by Anthony Blunt. When the art historian joined MI5 in May 1940, transferring from the Field Security Police after the Dunkirk debacle, he lost no time in pillaging the Registry for information that would prove his bona-fides to his NKVD controllers. One of the first items he passed on was information about a highly successful Soviet agent recruited years earlier by the legendary SIS professional Harold Gibson. Although in the Registry documents a weak attempt was made to protect the source with a code name, there was sufficient collateral data for the ruthless NKVD investigators to narrow the field of suspects, and according to the file released for publication in this volume, it was at this time that they extracted a confession from Nelidov.

The fact that 'Gibby's spy' had been arrested unexpectedly in Moscow was the first indication that the Soviets had developed a successful organisation in London with access to some of SIS's most vital secrets, but the signs had been ignored and misinterpreted, and it was only decades later that Peter Wright charged Blunt with having tipped off his contacts and thus sent Gibby's spy to his death. Reluctantly, Blunt had admitted his guilt, observing merely that the agent had been a professional and had known the risks he had run in working for Gibson. His attitude, in acknowledging that the Russian's fate had been little more than an occupational hazard, had revolted the molehunter and had served to demonstrate the very human dimension to Blunt's brand of treachery. In reality, unknown to either Wright or Blunt, Nelidov committed suicide in 1942, having confessed to two decades of collaboration with SIS.

The documents reproduced here represent the first indication of Nelidov's fate. He had fled to Turkey after the Russian Civil War and had become a skilled agent handler for SIS, operating across much of eastern Europe between 1922 and 1927. Nelidov then seems to have switched to working for the Germans, but in 1933 he was arrested by the Nazis and spent the next five years in a concentration camp. Upon his release he seems to have been in touch with SIS and to have learned something of the origins of the famous Zinoviev letter, or at least enough to try and interest a German publisher. (Supposedly a directive written to the Communist Party of Great Britain to encourage sedition in the British army, Grigorii Zinoviev's letter, once disclosed, was thought to have made a significant contribution to the Labour Party's defeat in the general election of 1924.) However, Nelidov's attempt failed, and he was in touch with the Americans when he was caught in Riga and deported to Moscow.

Nelidov's confession offers a fascinating glimpse into how the 'great game' was played in Asia Minor, and as a catalogue of British clandestine activities, it must have confirmed the worst fears of the NKVD's counter-intelligence experts, who saw SIS's apparently ubiquitous, nefarious hand behind every perfidy.

35 Confession of the SIS Agent Aleksandr S. Nelidov

In November 1917, I joined General Alekseev's volunteer army in Rostov on the Don, in Kornilov's [illegible]. After the so-called Kornilov campaign, i.e. the retreat to Ekaterinodar, I was attached to army headquarters as an officer for assignments with the Operations Section.

After the elimination of Denikin's army, I was detailed for duty with the commander of the Georgian units, General Artemiladze, to organise signals and supplies for General Fostikov's detachments, which were withdrawing to the

Batalpashinskii area. After the defeat of Wrangel's army in the Crimea, I worked at the headquarters of the Georgian Popular Guard, as aide-de-camp in the Service Corps. In the spring of 1921, I was evacuated to Constantinople, where, thanks to my acquaintance with members of the former English-French mission, I obtained a post in the Press Department of the British Secret Service. From there I was transferred to the Intelligence Department. In July 1921, I was sent to General Carr in London (chief of GHQ's Russian Department). In the same month I was sent to Boris Savinkov's organisation in Warsaw together with Captain Reilly.

Meanwhile, the British SIS was preparing an uprising in the Minsk region, where Savinkov's detachments were meant to operate. After an unsuccessful action in the Igumun region, I returned to London together with Boris Savinkov and Captain Reilly, and there I took part in meetings between Deterding, Churchill and Savinkov. In August, I returned to Constantinople with the special task of organising intelligence in the oil-drilling area (Baku, Groznii, Maikop). At that time, the British SIS in Constantinople was headed by Vice Consul Rogers and his assistant Christie (a Georgian by origin who had been given British citizenship).

The work of the British SIS at that time was organised as follows:

1. Monitoring the press, especially newspapers of the northern Caucasus and Transcaucasia
2. Questioning passengers arriving on steamers from Batum
3. Collecting information from sailors of the French Messengeries Maritimes and the Italian Lloyd Triestano steamer companies, which at that time held a monopoly over the Constantinople-Batum route
4. Dispatching special agents, mainly Caucasians who spoke Persian and had Persian passports
5. Dispatching special agents over the Turkish and Persian borders
6. Recruiting agents from among foreign trade officials
7. Dispatching special Turkish feluccas on various routes in the Black Sea

The most help in finding agents came from Mr Khoshtariia, a former owner of timber concessions in Persia. The entire Black Sea area was subdivided as follows: Odessa and Sevastopol were under observation from Varna, where Captain Hill was stationed. Captain Sinclair was responsible for the area from Sevastopol to Novorossisk. The Novorossisk-Tuapse region was covered by Captain HAG. The area Tuapse-Sukhum was observed by Gibson, the area Sukhum-Batum by Captain Roberts. All the captains mentioned were based in Constantinople. The general supervision of all areas was in the hands of Rogers and Christie. A support station was established in Trapezunde, run by Lieutenant Law. I was under the direct command of Rogers but also had to send information directly to Deterding. At this time, oil was the most important issue for the British SIS. In the spring of 1922, we had to establish the exact state of the oil wells and reserves in

Baku, Groznii and Maikop, the state of the Baku-Batum pipeline and the position regarding movement of oil by sea and rail.

My personal group of agents consisted of the following people:

1. The permanent Batum resident, Adzhari Mustafa. He had worked with the Adzharian activist Kuskin-Zade, who was killed by the Georgians after the British left Batum, and handed over to the Georgians. Living permanently in Batum and being very popular among the Adzharis, Mustafa was someone who could very easily find people to send to Baku, Groznii and Maikop. Communication with Mustafa was via Bordani, an engineer on a Lloyd Triestano steamer. Rogers trusted Mustafa so much that he allowed very large sums of money to be sent to him. In October 1921 Mustafa was sent about 10,000 Turkish lira.

2. The second most active agent was Khasan Karamaflei, born and raised in Batum, with a good knowledge of Russian, Persian and Turkish. He had a Persian passport and went to Batum-Baku under the cover of a trader.

3. Gabriel Khachaturov, formerly a lawyer in Groznii who left for Turkey after the revolution. He obtained information on the state of the oil industry from the Foreign Trade Office and official Soviet data published in the Soviet press.

   In 1921 and 1922, his information was the only means of checking intelligence data, since at that time it was very difficult to get newspapers from Baku, Groznii and Maikop in Constantinople.

4. We were in constant communication with Dzhakeli, the owner of a freight agency. At the time he was exporting manganese and was able to obtain information on the rail transport situation in Poti and Batum.

5. We also were in constant communication with [redacted]. As the owner of a business that was trading with the Caucasus, he often visited Tiflis and was able to give information on transport and the oil industry.

In 1921 and 1922 these were our principal assets for information on the oil industry. We also obtained information from other people who had managed to leave the Soviet Union, and bought a certain amount from a translator working for the French intelligence service named Delimarskii.

About a month before the Genoa conference, Captain Hill, who was dismissed from his work in Varna at that time, was sent to Batum and Groznii.

During the time of the Genoa conference, Captain Hill and I were called to Genoa to report to Deterding on this question.

While Lloyd-George was preparing for the Genoa conference, which a Soviet delegation was meant to attend, the British SIS tried to use the opportunity for a terrorist act. To this aim, Captain Reilly, Savinkov and Elmvengram received 100,000 francs from the Secret Service and 50,000 from Gustav Nobel, the industrialist who then lived permanently in Paris.

The first attempt was meant to be organised in the Berlin railway station. The head of station for the British Secret Service in Berlin, Vladimir Orlov, a former investigator of especially important matters at General Headquarters during the war of 1914–17, undertook to carry out the plan. Nothing came of this venture, owing to the vigilance of the Berlin police, who were very careful about giving out admission passes to the railway station. The arrival of Savinkov in Genoa was immediately discovered by the Italian police; he was arrested and expelled from Italy at once.

After the Genoa conference, the British SIS, infuriated by the Rapallo agreement, ordered the Constantinople station to do more active work, i.e. to organise acts of sabotage in Baku and Groznii.

Mustafa was to get in touch with insurgent units operating in Transcaucasia. The English were especially interested in Cholokaev's unit. Mustafa was also given the task of setting up small sabotage squads who were to blow up bridges and oil tanks. Mustafa was also told to organise a gang in the area of the Chiatur manganese mines. Arms for this were to be obtained from the British staff of the Constantinople occupation forces and then brought to the Trapezunde area by torpedo boat, where they were to be transferred onto Turkish feluccas, which would bring them to the locations specified by Mustafa. The British Embassy's interpreter, [Wilfred "Biffy"] Dunderdale, and Khasan Karamaflei were sent to Trapezunde to hire feluccas. Captain Sinclair was sent to Tehran to organise a gang in the Baku region.

Arthur Lander, the Amstrong-Vickers representative in Constantinople, undertook to supply the Secret Service with the necessary automatic pistols. The arms were transferred in small quantities. I took part in these meetings personally and was informed about all preparations. In July 1922, I was called to London to see Deterding. He expressed his dissatisfaction at the lack of activity by the sabotage groups and demanded that I go to Munich immediately and enter into negotiations with the Ukrainian Hetman Poltavets about attempts to organise similar sabotage groups in the Ukraine. During personal negotiations with Poltavets, it became clear that the only way to bring arms into the Ukraine was from the Romanian border, for which he needed the co-operation of the Siguranza (Romanian secret police). Poltavets also expressed the wish to speak to Deterding personally. A meeting was arranged in Paris, where Deterding gave Poltavets a trial advance of 30,000 francs. At the same time, he supplied Petliurov's organisation in Lvov with money via Captain Maclauren, the head of the British SIS in Warsaw. I personally brought £1,500 to Maclauren to give to Petliurov's people and then returned to Constantinople.

In November 1922 subsidies for sabotage groups were stopped, since London was not satisfied with their activities. In London they saw clearly that the hopes for an insurrection in the Cossack regions and in the Caucasus had failed, and therefore they decided to move on to new tactics.

The decision was made to create a large unit on the Persian-Turkestan border. The Constantinople station was ordered to begin recruiting soldiers and officers, mainly among the mountain peoples and the Georgians. With this object I went to Serbia, Bulgaria and Greece. Recruitment was stopped unexpectedly because Captain Sinclair in Tehran had successfully concluded negotiations with Khan Iumudskii, who undertook to organise a unit made up of local tribes from the region of the border with Turkestan.

I was sent to London once more. At that time, negotiations were held there with representatives of Petliurov's organisation in order to probe the ground in Hetman Skoropadski's circles on the possibility of collaboration with Petliurov's organisation. In Berlin, I conducted negotiations with Hetman Korostovets's secretary. The Hetmen categorically refused to collaborate with Petliurov's people but agreed to carry out tasks for the British SIS. From that time onwards, Korostovets kept in touch with the head of the British SIS via Captain Foley.

I returned to Constantinople, where I was moved to the Press Department, since observation of the oil industry had been transferred to the Tehran post. My agents were transferred to Captain Roberts, who used them for military intelligence.

A. Nelidov

27 August 1940

After the defeat of the Greek army in Asia Minor, the British SIS was ordered to abolish its Russian Department and to transfer all officers to Mossul. Only Rogers, Gibson and, as their consultant, the former Russian officer Vladimir Rykovskii remained in Constantinople. In Mossul, our group was responsible for the formation of Sheik Asen's units for actions against the Kemalists. Colonel Laurence directed all preparations. I stayed in Mossul for about six months and then was sent back to Constantinople. At the time, London was trying to organise Polish–Romanian action against the Soviet Union. I was sent to General Staff Colonel Pastia, the Romanian military attaché in Constantinople, to exchange information on the Romanian General Staff. Gibson was ordered to go to Bucharest and carry out intelligence work jointly with the Romanian colonel Tudosiu.

In Kishinev, an Anglo-Romanian intelligence post was set up, which was headed personally by Colonel Tudosiu. The direction and recruitment of agents was in the hands of Alexander Flemer, permanent resident of Kishinev and a German colonist. Since the Romanian–Soviet border was closed, agents crossed illegally. At that time I managed to recruit the Serb engineer Perich, who made several trips to Sevastopol and brought back information about the state of the Soviet navy and the work of the Nikolaev shipyards.

Meanwhile, Deterding was trying to draw the Germans into participating in the intended operations and to hold negotiations with General Hoffman. Two or three times I personally had to bring intelligence data from the Bucharest and Constantinople stations to Munich, where I handed them over to Lieutenant von Lessow, who gave them to Hoffman. On Deterding's instructions, Hoffman was also given intelligence data from Warsaw by Captain Maclauren, i.e. data from the Field General Staff and the British SIS station.

The negotiations with Hoffman were fruitless, since he made relaxation of the Versailles Treaty an indispensable condition, and Deterding, notwithstanding his connections, could not obtain agreement to this in Paris. In any event, the Polish and Romanian General Staffs thought public opinion was insufficiently prepared for such an operation.

London gave an order for the fabrication of false documents, leaflets, propaganda brochures and a whole series of other documents calculated to incense the public by scaring peace-loving bourgeois citizens with the 'Red Menace'.

The only success was the famous Zinoviev letter, all evidence about the preparation of which (documentary evidence) is held by the head of the British SIS at Riga, Vice Consul Hall.

Meanwhile, a series of proclamations in English were printed in Warsaw, calling on English sailors and dockers to strike, etc. Proclamations in Polish, Belorussian and Ukrainian inciting the population to riots and other disturbances were also fabricated there. Similar documents were, of course, produced in Bucharest, Constantinople and Athens. Attempts were made to frighten the Turks with the 'Red Menace', but they realised very quickly where these documents were coming from.

Specific orders also came from London. For example, we urgently had to forge a purported Soviet statement in the Monroe Doctrine and a supposed Soviet degree mandating obligatory deductions from Russian workers' salaries to support of striking English miners.

The forgeries did not have any success, since a lot of mistakes were allowed to slip through, and both the statement and the decree contained words spelled in the pre-revolutionary alphabet.

One of the copies fell into the hands of an English Labour MP, together with [Cogger's] evidence, and that story was very difficult to suppress.

Forgery 'laboratories' were set up at every British SIS station. In Constantinople, we merely gave instructions for what we needed; the texts were written by the lawyer Lysakovskii, and the typographical or lithographic work was done by the artist Tishko. When the text had to be in English, it was written by Captain Roberts or by Dunderdale.

A similar laboratory was run in Berlin by the head of station there, the British SIS man Vladimir Orlov. This did not succeed in frightening the Germans, however, since they quickly understood what was going on. Orlov was thoroughly compromised and dismissed from the Service.

Since there had been too many scandals about these forgeries, London ordered the 'laboratories' to be closed. Such forgeries were made in two or three copies and usually shown only to prominent figures. On rare occasions they were given to the press.

[Note:] The 'Arcos' case was prepared over a very long time but failed through the obstinacy of the Metropolitan Police, who assured the Secret Service that they could certainly find 'real' documents.

After this scandal, forgery operations were stopped. But agents continued to produce forgeries themselves and to supply their own intelligence services with them, and at that point London had to give the order not to buy any documents. The London 'laboratory' directed by Sir James Macleay continued operations, but the documents were no longer made public. Instead, they were given only to those people who had to be influenced in one way or another. The Berlin 'laboratory' mainly produced false instructions by the GPU to its departments abroad, signed by Triliser. The defector Bessedovsky also took part in the production of forgeries. In the first place, on orders from London he tried to prove the authenticity of Zinoviev's letter in his memoirs. Second, he issued a series of circular letters with the letterhead INO—which was supposed to mean the Foreign Department of the GPU. Third, he produced a series of documents in the 1930s testifying that Hitler's organisations were receiving money from Moscow.

The documents were published in a Berlin newspaper edited by Doctor Nuschke, but without success.

The documents were bought from Bessedovsky, but not because anyone believed in their authenticity. The British Foreign Service used Bessedovsky's name as a shield against possible suspicion.

Already in 1926, London conceived the idea of undermining the faith of Soviet citizens in the chervonets [a new currency unit] by issuing false chervontsy and sending them to Russia by courier. All stations were asked about the possibility of recruiting relevant specialists, people who would be willing for their names to be used to 'cover' the whole affair if it failed. In Constantinople, no specialists could be found. Bucharest and Warsaw also replied in the negative. The Berlin station undertook to organise this matter through an agent in Germany named Bell. He found a series of Germans who agreed to allow their names to be used as cover. Bell's mistake was that, besides Germans, he involved two Georgians in this affair. (I do not remember their names, but they all appeared in the Berlin trial.) When the chervontsy were ready, Bell divided them among the members of the group for safekeeping. One of the Georgians, who needed money, pawned his chervontsy with a wealthy German. The chervontsy were not got out of pawn in time. The German, needing money, decided to exchange part of the pawned chervontsy. At the bank they very quickly discovered the forgery, and all participants were put in the dock. If the prosecution had not suppressed this affair, the names of the initiators would be known. The court acquitted the accused, sentencing only the Georgian. Although the forged chervontsy were confiscated by the police, Bell managed to send some to the Soviet Union.

Bell was killed in 1933, after the Nazis came to power, when it was discovered that he had informed the German police as well as the British about Hitler's preparations in case Schleicher did not leave the post of *Reichskanzler* but mobilised the Reichswehr. After this scandal, the British SIS did not abandon the operation but decided instead to take it up again somewhere else. Once more, orders were given to the stations, and this time Gibson organised production in Romania. There were two consignments from Constantinople (as I was told by Dunderdale in 1928), but apparently these operations were not successful, since it was too difficult to get the money into the Soviet Union.

What things were like on the Romanian border I cannot say, but the only people through whom Gibson could carry out this affair were Colonel Tudosiu and Flemer.

According to Captain Maclauren, operations involving forged money were very easily run across the Polish border thanks to the agents of Petliurov's organisation.

Whether there were similar operations from the Baltic countries, I cannot say definitely, but I think there were, since a categorical order about setting up special agents as distributors was given to all SIS stations.

In June 1926 the reorganisation of the British SIS began. Colonel Thomson arrived in Athens, and all intelligence stations in the Balkans and in Turkey were subordinated to him. Meanwhile, Colonel Thomson began to create his own network of agents.

Agents' salaries were significantly reduced. Thus, until 1926, £100 plus travel expenses were paid for a trip from Batum to Baku. If material was brought back, the agent was paid extra. From 1926 on, payment for the same trip was only £50. The Control Commission (English-French-Italian) no longer existed, and the questioning of passengers became impossible. Captain Hill and X-2 were dismissed. I was transferred to the Egyptian Department, where I was to set up a network of agents for intelligence work against the former Egyptian khedive, Abbas Helmy, whose headquarters were in Constantinople.

The activity of the khedive greatly worried the English. His agents were supposed to have killed Sir Lee Stack, the British chief of staff in Egypt. London was convinced that the Soviet Union would enter this game and support the Khedivites in Egypt just as it supported the Kemalists.

There was no difficulty in finding agents. The former officers of the khedive's entourage were very communicative. Some of them had girlfriends among the local Greeks. But the information was of little value in that the agents did not manage to find even a trace of links between the Khedivites and the Soviet Embassy.

Simultaneously, a new order came from London, to obtain, at any cost, the text of the Soviet-Turkish treaty. This order was given to all agents, and the Turkish police very soon found out about it.

Accusations began. Turkish intelligence, relying on information obtained by questioning passengers arriving from the Soviet Union and from their own agents instead of the one we gave them, stopped liaising with us, alleging that we were engaged in espionage on Turkey.

At roughly the same period, the time given by the Turks to holders of so-called Nanssen [refugee] passports to remain on Turkish territory ran out. We had to either take on Turkish citizenship or leave the country. I moved to Berlin.

Our attempts at deceiving the Soviet intelligence service in Constantinople also need to be included in an account of my work for the British SIS. After the evacuation of Constantinople by the Allies and the arrival of the Kemalites, a Soviet repatriation commission and a Soviet consulate were set up in the city. Our agent Maikov managed to get in touch with the head of Soviet intelligence, Borisov. He was given completely correct information about the work of French intelligence and incorrect information about the work of the British. On instructions from London, incorrect information about the work of the Mussavatists in Azerbaijan was also given. Soviet intelligence very quickly figured out that they had been passed forgeries, and the connection was broken off. For this, too, I myself take full responsibility, since Maikov did not know that the material was forged.

I went from Constantinople to Berlin in order to replace Captain Ellis, who was transferred to Switzerland for work with the League of Nations. I was told from London that Soviet intelligence in Berlin was very strong and that I had to try and penetrate it. On the way to Berlin, I stopped in Vienna, where I met the head of Soviet intelligence, Müller, and offered him material. The material was entirely correct, about the preparation of an anti-Soviet action in Romania. As a condition of our further collaboration, I asked that he put me in touch with someone in Berlin. He agreed to my proposal, took my Berlin address and promised to send an agent to me for communication.

After I had arrived in Berlin and taken over from Captain Ellis, I realised that there was no material at all that might be used to interest Soviet intelligence. After conferring with Ellis, we decided to give information about plans for the future work of English intelligence and a cipher telegram supposedly sent by our station to Warsaw.

After a few days, a certain Bachman came to see me and took the material. We arranged to meet the following day.

The next day Bachman returned the telegram to me with a smile, declaring that no such message had ever been sent [to] Berlin. Our acquaintance finished with that, and I never saw Bachman again. Naturally, I carry full responsibility for this case, since I could easily have refused to carry out this assignment.

When I told Colonel Thomson, who came to Berlin shortly afterwards, about this case, he did not believe my report, since to establish whether a telegram had been sent or not while not in one's own country really took a great deal of skill.

After this I did not make any other attempts of this kind and did not come across representatives of Soviet intelligence until June 1933. Captain Ellis's work was not at all difficult. His main job had been to collect material about the Soviet Union from German sources in exchange for British information or for payments. His secondary task was to keep an eye on Indian students in Germany, for which he relied exclusively on the evidence of the German police.

Ellis had established connections. He introduced me to Kommissar Müller of the Fremdenamt (the police responsible for foreigners) and to Roy Weizel from the Political Police.

Both exchanged material with me with the permission of Vize-Polizeipräsident Weiss. We also exchanged information about the questions that we were interested in. Obviously, Weizel was a cover for German intelligence, since the police could have had no interest in our information about Russia and could not have given any. This connection was, of course, not official, although it was kept up with permission from above. Official connections between Scotland Yard and the Berlin Police Presidium were maintained by Vice Consul Foley.

There was an agreement between London and Berlin according to which the two police forces warned each other of the arrival of English Communists in Berlin and German Communists in London. At the same time, I was working with the political editor of the *Times*, Dr Wilson, and also with the correspondent of the *Daily Telegraph* in Berlin, Dr Wilcox.

My Personal Network of Agents in London

At the time of the preparation of the Schleicher–Papen affair, Bredow suggested that I set up a network of agents in London in order to find out about attitudes to Germany in the Foreign Office, at the General Staff Headquarters, in the Admiralty and also in the intelligence services of these institutions.

For this objective, I used the following people.

1. Captain George Hill had been dismissed by Seymour from the Secret Service on charges of having appropriated sums entrusted to him by Bruce Lockhart. Hill lived permanently in London. He needed money, his only income being as a freelance writer. He had written a book about the Soviet Union, which had not been a success. His articles were rarely accepted by the newspapers, and pay for them was small. He was bitter about everything and everybody. I asked him to help me find out about prevalent 'feelings' towards Germany in the Foreign Office and the Secret Service. He accepted eagerly. For £150 a month, he informed us about the work of the Foreign Office and the Secret Service. His work was reliable, and the RWM [Reichswehrministerium] raised his salary to £200. He sent us the information weekly with the help of special couriers that the RWM put at his disposal in my name.

2. Captain Francis, who had a post at the Secret Service Registry, was giving me information about Germany. From him we received (not always) the ambassador's and Foley's reports about the situation in Germany. Francis received £20 monthly in pay. When he sent an ambassador's report, his pay reached as much as £350 (each report—photograph—paid £100 or £50, depending on the content).

3. Villers, Jim, aide-de-camp to the military attaché in Berlin until January 1933, when he was transferred to the War Office's Department for Military Missions Abroad. He informed me about attitudes in the German Embassy and about

the military attaché's reports to London. He received £100 monthly during his time in Berlin and from £150 to £200 during his time in London. His information from London was considerably wider. The connection with him was kept up through the same courier as was used with Hill. Immediately before my arrest this connection was broken off.

24 October 1940
A. Nelidov

My Personal Network of Agents in London (continued)

The Villers collaboration did not enable us to obtain information about the attitudes of the leading figures in the War Office and the Imperial General Staff. He told us which questions the military attaché was asked from London, what he reported to London and also about attitudes in the embassy. It was known in the RWM that the head of the French military mission in Prague, General Fauché (to all intents and purposes the head of the Czech General Staff), was waging a bitter campaign against the RWM in London on the basis of Czech intelligence information, with the help of the Czech military attaché in London as well as the Czech ambassador himself.

The RWM felt it indispensable to get information about prevailing attitudes in the War Office and the Admiralty, since the influence of these two bodies in the Cabinet was very strong. At the RWM, they used to say that London was not Paris, where the military was put down by the politicians; in London the Admiralty had a very strong influence on foreign policy.

It was necessary to look for informers in these two bodies; trying to find traitors in London is always rather dangerous and for me personally was almost impossible.

One false step, in the sense of choosing the wrong person to approach about possible collaboration, and I would have been arrested immediately by Scotland Yard. In London they knew perfectly well where I was working, but on the basis of my continued visits to Deterding, everyone was convinced that I was still working for the Germans in the Russian Department.

My meetings with Hill and Francis could not arouse suspicion, since it was thought natural for people who had worked together for six years to meet.

I knew hardly anyone in the War Office and the Admiralty. The RWM was against making frequent appeals to Deterding for information on the prevailing attitudes in these bodies, since Bredow had reasons to want this channel used for different objectives.

As a consequence of all this, I decided to ask for the help of the former Russian émigré Boris MENSHIKOV, who had been naturalised in England. He was working for small newspapers and as a consultant on Russian questions for the political editor of the *Times*, Dr Williams, through whom I had met him back in 1927. Menshikov knew many people in London, and his income was very small.

Menshikov accepted my proposal but declared that he would work only as an informer on the attitudes of the War Office and the Admiralty towards the Nazis and the RWM. He would not give any information on other questions concerned with the set-up and organisation of the intelligence services of these institutions. I had to accept, since I could not find anyone else. Besides, the RWM at that moment was interested mainly in information on the prevailing attitudes. Menshikov spent a month organising this work. In the War Office, he enlisted the services of a civil servant called Greenwood and in the Admiralty those of a Mr Winter, who worked in the deciphering department there.

German intelligence tradecraft requires that an officer in charge of investigating an institution has to meet his informants at least once. Menshikov introduced me to these people without telling them that he was working for me.

I asked Bredow to establish the identity of these people. After verification, it turned out that Menshikov's information about the work of these people in the institutions we were targetting was correct. Greenwood worked in the War Office, in the minister's office. Winter worked in the deciphering department of the Admiralty. Both were trusted by their employers. Over the whole period of the operation, Menshikov's, Greenwood's and Winter's information was always correct, interesting and, most important, timely, which allowed the RWM to take certain measures aimed at achieving a fundamental change of attitudes in these institutions. They were paid £100 a month. After three months, these people expanded the scale of their work on their own accord, without any pressure from the RWM. They started giving information about the reports of military attachés and naval attachés in other countries, and also about the reports of the Military and Naval Intelligence services on Germany and on other countries.

At that time their pay was raised to £200.

In order to keep an eye on the circles surrounding the salons of Princess Vyazemskaia and Princess Obolenskaya, the same Menshikov found me two young ladies: Miss Olsbury and Miss Greves. I introduced them to the salons run by these ladies, who were the most zealous supporters and propagandists of Rosenberg's racist doctrines in London.

These two young ladies regularly informed Menshikov about everything that went on in these salons and about all the people from government circles who attended them.

All information about the work of these salons was given to von Balke and Gagarin, who tried to neutralise its effects with the help of the salon run by Deterding's wife.

Olsbury and Greves received £50 a month.

All these people worked uninterruptedly until 1933, when, in February, Bredow was forced to leave the ministry.

On leaving the RWM, Bredow instructed me to continue work with Hill, Francis, Olsbury and Greves. I was to continue connections with Menshikov and Villers, giving their information to Bredow personally, not to the RWM.

It went on like that until my arrest.

After Bredow's death, no one in the RWM knew from whom they received their English information.

I kept in touch with these agents through clubs:

1. with Captain Francis through 'The Albany', WI;
2. with Captain Hill through the Royal Society.

Both are beyond suspicion. Moreover, the Albany is the favourite haunt of the officers of the Russian Department and of medium-level Foreign Office officials. The Royal Society is a meeting place for political officers of the German Department and also the place where messages about the arrival of their agents were sent.

Contact with Menshikov was kept up through the editorial office of the *Times*.

My messages contained only the time of my arrival, which was the agreed-on sign for my agent to meet me at the indicated hour on that day either in 'The Albany' for Francis, or in the 'Royal' for Hill, or at the *Times* for Menshikov. I always gave out assignments verbally. Their work was given to them by couriers in the editorial offices of the *Times*, the *Daily Telegraph*, and the *Daily Mail*, where there were meetings every Saturday.

A. Nelidov

24 October 1940

The Secret Service makes it the duty of its political officers to try and get in touch with people holding responsible posts; it spares no expense and without any scruples promises such people any payment they may ask for.

The Secret Service seeks informers only among people who hold responsible posts or people who have links with such people. The Secret Service does not allow the use of mass espionage.

From 1921 to 1926 inclusive, Permanent Secretary Adams was the head of the Secret Service.

The head of the Russian Section was Colonel Thomson. The following individuals were political officers of the Russian Section:

1. in Helsingfors: Captain John Francis;
2. in Riga: Captain MacPherson;
3. in Warsaw: Captain Maclauren;
4. in Romania: Captain Hales;
5. in Constantinople.

Working for the headquarters of the occupation forces [in Constantinople]:

Captain Gibson
Captain George Hill
Captain Sinclair-Miller

Working for the High Commissioner in Constantinople:

Captain Douglas HAG

Working for the London headquarters of the Secret Service:

Vice Consul Rogers
Captain Christie
Midshipman Dunderdale, who also served as courier and translator at the
  consulate

Counter-intelligence functions were carried out by Captain [redacted]; he was responsible for the protection of the occupation force from Turkish and Soviet agitation.

Counter-intelligence functions were also carried out by the Allied police, which was headed in Constantinople by Colonel Maxfiend. The head of the counter-intelligence police apparatus was Captain Tramel.

Besides the political officers with responsibility for intelligence activities against the Soviet Union listed above, the head of the Russian Section of the Secret Service had under his command another three officers attached to him by Adam's special order: Captain Reilly, Captain Law and Captain Joyce.

These three officers travelled constantly through Europe in order to establish connections with émigré organisations, which at that time were beginning to develop their activities—for example, with 'Komuch' (Committee of the Constitutional Assembly) in Paris and with the centre of the SR [Socialist Revolutionary] organisation headed by Kerensky in Prague. They were also seeking to establish contacts with the recently formed General Staffs in Finland, Lithuania, Estonia and Poland.

Attempts were made to establish connections with the Czech General Staff, but since there was a very strong French influence there, the Secret Service had to content itself with connections to the Czech Foreign Ministry.

Czechia and Poland were assigned to Captain Reilly, Captain Joyce covered the Baltic countries, and Captain Law was sent to Romania to establish similar connections there.

In Warsaw, it was easy to establish connections between the Secret Service and the General Staff. This was due to Boris Savinkov's great influence on Pilsudski, who gave instructions to the head of the General Staff to put all the material of the intelligence unit of the Polish General Staff at the disposal of the Secret Service head of station in Warsaw.

For this 'courtesy', the Secret Service paid half the expenses of the intelligence unit of the Polish General Staff. Moreover, the Secret Service took over all expenses of the Polish Foreign Ministry, which in August 1921 came to one million Polish marks a day.

Simultaneously, the Secret Service acquired an agent to find out about Pilsudski's own 'attitudes' in the person of his aide-de-camp and liaison officer,

Colonel Dvoino-Sologub (count and former officer of the Semenovsky regiment of the Tsarist army).

Reilly also tried to establish connections with German military circles, but his attempts met with failure. Captain Foley was sent to Berlin as vice consul in order to establish connections with the Berlin police and to obtain information from them about any Russian matters. Through his senior agent, the former investigator Orlov, who was friendly with the head of the Foreign Department of the Berlin Polizeipräsidium, Consul Bartels, he was able to obtain information about the Soviet Union from the German Social Democrat Party. This material was valued highly in London in 1921. (In June 1921, I was put under the command of the head of the Russian Section, who sent me on a special assignment, the beginning of which I had already carried out back in Constantinople. It consisted of targetting the Polish Section in Paris to discover its government's thinking on the division of Silesia between Germany and Poland, which had been put to the decision of an 'ambassador's conference', to be called in Paris at the beginning of July. After that I was sent to Warsaw, and from there I went to London together with Savinkov. I returned to Constantinople at the beginning of October 1921.)

At the end of 1921, the division of the political officers in Constantinople into three groups was abolished. They were all assigned to work on the Soviet Union.

At roughly the same time, orders were received to set up intelligence stations in Sofia and Varna, and Captain Hill was sent to Bulgaria.

Major Edisson, who was assigned to organise work in Tehran, arrived in Constantinople from London.

In February 1922 all the political officers were called to London for a three-day meeting at 1 Adam Street. The meeting was chaired by the head of the Russian Section, Colonel Thomson, in the presence of Permanent Secretary Adams.

The attending officers reported about the work of their stations and the possibilities for an expansion of their work but in the end did not receive any new instructions; they all concluded that the real objective had been to allow Secretary Adams to see all the heads of stations personally. From his remarks it was clear that overall, he was satisfied with our work. However, he valued the information coming from Berlin more highly than that from the other stations.

The meeting also gave a picture of the relations established between the SIS political officers and the official institutions of the countries where they operated.

Captain Francis was connected to an important official of the Finnish police, Sinevar, who provided him with information and agents. He was closely connected to the head of the Finnish army staff.

Sinevar received £300 a month from Francis as his personal remuneration. Moreover, Francis paid all the expenses and salaries of the agents working with Sinevar on intelligence on the Soviet Union.

That the head of the Finnish army staff was being paid remained unknown to Sinclair; this delicate operation was handled personally by the British military attaché.

Captain MacPherson was connected to the head of the Latvian Political Police, Ozol, who was paid around £300 plus all expenses for his agents, which varied between £400 and £500 monthly.

MacPherson also had links to the Latvian army staff, who gave him intelligence about the Soviet Union. All expenses of the Latvian army staff related to intelligence on the Soviet Union were paid by the British Embassy, which also had ties to the Latvian Foreign Ministry.

Captain Maclauren received information from the Polish General Staff on the basis mentioned earlier. He also received information from Petliurov's organisation, whose centre was in Lvov, and from Bulak-Bulakovich's organisation. Savinkov's organisation no longer existed officially at that time, since he and the main figures had been expelled from Poland. What remained of the organisation without Savinkov was not of interest to the English.

Captain Hales in Romania had connections with the Siguranza and with individual officers on the General Staff of the Romanian army. His intelligence did not extend beyond Odessa but cost more than £700.

Colonel Thomson indicated that expenditures on the Romanians were not justified by the information received from them. Therefore he considered it necessary to close that station for some time, while Sir Henry Deterding tried to draw the Romanians into the preparation of a general front against the Soviet Union.

Captain Hales was to return to Constantinople.

Captain Hill, who had organised stations in Sofia and Varna, succeeded only in establishing connections with the Sofia and Varna police. He spent about £500 a month on these two bodies, whose intelligence was very low-grade, coming as it did from the owners of small boats and feluccas calling at the ports in the Crimea and Odessa. Before sending him to Bulgaria, Thomson gave Hill a specific assignment—to gather intelligence on the work of the shipyards in Nikolaev. So far, this has not been done.

Captain Sinclair-Miller, who obtained information by questioning incoming passengers and who was attached to the Allied [Control] Commission (which had police functions, including checking passports), did not have a fixed budget. His expenses varied from £109 to £150 a month. The information received from the passengers, most of whom came from Batum and Tiflis, mainly concerned the economic and political situation in Georgia and Azerbaijan.

Captain Gibson carried out intelligence work on Georgia. He was connected to the Georgian consulate in Constantinople, which gave Gibson agents and information. These agents were in most cases supplied with Persian passports and went in the guise of traders. The same consul put Gibson in touch with the trade companies Beridze and Djaneli, which carried out Gibson's assignments.

Gibson spent about £2,000–£2,200 on all this. The trips did not occur every month.

Captain Christie, considered the senior political officer in Constantinople, had connections with a spokesman, Kandarom (Organisation of Mountain Peoples of the Northern Caucasus) in Constantinople, and also with a representative of the Mussavatists there. He mainly ran intelligence operations against Azerbaijan and the northern Caucasus. He was also responsible for analysing all Soviet newspapers that arrived in Constantinople.

I do not remember his budget exactly, but it would have been something in the region of £1,000 a month.

Captain Douglas Hag was attached to the Allied Commission and assigned exclusively to the questioning of passengers.

It should be mentioned at this point that two-thirds of the lower-level staff of the Allied Commission were agents and officials of the Tiflis Special Branch (Political Police), the head of which was Kediia (former head of the Special Branch in Tiflis). Hag spent from £100 to £150 on his information.

My personal budget consisted of [redacted]'s remuneration of £500 monthly, Khachaturov's remuneration of £200 and Karamaflei's of £150. Altogether I received £1,000 a month, of which I had to pay £50 a month to Vice Consul Rogers according to the 'traditions' of the Secret Service. My personal remuneration was £100 a month.

Dunderdale did not carry out any intelligence and did not have a budget.

Work continued in this way until 1923, when a connection with the Romanians was established and Gibson was sent to Bucharest. I was attached to the Romanian colonel Basipa in Constantinople.

The personnel working against the Soviet Union at the intelligence posts of the Secret Service remained the same until June 1926.

The political officers were often sent to other countries for short periods, to the Genoa conference, to conferences in Geneva (Turkish-English negotiations in Mossul) and Mossul but always returned to their posts.

22 October 1940

A. Nelidov

The Organisation of the Secret Service

It should be added to all that has been said before that the political officers of the Russian Section in Constantinople carried out intelligence assignments against not only the Soviet Union but also Turkey (or rather those parts of it that were in the hands of the Kemalites). Moreover, we also had to do work on the former khedive of Egypt, Abbas Helmy.

Until the evacuation of Constantinople by the Allied occupation forces, a lot of information was received from the Allied Control Commission, which checked passengers arriving on boats and steamers from the Soviet Union. After the evacuation, these functions were taken over by the Turkish police, from whom Rogers had to buy this information.

After the evacuation, the position of the political officers became ambiguous. It was impossible to attach them all to the embassy to give them diplomatic status. Thus, some of them moved to Athens and made flying visits to Constantinople; others (Christie and Dunderdale) were attached to the consulate in Constantinople. Sinclair-Miller obtained a concession from the government to organise wild boar hunts on Turkish territory and export the meat. He opened an office, where the former officer Zelensky was asked to work as his assistant, organising groups of hunters and sending them to the Sametska and Trapezunde areas. As a Russian émigré, I was unlikely to arouse any particular suspicion from the Turkish side and therefore was left in Constantinople. Hill was travelling continuously between Sofia and Athens, and Sofia and London.

Gibson was in Bucharest. Moreover, on instructions from the head of section, Colonel Thomson, attention at that time was focussed on Angora, Soviet-Turkish relations, the preparation of Sheik Ali's units in Mossul and the activities of the former khedive Abbas Helmy, whose supporters in Egypt were supposed to have killed Sir Lee Stack (the commander in chief in Egypt). Meanwhile, the 'head of the naval base' in Athens (in reality, this was a cover for the Naval High Command for the British fleet in the Bosphorus, the Sea of Marmora and the Aegean Sea), Admiral Sinclair, demanded that the formation of the Arab units in Mossul be accelerated. Thus, all political officers were transferred there. Rogers, Christie and Dunderdale remained in Constantinople. All the officers who were transferred to Mossul handed their agents and links to other intelligence services over to them. Among these were links to Polish intelligence, which was led by the Polish consul, Klintsliand, and his assistant, the former Kuban officer Zinalov; to the translator of French intelligence Delimirsky and the Italian intelligence agent Giuriati; to Georgian intelligence; to the representative of the Kirillean organisation, Markovich; and to the representative of the Nicholean organisation, the former colonel Kreiton.

In Mossul, the formation of the Arab units was entirely in the hands of the political officers. Colonel Laurence was head of staff. The deputy to Commander in Chief Sheik Ali was Colonel Andersen.

Here I first learned that the Secret Service, on the model of the Imperial General Staff and the Naval General Staff, uses peacetime to plan its operations for war.

In planning their operations against a certain power or group of powers, the General Staff and the Admiralty give a general outline of the intended operations to the chief of the Secret Service. He, in turn, draws up an operational plan for the work of the intended operations for the head of the Secret Service during wartime. The first step is to set down how the Secret Service can facilitate the intended operations by:

1. The use of minority groups—those that contain nationalist-chauvinist currents—in the country of the enemy or enemies. The leaders of these currents are identified, connections are established with them beforehand, and they are supplied with means for propaganda. If such a minority or group of minorities is situated on or close to a border, stores of arms, explosives, etc., are set up in the neighbouring country and are transferred to the territory of the minorities in order to cause an insurrection or unrest at the moment of mobilisation. If such a minority is situated far from a border, the leaders of the nationalist-chauvinist currents are given means to produce explosives for blowing up railway bridges and railway beds, for the destruction of rolling stock, etc.—i.e. the Secret Service's first aim is to obstruct the mobilisation and concentration of the enemy's army units.

2. The use of illegal political organisations in the country of the enemy for carrying out propaganda, intelligence and sabotage work in the country of the enemy during wartime.

3. The use of pacifist elements in the country of the enemy for propaganda against those leading the war.

When war comes, all connections with these organisations are established through political officers who have never worked in that country during peacetime and therefore remain unknown to its police and counter-intelligence. (No officer intended for wartime work in a prohibited area will be used there in peacetime so that they cannot be exposed beforehand.)

All other points in the Secret Service's war plans are resolved at station level, for example, intelligence on the organisation of the opponent's army and navy and investigation of fortified areas, military supply bases, military industries and industries that can be used for military purposes and general intelligence tasks, such as intelligence on the mobilisation plans of specific divisions and corps—generally everything that may help to uncover the enemy's operations plans.

The chief of the Secret Service assigns the political officers required for carrying out the tasks mentioned under 1, 2 and 3 beforehand. The plan as well as the personnel intended to carry it out are kept absolutely secret.

If the Service does not have people among its staff to carry out a particular assignment, which happens particularly often in the areas of the Far and Near East, where there are many dialects, the chief turns to universities or special Oriental institutes for help and chooses people from the faculties. The candidates are carefully observed and vetted and, if they seem suitable, are trained for assignments. They are given the rank of captain or major and paid a salary; meanwhile, they retain their academic posts, thus remaining unknown even to the heads of stations.

In the beginning of June 1926, Secretary Adams retired, and Seymour was appointed to his post as head of the Secret Service.

He immediately began to reorganise the intelligence service, in particular the Russian Section. Colonel Thomson was dismissed from the post of head of section and replaced by Major Holmson. Colonel Thomson was assigned to organise a centre of Ukrainian, Caucasian and Transcaucasian intelligence in Athens. A number of political officers were dismissed or transferred to other posts. The first to be dismissed were Captain Hill, Captain Sinclair-Miller, Captain Roberts, Captain Francis and Captain Maclauren. (Captain Hill, who, after the occupation of Georgia by Soviet troops, was at the disposal of the head of section, stayed in the Baltic countries).

Some of those dismissed from their posts who threatened to publish material at their disposal remained with the Secret Service, but in less important posts. The only victim was Hill, whom Seymour suspected of having misappropriated money given to him by Bruce Lockhart in Moscow and which Hill did not hand over to the Secret Service, claiming that he had lost it when fleeing from Moscow. Sinclair-Miller was transferred to the German Section, but only for office work. Captain Roberts was transferred to naval intelligence owing to his connections. Captain Francis was appointed director of the Registry. Captain Maclauren was told to continue his work in the Russian Section but with a significantly reduced budget. To everyone's surprise, after a brief spell out of favour Captain Hill was appointed vice consul in the Baltic.

I was transferred to Berlin to replace Captain Ellis. Seymour had sent him to Geneva, where he was attached to the League of Nations in order to target Comintern agents in Europe.

Rogers, Christie and Dunderdale remained in Constantinople. Thomson and his aide-de-camp, Captain Harris, set up shop in Athens. Gibson stayed in Bucharest.

Seymour seduced the Vickers-Armstrong representative in Constantinople, Arthur Lander, working in the Russian Section, with the special assignment of covering Turkish-Soviet relations and following the activities of Khedive Abbas Helmy. Lander had large sums put at his disposal. He had very good relations with the representative of the Turkish Foreign Ministry in Constantinople, Artin Bey.

In Berlin, Seymour recruited the correspondent of the *Daily Telegraph*, Wilcox, and the correspondent of the *Manchester Guardian*, Voight, for work in the Russian Section.

Changes in the Secret Service over the Period from 1926 to October 1933

About two months after my arrival in Berlin, I left the British SIS and went to work for the Third Department of the German General Staff. This name had been a cover for the German intelligence service since the Versailles Treaty obliged the Germans to disband their General Staff and their intelligence service.

I learned about the changes in the Secret Service from German intelligence officers as well as from Deterding, with whom I had several meetings over this period. Also in meetings with Captain Hill, who was out of work and lived very modestly in London. His entire income consisted of the small fees he received for short newspaper articles on the Soviet Union.

Most of the changes occurred in London itself. Thus, at Deterding's urgent request, the political editor of the *Times*, Wilson, joined the Russian Section as a consultant in 1927. On Seymour's instructions, Macoghan, calling himself Prince Razumovskii, was taken on as a political officer of the Russian Section. Macoghan reported to Major Holmson and travelled regularly between London, Berlin and Warsaw.

On Seymour's instructions, Prince Vyazemskii and Prince Obolensky were included in the political officer staff as personal consultants to Major Holmson. These officers processed the material coming in from the stations. The main reason for their appointment was the fact that they were married to very rich and influential Englishwomen who ran political 'salons' that Seymour used for intelligence objectives.

I knew only two of the new political officers of English origin in the Russian Section. Deterding had introduced them to me. They were Captain Knox and Captain Helmsley, whose brother lived in Bremen and represented many English companies. He worked mainly with the 'Union of Heavy Industry'. German intelligence assumed him to be a political officer of the German Section of the Secret Service.

I do not know anything about the changes at the intelligence posts during this period.

Sinclair-Miller was transferred to Naval Intelligence. Captain Douglas Hag worked for the intelligence service.

Changes in 1938 and 1940

In the middle of July 1938, I came to Riga and visited Hill, who held the post of vice consul at the British consulate in Riga. He told me about the following new people among the political officers of the Russian Section: Berry, Backstone, Robinson-Kay and Marshall were working under his supervision. These officers supplied the Secret Service with information that they got from the Latvian and Lithuanian services. According to Hill, he himself worked with the Latvian Political Police, while the staff of the Latvian army had direct contact with the English military attaché. Backstone had ties to the Lithuanian Political Police and the Lithuanian Foreign Ministry. Links with the Lithuanian army staff were maintained personally by the military attaché, who went to Kovno from time to time. Robinson-Kay kept in touch with the Latvian press, and Marshall with Latvian industrial circles. In 1940, all these except Berry were still working. Berry had been recalled to London and Beritham appointed in his place.

Hill did not tell me about other changes, i.e. in other countries. According to him, since the beginning of the war he had also been responsible for intelligence in Germany and occupied Poland.

In Poland he was helped by the Riga consulate, which was under English protection.

The Work of the Intelligence Service

According to information obtained by German intelligence, the operations of the SIS in Germany were run by Captain King, who lived in Holland. He appeared in Germany once in a while and at one time was attached to the British military attaché in Berlin, Colonel House.

The intelligence service began to operate in Germany in 1932. Up till then, the intelligence service had operated on a legal basis by virtue of the right given to the Allies by the Treaty of Versailles to monitor German arms factories and the personnel and equipment of the Reichswehr as well as all German organisations of a military nature, such as the Stahlhelm, the Reichsbanner, the SA [Nazi Party stormtroopers] and the SS.

SIS began to operate in 1932 (although in fact the Allied Control Commission left Berlin much earlier).

The British Embassy employed a number of Germans as translators who in fact were then used mainly as agents. They were gradually ensnared by giving them a number of articles to translate from German which compromised Germany, written by Gerlach and Ossisky and placed in the German press between 1921 and 1929. The next stage was to obtain information from them about the SA, SS, Stahlhelm and Reichsbanner. After that came more serious assignments, such as finding out about the call-up periods for the Reichswehr, since the English knew that recruitment for the Reichswehr violated the Versailles Treaty and that the obligatory ten-year call-up period was constantly being violated. Similarly, they were asked to find out about the activity of factories, like RheinMetal, which, under the Versailles Treaty, had the right to produce arms.

After carrying out these assignments, the translators were asked to establish connections with members of the Reichswehr and with the navy. Some of the translators, apprehensive about the consequences but also afraid of losing their jobs, told the Reichswehr about this and passed information to the British with the latter's permission.

The Reichswehr soon realised that these tasks were of too low a grade to really be serious SIS assignments. They were seen as an attempt to divert the attention of German counter-intelligence away from an organisation that was running espionage operations on a very different basis and with different objectives. Only through German intelligence in London was it possible to find out about the methods of the intelligence service and to identify the people directing the operations.

The German Intelligence Section of the intelligence service was headed by

Colonel Philips. His heads of stations were Major Nicolson in Brussels and Captain King in The Hague. The agents run by these two heads of stations were Dutchmen, German inhabitants of the Mamel area (occupied by the Belgians from the time of the Versailles Treaty). These agents penetrated the Ruhr area and to the Rhine. They mostly investigated the work of the metallurgical and chemical factories and monitored whether any military installations were being set up in the demilitarised Rhine zone. Somewhat later, stations were established in Bern and Geneva, with Major Moore and Captain Alexander as heads of stations. Information was also received that Colonel Philips was establishing connections with Polish and Czech intelligence through the military attachés in Prague and Warsaw [to be used] for intelligence in Germany.

Moreover, German intelligence found out that the head of Russian intelligence in the intelligence service, Major Budget, who was responsible for intelligence on German-Soviet relations, also established connections with the Polish and Czech intelligence services with the help of Colonel Philips.

[It also found out] that Captain Sinclair-Miller and Major Douglas Hag are constantly travelling between Prague, Warsaw and London.

Also that the army staffs in Lithuania and Latvia carry out Philips's and Budget's assignments.

That is all I know about the work of the intelligence service.

November 1940

36   *British Deception Schemes, May 1944*

Deception During the Current War

Introduction

This report does not purport to give an exhaustive account of British deception in historical perspective or to show a full picture of the present situation. It aims to give a brief description of the structure of the British deception agencies and their work based on the current war-based material obtained by the First Directorate of the NKVD.

Accordingly, the report is divided into three sections:

1. Organisational structure, staff and functions of the British deception agencies
2. Deception during the preparations for the Allies' invasion of Sicily
3. Deception during the preparations for the opening of a Second Front

The report is based on intelligence material of the First Directorate of the NKVD for 1942–44.

The material at our disposal is most detailed on disinformation by dissemination of rumours, which plays an important role in the British deception system. There is very little material indicating the use of double agents for deception purposes. There is good coverage of the work of the TWIST and TORY [deception-planning] Committees, but not very much on that of the XX Committee.

In regard to the content of disinformation, we possess material on British deception work only in the area of strategic military plans.

The content of British disinformation in this area changes as the plans themselves change. At the first stage of the war, when Britain was threatened by an enemy invasion, the British tried to convince the enemy that they commanded sufficient forces to repulse any attempt of this kind. Deception was organised on a broad basis during the preparations for the invasion of Sicily and Italy. At present, the main thrust of deception operations in the area of British strategic military plans consists of disinformation about the time and place of the next Allied attack—in other words, in masking the preparations for the opening of a Second Front.

We know of the following deception methods used by the British:

a. Spreading of rumours.
b. Use of double agents and recruitment of German agents.
c. Use of British intelligence radio sets on German-occupied territories that have been captured by German counter-intelligence. The British circulate disinformation by pretending that they do not know this and continuing communications with their agents.
d. One-off initiative.
e. Statements by individual well-known British public figures and statesmen.

The following are the channels used in disseminating false rumours:

a. Diplomatic and other British representatives in neutral countries
b. Neutral diplomats in Britain
c. Foreign press correspondents in London
d. British and foreign press
e. Postal and telegraphic correspondence

1. Organisational Structure, Staff and Functions of the British Deception Agencies

The British deception agencies are organised as follows:

1. London Controlling Section

The main agency for deception in Britain is the so-called London Controlling Section (LCS), subordinate to the War Cabinet and part of the War Cabinet Office. The head of the LCS is the Controlling Officer for Deception, Colonel Bevan.

Bevan is directly subordinate to the Committee of the Chiefs of Staff (General Staff, Admiralty staff and air staff). Heading the LCS, he is also a member of other committees for deception, i.e. the XX Committee and TWIST. Besides, Bevan is in constant contact with the Americans who deal with deception issues, specifically with Colonel Dudley Clark, who directed deception work in the Middle East, and on Eisenhower's staff.

Besides Colonel Bevan, the personnel of the LCS consist of a number of officers from various military organisations whose task it is to maintain contact with these organisations on deception issues. Bevan's LCS deputy is Lieutenant Colonel Wingate; his personal assistant is Major Petavel. The latter is also the liaison officer between the LCS and the War Office. Besides those already mentioned, the following individuals on the LCS staff are known:

Captain Arbuthnot—liaison with the Admiralty.
Lieutenant Colonel Wheatley, Dennis—liaison with the Air Ministry. Wheatley is a former squadron Leader and is better known as the author of popular spy and crime novels.
Major Morley, Derek—liaison with the Joint Allied Command.
Hoare, Reginald—liaison with the Foreign Office. Hoare is the former British minister in Bucharest. Until 1943 he was the head of the Political Intelligence Department of the Foreign Office.

The main deception agency, the LCS, is responsible for:

1. Working out deception topics and defining deception tasks in accordance with the strategic plans of the British High Command and the overall military and political situation.
2. Obtaining factual information from various government bodies—for example, on troop deployment, the arrival in the UK of well-known public and military figures, new appointments, etc. The LCS needs this information, which it summarises, analyses and reviews in order to determine which components of it can be passed to the enemy without damage to the national interest, in order to include disinformation with it or in order to build a good reputation for a double agent. On the other hand, the LCS needs to know which information must be concealed—e.g. about the arrival of convoys, etc.—and avoid mixing it with the disinformation. It also needs all this to draw up deception plans. By manipulating it in the right way, it can be fed to the enemy in a form that, by corroborating other disinformation already in his possession, misleads him into over- or understating numbers, quantities, etc. The LCS develops the basic directives on deception, subject to ratification by the Chiefs of Staff Committee, and, in particularly important cases, by Churchill. These directives are then given to the other deception agencies for more detailed elaboration and implementation. In some cases, the LCS carries out certain of the more important tasks itself.

2. The TWIST Committee

The inter-departmental committee for deception known as TWIST was organised around September 1941. It followed the setting up of the LCS and of the XX Committee, and their predecessor, the W Board, which consisted of the heads of various British intelligence organisations and was subsequently reorganised. While the LCS is a directing body, TWIST was created as an executive organisation.

It is subordinated directly to the Committee of Chiefs of Staff and, in operational issues, to the LCS. TWIST is headed by the same person as the LCS, i.e. by the Controlling Officer for Deception, Colonel Bevan. The following are the committee members:

1. Colonel Robertson—head of Section B1(a) of MI5, the section in charge of work with double agents.
2. Major Blunt—assistant to the deputy director of B Division of MI5 (B Division is in charge of counter-espionage)
3. Major Masterman—secretary of the committee, chairman of the XX Committee, MI5 officer (Robertson's assistant)
4. Lieutenant Colonel WINGATE, member of the LCS
5. Major Petavel—member of the LCS at the War Office
6. Major Foley—the Secret Intelligence Service officer (works with double agents)
7. REGINALD Hoare—the Foreign Office official
8. LIONEL Hale—staff of Economic Warfare Intelligence (works with agents of this intelligence service abroad)
9. Montagu—naval officer
10. Lloyd—the Secret Intelligence Service officer, Foley's assistant

Colonel Bevan, Lieutenant Colonel Robertson, Major Blunt, Major Masterman, Major Foley and Lloyd are members of TWIST by virtue of their positions in the Secret Intelligence Service and the Security Service (MI5), since their main work in those agencies is directly connected to and interwoven with a number of the committee's functions (e.g. work with double agents, with agents in the diplomatic corps in London, etc.). If any of them moved to a different post within SIS or MI5 or left these agencies, they would automatically retire from TWIST and their position would be taken by their replacements. The other members of the committee are permanent representatives of their agencies—e.g. the Foreign Office (Hoare), the Ministry for Economic Warfare (Hale), etc.

TWIST has the following tasks:

1. Elaboration and implementation of the plans approved by the LCS for disguising military-operational initiatives or for deception in relation to these initiatives, using the special resources available to the committee.
2. Commenting on the credibility of specific deception or cover plans drawn up by the LCS before the latter finally confirms them.
3. The selection of material and the execution of special operations for giving disinformation to the enemy—e.g. Operation MINCEMEAT, more about which below. These operations are, of course, carried out with the full knowledge and approval of CSS and the director of MI5 and with the benefit of those organisations.

The committee's responsibilities are divided as follows:

1. Colonel Bevan is responsible for general supervision of the committee's work.
2. Lieutenant Colonel Wingate works with Bevan on this and also as a conduit between the committee and US deception operations (Dudley Clark and others).

   Note: Dissemination of disinformation in the Western Hemisphere, mainly spreading false rumours in Latin American countries, and also the use of double agents in America itself is handled directly by the Americans. They also deal with deception in the Middle East.
3. Major Masterman is secretary to the committee. He is also in charge of work with double agents.
4. Colonel Robertson deals with dissemination of disinformation through double agents. He selects and recommends double agents for the committee to use and also recommends methods of transmitting deception material to the enemy through them. He also selects, in the context of the overall plan, the rumours that can most effectively be transmitted to the enemy through double agents.
5. Major Blunt works on the dissemination of disinformation through MI5 channels in London, mainly via foreign diplomats and press correspondents. He conducts this work outside the MI5 network and is not accountable to his superiors in the Service in this regard. As one of the directors of the counter-espionage department, Blunt has the opportunity to use MI5 agents at his discretion for the purpose of spreading disinformation. Moreover, with the help of his agents, he often uses suitable foreigners as unwitting channels.
6. Lionel Hale is in charge of disinformation abroad, mainly in Spain, Portugal, Turkey and Sweden, through the agents of Economic Warfare Intelligence.
7. Reginald Hoare deals with disinformation, mainly in the form of rumours, through the heads of British diplomatic missions (ambassadors, ministers, etc.) abroad. He passes the rumours that TWIST thinks should be disseminated through these channels to [Victor] Cavendish-Bentinck, a counsellor at the Foreign Office and chairman of the Joint Intelligence Sub-Committee of the Chiefs of Staff. Cavendish-Bentinck draws up appropriate instructions for the dissemination of these rumours by British diplomatic representatives in countries regarded as fertile targets. Armed with these, the diplomatic representatives spread the rumours personally, as well as through their employees, etc.
8. Major Petavel has a special position as the representative of the LCS on the committee and assists Bevan and Wingate in directing the work of the committee. At the same time, he is in charge of co-ordinating the implementation of various deception measures with the War Office and supplies the committee with the relevant information.
9. Major Foley's duty is the transmission of disinformation to the enemy through double agents of the Secret Intelligence Service abroad. He also liaises with British intelligence on other issues to do with the work of the committee.
10. Captain Montagu liaises with the Admiralty and is in charge of the dis-

semination of misinformation through the Naval Intelligence channels. He is also engaged in researching special intelligence sources, particularly German radio intercepts, to find out which items and stories have been taken as credible. He feeds his findings back to the committee so that it can draw the appropriate conclusions and take the necessary action.

11. Foley's assistant, Lloyd, is responsible for scanning German diplomatic, intelligence and operational messages intercepted by the British. His summaries are used by the committee to assess what the Germans know about Allied plans, which deception initiatives have reached them and whether they believe them.

The normal course of TWIST's work is as follows:

1. The LCS submits to it weekly a list of specific issues to be tackled in the course of executing its various overall assignments.
2. The committee discusses these issues and, if necessary, amends them before handing them over to the appropriate organisations for implementation.
3. The LCS may, if it thinks it necessary, submit any preliminary plan to the committee for evaluation and for its opinion.
4. Topics confirmed by the committee for dissemination in the form of rumours are transferred to the TORY sub-committee.

3. The TORY Sub-Committee

This was created in March 1943, when it became clear that the spreading of deception rumours was taking a rather significant part of the overall TWIST agenda and that a special body was needed to focus specifically on this function. TORY is under TWIST's direct authority and is in effect a subsidiary of it.

Its basic function is, not to deceive the enemy directly, but to spread false rumours. Accordingly, it consists of those members of TWIST who are in control of channels for the dissemination of rumours.

The chairman of the sub-committee is the permanent representative of the Foreign Office in the LCS and in TWIST, Reginald Hoare. Other members are Major Blunt, Lionel Hale, Lieutenant Colonel Dennis Wheatley and Wintle, for whom Hale deputizes.

The members of the sub-committee divide the work as follows:

1. Reginald Hoare is in charge of spreading rumours through British diplomats abroad (through Cavendish-Bentinck; see above).
2. Major Blunt spreads rumours through MI5 agents in the diplomatic corps and foreign journalists in London.
3. Hale is in charge of disseminating deception rumours through the agents of the Ministry for Economic Warfare, and also through British businesses abroad.

TORY works as follows: It usually meets weekly. Its agenda will be a specific directive from TWIST around which rumours have to be created and disseminated. The sub-committee drafts the final form of these rumours, adds the necessary elements of credibility and discusses which channels are to be used for transmission. Its decisions are then submitted for approval to Colonel Bevan. If he is satisfied, he gives orders for them to be circulated to all members of TWIST, other than those belonging to TORY. The members of TWIST discuss these decisions and, if they endorse them, inform the TORY chairman of their approval. Points not approved are discussed at TWIST meetings, where a final decision is made (subject to formal approval by the Controlling Officer for Deception). The chairman of TORY is responsible for transmitting approved decisions to the appropriate organisations for implementation. As they are implemented, the results are reported back to the LCS.

4. XX Committee

The XX Committee is not a deception agency but a body that co-ordinates and controls the work of all British intelligence and MI5 departments that run double agents. One of its functions is censorship of all information given to the enemy via double agents—i.e. basically disinformation—which is why the XX Committee should be classified with the British deception agencies.

The XX Committee is subordinated directly to the Home Defence (Security) Executive and, on operational issues, to MI5. The committee is headed by Major Masterman of MI5. The committee has the following other members:

1. Lieutenant Charles Cholmondeley, secretary to the committee.
2. Colonel Bevan of the LCS and TWIST. Bevan is in charge of the committee's work in regard to the content of deception material transmitted to the enemy.
3. Major Foley of the Secret Intelligence Service.
4. A representative of Military Intelligence.
5. A representative of Naval Intelligence.
6. A representative of Air Intelligence.
7. A representative of MI5.

The XX Committee controls two groups of agents:

1. Double agents.
2. German agents landed in Britain by boat or parachute, arrested and recruited by the British for work against the Germans. Both groups of agents are used by XX to give the enemy disinformation that it has compiled to meet the directives of London Controlling Section or TWIST.

Another deception channel available to the committee is the use of the SIS radio sets that are known to be in German hands in occupied countries. Believing that the SIS is not aware that these sets have been captured, the Germans take the information transmitted over them by the British at face value and are thus deceived.

2. Deception for the Allied Landings in Sicily

After the German defeat in North Africa, the main objectives of the Allied Command for the first half of 1943 were landing in Sicily and then in southern Italy to force Italy out of the war. Deception plans were drawn up to match these objectives.

At the end of February 1943, at a meeting of the TWIST Committee (apparently there had already been a preliminary decision by the LCS), it was agreed that its main short-term task would be the deception of the enemy in this regard. In practical terms, this would involve diverting German attention away from the central Mediterranean and creating the false impression that the Allies were preparing an attack elsewhere.

The key issues around which the entire deception plan would have to be built were agreed to be:

1. The imminent invasion of Norway by Allied troops from Scotland and Iceland. Dissemination of this disinformation would be facilitated by the fact that the Germans had already received a great amount of intelligence information about preparations for such an attack.
2. An invasion of the Balkans. This version the Germans also took to be highly credible; they assumed that a base was being built on Cyprus for the invasion of Crete and Rhodes and then of the Balkan Peninsula.
3. The transformation of British and other Allied troops in the UK from defensive formations into units intended for offensive operations. The dissemination of this information, which was essentially correct, was to support deceptions 1 and 2.

Shortly afterwards, it was decided to add a point about the preparation of Allied troops for the invasion of France from the south and north. On the basis of these general directives, TWIST and its TORY sub-committee approved several detailed plans and lists of disinformation; these took much discussion and careful analysis and went through many different versions. The product was transmitted to the enemy mainly in the form of rumours through the different channels available.

At the end of February and the beginning of March 1943, several meetings of TWIST, with Colonel Bevan and the TORY sub-committee present, were held to draft a deception plan for the landing of British troops in Norway. The plan included:

* * * * * *

A. Measures in Stockholm

1. A quantity of cardboard boxes showing British and Norwegian national flags conjoined are to be manufactured in Britain and sent to Stockholm, with a

warning label on the box that they are on no account to be given to Norwegians in Sweden to wear. (Assigned to Economic Warfare Intelligence. Urgent.)

2. The British mission is to make the following strictly confidential inquiries of the Swedish Ministry of Foreign Affairs: If military actions began in Norway, (a) what would be the attitude of the Swedish government towards the transit of German troops through Sweden, and (b) what would be the position of the Swedish government towards Norwegian refugees of call-up age presently interned in Sweden, and would their return to Norway be considered? (Assigned to the representative of the Foreign Office.)

B. Legends—to be disseminated in neutral countries via channels leading to enemy intelligence, via the neutral embassies in London, via sailors in Britain and abroad, etc.

1. The British are secretly buying up Norwegian small change wherever they can—in Lisbon, Istanbul, Bern and Madrid. (Assigned to the representative of MI5, who is instructed to disseminate this through his links with Swedes in London, and the representative of the Ministry for Economic Warfare, through his connections in Lisbon, Istanbul and Bern. Very urgent. The dissemination of rumours in Istanbul has to be co-ordinated with the head of the American deception agencies in the Middle East, Dudley Clark.) Note: The following links of MI5 with Swedes in London are known: with the Swedish military attaché Klegel through the source LEMON. Also with Klegel's assistant Karlson through this source. With other journalists through the MI5 agent MONKEY, a Swedish journalist in London.

2. The real aim of 'X''s recent trip to Stockholm was to get samples of all the latest Norwegian currency notes in circulation. Although 'X' went undercover, he is in fact a technical expert for the banknote printers Waterlow and Sons. In London they did a rush job printing Norwegian notes. (The name 'X' is to be picked at random from the names of those Britons who have recently travelled to Stockholm.) (Assigned to the representative of the Ministry for Economic Warfare in Stockholm. Very urgent.)

3. Hangsten has recently visited the American troops in Iceland. (Note: Initially point 3 featured King Haakon, but since a visit by him was very unlikely in view of his age, he was replaced by Hangsten.) (Assigned to the representative of MI5, to be implemented through his Swedish and Turkish links in London.) (Note: A known link of MI5 with the Turks is MI5 agent TURBOT—a prominent British journalist with close Turkish contacts.)

4. Norwegian officers in Britain over fifty-five years of age are not happy with their assignment to the recently reorganised British Red Cross units. (To be included in a private letter of a Norwegian officer to Sweden. The letter is meant for the eyes of Swedish censorship. To be carried out by the representative of the Ministry of Economic Warfare.)

5. The Russian campaign will not be halted this summer. It will be doubled in scale in the north since the Murmansk route will be open. (Action by the representative of the Ministry of Economic Warfare for dissemination among journalists in Istanbul and Bern—in Istanbul in co-operation with Dudley Clark.)

6. The Russians have refused permission for the participation of British and American troops in their summer offensive after the opening of the Murmansk route. (Assigned to the representative of the Ministry of Economic Warfare, to be disseminated to journalists' circles in Bern and Istanbul—the latter with the knowledge of Dudley Clark.)
7. There will be no grounds for crews to demand hardship pay for the dangerous route to Murmansk. By the end of April it will be as safe or unsafe as any other. (Action by the representatives of MI5 for dissemination through sailors, etc. Implementation not urgent.)
8. 'My wife serves in an ATS [Auxiliary Territorial Service] unit assigned to the Norwegian forces. Her unit recently embarked on a ship under conditions of great secrecy. Damn strange thing, this war: the wife goes fighting while her husband sits at home in Aberdeen.' (Action by the representative of the Ministry of Economic Warfare in Aberdeen to be disseminated among Swedish civil airline pilots. Responsibility for this is to lie with the representative of MI5. Not urgent.)
9. 'We have been waiting two weeks now for GEORGE finally to come home from America, but he got stuck in Montreal for the past ten days. Those crazy Norwegians have been hogging all the aircraft.' (To be used in a private letter from Britain to Sweden. Meant for Swedish censorship. Action by the representative of the Ministry of Economic Warfare. Very urgent.)

C. The main commercial news agency in London sends out several business telegrams over radio every day en clair to its branches in Cairo and Istanbul. The telegrams are censored in those cities and may be intercepted by the enemy during transmission.

1. From London to Cairo and Istanbul: 'We are thinking about opening an office in Stockholm. The director assumes that it will have the potential to become one of our major centres. Could you reduce local expenses and also expenses related to the work of your correspondents in India, South Africa and South America, which in our view will become somewhat less significant in the future? Could you reduce monthly expenses by £200?'
2. Office in Cairo to London: 'Reducing expenses on South Africa and South America is not desirable; I do not object in regard to India. I would ask that my views on the inadvisability of opening an office in Stockholm be considered unless this becomes crucial.'
3. From London to Cairo: 'The new office will be of the highest importance. We will inform you of the opening date.' (Action by the representative of the Ministry of Economic Warfare. Not urgent.)

D. An agreement is to be made with Reuters new agency for them to send out the following telegram to their bureau in Stockholm: 'In co-ordination with COLBERS, we are assigning Quentin Reynolds to you to cover special news. [We are] sure you will co-operate with him while he is there; time presently open-ended.' Will be dated around 15 March. (Joint action by the representatives of the Secret Intelligence Service and the Ministry for Economic Warfare.)

E. A good channel for Sweden will be the Swedish press attaché Hammaling, who is currently in London but will soon leave for Sweden.

* * * * * *

5 May was chosen as the date of the invasion.

Parallel with this, but somewhat later, a plan for disinformation about Allied plans to invade the Balkans and France was drawn up. The aim of this plan, as of the first, was to disguise the preparations for the invasion of Sicily and to distract the enemy's attention away from the central Mediterranean.

During the first half of April, the following plan was developed at meetings of TWIST and TORY at the request of the LCS and in accordance with its guidelines. It was subsequently approved by the controlling officer, Colonel Bevan.

* * * * * *

Deception Policies in 1943. General Directive.

The rearmament of Britain is now complete; that of the USA is proceeding apace.

During the next few months strong land and air forces will be targeted at the final defeat of the Axis countries. Our only problem in providing enough ships for the job. Control of the Mediterranean enables us to use very large ships that were hitherto forced to take the long route around Africa.

Italy can be forced to leave the war by intensive bombardments. In any case, the Alpine barrier turns Italy into a dead end that cannot be used for our invasion of the Continent. For the same reason, attacks on Sicily and Sardinia will be futile. They are not bases for a further offensive. After the liberation of Tunis, new major operations will begin in the Mediterranean, possibly simultaneously in the west and the east. We will certainly attack the Dodecanese and Crete, and an invasion of Greece may follow. On the other hand, Giraud insists forcefully that we attack from southern France. However, the main blow has to come from the west. Only on the territory of Britain itself do the resources exist for the recruitment and rapid build-up of the strong expeditionary forces necessary for carrying out the final operation—the invasion of Germany.

The strength of the German air force is diminishing fast, and its fighter squadrons are no longer able to operate along the Continental coastline. This enables us to defend strong points simultaneously in at least two places as far apart as Trondheim and Bordeaux.

Our absolute air supremacy in areas close to Britain allows us to make airborne landings in the enemy's rear and to take several Channel ports. We have a hundred million people with a friendly attitude towards us on occupied territory, waiting for retribution. This will not be a military campaign but a massacre.

* * * * * *

Simultaneously, a detailed list of legends was approved for dissemination through private conversations. This is given as an appendix to the report owing to its large size.

The dissemination of the misinformation that formed the content of these plans was handled as follows:

1. Via MI5 channels (agents among foreigners in London and a limited use of double agents). The entire plan was intended to be used, with the exception of the part regarding an invasion of Norway.
2. Via Foreign Office channels. Reginald Hoare (via the Foreign Office counsellor and chairman of the Joint Intelligence Sub-Committee Cavendish-Bentinck) sent an abbreviated version of the plan to British diplomatic representatives abroad for them to use as they considered most appropriate.
3. The Ministry of Economic Warfare was given the task of disseminating the content of the main plan wherever possible and expedient, together with the content of the individual parts of the detailed plan, via its representatives in various parts of the world.

Shortly after these plans were developed and approved, a further scheme was drawn up to cover the Balkan and French legends. We cite it in its entirety:

* * * * * *

On the Balkans

1.
    a. The Graduates of the British School in Athens have been assembled and organised into a group of advisors. (For dissemination among Swedes in London via MI5 agents.)
    b. Excerpt from a letter: '. . . Even the old men do their bit. A couple of days ago I saw Professor Mayer, who is at least eighty years old, in New College. You must remember him from Athens. He was very excited, having been called to London to advise Whitehall.' (Action by the representative of the Ministry of Economic Warfare, to be run through Swedish censorship or sent by airmail to Switzerland.)
2. Something is going to happen in Greece on . . . (some suitable anniversary? . . . the anniversary of Byron's death? . . .)

On France

1. A new section has been created in the Royal Patriotic Schools to handle the British subjects repatriated from the south of France. (For dissemination in Sweden through the representative of the Ministry of Economic Warfare. For dissemination to the Swedish Embassy in London through MI5.)
2. French-Canadians are being formed into special units. (Via the representatives of the Ministry of Economic Warfare in Stockholm and Lisbon.)
    Excerpt from a letter: '. . . arrived together with other French Canadians. His life has taken a turn for the better after Madagascar and Dieppe.' (Via the Ministry of Economic Warfare. For Swedish censorship.)
3. Fighter squadrons from West Africa, which had been expected to transfer in North Africa or in the Middle East, have been sent home. ([Via the representatives] of the Ministry of Economic Warfare for Stockholm. The representative of MI5 for the Swedish Embassy in London.)
4. 'That bloodthirsty de Gaulle is always in a hurry. He raised formations in Savoy several months earlier than he should have.' (For dissemination among

journalists in the form of a rumour via the Ministry of Economic Warfare and in London through MI5.)

*   *   *   *   *   *

During April and May, TWIST and especially TORY drew up four other plans, roughly similar in content, for deception on the Balkans and France at the request of the Controlling Officer for Deception.

They each basically consist of a list of various legends specially selected and linked to one another in certain ways. The channels for their dissemination are the same as for the plans cited already. As a rule, the lion's share of the work on rumour dissemination is assigned to the Ministry of Economic Warfare. Legends to be transmitted to the enemy via double agents and recruited German agents seem to have been assigned according to a special plan drawn up by the XX Committee on the basis of general directives developed by the LCS and approved by the Security Committee. The effectiveness of these operations was obviously not that great, since rumours of any kind, and they are the principal weapon in British deception armoury, are treated with considerable scepticism by any counter-intelligence service, and the use of other channels was very limited. However, some of these rumours, which were spread in different places by different people, did reach the press in neutral countries and, having been corroborated by the reports of a number of agents, may have suggested to foreign intelligence that it was true or at least likely that an invasion of the Balkans or France by Allied troops was being planned, and may thus have thrown foreign intelligence somewhat off the track. The following three examples give a good flavour of the methods used by the British deception agencies in the run-up to the invasion of Sicily:

1. Capitalising on the popular support in the press for the opening of a Second Front and the promises of the Allies to the Soviet Union in this regard for deception purposes. The press and the statements of various public figures and statesmen were widely used for this. Many of the false rumours were adapted to respond to these popular attitudes. The following documents illustrate the point:

  a. A letter from Cavendish-Bentinck of 1 May 1943 to the British Embassy in Madrid:

  'I attach a memorandum on the general impression we are hoping to give to the enemy. We would be very grateful if you could use any opportunity to carry out this assignment.

  'We would also be grateful if the following information were passed to the Germans:

    'a) The new head of our military mission in Moscow was very well received, and it can therefore be assumed that his letter of recommendation from the prime minister to Stalin set out the principal points of our strategic plans for 1943. As a result, the Russian General Staff has become friendlier.

'b) Rearmament of the French forces in North Africa is on a very large scale and absorbs a significant part of the shipping tonnage that otherwise would be used for taking supplies to Russia. STALIN, however, fully approved of the delay in the delivery of these supplies when he learned why it was necessary to rearm the French so urgently.

'We would be very grateful for your general comments and in particular for a report on whether you succeeded in transmitting the above-mentioned information to the Germans.'

b. Letter from Cavendish-Bentinck no. D/D-6 of 1 May 1943 to the British minister in Lisbon, Balfour:

The beginning is the same as in the preceding letter.

'a) [French General] Catroux has reported on his way home that the morale of the French forces in North Africa is exceptionally high.

'b) [Lord] Beaverbrook does not take guidance from anyone and, as you know, has always pressed for the opening of a Second Front. The public therefore is now wondering what made him withdraw at the last moment his reply in the Commons to a question on this, which he had intended to table on 20 April.'

The conclusion of the letter is the same as that of the preceding one.

Analogous letters, only with different legends, were sent by Cavendish-Bentinck to the British missions in Turkey and other countries.

2. Peace feelers in regard to Italy

On May 1943 Colonel Bevan put forward a proposal that the Allies transmit peace conditions to the Italians via secret channels, with the aim of a 'bloodless' withdrawal of the latter from the war. According to this proposal, the British would promise that Italy could keep Cyrenaica and Tripolitania and guarantee that they would not use the Italian navy against Germany. In Bevan's view, the Italians would accept this proposal. The plan was confirmed by the Committee of Chiefs of Staff, but when it was discussed at a meeting of the War Cabinet, [Anthony] Eden expressed strong objections, and the Cabinet rejected it.

At that point, Bevan decided to implement his plan by other means. He put the following idea to the Chiefs of Staff: Peace proposals will be transmitted to the Italians with the aim of deceiving them—in particular, in order to divert their attention away from the Allies' intention to invade Sicily and in order to weaken their will to resist. In reality, Bevan hoped that if the Italians agreed to these proposals, they would approach the British themselves, and since the peace proposals would originate from them, Eden could agree to consider them. Bevan thus planned to bypass the foreign secretary.

This plan was submitted for discussion on 10 May 1943 at a regular meeting of one of the deception committees (apparently TWIST), with the main people in charge of deception attending. Bevan declared that he and his colleagues at the LCS considered the government's policy in regard to the complete defeat of Italy mistaken and that they were pressing for it to be changed. Citing the approval of the Chiefs of Staff of his plan, Bevan made the following arguments in its favour:

a. Deception would be useful to the British whatever happened.

b. If the Italians could be convinced to come forward with peace proposals first and if Italy subsequently left the war, this would be of great importance from a purely military point of view.

The committee agreed with Bevan's proposals and confirmed them as a deception plan. The committee then discussed which channels should be used for transmitting the peace proposals to the Italians.

After reviewing a number of candidates, the Spanish chargé d'affaires in London, Viscount Mamblaz, was chosen—a well-known member of the royalist party and a close friend and advisor of the ex-queen of Spain, with a strong influence on the pretender to the Spanish throne, Don Juan. Since Mamblaz was in touch with her, and she in turn was in contact with important individuals in Rome and in the Vatican, he was considered a good choice. The task of approaching Mamblaz on this issue was given to MI5 agent 1038 (a Spanish journalist in London, a Monarchist and close friend of Mamblaz's).

On 19 May, [agent] 1038 met Mamblaz and told him about the British proposals. Mamblaz was very interested but, as it turned out, was unable to transmit them to the Italians. He recommended the well-known Spanish lawyer and former finance minister, the Monarchist Ventoz, who was in London at the time. At the end of May, 1038 met him, and he agreed to transmit the proposals to Don Juan. Don Juan was to send his minister Lopez Olivan to Rome, and if successful, [Lopez Olivan would go on] to travel to Bern to see the British minister Norton with the Italian peace proposals.

Apparently subsequent events overtook the realisation of this plan, but it may have played some part in what happened in Italy.

3. Operation MINCEMEAT

During the spring of 1943, a dead body in the uniform of a British naval officer was dropped off a British submarine by the Spanish coast in the Gulf of Cadiz near Huelva. As expected, the body was washed ashore by the tide, picked up by the local Spanish authorities and subsequently handed over to the British naval attaché in Madrid. The dead man's pockets contained, among other things, top-secret letters (skilfully prepared by the British) from the deputy chief of the British Imperial General Staff, General Sir Archie Nye, to General Alexander and General Eisenhower and to the commander of the Allied naval forces in the Mediterranean, Admiral Cunningham. The most important of these was a letter addressed to General Alexander (the other letters apparently were of no great significance and served only as a 'frame', or as an indirect confirmation of the content of the first letter). This letter contained important (deceptive) information. The essence of the letter consisted of a debate between Nye and Alexander on British strategy. Nye claimed that the dissemination of rumours about plans for an invasion of Sicily could not be used to disguise operations in the eastern part of the Mediterranean, something that Alexander was supposedly insisting on. The reason given by Nye was that Sicily would be used as a cover for another operation. He did not say openly what this was, but it could be inferred from his comments that this was the invasion of the south of France. The letter also referred to plans for operations against the Cape of Araxos in the western Peloponnese.

In carrying out this operation, the British assumed that the documents found on the dead body would become known to the Germans and convince them that the Allies were intentionally spreading rumours about plans for an operation to invade Sicily while in fact preparing operations elsewhere. Even if these 'documents' did not convince the Germans, they would at least confuse them.

Intercepts of German operational and intelligence telegrams shortly afterwards showed clearly that the documents had indeed come into German hands and that they were very interested in them. Things were somewhat complicated by the fact that the papers ended up not with the Abwehr, as the British had calculated, but with the General Staff. The Abwehr suggested that the whole thing might be a British deception exercise. The final conclusion of the Germans is unknown, but the German General Staff apparently were convinced that the documents themselves were genuine.

Conclusions

British deception plans to mask preparations for the invasion of Sicily were focussed, purposeful and quite extensive. When the operation was launched, it was clear that the German and Italian Commands were somewhat taken by surprise and ill prepared to repel the attack. To some extent, this is evidence that the British and American deception agencies provided positive results.

3. Deception in the Run-Up to the Opening of the Second Front

According to our information, in September 1943 the British planned a major operation code-named COCKADE. Through a variety of deception measures and the corresponding concentration of military and naval forces, the British intended to convince the German Command that the Allied forces were planning to land a substantial force on the Continent. It was assumed that the Germans would send all air force units at their disposal to defeat the Allied landing fleet and repel the invasion. RAF fighters concentrated at special airfields on the southeast coast of England were to meet them in the air and destroy them. As part of the preparations for this operation, a special deception plan was drawn up, but it was not implemented, since the British later abandoned the operation.

At the beginning of October 1943, the Chiefs of Staff ratified a plan for an Allied invasion and occupation of Brittany as a base for a future major operation on French territory. Simultaneously, the General Staff tasked the LCS and TWIST via Bevan to work on a deception cover with the aim of convincing the Germans that the invasion of the Continent would occur in the Pas-de-Calais region. In carrying out these instructions, TWIST intended to use its channels to suggest to the enemy that the large-scale manoeuvres carried out in the Channel in September were a rehearsal for the actual invasion of the Continent.

The date for the beginning of operations for the invasion of Brittany was set for approximately mid-March 1944.

Around November 1943, British troops, notably the 50th and 51st Divisions, began to move from the Mediterranean to Britain. In order to disguise the true objectives of this move, the TWIST Committee proposed spreading rumours that this transfer was taking place so that battle-hardened troops could pass on their battle experience to younger soldiers at home.

At roughly the same time, the British began to spread rumours that the opening of the Second Front was delayed, that it might not happen at all, etc. For example, in November the British intercepted the following wireless messages sent from Lisbon to Bern:

1. 2 November 1943 from Ludovik to Kiro Bellicks and Khiob (in Berlin). OTTO (the head of Polish intelligence in Lisbon, with connections to the British and the Germans; he was giving the Germans false information that he received from the British) declared at the last meeting that the Polish consulate in London was very worried about the situation on the Eastern Front. The Poles know that now that the Russians have crossed the Dnieper, their divisions can be used for a westward offensive. The offensive now planned has already been rehearsed by German General Staff officers as well as by the officers of the Russian divisions; the many manoeuvres in these areas before the war, especially around Minsk, gave them a lot of practical experience. The danger of Bolshevism for Europe is realised by the Americans as well as by the British.

   The reason no landing has been made in France is that both feel it desirable to open a front nearer to the Russians—i.e. in the Balkans, in northern Norway and in Finland—so as to prevent the Russians from penetrating into those countries.

   The British and the Americans held negotiations on this issue with the ministers of Hungary and Romania in Lisbon.

   According to reports from London, 'neither the Germans nor the British were satisfied with the results of the Moscow conference'.

2. From Ludovico to Kiro 'Belliks' and Martin (in Berlin): 'OTTO has talked to a senior American officer who took part in the Moscow conference, who told him that the participants did not commit themselves to any definite obligations. One insignificant decision was made in relation to Austria. In the opinion of British and American military experts, the main task must be to try and stop the Russians. In connection with this, an attempt will be made to land troops in Norway, Finland and the Balkans. American and British politicians are supposedly in complete agreement on this. There is no point in a landing in western Europe. The Americans allegedly want to build an army of approximately ten million men with the objective of eliminating the Bolshevik danger and guaranteeing the existence of democratic Europe. De Gaulle's intelligence service is said to have been tasked to expose Communist elements and fight against them.'

In mid-January 1944, the LCS drew up a memorandum on the intentions of the Allies in 1944, outlining deception plans in response to instructions received by the LCS on the Allied strategy for the opening of a Second Front. At the beginning of February, the TWIST Committee drew up and confirmed a detailed plan. Both these documents are of great significance for an understanding of the nature of British deception operations generally and in relation to the future military operations of the Allies in particular. We therefore quote them in full:

* * * * * *

LCS Memorandum

1. The air bombardment of Germany seriously affected its military potential and, if continued, may lead to its complete defeat. In view of this, reinforcement of the Royal Air Force in the United Kingdom and in the Mediterranean has been given high priority, and the build-up of land forces in Britain has been relegated to second place.
2. All preparations to move on to the Continent if Germany is seriously weakened and retreats from western Europe have to be completed immediately.
3. During the spring, an attack on northern Norway has to be carried out jointly with the Russians with the aim of opening up access to Sweden. We then have to co-operate with Sweden to establish an air base in the southern part of the country from which we can mount co-ordinated operations by our bombers and fighters to cover a possible attack on Denmark from Britain this summer.
4. Since major cross-Channel landings will not be possible before the end of the summer, the Allies' main military efforts in the spring of 1944 will be directed against the Balkans. The following operations will be carried out:
   a. An attack by British and American troops on the Dalmatian coast
   b. An attack by British troops on Greece
   c. Landing operations by the Russians on the Bulgarian-Romanian coast
5. Turkey will be invited to join the Allies; this will increase available operational resources, including airfields, to be used to seize the Aegean islands as a precondition to an invasion of Greece.
6. Pressure on the German satellites to break away from Germany will be intensified.
7. The Anglo-American operations in Italy will continue. Landing operations will be carried out in the northwest and northeast. If these are successful, the 15th Army Group will move east through Istria to support operations in the Balkans.
8. Although Russian troops will be active all winter, they will not start their decisive summer offensive before the end of June.
9. Major cross-Channel operations will not begin before late summer, i.e. after the beginning of the Russian summer offensive. About twelve divisions will take part in the initial operation, with about fifty divisions engaged overall, given the strength of coastal fortifications and the number of German troops currently in France, Belgium and Holland.

* * * * * *

Main Characteristics of the Allied Forces and Their Bearing on the Distribution of Forces in the United Kingdom and in the Mediterranean

1. Lacking a sufficiently large pool of manpower, the British have been unable to bring up their army formations to full strength and have therefore been forced to reorganise. Some formations are still under strength or suffer from a lack of support units. Some of the American divisions that have arrived in the United Kingdom have not yet completed their training.

2. Some of the Anglo-American forces in the Mediterranean are returning to Britain for reorganisation and for new recruits.
3. Because of Allied operations in the Pacific, the supply of landing craft is still behind plan, and in view of this, the craft required for the initial cross-Channel invasion operation cannot be manufactured in Britain and America before the summer.
4. It is thought that some British divisions and landing craft can be moved from India to the Middle East. Fresh divisions from Britain and America will be sent to the Mediterranean.
5. To reinforce Allied troops in the Mediterranean, the defence of North Africa will be assigned to the French forces.

* * * * * *

Note: The memorandum cited is the basic deception plan for 1944. The LCS intended to place this document in the hands of the Germans as an authentic plan by the appropriate combination of agents.

The TWIST plan, containing a detailed elaboration of the memorandum, is cited below:

* * * * * *

TWIST Committee Plan

I. Air bombardment has seriously affected Germany's military potential and, if continued and intensified, may lead to its complete defeat. In this connection, such great importance has been attached to the building up of the air forces in Britain and the Mediterranean that concerns over the strengthening of land forces in Britain have taken second place.

Realisation:

a. When discussing military problems with representatives of neutral and Allied countries, diplomats and military attachés in neutral countries should express the opinion that the war can be won through strategic bombing and that we have to increase our efforts, since the results achieved recently have already exceeded all expectations. Execution: To be executed by the LCS through channels in Lisbon, Madrid, Stockholm and Bern. Colonel Robertson is to inquire into the possibility of using channels in London and to report to the LCS on what has been done in this respect and what can be done in future.
b. Look into the possibility of putting an article on this topic in the press and of the air minister's making a statement on this question during his regular fortnightly broadcast. To be executed by the LCS.
The decision about the possibility of using the press is to be delayed until the return of the prime minister. (This will be taken into account by the Controlling Officer for Deception.) Lieutenant Colonel Wheatley is to discuss the minister's broadcast with the Air Ministry.
c. B1(a) is to transmit the above in general terms through its channels. To be executed by B1(a).

d. Ask the air minister whether he might direct Bomber Command to augment its fleet with American long-range bombers, with the aim of having this information filter to the enemy through captured air crews. To be executed by the LCS. Note: The Air Ministry is not minded to give such a directive. It considers that the current airfield building programme in Britain is a sufficient demonstration of the underlying point.

e. B1(a) is to continue to send messages about the increase in airfield construction for long-range bombers and American reinforcements. To be executed by B1(a). See next point.

f. Washington is to be asked about the possibility of sending additional long-range bombers to the United Kingdom and the Mediterranean. To be executed by the LCS. Inquiry to be sent to Washington.

g. The LCS is to disseminate disinformation confirming point (e) in neutral capitals through non-diplomatic channels. To be executed by the LCS. See point (d).

h. Examine the possibility of getting the United States and Russia to co-operate over the use of Russian airfields in southern Russia by the Mediterranean Strategic Air Command. To be executed by the LCS. The Controlling Officer for Deception is to discuss this question in Moscow.

II. The Allies have to be prepared to take advantage of any serious weakening of Germany or the retreat of its troops from western Europe. All the required preparations must be completed urgently.

Realisation:

a. Bring details of the progress made on version 'S' of plan RUNKIN to the enemy's knowledge. Execution: The Joint Operational Staff of the Allied High Command will provide suitable excerpts from RUNKIN, version 'S'. A plan will be drawn up and executed by the LCS.

b. The following legends can be used:
  1. Army formations in the United Kingdom are not trained for landing operations and are under-manned; they are now being prepared for an invasion of the Continent if a German defeat occurs.
  2. If it does, merchant vessels are to return to the Continent. To be executed by the LCS.

III. In view of the fact that German coastal fortifications are very strong, and taking into consideration the number of German troops presently in France, Belgium and Holland, about twelve Anglo-American divisions will be needed for the initial stage of operations and about fifty divisions overall for the invasion of the Continent. This operation will not be started before the late summer (i.e. after the beginning of the Russian summer offensive).

Realisation:

a. Disseminate the following legends through diplomatic channels:
  1. It is obvious that in view of the risk entailed in carrying out combined land, sea and air offensive operations, we cannot open a Second Front until we are absolutely ready and until we possess overwhelming superiority. We cannot risk failure.

2. The number of Anglo-American divisions in the invasion operation has to be twice as large as the forces at the disposal of the Germans in France, Belgium and Holland.

3. It is said that the Russians have been given a good picture of the German coastal fortifications in northwest Europe and have now understood what huge efforts will be needed to overcome these fortifications.

4. As a result of strikes in the USA, the output of landing craft has been reduced, which apparently has a bearing on the timing of future operations.

   It may also be mentioned that General Eisenhower has expressed strong objections to sending some landing craft to the Pacific.

5. The nomination of General Montgomery was a cold shower for the optimists who expected the immediate opening of a Second Front, since it is well known that his invariable rule is carefully to prepare an overwhelming superiority of forces first and only then to act.

   Note: As proof that the British forces in the UK are not ready for combined landing operations in Europe, General Montgomery's recent statement that the 3rd Army is the only experienced army in the empire could be used.

6. The coming presidential elections in the USA have an increasing influence on the strategic plans of the Allies. Launching a huge and victorious offensive in Europe shortly before the elections would be a huge boost for the incumbent.

   Note: This statement can be reinforced by the following thought: 'The invasion of North Africa was too late to influence the last elections, but this time around, no timing mistakes will be allowed.'

7. Publication of the fact that the invasion of the Continent will be carried out by forces that are almost three-quarters American has greatly worried the British authorities, since the obvious delay in carrying out the operation and the evident disproportion between the invasion force and the perceived military efforts of the British to date has had a negative effect on British morale.

Execution: The LCS to transmit these legends to Lisbon, Madrid, Stockholm and Bern. Colonel Robertson and Major Blunt are to discuss measures for the dissemination of this paragraph through their channels in London and report to the LCS what has been done in this respect and what can be done in the future.

B1(a) is to give all possible assistance. On point 2, agent 1038 may be used. On point 6 the Americans are to be consulted.

b. Examine the possibility of transmitting maps or documents [illegible; possibly: 'of small' or 'of no'] national importance to the enemy. Execution: For consideration by the RACKET Committee.

IV. Lack of manpower has compelled the British army in the UK to resort to stop-gap measures, since some of its formations are not yet up to strength and do not have adequate administrative support. The number of Anglo-American divisions in the Metropolis that are fit for offensive operations is effectively smaller than the number needed for an invasion. Some American divisions that have arrived in Britain have not yet finished their training.

Realisation:

a. Detailed information will be provided by the Joint Operational Staff of the Allied High Command. Execution: The Joint Operational Staff of the Allied High Command is to draw up a plan. Major Clark is to maintain contact with the staff on this issue.

b. Ask Washington for co-operation on this issue, in particular in connection with the last phrase of the point. To be executed by the LCS. Approach Washington with this request after the Joint Operational Staff has drawn up a plan.

V. The personnel of some Anglo–American divisions that have been abroad for a long time will be replaced by fresh divisions arriving from Britain and the USA and will then be sent to Britain for reorganisation and used for training new soldiers.

Realisation:

Plan FOYNES.

VI. The lack of landing craft remains our main bottleneck, and the number required to carry the first twelve divisions for the invasion cannot be provided by UK and American production before the middle of the summer.

a. It can be indicated that one thousand craft will be needed. To be executed by the LCS. Ask Washington for information on landing craft production.

b. Explore the possibility of planting an indiscreet question in the House of Commons about the alleged lack of landing craft, which the government will refuse to answer. Execution: A final decision on the question is to be delayed until the return of the prime minister. (Action by the Controlling Officer for Deception.)

c. A clamour could be raised in the American press about the lack of landing craft. In order to spread rumours on this issue in the Canadian press, enlist the help of Canadian Naval Intelligence. Execution: Colonel Robertson and Captain Montagu are to submit a draft of a letter to Canadian Naval Intelligence asking for co-operation. Inform Washington about this. The Controlling Officer for Deception is to negotiate with the minister for information.

d. Explore the possibility of chartering ships from neutral countries to be in British ports by 1 July 1944. To be carried out by the LCS. Captain Finter will make inquiries and discuss the question with Captain Montagu.

VII. Carry out an attack on northern Norway jointly with the Russians during the spring of 1944 with the immediate objective of opening a route to Sweden. Subsequently obtain the active co-operation of Sweden in setting up air bases in southern Sweden to cover combined landing operations for the invasion of Denmark from the United Kingdom in the summer of 1944.

Realisation:

a. Anglo–American attack on northern Norway in the spring of 1944. (Preliminary plan pending a final version by the Joint Strategic Staff of the Allied High Command.)

   1. Inquire in Stockholm in regard to the *Tirpitz*. Can it be moved if necessary, in spite of the damages that it has sustained? To be carried out by the LCS. Not urgent. Captain Finter is to submit his views.

2. The Service ministries and Washington circulate a list of Scandinavian radio broadcasts. Action by the LCS. Ask the Service ministries whether this has been done already or when it is going to be done. Also inquire in Washington.

3. In view of the lack of airfields in northern Norway, find out whether the Air Ministry or Coastal Command can take any action that would indicate our intention to use sea planes more widely in 1944.

4. Explore the possibility of appointing the Norwegian crown prince to the Joint Strategic Staff of the Allied High Command or to the post of liaison officer with the Rosyth Force. Execution: To be submitted for consideration by the Joint Allied Staff.

5. Inquire of the Foreign Office about the possibility of convincing the king of Norway to take a friendlier attitude towards the Swedes. Action by the LCS. The Controlling Officer for Deception will make the appropriate inquiries.

6. Find out whether the Secret Intelligence Service can obtain current intelligence about Norway from the Norwegian government. To be carried out by the LCS. The Controlling Officer for Deception to make inquiries of SIS.

7. Find out about the possibility of generating a significant increase in diplomatic wireless traffic between Stockholm and Great Britain. Action by the LCS. The Controlling Officer for Deception is to make the appropriate inquiries. Should approval be given, Captain Finter is to draw up a plan and make agreements with the Radio Communications Committee.

8. Find out about the possibility of boosting the value of Norwegian government bonds. Action by the LCS. The Controlling Officer for Deception is to talk personally with Sir Findlater Stuart,

9. Military training of Norwegians in Sweden. Execution: The Controlling Officer for Deception is to discuss the issue with Strytson on 30 December 1943 and find out about his proposals.

b. Co-operation with the Russians. This question will be decided in Moscow. Action by the LCS. However, it will be possible fairly soon to demonstrate the presence of Russian officers at the General Staff in Scotland or at any other staff that may take charge of this operation. Execution: B1(a) will assist later.

c. Co-operation with the Swedes.

1. The LCS to agree with the Foreign Office about a well-timed, urgent recall of the military, naval and air attachés for consultations. Action by the LCS. The Controlling Officer for Deception is going to discuss the issue with Struts on 30 December 1943.

2. Find out whether the Air Ministry is able to tell the Civil Aviation Board that it considers setting up a more frequent and regular link with Sweden a matter of the utmost importance. Action by the LCS.

VIII. Although the Russians will probably continue their military operations all winter, it will hardly be possible for them to begin their summer offensive before the end of June.

Realisation:
The following will have to be indicated:

a. That the Anglo-American plans were drawn up in agreement with the Russians and that the staffs continue to hold talks simultaneously in Moscow and in London. Action by the LCS and B1(a).

b. That at the Tehran conference full agreement was reached on the timing for the beginning of the Russian-Anglo-American offensive, and there was a unanimous conclusion that any Anglo-American activities will not be of any use if they are carried out before the Russians are ready for their summer offensive. Action by the LCS and B1(a).

IX. Since large-scale operations across the Channel will not be possible before the beginning of autumn, the main military efforts of the Allies during the spring of 1944 have to be directed against the Balkans.

Realisation:

a. The operation will be carried out by the Expeditionary Forces. Execution: Inform Dudley Clark.

b. Request the Service ministries and Washington for lists of people appearing on radio in the Balkan countries. Action by the LCS. Make a request in Washington. Ask Brigadier General Dudley Clark whether he needs information on this point from the War Office, the Air Ministry and the Admiralty.

X. Anglo-American operations in Italy will continue, and combined landing operations will be carried out on the northwest and northeast coasts of Italy to hasten the outcome. If these operations are successful, the 15th Army Group will move to the east through Istria later.

Realisation:

The first part matches Plan AUCKFIELD. In analysing this plan, the first thing to notice is that it is significantly broader-based than earlier versions.

* * * * *

The scale, importance and nature of the measures themselves are also much broader. It is also characteristic that execution of the plan is assigned almost entirely to the LCS. Essentially, TWIST simply records the measures that the LCS and its head, the Controlling Officer for Deception, Colonel Bevan, intend to carry out. It is also interesting that a number of the measures the plan envisages involve the areas of responsibility of several ministries and other important government agencies simultaneously, often requiring practical steps that entail significant expenditures in terms of work and money. Finally, another fact of importance is that the measures to be carried out are being co-ordinated with American government bodies where necessary.

We do not have enough information to judge how this plan is being realised in practice or how effective it is. There is, however, some fragmentary information showing that the plan is being executed and already achieving certain practical results. In particular, the statements of several British statesmen and a number of articles on the topic of a Second Front frequently sound as if they are in harmony with the thoughts contained in the TWIST plan for 1944. We give a few examples:

1. On 2 January of this year, the well-known journalist [James] Garvin wrote in the *Sunday Express* that the appointment of Wilson to the post of Commander in Chief, Mediterranean, dispelled the last remaining doubts that a front was going to be opened in the Balkans in the air, at sea and on land. This event was bound to have a decisive influence on Turkish policy [he wrote]. Moreover, 'when the Western powers make contact with the Soviet armies via the Balkans, the last hour of Hitlerism has come'.

2. The Japanese observer Yasuo Yamada in a radio broadcast on a Second Front on 14 February this year said, among other things: 'The British as well as the Americans fear the heavy losses they will incur as soon as they try to land on the European continent. The Americans in particular know that they have to contribute 73 percent of the troops that will participate in the invasion, while Britain has to contribute only 27 percent. . . .' (There are very many statements on this topic everywhere in the world press.) '. . . The Anglo–Americans themselves are not completely unanimous on the question of the opening of a second front. The British are expecting the USA to make the greatest sacrifices, while the USA does not understand why Great Britain with its seven-million-strong army and large resources cannot begin the invasion itself. The fact is that Great Britain would be much happier to start acting in the Balkans. There it could fight not only against Germany but also against the Russian influence. The Americans naturally look with misgivings on these British plans, but the fact remains that when the time comes for an invasion, the Americans will contribute 73 percent of all troops invading the European continent. . . . Whether a second front will be opened in March or in July, it will cost immense sacrifices.'

3. The well-known American journalist Quentin Reynolds, speaking to the Toronto Press Club on 19 February and surveying the military situation, declared amongst other things that an invasion of Europe across the Channel was so difficult that it probably would never be undertaken. According to him, the defeat of Germany in less than three or four years is almost impossible.

4. From a speech by Churchill of 22 February on the air operations of the Allies: 'The air offensive is the basis on which our plans for an invasion of the Continent are founded. We will achieve a scale of air offensive that will surpass everything that has been done or imagined until now. The governments of the Allied powers will not countenance any suggestion that use of this most powerful weapon should be curtailed to create resources that will speed the end of the war.'

5. General Montgomery's answer to a woman who asked him in the middle of February of this year about when the Second Front would begin is well known: 'It has already begun,' he said.

6. At the beginning of April the *Daily Express* wrote that under present circumstances any attempt made to create a Second Front would be mad.

Any number of examples of similar statements could be given.

There is also a certain amount of intelligence information about British measures to execute the plan cited above. For example:

1. In March of this year rumours about a British invasion of Scandinavia in the near future were widespread in Sweden.

2. At the beginning of April of this year, the British minister in Stockholm approached the Swedish government with a request for the Allies to be permitted to use Swedish air bases. The British naturally did not count on Swedish consent, and this step had the aim of convincing the Germans that the target of an Allied invasion of the Continent would be Norway.

Conclusions

1. The British deception agencies are firmly established as a part of the British state security system.
2. These agencies are in close contact with the most important state institutions of military significance in Britain and enjoy broad support.
3. In preparing operations for the opening of a Second Front, deception is being used together with SIS and MI5 efforts as one of the means for ensuring that these preparations are successful.
4. Attention must be paid to the uncovering of British deception activities in regard to the Soviet Union, on which we do not possess any intelligence information so far.

19 May 1944

37   *MI5 Surveillance of Foreign Diplomatic Missions*

Information on MI5 Targeting of Foreign Missions and Diplomats

1. Structure of the British Counter-Intelligence Apparatus

Surveillance of the activities of foreign missions in the UK and also the investigation of foreigners and Communists is the task of what is called the Security Service. The divisions of the Security Service that deal directly with these matters have the following specific tasks:

1. To investigate and interdict espionage and other anti-state activity on the part of foreign intelligence services
2. Production of intelligence
3. Deception of foreign intelligence services
4. Recruitment of special agents for future use in intelligence work overseas

There are three divisions in the Service that carry out these tasks. The so-called B Division, which handles espionage; E Division, which runs surveillance on foreigners; and the division whose job is the prevention of subversion. The Service also has A, C and D Divisions, which handle other matters.

B Division

This is the cornerstone of the entire counter-intelligence apparatus. Its head is Captain Guy Lidell, who until 1931 worked in Scotland Yard's Special Branch. He is described as a capable and serious counter-intelligence officer of extremely reactionary views. His deputy is Dick White, an energetic intelligence officer who runs all UK operations against German espionage.

B Division has the following sections:

1. B1 (a) runs double agents. Headed by Colonel Robertson, who also represents counter-intelligence on the special inter-departmental committee on deception.
2. B1(l)—Counter-espionage work among British merchant navy crews and civil aviation maintenance staff. Headed by Stopford.
3. B1(b) runs counter-intelligence operations based on radio intercepts. Also runs special operations for examining diplomatic bags and clandestinely removing documents from foreign missions. It also processes the take from Special Camps 020 and 020R, where the most important foreign intelligence agents are held. Run by Hart.
4. B1(c) runs anti-sabotage operations, counter-measures against technical espionage and espionage conducted by former German businesses. Headed by Lord Rothschild.
5. B1(d), the so-called London Reception Centre. Employs specialists, officials with experience in investigative work who interrogate foreigners arriving in the UK. It is linked to the so-called Patriotic Schools, where foreigners arriving to settle in the UK are sent for quarantine and processing. The officers of this section have an excellent command of foreign languages. It is headed by Major Baxter.
6. B1(e) runs Camps 020 and 020R. Headed by Colonel Stevens, of German origin, a fervid reactionary and an anti-Semite.
7. B1(g) is responsible for counter-intelligence against the Spanish, Portuguese and South American services, focussing on the ways these channels are exploited by German intelligence. Surveillance of the relevant embassies. Headed by Brooman-White.
8. B4(b) runs counter-intelligence operations in industry and business and against economic espionage. It is headed by Crawfurd.
9. B1(h) works on Ireland [matters]. Its head is Cecil Liddell, brother of the head of B Division.
10. B3(a) processes the censorship product, examines and analyses intercepted correspondence, deciphers secret writing, conducts preliminary investigations of addressees and senders of mail suspected of espionage. Headed by Berg.
11. B3 liaises with the censorship organisations. Headed by Grogan.
12. B4(a) tracks and investigates POW camp escapees. Head, Major Whyte.
13. B signals, counter-intelligence, detects illegal radio transmitters. Liaises with Sigint [Signals Intelligence].
14. B3(c)—investigation of light signals and carrier pigeons used by enemy intelligence.

B and B3C are under the overall direction of the assistant to the head of B Division, Major Frost, who before 1940 was employed at the British Broadcasting Corporation.

B Division also includes B5, Investigations Section, headed by Hart, and B6, External Surveillance, headed by Hunter.

E Division

Conducts surveillance of foreigners and handles internment issues. It is headed by Brook-Bush and has the following sections and departments:

E1(a) consists of groups who conduct surveillance on the French (headed by Ramsbotham), the Belgian, Norwegians, Danes and Dutch and US citizens.

E1(b)—surveillance of foreign sailors landing in the UK. Headed by Chinnery.

E2—This section is headed by Major Stephen Alley. It has two departments:

E2(a) conducts surveillance on the Finns, Poles and citizens of the former Baltic Republics. Stephen Alley, who runs E2, heads this department as well. Alley lived in Russia for many years and speaks the language fluently. In 1914–18 he was an SIS agent working in the Counter-Intelligence Section of the Russian General Staff. Alley is extremely hostile to the USSR.

E2(b) watches the Hungarians and people from the Balkans. It is headed by Colford.

F Division

F Division's remit is the prevention of subversion. It focusses in particular on countering the Communist Party and Soviet intelligence. Its head is Hollis, who has worked in MI5 since 1934. Before that he was in China. He has been working on the Communist Party since 1938, knows many of the British Party's prominent activists well and has personally run the targeting of the British Party for a long time.

The division has the following sections:

F1 undertakes counter-intelligence work in the army and in government establishments, targeting Communists and Communist sympathisers. It is headed by Lieutenant Colonel Alexander.

F2 operates against the Communist movement. It is run personally by Hollis, the division head. F2 has three sections:

F2(a), which targets the British CP [Communist Party]. It is connected with the agent-running section of the BSS's [British Secret Service] General Staff. It is headed by Maxwell Knight. The department's investigation of the British CP is active; in particular, a major effort has been made to infiltrate agents provocateurs. The department's head is Clark, and his assistant is Miss O'Reilly.

Department F2(b) investigates the activities of the Comintern as a whole, as well as those of Communists and émigrés. One of its principal officers is Miss Bagot, who has headed work on the Comintern in MI5 for many years.

Department F2(c) undertakes MI5 operations against the Soviet intelligence services. Until mid-1940 its head was Mrs Archer (who presently heads SIS's Irish Section). From 1940 to the beginning of 1942 the department was headed by Pilkington. At the present time, F2(b) and F2(c) are run by Shillito.

Section F3 investigates various Fascist nationalist organisations, as well as right-wing organisations and groups and pro-German and defeatist elements. Until recently this section was headed by Aiken-Sneath, but he has now been transferred to the RSS staff, and Bedford is now in charge.

The Service grew significantly during the Second World War. In that period, most of its effort went into countering foreign espionage. The British liquidated the Nazi Party (BUF) organisation, which was thought to have had some thirteen hundred members. Special measures were taken against persons suspected of being linked to German intelligence. Refugees from enemy-occupied territories—thought to total some thirty-four thousand people—were screened, leading to three hundred arrests.

When the threat of German invasion loomed in 1940, a group of counter-intelligence officers was specially attached to the staff of the defence forces.

When and if the time came, these officers were supposed to work closely with local police forces.

2. MI5 Operations Against Foreign Missions

We have specific evidence of British operations against the missions of the Argentine, Brazil, Greece, Germany, Egypt, Spain, Iran, Colombia, Peru, Portugal, Siam, the USSR, Turkey, Chile, Switzerland, Sweden and Japan.

We do not have detailed evidence of operations against the diplomatic missions of Belgium, Holland, Norway, Poland, the USA, France or Czechoslovakia, but we do know that the British have utilised the intelligence services of those countries for their own intelligence purposes and that certain of these— e.g. the Polish and Czech services—are involved in operations against other foreign missions in the UK. The British make especially effective use of the Polish service to this end.

Nevertheless, despite the fact that the Polish government in exile is totally dependent on, and subordinate to, the British, British intelligence organisations illegally monitor the activities even of such individuals as the former Polish premier, General Sikorski, the Polish ambassador to the UK, Raczynski, and others. We have information on the tapping of their telephone conversations, British inspection of secret Polish diplomatic mail, etc.

This shows that the British spare no one in their targeting of diplomatic establishments situated in the territory of the British Empire. From the outset of the Second World War, one of MI5's major tasks has been the detection and interdiction of espionage or subversive activity undertaken by Germany and its allies via the foreign missions of neutral countries and other channels.

The British use a wide variety of techniques in operations against foreign missions: agents (foreign sources, agents on the mission's staff), technical methods, external surveillance, telephone taps, bugging of embassy premises and of public places visited by foreigners and of their private homes, interception and reading of plain-language diplomatic mail, the clandestine removal and replacement of codes and other secret documents, deciphering of coded correspondence, radio intercepts, using agents to 'honeytrap', or compromise, individual foreign mission staff members, etc.

For their targeting of foreign missions, the British have a very large number of agents at their disposal, drawn from an extremely wide range of professional and social backgrounds. They include ambassadors, military attachés, first and second secretaries, counsellors, service and maintenance staff, typists, caretakers, cleaning women, doormen, drivers, etc.

The British also make extensive use as agents of people of some political, social, scientific, literary or similar prominence who have the right sort of background; they also use people from major industrial, banking and trading concerns.

In targeting the Spanish Embassy, for instance, British counter-intelligence used the following agents: the Spanish military attaché, Barra; the chargé d'affaires, Vernon Manes; the press attaché, Brugada; the head of Chancery, Cavernon; Miss McDonald, the counsellor's secretary; the embassy official Arthur Kelber Pinisto; the professor of Spanish at London University, Pastor; the journalist Armesto; the émigré Republican [illegible] and the former Spanish consul in London, Machedo Miguel.

Agents used in targeting the Swedes: The military attaché at the Swedish Embassy, von Rozen;, the assistant military attaché, Marlom; the military attaché's secretary, Miss Maxwell; the former air attaché; the embassy employee Dig. The British used a Czech, Shakhvamer, as their cut-out in dealings with von Rozen and the other agents.

Agents used against the Turkish Embassy: Miss Philipson, the ambassador's private secretary (who was planted on the Turks by MI5); the secretary to the Turkish military attaché, a Turk by [illegible], who was recruited in place and who was run against the military attaché; as well as the embassy charlady.

Employed against the Swiss mission were: the military attaché at the Swiss mission, Schlegel; the press attaché, Kessler; the Swiss businessman Roy [illegible]: the latter was also used by British counter-intelligence as a travelling agent.

In the Chilean Embassy the British used the ambassador and the military attaché; in the Brazilian Embassy, the ambassador, Senhor Mon de Arago, the military attaché and the doorman; in the Argentine Embassy, Don Ricardo Siri, the first secretary. Against the Egyptian mission the British used Lady Dalrymple-Champneys, wife of a senior Ministry of Agriculture official, whom they had enlisted for targeting the Egyptian ambassador and his circle; they also used the ambassador's chauffeur. For the Peruvian Embassy the British used the third secretary, the secretary to the military attaché, Doides, and also the embassy employee Ber Valno, who provided information on the ambassador's activities.

For the Colombian mission the British used a secretary whom they had infiltrated. According to our information, the British have only one agent, the first secretary's servant, involved in their surveillance and investigation of the Portuguese Embassy.

Although the British are well aware of the Portuguese ambassador's pro-British leanings, they are nevertheless making an effort to increase the number of agents in the embassy. The British also use other means to monitor what goes on at the embassy.

Prince Chila is used in the case of the Siamese mission. He is a member of one of the special commissions. He passes to the British information on the attitudes of the country's ruling circles.

We know that the British have an agent in the Iranian Embassy, among the support staff, who supplies them with drafts of official correspondence and also gives them information on all the ambassador's visitors.

The British sources at the Greek Embassy are Moniley, who is on the military attaché's staff, and a British officer, Matthews, who has been seconded to the attaché's staff.

We do not have hard information on the agents deployed by British counter-intelligence before the war in the Japanese, Hungarian, Romanian, Bulgarian, Italian or Finnish Embassies, but the First Directorate has at its disposal extensive evidence that the British were actively targeting these embassies' personnel.

It has been established that British counter-intelligence runs the following agents against members of the Soviet Embassy and other Soviet organisations in the UK: Count Romer; Bara St Golberg; Lady Listowel; the journalist Morton, nicknamed 'Brit' (who provided information on the military attaché Oklyorov and on Counsellor Benko), former Counsellor Novikov, former first secretary Korzh and a number of the Soviet officials; the former Czech Communist Miller-Lozany; the White officer [Kotsov]; the White officer Ustinov and others.

The foregoing certainly represents only a partial list of the British counter-intelligence agents deployed against Soviet citizens. The Soviet organisations in London have on their staff some forty British subjects, a significant number of whom have doubtless been recruited by the British to report on those organisations and their personnel.

British counter-intelligence has also tried several times to run its Bulgarian, Czech, Polish and other agents against individual members of the Soviet Embassy staff.

At the end of September 1941, two Bulgarians named Todorov and Mazabilyev attempted to make contact with the former Soviet Embassy counsellor Novikov, whom the British suspected of involvement in intelligence work. It was later established that both of them were British counter-intelligence agents.

A similar thing happened on 1 April 1942. An unknown Pole telephoned the Soviet Embassy saying that he was a former Communist now serving in the Polish army in Scotland, who had come to London on official business and wanted to meet an official of the embassy to pass on very important information.

It later transpired that the Pole and two other people whom he managed to put in touch with members of our embassy were agents of the Polish or British counter-intelligence services. Many British turn up at the Soviet Embassy under various pretexts to offer their services. They certainly include British counter-intelligence penetration agents.

It has been established that the British maintain active surveillance on the staff of Soviet establishments not just in the UK but also in other countries.

We know, for instance, of a case where one of our officials who had previously worked in Sweden and was to be transferred to the UK for operational reasons, could not get a visa for a long time. It was later established via an agent that British counter-intelligence, which had received quite extensive information from Sweden about this official, used various pretexts to delay giving approval for a visa. Subsequently, as soon as the official arrived in the UK, he was immediately put under investigation. This shows that having targeted one of our officials in one country, British counter-intelligence puts his name on a central register and keeps him under observation wherever he goes.

Information available to us suggests that for the most part, British counter-intelligence recruits its agents on the basis of:

a. In the case of British subjects, patriotism.
b. In the case of foreigners, hostility towards the political systems that have come to power in their native countries (German anti-Fascists, Spanish Republicans and Monarchists, White Russian émigrés).
c. In a third category are those recruited for counter-intelligence work on the basis of their material interest in co-operation with the Service, or their dependence on it—e.g. landlords; hotel owners; pub landlords; restaurant, bar and cafe proprietors, etc.
d. In a fourth category are people who have somehow compromised themselves or been compromised by the British, who take advantage of the opportunity to recruit them.
e. In a fifth category are the agents of other intelligence services, who often have diplomatic passports and who collaborate with the British to exchange intelligence unbeknownst to their own governments.
f. Finally, there are agents of other foreign intelligence services who have been exposed by the British and 'turned'.

We know of a number of cases where a British subject has become aware that someone he knows is behaving suspiciously; or he may be asked to obtain some secret information or a secret document. The British individual concerned has reported the matter to his superiors, who in their turn have informed the counter-intelligence service.

In such instances the Service quite often co-opts the person making the report and involves him in their investigation of the target. The Service recruits extensively among people whose position or whose special knowledge makes them valuable in targeting foreign missions and foreigners generally. In most cases, these people are run against secretaries, interpreters, guides, maintenance staff, and so on. People of prominence in British society are also used in this direction. People in the latter category are run by the British under the cover of all sorts of cultural, scientific and other organisations or bodies that are in close contact with foreign missions and individual foreigners.

A typical example of British exploitation of compromising materials for agent recruiting is by their enrolment of a number of Spaniards in London. The British became aware that José Brugada, the press attaché at the Spanish Embassy and the member of a well-to-do family of Monarchist sympathisers, had once embezzled money from the Press Office funds.

Trading on his moral and political unreliability, and also the fact that his mother was British, MI5 recruited him. They established after the fact that he had earlier been recruited by the Germans. While collaborating with the British, Brugada gave them valuable intelligence on his recruitment by the Germans, on all the tasks given to him by the Germans (both directly and via Alcazar, an official of the Spanish Embassy), and also betrayed to them two Spanish double agents, Martin Casabar and Onofre Garcia Tirado, intelligence agents of the British Ministry of Economic Warfare who had been recruited by German intelligence. The British recruited the former Spanish consul in London, a Basque and a long-time member of the Falange Party. During the Civil War, Lajendia was in Chile, where he was very active on the part of the Falangists. In recruiting him, the British assessment was that he did not have firm political views and had a vain and ambitious personality.

The Chilean ambassador in London, Don Manuel Bianchi, was suspected by the British of spying for the Germans. Illegal financial operations on his part led to his being compromised and then recruited by the British.

When targeting officials at a foreign mission, the British often lure them deliberately into drunkenness and debauchery. They then blackmail them over their financial difficulties or other misbehaviour and recruit them directly or under threat of being expelled from the UK.

It is well known that for various reasons a number of officials in diplomatic missions, especially those whose job it is to obtain intelligence (e.g. military attachés), are not always able to do their jobs. Knowing this, the British entice military attachés to collaborate with them in exchange for intelligence, which the British provide.

We are aware that the British are exploiting the Chilean military attaché, air force captain Don Ricardo Garcia, in this way, as well as the Brazilian military attaché.

Regardless of the extent to which they trust their agents, especially foreigners, the British check on them regularly via a parallel agent network and investigate them thoroughly using all available techniques.

We know the following for a fact. The former Russian naval captain Nikolai Mukalov, a Russian born in Kiev in 1876, lives in London with his wife. Our organisation shot Mukalov's brother during the Civil War. Mukalov comes from a shipowner's family and is anti-Soviet. He has been collaborating with British intelligence for a long time. Nevertheless, MI5 continues to keep him under active investigation. Indeed, from information at our disposal, they have had him under investigation for twenty-seven years.

MI5 will base a decision to classify someone as an active target for its agents on the following information:

a. Reports from British intelligence sources abroad that persons suspected of spying or who are established spies are headed to the UK
b. Suspicious behaviour by an official of a foreign mission while he is in transit to the UK or while he is in the country
c. Intelligence obtained from telephone taps or microphones
d. Intelligence obtained from radio intercepts, from opening diplomatic mail or by ISK
e. Contacts by foreigners with persons known to the British to be involved in some sort of subversive activity
f. Information from inside agents or informers about subversive activity on the part of officials of foreign missions or persons connected with them
g. Evidence from arrested spies about persons connected with their intelligence operations

There follow some examples of British agent investigations:

The de Menezes Case

In 1942, de Menezes arrived in London to take up a post with the Portuguese Embassy. The British subsequently received a report from a source overseas that de Menezes was an agent of German intelligence. Despite thorough MI5 surveillance on de Menezes, no hard information was obtained about his involvement in espionage activity. The only thing that aroused their suspicion was that he had bought soda, which, they suggested, might be used for making invisible ink for secret writing.

On examining the diplomatic mail sent by the Portuguese Embassy to Lisbon, the British established that de Menezes had used secret writing to put some information on the backs of papers he was sending out. The British, worried about damaging diplomatic mail through their own processing, were unable to read the secret writing and thus establish the exact nature of the information. However, the British exploited the friendly attitude of the Portuguese ambassador and with his co-operation exposed the secret-writing techniques and charged de Menezes with spying for Germany.

The Herman Case

Herman was *resident* of a foreign intelligence service working in London undercover as the manager of the London office of the Federated Press of America. He was targeted as a consequence of his own carelessness, and as a result, he had to cease operating, and some of those connected with him in the intelligence operations were neutralised by the British.

He was 'blown' because:

Persons connected with Herman visited a foreign embassy.
Police who had these people under observation were themselves discovered to be under counter-surveillance.

For the entire time that the Federated Press of America office operated, it received not a single item of journalism-related mail, and not one Federated Press of America correspondent ever visited its office.

The Macartney Case

In 1927 an official of a City firm told MI5 that his friend Macartney had suggested to him that he might earn some money by collecting material on military aviation by filling in a special questionnaire. After photographing the questionnaire, the British established by expert analysis that it was so thorough and all-embracing that it could not have been compiled by one individual but had to be the work of a number of intelligence officers who specialised in aviation. The experts who investigated came to the conclusion that the questionnaire had been translated from Russian into English. Further investigation allowed the British to uncover, and then eliminate, a group of individuals working for the USSR.

The Case of Glading and Others

All these individuals were known to the British as Communists. The last two were engineers at the Woolwich Arsenal.

Glading, previously the most active Communist in the group, but who had suddenly severed all his connections with the CPGB [Communist Party of Great Britain], was targeted by Miss X, a senior MI5 agent. In order to get close to Glading, Miss X, on the instructions of MI5, joined the Anglo-Russian Friendship Society, where she got to know and later became friendly with Glading, who employed her as a typist. As she gained his confidence, he began to give Miss X special assignments and finally ordered her to rent a flat for clandestine use; she reported this straightaway to MI5, and surveillance by the British on the flat established that Glading was using it to meet Woolwich Arsenal employees who were bringing him secret material, which he then photographed.

At one of those meetings the British arrested Glading, Williams and Bowman. A search of the flat revealed photographic negatives and film of drawings of secret aircraft designs, and they also found other substantive proof implicating the group in intelligence activity.

The Case of the Spanish Journalist Calvo

In targeting foreign missions and foreigners, the British attach high importance to external surveillance. The MI5 surveillance manual states: 'In many cases external surveillance is the only way to establish a suspect's connections and to obtain substantive evidence enabling charges to be brought.'

For a target to come under surveillance is one of the main indications that he is under active investigation.

The British make extensive use of surveillance against foreigners and their connections, as evidenced by the fact that in just the period from May to November 1941, according to information in our possession from surveillance reports, seventy-three people were deployed on external surveillance of Soviet Embassy personnel.

Material at our disposal on how agent-based investigations were handled operationally shows that the active use of external surveillance played a large part in bringing the investigations to a conclusion.

The surveillance manual shows that the British are endeavouring to raise the level of skill of their officers and to improve the selection and training of personnel so as to raise, in turn, the quality of external surveillance.

To give a picture of how external surveillance is actually run, we set out below a copy of an MI5 surveillance report on the Soviet journalist Bondarenko.

Report by NN on Leonid Petrovich Bondarenko, 49 Highstone Street.
20 March 1942.

External surveillance on the above address was established on 1 March, but Bondarenko was not seen. We therefore had to double-check the address. At 9.10 a.m. on 16 March he headed for Saxby's leather-goods shop in Candeman Street, where he purchased a leather suitcase. He then walked to the Reuters Building on Fleet Street, where the TASS Agency is located. At 11.20 he came out and walked along the Embankment. He returned to Fleet Street, where he jumped on a bus headed for Aldwych. From there he went up Kingsway, then suddenly ran for a moving bus. He ran many yards before boarding it and travelling to Russell Square, where he visited the Ministry of Information. He was there from 12 noon to 1.15. He then returned to his Fleet Street office. At 1.20 he went out with two men, evidently colleagues; they went to the Flagstaff Restaurant, where they lunched together. They came out at 2.50 p.m. and all returned to the Reuters Building. One of Bondarenko's companions departed. The following are the distinguishing features of the latter, to whom we shall henceforward refer as 'A': age about forty-five, height 178 centimetres, medium build, clean-shaven, brown hair, wears tortoiseshell-framed glasses, blue suit, light-coloured coat, soft black hat. After leaving Bondarenko, he proceeded to Cone Street, to the editorial office of the *Daily Sketch*. He remained there till 3.28 p.m., when he returned to the Reuters Building. Meanwhile, Bondarenko saw the second man, whom we will designate as Target B, who had gone back into the Reuters Building. B's distinguishing features are: age around fifty, height 173 centimetres, stout, weak-looking, black hair, moustache, wearing a black suit, a dark coat. Possibly Russian. At 5.10 p.m. he came out and hailed a taxi, and we lost him.

On 17 March, Bondarenko arrived at TASS at 9.50 a.m., remaining there until 1.40 p.m., when he went to the Ministry of Information. He left there without being spotted. At 4.20 p.m. he was observed returning to the Reuters Building with a woman who was evidently his wife. At 6.50 p.m. he came out and went home. Although he seemed to be alone, it is possible that his wife accompanied him. There was no further sighting of him that day.

On 18 March, Bondarenko left home for the Reuters Building at 8.50 a.m. At 11.00 a.m. he left there with Sverlov and an unknown man (whom we will refer to henceforward as 'C') for the British News offices in Soho Square. He remained there till 12.12 p.m., then returned to 85 Fleet Street.

C's distinguishing features: age forty-four, height five feet eleven inches, running to fat, dark brown hair, gold-rimmed glasses, clean-shaven, swarthy.

At 1.05 p.m. Bondarenko came out with Target C and went to the Soviet Embassy in Kensington Palace Gardens. They entered at 2.00. We did not establish the time they left. It cannot be ruled out that they departed in an official vehicle. At 3.55 p.m. Bondarenko was observed re-entering 85 Fleet Street [but] with a woman, evidently his wife, but the latter came out again almost immediately and departed in the taxi in which she had arrived. Bondarenko came out at 5.00 p.m. and headed for the *Daily Express* headquarters; he made his way to the room occupied by the *Evening Standard* and went in. At 5.25 p.m. he visited the World News office on Bouverie Street, where he remained until 7.15 p.m.; he then went back to the Reuters Building. He remained there until 17.45 p.m., when that day's surveillance terminated.

On 19 March, Bondarenko left home at 9.40 a.m. for 85 Fleet Street, where he stayed until 11.55, when he came out and hailed a taxi, and we lost him. Up till 4.35 p.m. there was no sight of him at Fleet Street or the Ministry of Information. At that time he was sighted on Fleet Street heading towards the tailors M. Dennett, where he remained until 4.55 p.m. He then returned to 85 Fleet Street.

His connections B and C came out of the building at 7.40 p.m.

At 8.15 p.m. it became impossible to maintain surveillance. Up till then, Bondarenko was evidently in the Reuters Building. Surveillance is continuing.

In their targeting of foreign missions the British make extensive use of secret examination of diplomatic and other mail; material is also actually clandestinely extracted. For this reason the British pay careful attention to the ways and means by which diplomatic mail is sent. MI5 has compiled a special handbook including a summary of the methods used by foreign missions in dispatching their mail and also the ways in which MI5 examines secret mail.

We know that in examining the Portuguese Embassy's diplomatic mail, the British did not limit themselves to photographing papers of interest to them. They also treated the mail with chemicals or put it under UV light. The thoroughness of their examination enabled the British to establish that the Portuguese diplomatic mail was being used to transmit secret information to German intelligence.

British examination of the diplomatic mail is sometimes clumsy. One consequence was a request by the representatives of the Polish government in London to desist from this sort of operation.

One of the Spanish Embassy surveillance reports indicated that the British had twice clandestinely removed Spanish ciphers. In addition, the British had broken several codes used by the Spanish by tackling it analytically.

The British stop at nothing, even physical force, to get hold of papers of interest to them, as in the case of the Arcos raid in 1927.

In 1942 an attempt was made to get hold of papers of interest to the British by staging break-ins at the flats of Bogomolov, the Soviet ambassador to the Allied governments, and the military attaché Colonel Sklyarov. It is interesting to note that the 'robbers' were looking only for documents and did not lift anything of value.

In their operations against foreign missions and in investigating foreigners and Communists, the British make extensive use of telephone taps and the bugging of foreign missions and the homes of those targeted for investigation.

Documents in our possession indicate that all telephone conversations in foreign missions are permanently monitored by MI5. This is also true of the home phones of foreigners targeted by the British. Reports on monitored calls are kept in the targets' files.

The British make a special effort to monitor the telephone conversations of employees of Soviet establishments, who all too frequently forget they are being overheard and thus provide the British with valuable material and enable them to plan specific operational measures. The taped conversations also provide the British with information on Soviet institutions' contacts in the UK. For example, one tap report contains the following notes: '21 November 1941. 1542 hrs. Soviet Embassy staff member Yakubovnik rang a restaurant and booked a private room for a meeting with Bogomolov.'

A file note of 19 September 1941 indicates that at 1550 hrs the Soviet military attaché, Colonel Sklyarov, agreed to have breakfast with the Swedish military attaché, von Rozen.

A file note of 23 May 1942 established that the Soviet Embassy official Korzh had set up a meeting in a restaurant with Morgan. The British then set up external surveillance. We have information that the British intended to recruit Morgan to target Korzh. Based on intercepted telephone conversations of the Soviet Embassy official Annie Aptekar, the British concluded that she worked for Soviet intelligence and put her under intensive surveillance. We know of cases where the British tap the phones of people who have not yet come to notice, and then decide to subject them to a thorough check or even at times to investigate them on suspicion of espionage. The British tapping operation is highly sophisticated. Their recorders clearly incorporate a time clock, since the file notes of monitored conversations pinpoint the times to the nearest minute. All conversations are recorded on tape and then scanned; where necessary, translations are made. We know of a number of cases in which, by planting microphones, MI5 has obtained extremely important operational intelligence. For example, they are attempting to use this technique to get information on links between the Communist Party and official Soviet institutions in the UK. For instance, MI5 planted a microphone in one of the flats rented by the CPGB for visits by Party organisations and soon discovered that one of the reasons the flat had been rented was to receive secret intelligence by questioning Communists who were serving in the army.

On 7 January 1942, MI5 monitored a conversation taking place in one of the CPGB members' flat with a Soviet Embassy official. MI5 also bugs the homes of CPGB officials. Using a microphone in the CPGB's headquarters, they established that the courier between the CPGB and one of the Comintern's organisations was an official of the Chilean Embassy in London. In their surveillance of foreign missions the British also examine and analyse, on a broad scale, all non-secret incoming and outgoing mail. They also scrutinise the mail of persons under investigation. Such mail is always photographed, sometimes treated chemically, and also translated, and copies are kept in the targets' files. If correspondence refers to individuals who have already come to notice, extracts are taken or memoranda prepared, which are passed to the relevant authorities.

The Post Office and [various] companies are involved in the mail intercept programme. It is also worth noting that in addition to the methods described above, in targeting the Soviet community the British also exploit the opportunities presented by the structure of government and other bodies, all the more since the links between representatives of these bodies and the Soviet community have recently been growing.

In order to bring intense and skilled focus to the targeting of Soviet citizens, MI5 has created special sections, the so-called Russian sections, in a number of ministries and government departments, whose real task is intelligence and counter-intelligence—in particular, vis-à-vis the Soviet community in the UK. In addition to their counter-intelligence functions, these sections are also tasked with taking extensive precautions in industrial and military establishments, military depots and other targets visited by Russian officials to prevent the latter from getting to know anything about secret or new armaments.

The most important of these sections are in the War Office, the Admiralty, the Air Ministry and the Ministry of Information.

The staff of these sections are drawn from among people with intelligence experience who have spent time in Tsarist Russia or the USSR and who, in most cases, speak Russian well. As a rule, those who work in the Russian sections are first sent to Oxford for a special training programme, with particular emphasis on improving their Russian. Each student gets a bonus of £80 for passing the course.

(a) War Office Russian Section

This section's official task is liaison with the Soviet military and trade missions in the UK on matters relating to military shipments to the USSR. It also is in de facto control of all links between these missions and various British establishments, commercial firms, depots, industrial enterprises, port authorities, etc. MI5 has seconded senior officials to all the principal posts in the section. It is headed by General Staff Brigadier Firebrace, who served as military attaché in Moscow in 1937 and in Riga prior to that. Although he is getting on in years, he is described as an energetic and capable intelligence officer with a hostile attitude towards the USSR.

We know that the following counter-intelligence personnel work in Firebrace's section—Lieutenant Creighton, Sergeant Kaplan and Lieutenant Raymond.

(b) Air Ministry Russian Section

This is headed by an RAF officer, I.E. Pennington. We know the following are members of the section:

Lev Arnoldovich Coxon, fifty-four, born in Russia, had a capital fund there of some 60,000 roubles at the time of the October Revolution. Speaks excellent, accentless Russian. Took part in the [Anglo-Franco-American] Intervention [in the Russian Civil War], after which he worked for British tourist organisations. He has been to the USSR twice, in 1936 and in 1941–42. Extremely interested in Soviet art and literature. Attempts to present himself as a friend of the USSR and someone who is dissatisfied with the British.

Viktor Yegorovich Cottam, aged approximately forty-eight or forty-nine. Father lived in Russia for about twenty years, was co-owner of a cotton mill. According to Cottam, his family lost three million roubles as a result of the Revolution. He lived in the USSR until 1916. He served in the RFC [Royal Flying Corps] / RAF from 1916 to 1925 and then became a cotton merchant. As a Russian speaker, he was sent on an intelligence course in 1939 and then served as a military intelligence officer. He has been to the USSR twice in 1941–43. In talking to our officers he jokingly refers to himself as 'the Gestapo' and makes no attempt to conceal the fact that he is an intelligence officer.

Mikhail Semyonovich Father, about fifty, born in Russia, father Russian. His wife was also born in Russia. Father lived in Russia until 1919, graduated from Moscow University, served in the Persian army as an artillery officer, and then became a staff officer to General Denikin in the British mission. Speaks accentless Russian. After the outbreak of war, Father completed a course at the Intelligence School and, before his transfer to the Air Ministry, worked as a military intelligence officer. Father has extensive connections among the White Russian community in the UK. He is described as a cunning man who lives simply, is well liked, educated and relatively well informed about the situation in the USSR.

The Russian sections keep a close eye on all Russian officials, their jobs, their behaviour, etc., and on everything related to the official tasks of the military and trade missions.

One of our agents (a Soviet citizen in the UK) has reported that on a visit to the Russian Section of the War Office in connection with visits by trade delegation representatives to British factories, he happened to see that one of the section's officers had a big sheet of paper on which was a chart of the trade mission's engineering section, showing the names of every one of our engineers; against each name were notes of the visits and trips they had made to British businesses.

Another of our agents has told us that when he was in the same section, one of the secretaries carelessly dropped on the floor a file she was taking out of a fireproof cabinet. Out of it fell papers, seals, stamps, envelopes and various blank forms. Our agent went to help the secretary to pick them all up, and when he took a quick look, he saw that [next sentence illegible]. Soviet officials visiting British firms are never left unobserved. Wherever they are likely to appear, people are stationed there, Russian speakers who listen to every word our officials say.

Knowing that some of our officials, especially some of our pilots who are in Britain to ferry back British aircraft, are fond of a drink, the British take every opportunity to entice them to take a glass or two, using various excuses to try to get them drunk and hoping to take advantage of any careless talk that might result.

MI5 Deception Operations

The importance that the British attach to deception is underscored by [the fact that] an MI5 [representative] sits on the so-called Inter-Departmental Committee, whose members include representatives of the [Secret] Intelligence Service, the MEW [Ministry of Economic Warfare]'s Intelligence Department, Military Intelligence and the FO [Foreign Office]. Lieutenant Colonel Robertson of B Division of the Security Service has a special department, B1(a), whose task is to run a network of double agents who are used for deception operations against enemy intelligence services. Lieutenant Colonel Robertson is in charge of this department.

In 1927 a GRU officer attempted to get hold of the RAF secret manual. This came to the attention of British counter-intelligence, which took the opportunity for a deception operation. It had in fact been proposed at that time that a new manual should be developed for the RAF, although this was known only to a handful of senior people. The British decided to use an agent to pass a copy of the *old* manual to the GRU officer. The British conceived a script that enabled them to explain to the GRU officer how the manual had been acquired and eventually put into his hands without arousing any suspicion on his part that, in fact, he was the target of a deception ploy. The operation also gave them the opportunity to subsequently target the officer concerned.

Shortly before the British and Japanese went to war in 1941, the British became aware of the close ties between Professor Derazville, who had once worked at the Foreign Office, and the Japanese Embassy. A check established that Derazville was a close friend of Sir Edward Grigg, MP. It was also established that Derazville was passing on to the Japanese information of interest to them, which he had obtained through his personal ties with highly placed people. MI5 took steps to warn Grigg and then used him as a channel for deception against the Japanese.

In 1941 two German agents, Norwegian nationals, were landed in Britain to carry out sabotage at power stations. The British turned them and communicated to the Germans that their agents had got work at a power station near Basingstoke and now needed the equipment and material required for their sabotage work. The Germans replied that everything they required would be parachuted to them. In order to deceive the Germans even further, the British evolved a phoney sabotage plan.

ZIGZAG landed by parachute near Thetford to carry out sabotage at the de Havilland Mosquito [airplane] plant. He was turned and sent back to Germany via Lisbon to pass false intelligence to the Germans and get a new assignment to spy in the UK.

The first secretary at the Portuguese Embassy was known to the British as a German agent, and he was fed deception material. Officials at the Spanish Embassy working for the Germans were fed a false list of codes. They were also fed information about opportunities for sabotage and duped into asking for explosives.

The Royal Patriotic School

This is officially known as the London Reception Centre. It takes in and vets émigrés arriving from German-occupied countries and also those seeking to join the military units of Allied governments in exile. Its main purpose is to prevent enemy agents from penetrating the UK, as well as to collect intelligence.

After being vetted at the school, some of the foreigners, particularly those determined to be agents of hostile intelligence services, as well as people suspected of espionage, are sent to special camps, either to sit out the war or to be further processed.

Some 155 foreigners passed through the school in January 1941. In September of the same year, it handled 942. All those employed at the school work for MI5. The school is divided into sections—i.e. Europe (Belgium, Holland, Switzerland, Luxembourg), which is headed by Thompson, cover name 'Terry'; the French and French Colonies Section, headed by [illegible], cover name [illegible], the Scandinavian and Finnish Section, headed by Captain [illegible], cover name 'Slocombe'; the Spanish and Portuguese Section, headed by Green, cover name 'Prior'; eastern Europe, headed by Kingsford, cover name 'Coyle'; and the Polish Section, headed by Captain Scott, cover name 'Stokes'.

The British pay very close attention to individuals arriving from the USSR (especially Poles), since they suspect a significant number of Soviet intelligence agents are included among them. In addition to the country sections, the school also has information and technical departments, including photography, registry, housekeeping, etc.

38   MI5's Targeting of Foreign Diplomatic Missions in London

TOP SECRET

MI5 targets foreign missions accredited to the British government in London. We have information that they have targeted the Swedish, Swiss, Spanish, Turkish, Portuguese, Egyptian, Brazilian, Chilean and Peruvian missions.

Since the start of hostilities with Germany, MI5's main objective has been to determine what espionage activity was being carried out via the missions for the benefit of their home countries and, above all, Germany.

MI5 focussed most heavily on the Spanish and Swedish missions and has a considerable network among the staff of the Spanish mission. The following are known to be British agents:

Barra, the military attaché
Vernon Igles, chargé d'affaires
Brugada, press attaché
The counsellor
The secretary to the counsellor
Bill de Pimego and Arthur Barriento Bilber, colleagues of Miss Pastor, professor of Spanish at London University
Ardesto, a journalist
Gardiano, a Republican in Negrin's circle, and others

In targeting the Spaniards through agents, radio intercepts, telegram decrypts and opening diplomatic bags, MI5 established that in 1940 a Spanish spy network was set up operating on German orders. The network was initially run by the embassy's second secretary and later by the journalist Luis Calvo.

It is clear from information available to us that the British have uncovered a significant amount about this organisation. They established that Olivares Sugreta came to London at the beginning of 1940 to set it up. He remained until April. He recruited Miguel de Lojendio as his main agent. The Spanish consul in London and the embassy's second secretary, Miguel de Lojendio, was recalled to Spain at the end of 1940 under suspicion of ties with MI5 and sent for trial. In January 1941, Alcazar de Velasco came to London twice under the cover of embassy press attaché. His special assignment was to activate Spanish espionage work in the UK, and during his second visit he recruited the press attaché Brugada and the journalist Luis Calvo as his main agents. In turn, MI5 stepped up operations against the Spaniards, and they ran double agents against Calvo, including a Welshman named Williams, under the code name GW, who was deployed against Alcazar; and Luis Calvo was arrested. The following were used as double agents: Arthur Ignacetto & Cellier—to provide information on what Alcazar was sending out and on communications techniques; he was also used for deception material. GW was used to uncover the agent network and the nature of its assignment, and [he] exposed Miguel Pivovih de Joso, the journalist; Segundo Bertasco, an embassy doorman; and the journalist Luis Calvo.

Tasks he was given by the Spaniards included procuring of intelligence on ship and cargo arrivals, disruption at military plants and production levels. On MI5's instructions GW suggested to the Germans that his main task should be sabotage. He asked them to send him explosives and instructions. He gave them phoney lists of codes and ciphers, for which he asked £500. He appropriated £3,900, which Pirnaukh had given him for safekeeping.

During MI5's interrogation after his arrest, Calvo identified as spies: Itturande, the commercial attaché; Ramiro Pinelo, the commercial attaché's secretary; Garcia Gastrilo, a fruit merchant; Count Arthoz, the Spanish consul in Cardiff, and others. According to Calvo, the Spanish espionage network covered the whole country.

Most of the Spanish Embassy staff in London worked for the Germans, but as a result of MI5's efforts, many of them are now in fact working against Germany in the British interest.

TONY meets these agents and manages and directs them. He obtains material, some of which he passes to us, but he does not tell us in detail about his work with them. We need to take into account what we know about MI5's operations against foreign missions in our own counter-intelligence work in the Soviet community in London.

Attention must also be drawn to the fact that we have not received from TONY, or from our other sources, any serious material on MI5's operations against Soviet establishments.

Khrantsov

39   Elena Modrzhinskaya's Report, April 1943

I. British Intelligence Assessments of the USSR

Shortly before the German attack on the Soviet Union, 'intelligence services' [IS] circles began to turn their minds to a possible Anglo-Soviet war. In that connection a special IS bureau was set up to study the situation in the Caucasus, the Ukraine and Bessararabia. The Russian Bureau staff includes such British intelligence experts on Russia as Clively (who presently heads the Russian Section of the British Ministry of Economic Warfare's intelligence organisation), David Roberts (who, according to information at our disposal, has worked in British intelligence against the USSR since 1926 and who is now air attaché in the [British Embassy in the] USSR), Allen, a specialist on the Caucasus, and others.

At a very early stage in the war (August 1941), an appreciation by the Joint Intelligence Committee of the Combined Chiefs of Staff of the prospect of a German-Soviet war showed that British intelligence underestimated the strengths of the USSR. Their papers showed that the British envisaged a retreat by Soviet forces beyond the Urals and expressed the view that while it might be possible for the Soviets to retain power, this would be only temporary. 'Despite the fact that there is dissatisfaction with the regime inside the country, it might be able to hang on until the following summer.' They appreciated that in the best case, if Moscow and the Donbass were lost, the Soviets would still be able to field sixty or seventy divisions, including those in the Far East, but that resistance to the Germans could not be of an offensive nature.

According to agents' reports, in his instructions to Cripps in the first months of the war, Eden suggested that steps be taken to set up British consulates in Baku, Tbilisi, Astrakhan, Novosibirsk and Vladivostok so as to have British representation in these points of special importance to the British 'should Soviet resistance crumble'.

As always, Soviet oil was the focus of keen British interest. In 1941 the British War Cabinet undertook a special review of a plan to destroy the Baku oilfields. The plan was written by MacPherson, an official of the Air Ministry, a personal friend of Churchill's and a leading specialist in oil matters. It was felt desirable to avoid putting pressure on the Soviet government over this question, but the Cabinet also felt obliged to offer the Russians credit, 'otherwise, the Russians will not resolve to put themselves in an economically and hence politically subordinate position vis-à-vis the western European powers by the destruction of a vital part of their oil industry.'

The British decided that if the USSR did not agree to destroy the fields, the British would do it themselves by sabotage, an approach considered more effective that air raids. MacPherson's note states clearly that the Russian oilfields are 'vulnerable to well-organised, systematic sabotage, in the wake of which the country's industry would be significantly stalled for many years, since Russia's entire economy depends on oil'.

To support the implementation of their plans the British intensified their espionage in the Caucasus both directly and via Iran, Turkey and Egypt. Their expectations coloured by the interpretation of the situation in the USSR provided by their anti-Soviet agents, the British supposed they would see signs of internal dissension and disturbances. But after the first few months of war they were compelled to admit that 'the solidarity of the regime, which was doubtful at the outbreak of war, is no longer open to question'.

As the war unfolded, British intelligence in the USSR has devoted its attention to the internal situation, Soviet economic and military power and the state of our reserves, drawing heavily in the process on material provided by other Allied intelligence services. We know, for instance, that in September 1942 representatives of the British Ministry of Economic Warfare and the General Staff had talks with American intelligence about the USSR's military potential.

On 15 February 1943 the Joint Intelligence Sub-Committee circulated a paper on the military situation on the Soviet-German front. It noted the numerical superiority of the USSR in troops, the satisfactory supply and transport position and the Red Army's high morale. It pointed out the big German losses and stressed that the situation could arise where German resistance was broken and Germany would face the threat of anarchy. The British appreciated that in that event, they might even be obliged to ask their Allies to send troops into Germany. The same paper notes the risk of post-war Soviet influence in Bulgaria, Romania and Hungary. The entire paper is testimony to a fear of the Red Army's success and the growth of the Soviet Union's influence.

[II.] Senior British Intelligence Personnel Working Against Us

The senior levels of the British intelligence organisation include bitter enemies of the Soviet Union who have been involved in work against us for many year.

Work against the USSR within SIS is run by Department P-10 of the Intelligence Directorate, which is headed by Denny. The SIS Security Directorate, which is responsible for counter-intelligence work overseas, is headed by Colonel Vivian, the deputy to the chief of SIS, Menzies. Vivian worked with Kolchak in the past and is considered to be an authority in the struggle against Bolshevism. The SIS representative on the Joint Wireless Committee is Major Ferguson, who accompanied Eden to Ankara in early 1941 and is a senior SIS officer dealing with the Near East and the USSR; in the past he was close to Shell chairman Sir Henry Deterding. The head of the SIS French Section is the former HoS [head of station] in Paris, Dunderdale, who was born in Nikolaev and is the son of the former manager of the Vickers works in Kronstadt and Countess Demidov. As far back as 1921, Dunderdale was on the staff of the British station in Turkey, running operations into the USSR. He speaks Russian and has White Guard connections. A senior British intelligence officer, Paul Dukes, is involved in training intelligence personnel on Soviet matters. Before the war he spent some time in Berlin, where he is said to have been linked with Goebbels; in 1939 he attempted to re-enter the USSR, citing his 'pro-Soviet' views.

Elisabeth Hill, a White émigré and the daughter of General Miller, plays a leading part in teaching Russian to British intelligence personnel. Hill is connected to the reactionary 'Imperial Policy' group. She believes that the Russian people should soon get rid of the Bolsheviks and that if they did, the British would come to their aid.

MI3, the Russian Section of British Military Intelligence, is headed by Captain Tamplin. He speaks excellent Russian, having been born in St Petersburg and lived in Russia until he was nineteen; his parents had a paint and varnish factory there. After the German attack on the USSR, Tamplin stated that the war would not last more than one–two months. Both Tamplin and his assistant Sillem stand out even among the reactionary officer corps in Military Intelligence by virtue of their acutely anti-Soviet views. Sillem's pro-German attitude is especially marked; as far back as 1918–20 he was involved in anti-Soviet operations in the Baltic States.

Firebrace, a career military intelligence officer and a former British military attaché in the USSR, heads a special Russian Section of Military Intelligence that handles liaison with the Soviet military mission in the UK and the Soviet organisations dealing with the British on matters of military and economic aid. He plays an active part in decisions about shipments to the USSR. In his opinion, it is the Bolsheviks and not the Germans who are Britain's main enemy. He has a good knowledge of Russian, and his section handles surveillance of the Soviet trade mission, our shipment inspectors, etc.

British intelligence created a special organisation to undertake espionage operations in the Caucasus. According to an informant, this is the Central Asian Bureau (an intelligence section set up among the staff of the British Armed Forces Middle East). Its head is said to be Colonel Adrian Simpson, who is based in Cairo.

Simpson was posted to Cairo in 1940 and tasked with running sabotage operations in the Caucasus to prevent oil being shipped to Germany. According to other agent information, British intelligence operations in the Caucasus were run until 1941 by a special bureau headed by Oliver Baldwin, son of the former prime minister. It is claimed that during Intervention, Baldwin was in the Caucasus and linked with the Dashnaks [Armenian Political Society]. A leading officer of this bureau was Phillip Thornton, who was apparently in Soviet Armenia shortly before the war as a representative of a British trading firm.

Thornton went there again on Baldwin's order in June 1941, crossing the Soviet-Turkish frontier illegally to establish contact with Caucasian nationalist organisations. (At the present time Thornton is formally on the staff of the British Ministry of Information.) Allen, a career intelligence officer and a former BUF (British Union of Fascists) member who had close personal ties in the past to Goebbels, is a British military intelligence specialist on the Caucasus. Allen currently has a close relationship with Lord Phillimore of the 'Imperial Policy' group. According to agents' information, Allen believes that Soviet Georgia should be annexed to Armenia, and he makes periodic trips to Iran. In the UK he was linked with anti-Soviet representatives of the Caucasus émigré community. He is married to a White émigré.

Diplomatic intelligence is handled by the Research Department of the Foreign Office; the department's Russian Section is headed by Brigadier Scaife.

The Russian section of the intelligence organisation of the British Ministry of Economic Warfare is run by Clively, who has been involved in work against the USSR since 1921. He was born and raised in Russia (his father was a British consul). Clively expressed the view, shortly before the Soviet-German war started, that it would lead to the Soviet Union's dismemberment.

Clively has links on intelligence matters with Finns and the Poles. The White Russian émigré Konstantin Postan works in the Ministry of Economic Warfare, running a special section that collects information on military and economic targets in the USSR, which it passes to SOE. (Postan is currently employed in the War Cabinet Secretariat and is also a member of a secret committee of the Royal Institute of International Affairs that prepares papers for the government on future Anglo-Soviet relations and likely Soviet post-war policy.) One of SOE's principal operators, George Hill, spent his childhood in Russia, is fluent in Russian and has worked against Russia in the past together with Sidney Reilly, Paul Dukes and Robert Bruce Lockhart. In 1921 he operated against the USSR from Bulgaria and later from the Baltic States. At one time he worked at the Head Office of British intelligence in the Section D area (sabotage and terrorist operations). At the end of 1940, Section D was taken out of SIS and transferred to the Ministry of Economic Warfare, where it became SOE, the major intelligence and sabotage centre. Hill transferred to SOE along with all the Section D staff and worked there until June 1941, when he was sent to the USSR as its representative.

III. The Organisation of the British Agent Network in the USSR

Since July 1941 the SIS station (95000) in the USSR had been headed by George Berry, the third secretary at the British Embassy. Berry is known to have run intelligence operations against the USSR from Riga in 1938; he was recalled to London in 1940.

We have the following information on the other staff of the station:

Corrigan, wireless operator, paid £450 per annum plus £100 for personal expenses.

Alec Parker, Berry's secretary, salary £400 per annum plus £200 lump-sum expense allowance.

O'Leary, salary £400 per annum

Berry and Atkinson are paid £350 per annum plus a living allowance and 5 shillings per day for personal expenses.

Berry's assistant used to be Cheshire, who previously operated against the USSR from Helsinki; he is to be succeeded by David Roberts.

Berry had intelligence links with the Poles, Czechs and Americans. In September 1942, Berry reported to his head office regarding his liaison with the Poles: 'The recall of the Polish liaison officer, the departure of Polish troops and the arrests mean the loss of almost all Polish sources. I am in close contact with the Polish consul in Kuibyshev, Rozmanski; from whom I plan to get intelligence. I will refer to Rozmanski as 95000/B'.

In the same month Berry also reported that he had been in touch with Henderson in the American Embassy (deputy head of the Russian Section, State Department; Henderson had earlier been a secretary at the American Embassy in Riga). He promised Berry he would set up systematic contacts on intelligence matters for the British with the appropriate members of the American Embassy staff.

Berry uses the following symbols in his communications with Head Office:

X is a section at SIS Head Office.
Z is a ministry or department with which SIS is in touch.
Y is a British embassy or mission overseas.

These four letters—W, X, Z and Y comprise one group of symbols.

P stands for 'political, A—'aviation', B—'the police or counter-intelligence department', S—'blockade or economic warfare', T—'trade', M—'military', N—'naval'. These seven letters make up the second group of symbols.

The two groups of symbols are used jointly. A code letter from the first group also precedes one from the second. For example, XP is the Political Section at the Head Office of SIS, Section 1 ZN is the British Admiralty, [and] Soviet WR means either the People's Commissariat for Foreign Affairs or the Soviet Embassy. YP Madrid stands for the British ambassador in Madrid, ZB is MI5, while WB is the NKVD. ZS stands for the Ministry of Economic Warfare. These symbols are used in SIS station wireless traffic.

IV. The British Agent Network Operation Against the USSR

The British take great care to keep their agent network hidden, observing all the tradecraft requirements to do so. As a rule, agents' reports and documentary information at our disposal give only the code numbers of sources; in several cases, though, some other information is also included. In addition to agents' information, we have received copies of a number of messages from the USSR station to Head Office and other documents describing British intelligence operations.

These messages relate mostly to 1941, and some are from 1942. This material without doubt represents no more than a fraction of the intelligence that the British obtain from their agents on Soviet territory, but it is nonetheless interesting, primarily for what it reveals about the sources of British intelligence in our country.

1. Letters of the HoS

We have the following letters from the British HoS about the internal situation in the USSR:

1. Dated 28 October 1940. The source of the report is not given.
2. Dated 17 July 1942. There is an indication in the text that the information was obtained from a Soviet source in Moscow.
3. Dated 1 July 1940. In an explanatory note on the document there are indications that the information was received by a British businessman from his trading counter-part. It is evident from the text that this counter-part is linked to the Hungarians and has been in contact with a German trade delegation. This leads us to conclude that the source of the information was a journalist or someone inside Vneshorg (Foreign Trade Organisation) or Intourist.
4. Dated 1 August 1940. Information from the same source. The latter is reportedly in touch through his work with Iranians, Swedes and Hungarians.
5. Dated 17 July 1940. The text contains references to the information from the ZIS factory and a conversation with a leading doctor; an explanatory note mentions one 'Noskov'.
6. Dated 10 July 1940. About the arrest of Dr Aslanov, allegedly a friend of the Kaganovich family. Refers to the information having been obtained indirectly from a good source in Moscow.
7. Dated 21 January 1941. The message text matches extracts from an attachment to a letter sent in November 1940 from Moscow to British intelligence by an individual connected with Reuters Agency. It may be concluded from this that one of Reuters correspondents stationed in Moscow at the end of 1940 was an informant for the British station.

Our files show that the British station sent to Head Office on 23 July 1940 a review of the Soviet press and on 18 July 1941 a detailed list of Soviet official bodies. After Berry received instructions from Head Office in a telegram that came on 23 June 1942, tasking him to recruit six Malay-speaking agents and two radio operators with access to Communist circles. The telegram states that these people are possibly required for India. This shows that the British are using their station in the USSR to penetrate Communist circles linked to the Comintern and to infiltrate their agents provocateurs into these circles.

2. Operations via the Poles

From the correspondence of the British HoS with Head Office in 1942 we can see that the British received a significant proportion of their information from the Poles. Thus, for example, in February 1942 British intelligence received a report from Agent PERCH on artillery units in Totskoye, east of Buzuluk, and in Tatishche, forty kilometres from Saratov, and also information from Agent TROUT on the railway situation in the Cheliabinsk-Chkalovoa-Burguruslan region on the anti-Soviet attitudes of Ukrainians returning to German-occupied territory.

On 24 January 1942, Berry informed Head Office he had received 72,000 roubles to cover PERCH's expenses.

One of the main Polish sources identified in Berry's correspondence is 95038. For example, on 28 March 1942 he reported information on attitudes in the USSR. The correspondence also shows that on 15 March, 95038 introduced Berry to a Major Tatchin or Ilamchin (a Pole who was given the code number 95038/a). On 21–22 March, 95038 was supposed to have left Kuibyshev for Moscow. In July, Berry reported that 95038 had to leave for Tehran, and finally, on 2 August 1942, according to a message from Berry, he eventually managed to make contact with 95038 during the latter's brief visit to Kuibyshev before he left the USSR to join General Anders (Yatsin, Polish military attaché in Kuibyshev, expelled from the USSR in 1942). In May 1942 source 95038/a gave British intelligence information on the situation in Vladivostok at the beginning of 1942, about the 5th Fighter Aircraft Regiment in the town of Kinel, about the IL-3 aircraft and M-87 aeroengine and about the situation in Pavlodar in May 1942.

On 19 May 1942, Berry received instructions from Head Office to ask 95038/a to provide information on the calibre of all Soviet guns, especially anti-tank and anti-aircraft guns. In July 1942 the British were told by 95038/a that the Russians required him and his assistant, an officer of the Polish military mission, and General Wolikowski, to leave the USSR.

The assistant to 95038/a passed information to the British in July 1942 about Factory no. 525. He said the reason for 95038/a's expulsion from the USSR was the inappropriate behaviour in a Soviet restaurant of the Polish deputy military attaché, Major Yatsin, who got disgracefully drunk. On 6 July 1942, Berry told Head Office that the relationship with 95038/a was unsatisfactory. This had nothing to do with the latter personally, but arose from the suspicious attitude of the Soviet authorities, the departure of Polish officers from many observation points and the fact that the locals did not trust Poles. Later in his message Berry mentions sources 95038/11 and 95038/c. In June 1942 the former reported to British intelligence on the food situation in Samarkand; the latter gave Berry information in December 1942 about an explosion in the Cheliabinsk Tank Works, as well as information from a Polish officer who had earlier lived 110 kilometres north of Ukhta about the construction of a military factory at the railroad junction in Ukhta.

In December 1942, Berry reported that he had established from three Polish delegates who had been arrested that some of the arrested Poles had confessed to collaborating with the Poles in British intelligence. Based on Berry's report, the presence of the former Polish army captain and delegate in Pavlograd, Likindorf, is further evidence of the connection between the British and Polish intelligence services both in the USSR and in London.

Zelenski, Polish delegate for Vladivostok, is said to have been questioned about the connections between Polish intelligence and the Americans.

In their operations in the USSR, the British also work with other services, in particular the Czechs and the French. Thus, for example, in June 1942 the British representative at de Gaulle's HQ reported that on 16 June 1942 information was received (from French army HQ) that had been obtained from an officer in the Soviet General Staff in Baku on the prospects for an attack by the Red Army and on the latter's reforms.

3. Operations via Iran

The SIS station in Tehran (83000) is actively involved in intelligence operations against the USSR. Until recently the HoS was the British Embassy's first secretary, Wilfred Hindle. Hindle, a Russian-speaking former journalist for the *Times* and the *Morning Post*, has had previous postings in Budapest and Prague. Hindle's assistant, Sedcole, is on the staff of the British consulate in Tehran; he too speaks Russian. The SIS representative in Isfahan, Captain Harris, also works against the USSR, recruiting agents among the Armenians. In addition to the SIS station, which operates under diplomatic cover, the British also use an extremely wide range of representative offices and business firms in Iran as 'cover' for intelligence operations. These include 'The British Transport Section' cargo shippers, run by Brigadier General Rhodes and the representative office of the British Commercial Corporation, which is headed by one Simonson, who some years back represented the British High Command in supplying ammunition and equipment to the White armies. Also located in Tehran is the representative office of the British Bible Society, which operates in the Causcasus and Turkestan under the guise of supplying religious material.

The Iran station makes much use of Czechs and Poles in its operations against the USSR, especially Poles arriving in Tehran. For example, the 83000 station received the following information:

1. On 3 June 1942 via source 83036 from the Pole Edward Skismund, an anti-Soviet review of the situation in Russia.
2. On 11 June 1942 via source 83900 from a Polish ex-POW in Russia, an anti-Soviet review of the internal situation in the USSR.

At the end of June 1942, British agent 83917 travelled to Kuibyshev and, on his return to Iran via Baku, gave the British information on the Baku anti-aircraft defences.

The SIS exchanges for 1942 mention 22501/c, 22501/j and 22501/ja as Hindle's Czech sources. According to our information, 22501/j has studied the USSR for twenty-five years. Otherwise, we know only that in August 1942 he had a conversation with the Soviet military attaché in Iran about the situation in the Caucasus. In mid-1942, Hindle's other Czech source, 22501/c, reported that a certain Dneprov with whom he had discussed the situation on the Caucasus front took an optimistic view of what was happening. On 11 August 1942, Hindle told Head Office that he had made contact with Gaspar Kleber Pathi, a Czech who had transferred to Kuibyshev from Tehran on 8 August. Pathi had been recruited in Budapest and given the symbol 22501/ja.

In June 1942 the Tehran station told Berry that 43300—a friend of the former 43000 (the symbol of Giffey, the former HoS in Tallinn)—was heading for Kuibyshev and that he was an extremely capable agent. After additional steps were taken, information was obtained that was good grounds for identifying 43300 as Frederick John Owridge, who speaks fluent Russian, whose passport was issued in Tallinn and who at the time was actually heading from Tehran to the British Embassy in Kuibyshev.

In August 1942 the Tehran HoS informed Laura [O'Leary, an SIS station officer in Moscow] that he proposed to recruit Boris Shapiro, a Latvian who held a British passport. He was a fur trader who had previously represented an American fur house in Moscow. Shapiro may be sent into Turkestan under trade cover.

Malcolm McLaren, a British career intelligence officer, is actively involved in operations against the USSR; his present official position is vice consul in Tabriz. McLaren is presently in Cairo and is the link between 87000 (the Far East HoS) and the trade attaché in Rangoon. McLaren is married to a Russian, is fluent in the language and was formerly an illegal in Warsaw, where he also ran intelligence operations against the USSR.

After the fall of Poland, McLaren—22310—escaped to Turkey, where he stayed from March 1940 to March 1941 and continued to work against us under the direction of Gibson, the Istanbul HoS. According to agents' reports, the British Intelligence Centre in Istanbul had marked 23310 to be the British Consul in Baku should the Soviet government agree to the opening of a consulate there. We have a quantity of material obtained by British intelligence from 22310's subordinate 22310/c and from informer 22310a. Despite the fact that McLaren's station has a network on Soviet territory, the station operates independently and is not subordinate to the IS HoS in the USSR, Berry.

The following were obtained through 22310/c:

1. Report of 12 May 1942 on the health of Comrade Stalin.
2. Report of 18 January 1941 on alleged friction between Comrades Molotov and

Vyshinsky. Both of 22310/c's reports came from one Bykovshy or Bykhovsky, who is employed in the People's Commissariat for Foreign Trade or possibly somewhere in its system.

3. A report of 20 April 1940 on the Communist Party plenary session—in particular, on the speeches of Comrades Yaroslavsky and Mikoyan. This came from one Donamitsky, who works in the Party's Propaganda Section.

4. Reports on 23 November 1940 and 26 December 1940 on the position of Comrade Timoshenko and on the purge of senior Red Army officers, plus a commentary on this report. The report on 23 November indicates that the material was obtained from a Soviet source in an official position in Moscow, while the second is marked 'Received from Bollinger'.

Informant 22210/n provided a report on 29 September 1940 on illegal strikes and anti-Soviet organisations. Another document explained that this information came from a technician in a factory in the south of the USSR who was in Moscow in September 1940. 'This is a new source . . . but our intermediary considers him reliable.'

We also have the following messages to Head Office from 22310:

1. Dated 15 August 1942, on labour unrest in the USSR (source not indicated).

2. Sometime in August 1942, on the Soviet Union's military preparations, on public opinion and on relationships between political leaders. The information is indicated to have come from Poles connected to German circles in Poland and Romania.

4. Operations via Turkey

The Istanbul station is active in operations against the USSR. These include infiltrating agents across the Turkish and Iranian frontiers, recruiting Soviet officials abroad, questioning passengers arriving by ship from the USSR, receiving information received from foreign sailors and through study of the Soviet press (especially regional newspapers).

Close attention is paid to information on the Black Sea coast, which has been split up into segments among the staff of the station as follows:

1. from Odessa to Sebastopol
2. from Sebastopol to Novorossisk
3. from Novorossisk to Tuapse
4. from Tuapse to Sukhumi
5. from Sukhumi to Batumi

According to information received in 1941, the HoS in Istanbul was in contact, jointly with Turkish intelligence, with an underground organisation Tbilisi styles 'The Georgian National Committee'.

Information in May 1942 identified the IS HoS in Istanbul as Gibson, who runs SIS agent infiltration units into the USSR, the Balkans, Germany, Italy, etc. Liaison with Turkish intelligence is the job of a station officer, Major O'Leary.

At the beginning of 1942 the IS HoS in Istanbul recruited a Soviet citizen, Colonel Nikolaev (a former press attaché at our embassy in Turkey), who was working for the 'Military Neighbours' Organisation [GRU]. On 12 February 1942, Nikolaev gave the British a report on the internal political situation in the USSR and asked the British to help him publicize Soviet atrocities and protect him from any retaliatory action against him for his 'democratic views'. On 19 June 1942, [agent] 18000 informed Head Office that Nikolaev was under suspicion and had been recalled to the USSR.

In addition to documents on Nikolaev, we have the following messages about the USSR, received by the British station via Turkish intelligence:

(1) Dated April 1940, a message from source 18060/m about actions against enemies of the people and wreckers. Judging by the report, whoever wrote it had information about the Transcaucasus and was connected with the Georgian nationalists.

(2) Dated 16 August 1940, a message from source 18500 on the situation in the USSR, based on information from Turkish intelligence.

(3) Dated 11 July 1942, a message from source 18860 and information received from Ilyami Bayram Ogli about public opinion in Kuibyshev.

5. Operations via Bulgaria

In November 1940, IS received from Sofia a translation of a letter said to have been written by a Hero of the Soviet Union, Major General Naneishvili. We do not have the letter itself, but the message to IS indicates that it was written by Naneishvili to aviation Major General I.G. P'yatykin and also that while he was in Georgia in May 1940, Naneishvili met Major General Zumanovich, OC [Office Commanding] Supplies of the Transcaucasian Military District, who shared with him a number of items of secret information.

British intelligence took a keen interest in Naneishvili; they established his biographical profile, his service career, etc. The document also shows very clearly that the British read the local Soviet press carefully, have biographical details on all Soviet generals, track their postings, and so on.

6. Operations via Greece

An SIS document in our possession, received from Greece (Station 41000) states that in the middle of July 1940 a certain Captain Slavonis, who is connected with British intelligence, shipped to Piraeus from Istanbul a Russian refugee who provided information on the USSR. The refugee had left Odessa on 12 July 1940; the document does not indicate whether the individual left the USSR legally or illegally.

7. Operations via Romania

In the first half of 1940 British intelligence received from its HoS in Romania (14000) a review of the Communist Party's Plenary Session. The source of the information is unknown. SIS also received from 14000 messages from his agent Teodorovich, who, from the attached document, works for Reuters. Their agent reported on the situation in Bukovina.

8. Operations via Finland

Of the papers we have on the British agents deployed against us from Finland, the most interesting are those on group member 21069 and his network.

21069 was a Russian who had taken Finnish citizenship in 1936 and who, from 1939, on the orders of British intelligence, infiltrated agents across the Soviet-Finnish border into Murmansk.

In February 1940, [agent] 21069 began work in the Russian Section of the Finnish Ministry of War, where he personally handled interrogation of Soviet POWs. He is known, for example, to have recruited the Soviet POW Bolshakov, Ivan Petrovich (21069/n), who was sent into the USSR on an assignment for British intelligence. We know that Bolshakov had earlier served in the frontier troops on the southern border, that his first cousin works in Moscow in civil aviation and that he has a friend in the NKVD in the Archangel region.

Another source connected with 21069 gave British intelligence a report on the internal situation in the USSR in February 1942. Comments on the report indicate that its author is a Communist Party member who completed graduate studies at a Soviet university, received a professorship and was a POW in Country 21 (Finland).

In the course of January 1941, [agent] 21000 sent to Head Office forty-two reports on the Red Army received from 21069, based on POW information. In 1940–41, [agent] 21069 was receiving £20 a month from the British.

In total, eighty-nine agents for whom we know the symbols or on whom we have some other information were operating against the USSR for the SIS station in Helsinki.

Among them were a number of officials. For instance, 21920 is the former chief of the Finnish Political Police, 21930 the former Finnish military attaché in Moscow, 21932 an official on the Finnish General Staff, dealing with ciphers and wireless intercepts (recruited in 1940), and 21482 is a secretary in the US Embassy in Helsinki (recruited in September 1941).

The Helsinki station makes extensive use of foreign vessels calling in Soviet ports and of trading firms. For instance, group members 21018, a Russian by origin, a British agent since 1926 and co-owner of the John Sunoval tool works, has the following agents in his network: 21018/a, a former Russian, now Swedish, citizen, works for a Stockholm export firm and deals with the USSR on trading operations; 21018/al is the captain of the Estonian steamer *Sulev;* 21018/n is the captain of the steamer *Unto;* 21018 is the former Russian naval officer who is now second navigator on the steamer *Regina.*

British agent 21107 is a Finnish antique dealer living in the Terkok area who often visits Leningrad. In 1938 he moved to Petsamo, where he worked on collecting information about Murmansk. He had a sub-source in Leningrad, a Karelian, who worked in an aviation fuel dump.

Among the Finnish intelligence sources known to us by their symbols is 21106, a Soviet citizen form Leningrad, about whom we have enough information to have established his identity as a former employee of the Leningrad office of Sovtorgflot [Merchant Marine] and a member of Sovtorgflot's technical commission overseeing the construction of the vessels for the USSR in western Europe. He lived in Leningrad but travelled abroad frequently; he is on the Naval Officers Reserve list. His father was shot during the Soviet regime. In the SIS estimates for 1940–41, [agent] 21106 was allotted £25 a month. The British noted that he always provided valuable information on naval matters, which he got from 'unwitting' informants.

British intelligence received a report on 12 May 1940 from 21400, a source whose identity has not been established, about disturbances in the USSR.

9. Operations in the Baltic States

We have in our possession the following messages received by British intelligence from its agents in the Baltic States in 1940–41.

1. Dated 16 November 1940, about the situation in Riga and Tallinn.
2. Dated 1 and 16 September 1940, from 31000 about a trip from Riga to Vladivostok. This report is an anti-Soviet review of the situation in the USSR. The author of the report is the man who made the trip, the British HoS in Riga (31000).
3. A report dated 23 April 1941 about German activities among the White émigré community, received from the former Estonian source 43931 via Sweden.

For the Estonian (Tallinn) station—43000—we know the symbols or a certain number of the informants for fifty-five agents; in the case of the Riga station— 312000—the number is twenty-five. A significant number of them are various senior officials of former Estonian and Latvian government departments. Examples include:

43447	Former head of the Estonian government and last Estonian envoy to Moscow. Recruited in June 1941 while living in Stockholm; received £30 a month.
43450	Former Estonian ambassador and envoy to Stockholm; recruited in August 1941.
43470	Former Estonian ambassador in London; recruited October 1941.
43920	Former chief of the Estonian secret police. Received a special payment for setting up an intelligence organisation on the Soviet frontier. Considered a valuable agent.
43431	Colonel Mazans, former chief of Estonian military intelligence. In 19373–8 he was paid £50 a month. The British have established contact with him again in Stockholm.

43996	Former head of the Operations Section of the Estonian General Staff; recruited in 1936.
43941	Former Estonian military attaché in Moscow; recruited in April 1940. In 1941 he was paid 400 crowns a month.
43915	Former head of the Russian Section of the Estonian General Staff; recruited in May 1940; received $(?) a month.
31850	Former harbourmaster in Libau; recruited in May 1940.
31920	Former head of the Latvia Political Police.

The Estonian agents with official positions in the Baltic States took advantage of their connections and their opportunities to work against the USSR. For instance, source 43932, former assistant head of Estonian military intelligence, was connected with 43711, a helmsman on an Estonian steamer that called at Leningrad. 43741 recruited in Leningrad a Russian inspector of the Baltic fleet steamship engines, who became 43711/a. This Soviet source provided the British with valuable intelligence. We do not exclude the possibility that 43711/a is an old acquaintance of 43711, since the latter attended the Leningrad School of Engineering. A significant number of British intelligence agents in the Baltic States were focussed specifically on the USSR; 43281, for example, was a senior Estonian naval officer recruited in March 1940. He gave the British regular information on Soviet vessels entering Estonian waters. 43311, an Estonian Territorial Army instructor on the island of Sorema, also provided intelligence on the Soviet navy.

43250 is an Estonian radio-operator in Helsinki handling Soviet wireless intercepts. 43681, a Polish expert on Russian army matters in the Finnish General Staff, was recruited at the end of 1940 and worked for the Finnish General Staff interrogating Soviet POWs in 1939–40, passing information on to the British. 12022 was the representative of the Association of Latvian Timber Merchants and the director of a plywood factory; he worked through his nephew, who was an employee in the Eastern Section of the Latvian Foreign Ministry. 21022 passed information to the British on Soviet-Latvian and Soviet-Romanian relations.

According to our most recent information, the Germans are rolling up the British agents in the Baltic States. In November 1942, British intelligence learned that in the process the Germans had, with the help of Malkov Papin (?) and Alexander Rett, identified the connections of Giffey (42000), the previous British HoS in Estonia.

The British feared that the following sources would thus be compromised: 43300 (Tart), who was said to be living in the USSR; 43250, a radio operator who worked in the same house as Giffey; 43290, a former police chief said to be living in the USSR (per our inquiries, condemned to death); and 43933, the former Estonian military attaché in Finland.

10. Operations in the USA

British intelligence pays a great deal of attention to what Comrade Litvinov does and thinks. In mid-December 1940 a source of the Stockholm station (43900) received information in a conversation with a diplomat who was accompanying Comrade Molotov in Berlin, that Litvinov was once again playing an active role in deciding foreign policy, had access to government information and was a consultant to the Politburo on foreign policy matters, but was allegedly barred from meeting foreign diplomats.

Later, in March–June 1942, British intelligence received from its US station (see attachment 34037) the following messages regarding Comrade Litvinov:

1. Dated 26 March 1942, on Litvinov's conversation with the former Spanish foreign minister Del Vayo on the question of a Second Front.
2. Dated 23 April 1942, on Litvinov's conversation on the military situation with an American whom he knew from Geneva.
3. Dated 28 May 1942, on his talk with de Yerillson about a Second Front.
4. Dated 12 June 1942, on views expressed by Litvinov at a breakfast with Lord Morley at the Soviet Embassy. These documents leave us in no doubt that Comrade Litvinov is being given blanket coverage by British agents.

11. British Intelligence's Operating Methods in the USSR

The documents attached do not, of course, provide grounds for definitive conclusions either about the way British intelligence operated before the war or about the changes that were made to their operational techniques within our borders as a result of the war situation. We can, however, make a few observations. Before the war the British were primarily interested in the internal political situation of the USSR, in public opinion, in expressions of anti-government sentiment, in the state of our economy (industry and agriculture), in the situation in the newly annexed regions and in the foreign policy area—the state of Soviet-German relations.

Because intelligence on these matters came from agents of a markedly anti-Soviet bias and because direct contact by the British with the realities of Soviet life was quite restricted, there is no doubt that the British had a wrong picture of the overall situation in the USSR; they reckoned that it would lose the war and that the Soviet regime would collapse. Some of the messages (see attachments 16 and 17) confirm that the British were badly informed; indeed, the contents are so absurd and pointless that one can do no more than express astonishment that the IS centre regarded them as 'valuable'.

In providing help to the USSR, the British were merely hoping to prolong the time for which the Red Army might hold out; this served their own interests by sapping the strength of a future enemy to the maximum possible extent.

As this unfolded, the British continued to focus on the political and economic situation of the USSR—above all, its military potential. Agents as well as staff intelligence officers—whose numbers increased significantly—were asked very detailed questions about the armed forces, the Red Army's armaments and the state of our transport. In addition, the British were interested in how strong our rear was, especially the food situation and manifestations of anti-Soviet feelings. Since they have had more opportunities open to them, the British now have a more objective picture of the situation in the USSR than before and in a number of cases are adding comments about the subjective approach of the sources to reports made with a heavy anti-Soviet bias.

A considerable number of British stations are targeting the USSR, both on Soviet territory and from neighbouring countries. Each HoS has sent Head Office regular reports with an assessment of how things stand on the most important issues. These reports reflect the personal opinion of the HoS and his observations, as well as press reports and agents' information.

The British have a wide variety of agents in the Soviet Union; the attached documents identify a professor, a prominent doctor, a worker in the ZIS plant, a factory technician, people close to leading party and military circles, etc. When leading Soviet officials travel abroad, the British cover them thoroughly with their agents, as seen, for instance, in the case of Comrade Litvinov.

Intelligence documents generally mention only agents' symbols, although sometimes their surnames are included. However, it is not always clear whether a particular item of intelligence was obtained unwittingly (by taking advantage of these individuals' garrulity) or whether the informant was aware of the destination of the information (e.g. Bykovskii and Donamitskii were perhaps used unwittingly; see attachments 11 and 12).

To legitimise its meetings with agents, British intelligence used the business connections of British individuals in various Soviet establishments. This is borne out by, for instance, the material obtained by the station from a British businessman who was evidently in contact with a whole range of Soviet citizens, staff of foreign trade organisations, and tourists, etc. Some element of the British agent network has access to secret Party papers. At the same time, some reports have a purely gossip-mongering flavour.

Agent reports sent from stations to Head Office are carefully reviewed, assessed and re-checked there. British annotations on individual documents show that Head Office keeps a close eye on opportunities and on appointments and studies the central and regional press and other official publications.

The stations operating against the USSR from neighbouring countries use a wide variety of techniques. Ex-politicians from the Baltic States and senior members of their intelligence services were taken onto the British payroll for operations against the USSR (which, by the way, they continue today from exile). Individual travellers arriving from the USSR were questioned in several different ways. During the Soviet-Finnish War British intelligence incorporated its agents into the operations of the Finnish intelligence organisation and recruited among POWs; they also used POW interrogators to obtain information.

They systematically infiltrated agents into the USSR using trading firms and shipping companies as conduits.

With the outbreak of war British intelligence significantly stepped up its operations based on the relationships that it had built up with its allies. The SIS station in the [British] Embassy was reinforced and enlarged; in addition, an SOE representative was appointed, and Military Intelligence stepped up its efforts, organising its own staff via the various British missions and representative offices on our territory.

Liaison with Polish intelligence in agent operations became very close indeed. The Poles put at the disposal of the British all their opportunities and contacts in the USSR. Several documents also point to some kind of connection with the French and Turkish services. British stations in the Baltic States whose normal functioning was disrupted by the German occupation are continuing their operations under the new conditions and communicating with Head Office through Stockholm.

British intelligence set itself the task of taking advantage of wartime circumstances and the anti-Fascist activities of the Communists to penetrate a number of Communist Parties under the pretext of using them in the fight against the German espionage networks. They envisaged effecting this penetration with the help of their station in the USSR; this explains their instructions to the station about recruiting individuals with access to the Communist circles in India and Malaya, as well as the great interest shown by the British in the activities of the Comintern and the whereabouts of its officials on Soviet territory.

The British are presently sending a large number of their agents and professional intelligence officers to the USSR on the pretext of having friendly relations and meeting the need to carry out various tasks connected with the military assistance and collaboration.

Over the last year, the vetting of British travellers to the USSR has identified among them a large number of individuals listed on our Special Intelligence Register as knowing Russian, as having completed special intelligence courses, etc. There have been several instances where the British have sent White émigrés and active participants in the Intervention to work on Soviet territory. The following examples are typical. In September 1941, Private Sergei Leontyev was released from the army by the War Office. He was given the rank of lieutenant and captain's pay and issued a passport in the name of J. Graham. The father of Leontyev-Graham is known to have served in the Tsarist Guards. J. Graham arrived in the USSR to work as assistant to Hill (SOE's representative).

In March 1943 the British asked the NKVD about a Soviet entry permit for F.T. Sven, the former assistant of Firebrace, head of the Russian Liaison Section of Military Intelligence. Sven is a rabid anti-Soviet who speaks English with a Russian accent since he was born in Russian and spent many years there. During the Intervention years he played an active part on the side of our enemies and was in the British Expeditionary Forces in Archangel and Vladivostok. He worked as a signals officer in Denikin's army, he was with Wrangel in the Crimea, etc. He is known to have been close to German diplomatic and military circles in 1939–40.

Via our Sixth Section we have kept the Second Directorate regularly informed of information at our disposal on British individuals dealing with the USSR.

12. Our Tasks

To facilitate more detailed investigations of British intelligence personnel operating against the USSR and to gain a fuller understanding of the activities of British intelligence organisations, we have raised the following questions:

What basic changes in specific British intelligence activities against the USSR have been brought about by the military situation?

1. What are the main tasks assigned by SIS Head Office or the directorates of the specialist intelligence services in their operations relating to the USSR?
2. How are British deception operations organised in relation to the USSR: in what forms and by what methods?
3. What specific tasks have been given to the SIS station at the British Embassy and to the SOE representative, and what are they actually doing?
4. What tasks have been given for British intelligence operations in the Caucasus? How is the work organised from a practical standpoint, and what specific operations are being conducted?
5. What specific USSR-related tasks have the British given their stations in Iran, Finland, Turkey, Cairo, Afghanistan and the Baltic States?
6. What liaisons exist between the various stations operating against the USSR, and how is it implemented?
7. How do the stations in countries bordering the USSR communicate with their agents on Soviet territory?
8. How do the British liaise in their operations against the USSR with other Allied services (Polish, Czech, French, etc.), and what concrete results are produced?
9. What British intelligence personnel are on Soviet territory either on the staff of official diplomatic and military missions or as illegals?
10. Who do the British have by way of Soviet citizens currently operating as agents on Soviet territory (agents previously recruited but only recently activated)?
11. Methods of recruitment.
12. Counter-intelligence work by British intelligence bodies in the USSR.
13. The number and personal profiles of personnel working in the sections and departments dealing with the USSR in the SIS Head Office.
14. Conclusions and assessments of British intelligence bodies relating to the Soviet Union, based on agents and other information.

Elena Modrzhinskaya

Head of Department 1, Third Section, of the First Directorate

10 April 1943

40   *Dossier on Harold Gibson, September 1949*

Information on Harold Gibson (Compiled from File Records)

Gibson, Harold Charles Lers, was born in 1897 in London, a British citizen.
Statements by a British intelligence agent Vasiliev in 1945, however, indicate
that Gibson was born in 1894, in Moscow.

Speaks many foreign languages fluently, including Russian. Educated in England. Hates the USSR and the People's Democracies. Something of a loner.

Source PAVLOV stated in 1944 that as a child, Gibson lived in Russia with his
parents. He served in the Russian army in the First World War as a soldier and a
junior officer. Gibson's father is dead. His mother lives in London. During the
Second World War his brother, Archibald, lived in Turkey and Romania. He
currently lives in London and is an intelligence officer.

Harold Gibson's first wife, a Russian, died in 1947. His second wife, also
Russian—Alfimova, Ekaterina Alekseevna—was born in 1920. Her father, Alfimov, born in 1886, also Russian, is a doctor and lives in Bucharest. Her
mother—Alfimova, Ekaterina—was born in 1880 and died in Bucharest in 1945.
She has a step-brother who has lived in Romania since 1936 and who was arrested by the Germans during the war.

Ekaterina Alfimova, a dancer, speaks Russian, French, Romanian and a little
Turkish. From 1941 to 1945 she lived in Turkey as the wife of the British journalist Morton Allen Mackintosh, the correspondent of the *Daily Telegraph*. Alfimova was in the UK from 1945 to 1947.

Gibson met Alfimova in Turkey in 1941 and re-married in 1948.

From 1945 to 1948, Gibson worked as first secretary and head of the PCO of
the British Embassy; he resided at 21 Smono Street, Prague I. He left Czechoslovakia for the UK in 1948. According to our latest information, Gibson is in
Berlin on the staff of the British military government.

A dossier on Harold Gibson compiled in May 1947 by the Czech security
organisation on the basis of case files indicated that in 1917, while Gibson was in
St Petersburg and Moscow, he played an active part in a plot against the Soviet
regime. In November 1918, Gibson left Russia for England.

In 1922, Gibson was tasked by the chief of the Secret Intelligence Service to
organise intelligence operations in south-east Europe, as a result of which he
and his 'Intelligence Group' moved from Turkey to Bucharest, where he undertook major intelligence operations against the USSR, establishing SIS stations
in Romania, Bulgaria and Poland.

In the period 1922 to 1935 the structure of Gibson's Intelligence Group for
southeast Europe was as follows:

1. Group head—H. Gibson
2. Assistant and secretary—A. Gibson

3. Assistant for agent handling—Viktor Vasilievich Bogomolets
4. Assistant for military matters—Rostovskii-Bryukhatov
5. Courier/recruiter—Ismal Ali Ogly, an ex-officer and an Ossetian national

Gibson's *rezident* in Romania was the former Russian General Staff officer Colonel Vladimir Arnoldov. Gibson sent to Bulgaria as the SIS *rezident* Vladimir Shosti, born 1894, an ex-officer in the Russian army; he fled to America in 1922, scared that the Bulgarians were on to him.

The Warsaw *rezident* was Nikolai Vasilievich Ilyichev, born in 1900, a former volunteer in Kornilov's regiment.

From 1928 on, SIS made extensive use of Romanian intelligence organisations in its espionage operations against the USSR. With Romanian help, a large network of British agents was recruited on Soviet territory. The British intelligence agents then bribed the head of the Sigurante in Kishinyov and the head of the ROVS [White Russian] intelligence group there, General Leontovich, with whose help information of an intelligence nature was obtained on Soviet Russia. Gibson also bribed a number of senior people in Romanian intelligence. The Romanian intelligence organisation was then reorganised in line with SIS instructions.

In 1930, SIS posted Gibson to Riga to organise intelligence operations against the USSR and Germany. The British agent Goltz, born in Kalinin in 1894, was transferred from Romania to help Bogomolets in running intelligence operations against the USSR and Germany. Goltz was a former colonel in the White Army who in exile worked as a jazz musician.

In 1922, Bogomolets was transferred from Riga to Paris to work among Russia émigrés, as well as to make contact with the French socialist parties in order to use them in the interests of British intelligence.

The SIS directorate sent a representative to Estonia who set up a beachhead there for operations against the USSR.

On Gibson's orders, Bogomolets established contact with the head of the Eastern Department of the Second Section in 1930 via the Warsaw *rezident* Ilyichev and agreed with him that British intelligence would be given opportunities to organise intelligence operations against the USSR from Polish territory. The Second Section of the Polish General Staff gave British intelligence official permission to base a *rezident* on Polish territory, specifically in Warsaw, who was authorised to conduct intelligence operations against the USSR under the cover of Polish intelligence.

British intelligence was allowed to bring its agents into Poland from abroad for subsequent infiltration into the USSR; the Second Section of the Polish General Staff agreed to provide the agents with technical and other assistance. The Second Section allowed the British *rezident* to use Poles as agents to organise an espionage network on Soviet territory for communication with his agents.

For his part, the British *rezident* in Poland undertook to co-ordinate all his intelligence operations against the USSR with the Second Section and to share the 'take' with them.

Up to 1932 the main task of SIS agents sent into Soviet territory was to collect predominantly military intelligence.

From 1932 onwards, SIS sought to get a better and more detailed understanding of the internal and foreign policy of the USSR, its industrialisation and the development of aviation; to develop approaches and routes for penetration; and to get a better picture of the opinions and the work of the leaders of the Party and the Soviet government.

In the spring of 1932 the directorate of SIS sent Gibson to Prague to organise intelligence operations against the USSR and Germany.

The Work of the British Head of Station in Warsaw, 1930 to 1935

The British intelligence station handled the recruiting, training, infiltration and debriefing of agents and processed their product; it interrogated the Soviet defectors and studied the Soviet press and technical publications.

In 1930 the British station sent to Moscow two agents who were employed in Gosplan, Volodya (a Pole) and Luka (a Ukrainian who sold newspapers in Warsaw). When they returned, they brought with them valuable information on the Soviet Five-Year Plan.

The British intelligence officers recruited émigré Kulaks, members of the White Russian nationalist organisation, former German settlers in Russia, sons of Tsarist army officers, pilots who had defected to Poland from the Belorussian Military District, movie actors, Poles and Soviet sailors whom the Poles had persuaded to jump ship.

The British also engaged as agents the relatives of White Russian émigrés who were still living in the USSR. They also obtained intelligence on the USSR from foreign specialists who were working there and from staff of the Soviet trade mission in Warsaw.

The British intercepted or got by bribery material of interest to them from the Polish, Japanese, Romanian and other intelligence services. They used for intelligence purposes the White émigré organisation 'Peasant Russia', Ukrainian nationalist groups in Poland, Trotskyites, members of the Polish Peasant Party, Germans living in the USSR, Soviet citizens working in the print shops of the Armed Forces Ministry, the children of 'Kadets', etc.

In 1941, Gibson was in Turkey, where he ran British intelligence in the Balkans and against the USSR.

Gibson had ties to Czech émigrés. He organised the escape of Czechs and Slovaks to the west through Yugoslavia and Turkey, supplying them with British papers via the Passport Control Officer in Belgrade, Lethbridge; the Czech military attaché; and the British Embassy in Belgrade.

It has been established that in this period, Gibson was in contact with the following persons:

Lipa—a Czech envoy in Belgrade
Minovskii and Bakhitik—members of the staff of the Czech Embassy who were in touch with Yugoslav nationalists (Dimitri Dule)
Gannik—a colonel, member of the Czech army staff
Fritschler—a Czech colonel
Stoy—a Czech colonel
Gak—head of the Czech Military Group

Gibson's Intelligence Work in Czechoslovakia, 1945 to 1948

While in Czechoslovakia, Gibson was connected with the following:

Georgy Cherikha—a manufacturer.
Roza Moravcova—housewife, born in 1894 in Kovani Gradistenski District Circle. Widow. Has two sons; the elder, Svyotoslav Moravec, works for the ZNV. Her husband used to work in the consular section in Paris. He was a member of the Popular Socialist Party. Mentally ill since 1945.
Ivan Mateichik—born in 1876. A doctor. Former Czech consul in Hamburg. His son, Ivan Mateichik, born in 1926, studied at Prague University. He lives at 21 Slyumna Street, Prague. In 1946 he planned to emigrate to Switzerland. In 1947 he was given permission to leave for London. The younger Mateichik works at the Radio Committee (Prague). He was a member of the Popular Socialist Youth Organisation and later a member of the Social Democratic Youth Movement. Speaks English and French.
Bozena Klarova—forty-three years old, a widow, childless; receives her husband's pension.
Anyuta Bules—a domestic servant, a White Russia émigré. Asked Gibson to exfiltrate her to London, for she feared the Czech authorities would hand her over to the Soviet army. She intended to become a British citizen.
Rujana Shandarova—born in 1909 in Bradlo, Iglowski District; now living at 21 Slyumna Street, Prague. Gibson's maid. Shandarova is the wife of Jaros Antoniya, a Gestapo agent in Prague, who was sentenced to five years' imprisonment. She is a German citizen and was expelled by the Czech authorities to Germany, but escaped and has been working as Gibson's maid since 1 October 1946. She does not get ration cards. Has three married brothers and a sister. They all live in Moravia. She is seeking Czech citizenship.

Shandarova keeps herself to herself. When he was out of Prague, Gibson used to write to her. He never allowed her to go into the centre of Prague by tram but always took her in his own car. She entered Gibson's service with the help of Beril Vidman Sedlintskeno (a member of the count's family).
Wolfgang Bretholz—born in Brno in 1904; a doctor; lived in Berlin; became a Czech citizen in 1935 and lived in Prague until the war, editing one of the newspapers. After the Prague press was shut down, he went via Poland to Turkey. During the war he passed information to the Czechoslovak State Council in Lon-

don. He is currently a correspondent for the newspapers *Baslet* and *Sveiska*. Speaks Czech, French, English, Italian and German. He has visited Athens, Sofia, Belgrade and Italy. Discontented with Czechoslovakia's friendship with the USSR.

Bretholz got to know Gibson in Turkey. He met him in Prague in 1947.

On 5 March 1948, Bretholz met fifteen foreigners at the apartment of Eiplyande. On 6 March 1948 he left for France in a diplomatic vehicle.

Bretholz has recently been meeting Singal Sambosadi and Weberau. He lives in the Eksplande and spends time with Dr Filits in the 'Palats' SIS.

Utiber Bubel—born in Vienna in 1890. Lives at 6 Generdor Street, Prague. Speaks Czech, German and English. Before the war he worked in the consular section in London.

Currently employed in the Chemists' Union of the Nationalised Industries in Prague. Bubel joined the National Socialist Party. He received many letters in English. He visits many foreigners, especially women. Was hostile to the nationalisation of industrial concerns. Bubel has contacts with the foreigners Glisnikowski and Bautovanski. The latter, an American, is a White Guard.

It has been established that after the events of February 1943, Bubel met Gibson almost every day in the Passport Section. Bubel, in turn, very often received visits from members of the British Embassy. On 10 February, Bubel was together with Captain [name redacted].

Jan David—born in 1912, a Czech, a Catholic, a bachelor; graduated from the Mercantile Academy. Was in England in 1936. In 1937 he left England for Portugal.

In 1940 he was sent by the British to Calcutta, from where he returned in March 1942. Speaks English, Spanish, German, Arabic and Italian.

Vladimir David—born in 1922, a student of Brno Higher School.

Adel Sallinger (née Davidova)—born in 1915, wife of the manufacturer Sallinger in Omulc. German by nationality, now in the US zone in Germany.

Ruthena Gaikova (née Goudenova)—born in 1900, a Czech citizen, a widow; lives at 69 Legarova Street, Prague. In 1940 she lived in England with her husband, Colonel Gaikov. While there she worked at the Radio Broadcasting Committee, where her colleagues included Tigrid and Grushakov. Her son, Fyodor, attends the Higher Mercantile School. She speaks English, French and Serbo-Croat. She works as a radio announcer in Prague; she has acquaintances in the army. She receives Englishmen and Americans at her home.

Pavel Govash—born in 1913, a Slovene, a former Czech pilot in England. His wife is Maria Ramlerova, born in 1918. He lives at 574/3 Minkovtseva Street, Prague. Govash works in Section IV of the Ministry of Foreign Trade.

In 1946 Govash helped British servicemen find billets in Czechoslovakia. Captain Rickson, an Englishman, lived in his house with Govash's sister-in-law Yusta Kolousova in 1947 without the permission of the Czech police.

Kamil Genner—a professor of medicine living at 20 Stepanskaya Street, Prague. A member of the Social Democratic Party. Genner is known to meet Neniliya Kalanova, born in 1910, a Russian émigré, who lived in Czechoslovakia before the war. Her husband, Vladimir Kalan, died in London. She arrived in Czechoslovakia from London on 1 November 1945 and spread rumours that she had been in the Resistance. In 1947, Kalanova received Englishmen almost daily, some of them at night. She speaks Czech, English, German, French, Russian, Turkish and Hungarian. According to reliable sources, Gibson met Kalanova frequently.

In 1946–47 Kalanova was awarded medals by the British for services to HMG.

On 20 June 1948, Kalanova left Czechoslovakia illegally for Switzerland, having left all her possessions to her nephew Marcel Bergetov, a member of the Czechoslovak CP living on Oplatov Street, Prague; he is of Sudeten origin.

Kalanova's Connections

1. Stanislav Voitasek, born in 1889, a doctor, from a prince's family; worked in the Passport Section of the Prague police from 1920.
2. Yaroslav Lipa, born in 1890, living on Lechin Street, Prague XVI, a former Czechoslovak envoy in Belgrade. During the German occupation of Czechoslovakia, Lipa was in England. Doctor Benes and Jan Masaryk called on him.
3. Emil Smetanka, born in 1875, a professor, unemployed. Lives at 1110/5 Saptoneko Street, Prague XVI.
4. Karl Nigrin, born in 1904, a professor. Lives at Kresny Dvor 294/4, Prague XIII. Works as a chief counsellor. Went to England before the war and remained there until July 1945. Englishmen often visited Nigrin's apartment. There were CD [Corps Diplomatique] plates on their cars.

   At the beginning of 1947 he visited France, Spain, Portugal, Switzerland and Britain, allegedly on official business. Nigrin is a member of the Popular Socialist Party and has pro-Western sympathies.
5. Yaroslav Kaspar, born in 1908, a colonel of the General Staff; lived in England, 1937–45. Now living at Komarnitka Street 1498/12, Prague. Was hostile to the USSR.
6. Karl Janacek, born in 1898. A general. Attempted to flee Czechoslovakia on 30 April 1948 with the collaboration of the British air attaché, Captain Merton, but was detained by the security organs at the frontier and handed over to the military.
7. Stanislav Knor, born in 1888, a doctor, dean of faculty (of which institution is unknown).
8. Vladimir Kobylka, born in 1887. Lived in Turkey in 1922.
9. Vera Kruibash, born in 1915, a native of Leningrad, a widow, with a Dutch passport. Her husband, Kruibash, born in 1905, was a Russian merchant. He died in 1947. It is not known why she came to Prague. She frequently visited the engineer Igor Gortinsky, born in 1918, a native of Mogilyev. His wife, Elena Chervenkova, born in 1921, is Czech, a daughter of General Chervenkov. His father was Vladimir Gorinsky, and his mother was Alexandra Sudsilovskaia (maiden name).

   In 1918 they fled from Russia to Turkey, then to Bulgaria, where they lived until 1928. They arrived in Riga in 1931 and in Prague in 1938. Worked against the Germans during the war. Took part in the 1945 Prague uprising against the Germans.

   Vera Kruibash met Gibson on 9 September 1947.
10. Egor Levit, a doctor of medicine, emigrated to England with his wife and

daughter in 1939, before the occupation. A member of the Social Democratic Party. His son, Karl Levit, emigrated to France and then to England. He returned to Czechoslovakia via the USSR in 1945. Dr Levit works in the Ministry of Health. At the end of 1945 he declared his intention to leave for England. In 1946 his wife, Hedwiga Levit, joined the Czechoslovak Communist Party. Their son, Karl Levit, is married to an Englishwoman, Iris Irwin.

Before the war Dr Levit treated a member of Gibson's family.

11. Frantisek Maly, born in 1908, a Czechoslovak citizen, a radio mechanic and a pilot for the émigré government in London. Married to an Englishwoman, Joan Angel, born in 1913. Lives at 35 Cheshskaya Street, Prague. Works as a pilot for one of the Czechoslovak airlines (precisely which one has not been established).

Maly meets former officers of the Western Army. His wife often goes to the villa of the former pilot Lieutenant Adolf Yurman, who lives at 1931/21 Cheshskaya Druzhina Street, Prague. Yurman is studying law and works for the Export Union. His telephone number is 458-55. In June 1947, Yurman's wife flew to England with their children. Also at the same address is Georgyi Pawelka, who is married to an Englishwoman. He was in England during the war. He is studying in Prague to be a construction engineer.

Yurman and Pawelka have a hostile attitude towards the People's Democracy Regime.

One Potsel't, who is married to an Englishwoman and who has emigrated (where and when, we do not know), also lived with Yurman and Pawelka.

Maly meets with Gapak, a former soldier with the émigré government in London. He is married to an Englishwoman. They live on Studenskaya Street, Prague XIX. He is connected with Kurkow, a civil aviation pilot, who lives at 1935/35, Cheshskaya Druzhina Street.

12. Vladimir Mateika, born in 1923, lives in Prague and works in the rubber and leather trade. A member of the Socialist Party. He is visited by Englishmen.

13. Vaclav Modrak, born in 1909, a pilot, was in Poland, France and England between 1939 and 1945. Works as a radio operator in a Czech army unit.

1. Vladimir Nosek, born in 1895, works in the Foreign Ministry. His wife is English. From 1932 to 1939 he was a counsellor in the Czechoslovak Embassy in Brazil.

2. Lyubsha Kovakava-Bartonova, lives in XXX Street, Prague. Gibson visited her flat on 20 February 1948.

3. Vladimir Petrassi—born in 1920, an architect. Emigrated (destination unknown).

4. Elsa Tostimova (née Polyanova)—born in 1904. Was in Auschwitz during the war.

5. Regor Vasiliev—born in 1908, a merchant, his father a general in the Tsarist army. Lives at 591/7 Prava Street, Prague. His wife, a countess and a Jewess, died in the ghetto. A member of the Agrarian Party. Mixes with Gibson. In the evenings Vasiliev is sometimes visited by foreigners. Works in the personal technical office (*sic*) in Prague II.

Vasiliev's Connections

Alberta Rulichkova—born in 1929, a former German national who is seeking Czech citizenship.

Viktor Bekk—born in 1909, married, a singer and a journalist. German. Sent back to Germany in administrative exile 28 June 1946.

Elizaveta Nikolskaya—born in Vladivostok in 1904, Russian, lives in Prague, has a theatre in Germany (in the American zone).

Nikolai Savinkov—born in Sukhumi in 1910, a doctor; his wife is French, Ordette Dueleitov (*sic*), born in 1912. Lives at 30/71 Rasinava Embankment, Prague VI. Fought in Africa. Meets Gibson often.

Robert Smit—a priest; is visited mainly by Englishwomen; delivers sermons against the People's Democracy regime.

Karl Staller—an engineer, born in 1893, worked as technical director of a military factory. In 1946 was appointed director of a state-owned metal workshop.

Robert Stross—born in 1899, a merchant, works as director of the International Union. Speaks Czech, German and French. His son Petr is correspondent for an English newspaper.

Nikolai Barger—born in 1907, a Jew. Lives in Prague. Was in England during the war. Returned to Prague in 1945; left again for England.

Yaromir Shebest—born in 1901. Lives in Prague. Fled to Yugoslavia in 1939 and then lived in India. Arrived in Prague in 1947. A trader.

Gerann and Shebest (sic)—merchants.

Papek—merchant, nationalist.

Karl Shebest—born in 1889, a merchant.

Josif Tural—born in 1890 in Odessa, a Turkish citizen. An employee of the Turkish Embassy; he often visits Gibson. Present whereabouts unknown.

Vaclav Beran—born in 1916, a doctor, a bachelor, lives in Prague. A wholesaler. Speaks English, Turkish and German.

Vilgortits—a dental technician. Lives in Prague. Connections with Gibson and Hill.

Yudr Shimmerkal—born in 1889, a doctor. Was deputy minister of defence for legal matters during the war. His son is studying in Paris.

Arno Preis—born in 1908. A Czech army doctor in England. Works in a clinic.

Marian Khakhula (Andre Bozga)—born in 1920. Met Gibson on 26 January 1943. Presently living in an SIS accommodation, domicile unknown.

Oscar Klinger—a doctor, Benes's personal physician. Met Gibson first in March 1948; thereafter saw him several times. Klinger left for England and did not return.

It has also been established that the following have connections with Gibson:

K.V. Kral
Neprash, a Prague tailor
Prokes
Mareshova
Svoisin, a doctor
Georgii and Marut Cherylek

Georgii Diamant
M. Mashinova
Alois Kibit, a brigadier general
N.I. Kalla
Hubert Ripka
Vaclavai Kaitora

In carrying out his intelligence work in Czechoslovakia, Gibson relied on merchants, former plant and factory owners, princes, members of the Czechoslovak diplomatic service, members of the Popular Socialist Party, Social Democrats, Fascists, White émigrés from Tsarist Russia, persons owing allegiance to Germany and hostile to the USSR, newspaper correspondents, Czechs and Slovaks who spent the war in England, scientists with reactionary attitudes, heads of nationalised enterprises, staff members of the Turkish Embassy and medical workers employed in civilian and military establishments. We also know from Gibson's diary that he was in Czechoslovakia in December 1933; September 1936; January 1937; August 1937; February, July and August 1938; and September, October as well as April 1939.

The diary also shows him to have visited the following cities:

1927—Bucharest, Belgrade, Milan, Budapest, Vienna, Berlin and London
1928—Bucharest, Pisa, Turin
1930—Bucharest, Vienna, London, Milan, Lugano, Paris, London, Milan, Bristol, Brussels and Bucharest
1931—Bucharest, Budapest, Vienna, London, Riga (six times), Paris, Berlin, London, Warsaw and Berlin
1932—Riga (ten times), Berlin (four times), London (twice), Paris, Warsaw, Stockholm and Stettin
1933—Riga (twelve times), Tallinn (three times), Helsinki (twice), Berlin, Paris (five times), Hamburg, Stockholm, London (four times), Warsaw (twice) and Prague
1936—Prague (twice), Vienna (twice) and Godieng
1937—Prague (six times), Vienna, Paris (twice), London (twice), Nuremberg, Salzburg, Munich, Lausanne, Geneva, Rouen, Versailles, Bologna, Narvik, The Hague, Düsseldorf, Marburg, Frankfurt, Weimar, Jena, Hof, Hebb and Karlovy Vary
1938—Prague (eight times), Vienna, Geneva, London (three times), Brno, Katourice, Lvov, Bucharest, Paris and Bucharest
1939—Prague (three times), Zurich, Paris (twice), London (twice) and Geneva
1940—London (twice) and Paris
1941—London, Borremond, Lisbon, Las Palmas, Frestovi, Ankara, Istanbul (eight times), Sofia, Belgrade, Athens, Ankara (three times), Aden (twice), Port Said, Oaudd and Jerusalem

Index

A (SIS symbol for Communism), 133
A 168. *See also* Davis, B.A.P.
A1, 168. *See also* Taylor, Capt. H.P.
A2, 168. *See also* Hiles, Maj. G.D.
A3, 168. *See also* Wallerstein, Maj. L.J.D.
A4, 168. *See also* Pearse, Cmdr R.
A5, 168. *See also* Quinn, Capt. F.A.
A6, 168. *See also* Niall, Col. F.W.
A Advisory Selection Board, 168
Abbas Helmy, 267, 270
Abteilung S.V., 53–55
Abwehr, 32, 53, 54, 56, 69, 79, 98, 288
    Hamburg Abwehrstelle, 75, 76, 86
ACSS (Assistant Chief of SIS). *See* Easton,
  Wing Cmdr James
Adams, Maj., 113
Adams, Permanent Secretary, 263, 265, 269
Admiralty, 6–13, 40–42, 262, 268, 277, 311
Advisor on Financial Policy (AFP), 186. *See*
  also Sykes, Percy
Advisor on Security Policy (ASP), 188. *See also*
  Vivian, Valentine
AFHQ (Allied Forces Headquarters), 158
AFP. *See* Advisor on Financial Policy
Aiken-Sneath, Francis, 301
Air Ministry, 9, 37, 47, 64, 91, 167, 182, 185,
  209, 212, 227, 243, 244, 275, 291, 292, 295,
  296, 311, 312, 317
    Director of Intelligence, *see* Boyle, Air
      Commodore Archie P.
    Russian Section, 312
Alcazar de Velasco, 305, 316
Alekseev, Gen., 251
Alexander, Col., 300
Alexander, Gen. Sir Harold, 287

Alexander, Maj., 273
Alexandria, 109
Alfimova, Ekaterina, 335
Aliens Restriction Order (ARO), 47
Aliens Tribunals, 216, 229
Allen, Harry I., 209, 226
Allen, Maj., 317
Allen, W.E.D., 60, 320
Alley, Stephen, 300
Allied Control Commission, 266
Allied Forces Headquarters (AFHQ),
  158
ALPACA, 19, 23
Alvear, Lezica, 19, 23
American Naval Review, 41
Amis, 205
Anders, Gen. Wladyslaw, 322
Andersen, Col., 268
Andersen, Miss K.J., 169
Anderson, Sir John, 58, 59, 211
Andrew, Prof. Christopher, 26
Angel, Joan, 341
Anglo-German Circle, 74
Anglo-German Club, 10
Anglo-German Fellowship, 33, 74
Anglo-German Fraternity, 74
Anglo-German Friendship Society, 74
Anglo-German Information Service, 74
Anglo-Russian Friendship Society, 307
ANKER, 108
Antoniya, Jaros, 338
Aptekar, Annie, 310
Arbuthnot, Capt., 275
Archer, Col. Liam, 85
Archer, Jane, 118

Denney, Patrick, 175
Denniston, Alastair, 135
Denny, Maj. 318
Dennys, Rodney O., 116, 120, 135, 166, 184
Deputy Director Administration (DD/A),
    186. *See also* Slocum, Frank
Deputy Director Finance (DD/F), 186. *See
    also* Sykes, Percy
Deputy Director of Military Intelligence
    (DDMI), 84
Deputy Director of SIS (DD), 182
Derazville, Professor, 314
Dernighofen, Freitag von, 56
De Salis, Charles, 117
Deterding, Sir Henry, 254, 261, 266, 270,
    318
Deutsche Arbeitsfront, 83
Deutsche Uberseedienst, 56
Deuxième Bureau, 64, 96,
    Section M, 115, 144
Diamant, Georgi, 343
Dicker, Miss M.I., 233
Dickson, J.G., 21, 22, 24
Dig, 302
Direction de Securité Militaire (DSM), 132
Director/Directorate of Military Operations
    (DMO), 38, 45, 48
Directorate of Training and Development
    (DTD), 187, 188
    Head of, *see* Munn, Col. John W.
Director B Division (DB), 26. *See also* Harker,
    O.A.; Liddell, Capt. Guy
Director-General of the Security Service
    (DGSS). *See* Kell, Vernon
Director of Air Intelligence (DAI), 196, 197,
    210, 227. *See also* Bass, Air Commodore;
    Boyle, Air Commodore Archie P.
Director of GCCS (DD/C), 131
Director of Military Intelligence (DMI), 71,
    183, 197, 215. *See also* Beaumont-Nesbitt,
    Gen. F.G.; Sinclair, Gen. John
Director of Naval Intelligence (DNI), 215, 227.
    See also Godfrey, Adm. John
Director of Public Prosecutions (DPP), 103,
    210. *See also* Atkinson, Sir Edward
Director of Security (DD/SP). *See* Vivian,
    Valentine
DMI. *See* Director of Military Intelligence
DMO. *See* Director/Directorate of Military

Operations; Operational Section, First De-
    partment of the Anglo-Indian Army HQ
Dneprov, 325
Doides, 303
Dominions Office, 212, 225
Donamitsky, 326, 332
Donovan, William J., 118
DR. *See* Head of SIS Information Department
DSM. *See* Direction de Securité Militaire
DTD. *See* Training and Development
    Directorate
DUCK, 22
Dueleitov, Ordette, 342
Dukes, Sir Paul, 319
Dulanty, John, 85
Dule, Dimitri, 338
Duncombe, Mrs, 77
Dundas, Charles D., 166
Dunderdale, Wilfred, 118, 170, 254, 264, 267,
    318
Dunlop Rubber, 75
Dunn, 86
Dutch Embassy, 22–25, 301
Duvier, C.F.E., 128
Dvoino-Sologub, Col., 265
Dzhakeli, 253

E (SIS symbol for Soviet Communist Parties),
    133
E1(a), 300
    Head of, *see* Ramsbotham, Peter
E1(b), 300
    Head of, *see* Chinnery
E2, 300
    Head of, *see* Alley, Stephen
E2(a), 300
    Head of, *see* Alley, Stephen
E2(b), 300
    Head of, *see* Colford
EAM, 157
Easton, Wing Cmdr James, 166, 188
Eden, Anthony, 286, 317, 318
Edenhofer, 81, 82
Edisson, Maj., 265
Edmonds, Col. James E., 38, 39
EDWARD, 189. *See also* Cairncross, John
Edward VIII, King, 68, 102
Edwards, Arthur, 10
Edward the Confessor, 29

Hankey, Lord, 35, 36, 189, 209
  Report by, 189–233
Hardinge, Sir Charles, 40, 42, 192
Hardt, Paul, 247
Harker, O.A., 58, 91, 209, 228
Harland and Wolff, 129
Harpenden, 109
Harris, Capt., 270, 324
Harris, Leonard, 166, 184
HARRY, 105
Hart, Herbert L.A., 26, 110, 299, 300
Hastings, Edward, 118, 135
Hatton-Hall, Col., 182
Head, Francis, 166
Head Office (HO), of SIS, 154, 162–64, 175, 180, 322, 323, 332–34
  Intelligence Department, 179
Head of SIS Information Department (DR), 166
Heal, 118
Hebble, 187
HEDGEHOG, 7
Heliopolis, 109
Helmsley, Capt., 271
Henderson, 321
Henry, Sir Edward, 192
Herman, 307
Heydrich, Reinhard, 112
Hiles, Maj. G.D., 168
Hill, Elisabeth, 319
Hill, George, 172, 253, 258, 260–63, 271, 320, 333
Hilu, Farajalla, 155
Himmelmann, 83
Himmler, Heinrich, 32, 70, 83
Hinchley-Cooke, Edward, 86, 230
Hindenburg, 60
Hindle, Wilfred, 324, 325
Hinton, Geoffrey, 167
Hitler, Adolf, 18, 35, 60, 63, 66–75, 257
Hitler Youth, 62, 73
HO. See Head Office (HO), of SIS
Hoare, Reginald, 166, 184, 275, 276
Hoare, Sir Samuel, 80
Hoffman, Gen., 255
Holbein, 205
Holland, W., 169
Hollis, Roger, 26, 106, 249
Holmson, Maj., 270, 271

Holt-Wilson, Sir Eric, 42, 47, 58, 95, 209, 224, 225
Home Defence (Security) Executive, 279
Home Office, 11, 207–11, 213, 220, 225–27, 229, 231
  Permanent Secretary. See Maxwell, Sir Alexander; Scott, Sir Russell
  Warrants (HOW), 19, 58, 75
Hoover, J. Edgar, 86
Hopkinson, Henry, 143, 161
HOTEL (Soviet code name for SIS), 234
House, Col., 272
HOW. See Home Office: Warrants
Hudson's Bay Company, 126
Hugo, Squadron Leader, 166
Hungarian Embassy, 303
Hunter, Harry, 300
Hunter, Pamela, 7
HUT (Soviet code name for MI5), 235

I (SIS symbol for Soviet intelligence), 133
IBIS, 108
Igles, Vernon, 315
Ignacetto, Arthur, 316
Ilamchin, 323
Ilyichev, Nikolai V., 336
Imperial Chemical Industries (ICI), 75
Independent French Agency, 22
Indian Political Intelligence (IPI), 113, 212
Inland Revenue, 222
INO, 239, 257
Intelligence Corps, 117
Intelligence Planning Bureau, 175
International Brigade, 241
Inter-Services Liaison Department (ISLD), 151
Intourist, 322
IP Club, 211
IRA. See Irish Republican Army
Iranian Communist Party, 152
Iranian Embassy, 303
Irish Republican Army (IRA), 230
Irwin, Iris, 341
ISK, 118
ISLD. See Inter-Services Liaison Department
ISOS, 108–10
Italian Communist Party, 159
Italian Embassy, 303
Italian Overseas Youth Organisation, 88
Itturande, 316

Morton, Michael, 166
Morton Evans, Kenneth, 110
Mosley, Sir Oswald, 59, 60, 66, 74, 101
Mukalov, Capt. Nikolai, 306
Müller, Kommissar, 259
Munn, Col. John W., 187, 188
Muños, Alvaro, 19
Munthe, Malcolm, 166
Murray, Gen. A.I., 192
Murray, Sir George, 192
Muslim Union, 147
Mussolini, Benito, 35, 60, 66, 101
Musson, 169, 188
Mustafa, Adzhari, 253
My Silent War, 1

N (SIS symbol for Poles), 133
N. *See* Press Department
Nachrichtendienst, 38, 50
Naneishvili, Gen., 327
Napoléon, 40, 41
Narkevich, 118
Naval Intelligence Division (NID), 132, 278
Nazi Party (NSDAP), 37, 59, 61, 67, 71, 73,
    80–83, 87, 95
Negrin, Juan, 315
Nelidov, Aleksandr S., 250, 255, 261, 263, 267
Neprash, 342
Neurath, Konstantin von, 81
Newsam, Frank, 209
Niall, Col. F.W., 168
Nicolson, Maj., 273
NID. *See* Naval Intelligence Division
Nidda, 81
Nigrin, Professor Karl, 340
Nikolai, Col., 32, 52–54, 205
Nikolayev, Col., 327
Nikolskaya, Elizaveta, 342
NKVD, 3, 149, 161, 164, 165, 170–73, 207,
    189, 235–40, 247, 248, 251
    First Directorate, 273
    Second Directorate, 170
Nobel, Gustav, 253
Noble, Capt. A., 7
Norton, 287
Norwegian Embassy, 301
Nosek, Vladimir, 341
Noskov, 322
Noulens, Hilaire, 146

Novikov, 303
Nuntia Bureau, 56
Nuschke, Dr, 257
Nye, Sir Archie, 287

O (SIS symbol for seaborne operations), 183
Obolensky, Prince, 271
Obolenskaya, Princess, 262
O'Brian, 114
Office of Strategic Services (OSS), 150, 159
Official Secrets Act (OSA), 41–43, 246
Ogly, Ismal Ali, 336
OGPU, 149, 235–40, 246
Oklyorov, 302
O'Leary, 171, 321, 325, 326, 426
Olsbury, Miss, 262
One-Time Pad (OTP), 20
Operational Section, First Department of the
    Anglo-Indian Army HQ (DMO), 131
OPEROD, 238
ORANGE, 23
O'Reilly, Miss, 300
Orlov, 205
Orlov, Vladimir, 253, 265
OSA. *See* Official Secrets Act
OSS. *See* Office of Strategic Services
Ossisky, 272
Ostdienst, 56
Ota, 90
OTP. *See* One-Time Pad
Ottley, Bruce, 126
OTTO, 289
Overseas Control, 95
Owens, Arthur, 75
Owridge, Frederick J., 325
Oxenstierna, Johan G., 5–8, 12
Ozol, 266

P1, 184
    Head of, *see* Morley, John
P2, 165, 184
    Head of, *see* Bristow, Desmond
P3, 166, 184
    Head of, *see* Bide, Peter; MacKenzie, Lt
        Cmdr
P4, 184
    Head of, *see* Folkes, Capt.
P5, 184
    Head of, *see* Harris, Leonard

SA, 272
Saarsen, Col., 112
Saffery, 20
Sale, George, 11
Sale, Tilney, 11
Sallinger, Adel, 339
Sandridge, 109
Sarafand, 109
Sartorius, Col., 12
Saudi Arabian Embassy, 10
Saul al Sharq, 154
Savinkov, Boris, 252, 264, 266
Savinkov, Nikolai, 342
Scaife, Brig., 320
Schirach, Baldur von, 62
Schlegel, 302
Schleicher, 257
Schulenberg, Graf Werner von der, 70
Schutzstaffel (SS), 68
SCI. *See* Special Counter-Intelligence
SC1, 186
SC2, 186
SC3, 186
SC4, 186
SC5, 186
SC6, 186
SC7, 186
SC8, 186
Scotland Yard, 34, 51, 57, 58, 209–11, 218, 299.
    See also Game, Sir Philip; Kendal, Sir Norman
Scott, Capt., 315
Scott, Sir Russell, 60
Scottish Nationalists, 101
SD. *See* Sicherheitsdienst (SD)
SEAGULL, 23
Seccia Maria, 159
Secret Intelligence Service (SIS), 1, 2, 20, 27,
    96–99, 104–208, 212, 231, 233, 235, 251–73,
    298–316, 318–43
    Administrative Directorate, 169
    Budget, 203
    Central Registry, 98, 181
    Chief of, *see* Cumming, Sir Mansfield;
        Menzies, Stewart; Sinclair, Gen. John
    Economic Section, 175
    Finance and Administration Directorate,
        186. Head of, *see* Musson
    Information Department, 170
    Intelligence Directorate, 185

Irish Section, 301. Head of, *see* Archer,
    Col. Liam
Registry, 98
Reorganisation of, 169–82
Section I, 113
Section V, 58, 95, 97, 99, 104, 106, 107,
    114, 116, 142, 176, 233. Head of, *see*
    Cowgill, Felix; Philby, H.A.R.
Section VI, 183. Head of, *see* Limpenny,
    Adm.
Section VII, 110
Section VIII, 103, 135, 186, 199. Head of,
    see Gambier-Parry, Richard
Section IX, 113–18, 142, 200, 201, 233,
    235. Head of, *see* Curry, Jack C.; Philby,
    H.A.R.
Section X, 118
Section Y, 188
Special Communications Directorate, 185,
    186
Subversive Movements Section, 181
Technical Research Section, 175
Training Section, 175
War Planning Department, 170
War Station, 199
Secret Service Bureau, 41
Section D, 2, 231, 320
Security Executive, 279
    Chairman of, *see* Swinton, Lord
Security Intelligence Middle East (SIME), 100,
    153, 164
Security Liaison Officer (SLO), 92, 95
Security Service (MI5), 1–6, 11, 190–233,
    276–79, 281, 282, 284, 298–316
    A Branch, 58. Head of, *see* Phillips, Maj.
    B Branch, 58, 61, 64, 67, 73, 91. Head of,
        see Harker, O.A.
    D Branch, 37
    G Branch, 48, 57
    A Division, 298
    B Division, 96, 99. Director of, *see* Lid-
        dell, Capt. Guy
    C Division, 298
    D Division, 298
    E Division, 96
    Budget, 221, 222
    Curry history, 26–103
    Registry, 98, 232, 230, 250. Head of, *see*
        Payton Smith, Miss

VP. *See* Adams, Maj.
VX. *See* Foley, Frank
Vyazemskaya, Princess, 262
Vyazemskii, Prince, 271
Vyshinsky, 326

Wallerstein, Maj. L.J.D., 168
Walshe, Joseph, 85
Waltham Abbey, 231
War Cabinet, 201, 203–14, 223, 286, 317, 320
War Office Agent, Intelligence Section (MID),
    131
War Office Police, 209
    Commandant of, *see* Kell, Vernon
War Office Y Group, 109
Waters, Lt Cmdr R.K., 187
WB (SIS symbol for the NKVD), 156
Welles, Priscilla, 117
Wellington, Duke of, 34
Welsh, Eric, 167
Welsh Nationalists, 101
Whaddon Hall, 188
Wheatley, Dennis, 275, 291
Whinney, Patrick, 165, 188
White, Dick, 299
Whitestone, 167
Whyte, Maj., 299
Wilcox, Dr, 260, 270
Wilkie, Helen, 247
Williams, Albert, 307
Williams, Dr, 261
Williams, Gwylym, 316
Wilson, Dr, 260, 271
Wilson, Gen. Sir Henry, 16
Wingate, Col. Ronald, 275, 276
Winter, 262
Winterbotham, Fred, 182
Wintle, 278
Wirtschaftsdienst, 56
Witty, F., 166
Wolff, Johanna, 83
Wolikowski, Gen., 322
Women's Royal Naval Service (WRNS), 7
Wood, 166
Woodfield, T., 168
Woods, Christopher, 166
Woollcombe, Malcolm, 182, 198
Woolwich Arsenal, 228, 307

Worke, Kenneth, 167
World Crisis, The, 43
Wormwood Scrubs, 210, 213
WP (SIS symbol for US State Department), 132
Wrangel, Gen. Piotr, 252, 334
Wright, Peter, 2, 251
Wyatt, Phillip, 166
Wymondham, 109

X, Miss, 307
X (SIS symbol for Head Office section), 321
X (SIS symbol for telegraph and telephone
    communications), 131
X-2, 149
XB (SIS symbol for counter-intelligence infor-
    mation), 132
X Council, 93
XK (SIS symbol for Communist activity), 133
XP (SIS symbol for political intelligence), 132
XS (SIS symbol for economic intelligence), 132
XS/F, 121–30. *See also* Farrar, Lord
XX Committee, 93, 274, 279
XXX (TRIPLEX), 1

Y (SIS symbol for a British embassy), 321
Yakubovnik, 310
Yamada, Yasuo, 297
Yaroslav, Kaspar, 340
Yaroslavsky, 326
Yatsin, Maj., 322
Yerillson, de, 331
YP (SIS symbol for US Embassy in London),
    132
Yurman, Lt Adolf, 341

Z (SIS symbol for government department),
    321
ZB (SIS symbol for MI5), 321
Zelenski, 324
Zelensky, 268
ZIGZAG, 314
Zinalov, 268
Zinoviev, Grigorii, 250
    Letter by, 250, 256, 257
Z Organisation, 176
ZS (SIS symbol for the Ministry of Economic
    Warfare), 321
Zumanovich, Gen., 327